'The flesh is frail'

BYRON'S LETTERS AND JOURNALS
VOLUME 6
1818–1819

'Tis a sad thing, I cannot choose but say,
   And all the fault of that indecent sun,
Who cannot leave alone our helpless clay,
   But will keep baking, broiling, burning on,
That howsoever people fast and pray,
   The flesh is frail, and so the soul undone:
What men call gallantry, and gods adultery,
Is much more common where the climate's sultry.

DON JUAN, 1, 63

BYRON.   Pastel drawing by G. H. Harlow, Venice 1818
(*From a private Collection*)

'The flesh is frail'

BYRON'S LETTERS AND JOURNALS

Edited by
LESLIE A. MARCHAND

VOLUME 6
1818–1819

*The complete and unexpurgated text of
all the letters available in manuscript and
the full printed version of all others*

THE BELKNAP PRESS OF
HARVARD UNIVERSITY PRESS
CAMBRIDGE, MASSACHUSETTS

1976

© Editorial, Leslie A. Marchand 1976
© Byron copyright material, John Murray 1976

All rights reserved. No part of this
publication may be reproduced, stored in
a retrieval system, or transmitted, in any
form or by any means, electronic, mechanical,
photocopying, recording or otherwise,
without the prior permission of the publisher.
ISBN 0-674-08946-4

Library of Congress Catalog Card Number 73-81853
Printed in the United States of America

CONTENTS

EDITORIAL NOTE

As in previous volumes, the statement concerning editorial principles and annotation is repeated at the end of this note. And the acknowledgments, the Byron Chronology, the index of proper names, and the appendixes are all intended to make the volume as self-contained as possible. The general index and subject index will appear in the last volume of the series.

ACKNOWLEDGMENTS. (Volume 6). My debt to my publisher John Murray accumulates not only for his meticulous editing, but for his personal interest and continued enthusiasm for the project and his zeal in looking for new letters. I am again indebted to the National Endowment for the Humanities for a Research Grant which has facilitated the work on this volume by giving me means to travel to libraries and to employ clerical and typing assistance. I want to thank Arthur Rosenthal, Director of the Harvard University Press, and Mrs. E. T. Wilcox, Editorial Chief of the Press, for their encouragement and help in connection with the American edition. Doris Langley Moore has been a source of great help with her untiring answers to questions. The Carl H. Pforzheimer Library has been most helpful in many ways, and I am particularly grateful to Donald H. Reiman, Editor of *Shelley and his Circle*, and to Doucet D. Fischer, Coordinating Editor. John Gibbins of John Murray's has given valuable assistance on proofs.

I want to express my deep appreciation to the Marchesa Iris Origo for her permission to use her translations of Byron's Italian letters following the Italian texts. These letters and her translations first appeared in *The Last Attachment*. I am also grateful for permission to quote facts and commentary in that volume in my notes. I am indebted to Professor Nancy Dersofi of the Italian Department of Bryn Mawr College for the translation of a few letters from other sources.

For permission to get photocopies of letters in their possession and to use them in this volume I wish to thank the following libraries and individuals: Beinecke Rare Book and Manuscript Library, Yale University; Henry E. and Albert A. Berg Collection, New York Public Library; Biblioteca Classense, Ravenna; Biblioteca Nazionale

Centrale, Florence; British Museum (Department of Manuscripts); Cornell University Library; Historical Society of Pennsylvania; Houghton Library, Harvard University; Keats-Shelley Memorial, Rome; Lord Kinnaird; University of Leeds Library; The Earl of Lytton; Pierpont Morgan Library; Mr John Murray; Nottingham Public Libraries; Carl H. Pforzheimer Library; Roe-Byron Collection, Newstead Abbey; Stark Library, University of Texas; Robert H. Taylor Collection, Princeton University Library; D. S. M. Watson Library, University College London.

For assistance of various kinds I wish to thank the following: Susan E. Allen; Betty T. Bennett; Cecil Clarabut; John Clubbe; Ian Donaldson; Philip Flynn; Paul Fussell; Lady Ann Hill; Jerome J. McGann; Rae Ann Nager; John O'Connor; Stewart Perowne; Contessa Maria Luisa Cini di Pianzano; Anthony Powell; Gordon N. Ray; Brian Rigby; Charles Robinson; William St. Clair; David Ventura; Keith Walker; John Wardroper; Carl Woodring; W. B. Yapp.

* * * * * *

EDITORIAL PRINCIPLES. With minor exceptions, herein noted, I have tried to reproduce Byron's letters as they were written. The letters are arranged consecutively in chronological order. The name of the addressee is given at the top left in brackets. The source of the text is indicated in the list of letters in the Appendix. If it is a printed text, it is taken from the first printed form of the letter known or presumed to be copied from the original manuscript, or from a more reliable editor, such as Prothero, when he also had access to the manuscript. In this case, as with handwritten or typed copies, or quotations in sale catalogues, the text of this source is given precisely.

When the text is taken from the autograph letter or a photo copy or facsimile of it, the present whereabouts or ownership is given, whether it is in a library or a private collection. When the manuscript is the source, no attempt is made to indicate previous publication, if any. Here I have been faithful to the manuscript with the following exceptions:

1. The place and date of writing is invariably placed at the top right in one line if possible to save space, and to follow Byron's general practice. Fortunately Byron dated most of his letters in this way, but occasionally he put the date at the end. Byron's usual custom of putting no punctuation after the year is followed throughout.

2. Superior letters such as S‍ͬ. or 30ᵗʰ have been lowered to Sr. and 30th. The & has been retained, but &ͨ has been printed &c.

3. Byron's spelling has been followed (and generally his spelling is good, though not always consistent), and *sic* has been avoided except in a few instances when an inadvertent misspelling might change the meaning or be ambiguous, as for instance when he spells *there* t-h-e-i-r.

4. Although, like many of his contemporaries, Byron was inconsistent and eccentric in his capitalization, I have felt it was better to let him have his way, to preserve the flavour of his personality and his times. With him the capital letter sometimes indicates the importance he gives to a word in a particular context; but in the very next line it might not be capitalized. If clarity has seemed to demand a modification, I have used square brackets to indicate any departure from the manuscript.

5. Obvious slips of the pen crossed out by the writer have been silently omitted. But crossed out words of any significance to the meaning or emphasis are enclosed in angled brackets ⟨ ⟩.

6. Letters undated, or dated with the day of the week only, have been dated, when possible, in square brackets. If the date is conjectural, it is given with a question mark in brackets. The same practice is followed for letters from printed sources. The post mark date is given, to indicate an approximate date, only when the letter itself is undated.

7. The salutation is put on the same line as the text, separated from it by a dash. The complimentary closing, often on several lines in the manuscript, is given in one line if possible. The P.S., wherever it may be written in the manuscript, follows the signature.

8. Byron's punctuation follows no rules of his own or others' making. He uses dashes and commas freely, but for no apparent reason, other than possibly for natural pause between phrases, or sometimes for emphasis. He is guilty of the "comma splice", and one can seldom be sure where he intended to end a sentence, or whether he recognized the sentence as a unit of expression. He does at certain intervals place a period and a dash, beginning again with a capital letter. These larger divisions sometimes, though not always, represented what in other writers, particularly in writers of today, correspond to paragraphs. He sometimes uses semicolons, but often where we would use commas. Byron himself recognized his lack of knowledge of the logic or the rules of punctuation. He wrote to his publisher John Murray on August 26, 1813: "Do you know anybody

who can *stop*—I mean point—commas and so forth, for I am I fear a sad hand at your punctuation". It is not without reason then that most editors, including R. E. Prothero, have imposed sentences and paragraphs on him in line with their interpretation of his intended meaning. It is my feeling, however, that this detracts from the impression of Byronic spontaneity and the onrush of ideas in his letters, without a compensating gain in clarity. In fact, it may often arbitrarily impose a meaning or an emphasis not intended by the writer. I feel that there is less danger of distortion if the reader may see exactly how he punctuated and then determine whether a phrase between commas or dashes belongs to one sentence or another. Byron's punctuation seldom if ever makes the reading difficult or the meaning unclear. In rare instances I have inserted a period, a comma, or a semicolon, but have enclosed it in square brackets to indicate it was mine and not his.

9. Words missing but obvious from the context, such as those lacunae caused by holes in the manuscript, are supplied within square brackets. If they are wholly conjectural, they are followed by a question mark. The same is true of doubtful readings in the manuscript.

Undated letters have been placed within the chronological sequence when from internal or external evidence there are reasonable grounds for a conjectural date. This has seemed more useful than putting them together at the end of the volumes. Where a more precise date cannot be established from the context, these letters are placed at the beginning of the month or year in which they seem most likely to have been written.

ANNOTATION. I have tried to make the footnotes as brief and informative as possible, eschewing, sometimes with reluctance, the leisurely expansiveness of R. E. Prothero, who in his admirable edition of the *Letters and Journals* often gave pages of supplementary biographical information and whole letters *to* Byron, which was possible at a time when book publishing was less expensive, and when the extant and available Byron letters numbered scarcely more than a third of those in the present edition. Needless to say, I have found Prothero's notes of inestimable assistance in the identification of persons and quotations in the letters which he edited, though where possible I have double checked them. And I must say that while I have found some errors, they are rare. With this general acknowledgment I have left the reader to assume that where a source of information in the notes is not given, it comes from Prothero's edition, where additional details may be found.

The footnotes are numbered for each letter. Where the numbers are repeated on a page, the sequence of the letters will make the reference clear.

In an appendix in each volume I have given brief biographical sketches of Byron's principal correspondents first appearing in that volume. These are necessarily very short, and the stress is always on Byron's relations with the subject of the sketch. Identification of less frequent correspondents and other persons mentioned in the letters is given in footnotes as they appear, and the location of these, as well as the biographical sketches in the appendix, will be indicated by italic numbers in the index. Similarly italic indications will refer the reader to the principal biographical notes on persons mentioned in the text of the letters.

With respect to the annotation of literary allusions and quotations in the letters, I have tried to identify all quotations in the text, but have not always been successful in locating Byron's sources in obscure dramas whose phrases, serious or ridiculous, haunted his memory. When I have failed to identify either a quotation or a name, I have frankly said so, instead of letting the reader suppose that I merely passed it by as unimportant or overlooked it. No doubt readers with special knowledge in various fields may be able to enlighten me. If so, I shall try to make amends with notes in later volumes.

I have sometimes omitted the identification of familiar quotations. But since this work will be read on both sides of the Atlantic, I have explained some things that would be perfectly clear to a British reader but not to an American. I trust that English readers will make allowance for this. As Johnson said in the Preface to his edition of Shakespeare: "It is impossible for an expositor not to write too little for some, and too much for others ... how long soever he may deliberate, [he] will at last explain many lines which the learned will think impossible to be mistaken, and omit many for which the ignorant will want his help. These are censures merely relative, and must be quietly endured."

I have occasionally given cross references, but in the main have left it to the reader to consult the index for names which have been identified in earlier notes.

SPECIAL NOTES. The letters to Thomas Moore, first published in his *Letters and Journals of Lord Byron* (1830), were printed with many omissions and the manuscripts have since disappeared. Moore generally indicated omissions by asterisks, here reproduced as in his text.

Byron's letters in Italian to the Countess Guiccioli (and to a few other correspondents) I have transcribed from the original autograph manuscripts in the Biblioteca Classense, Ravenna. The Italian text is followed immediately by the English translation as printed by the Marchesa Iris Origo in her *The Last Attachment*. The translations of a few letters from other sources, not included, or only partially included, in that volume, have been made for me by Professor Nancy Dersofi of the Italian Department of Bryn Mawr College.

BYRON CHRONOLOGY

1818 Jan. 8—Hobhouse left for England with the MS. of Canto 4 of *Childe Harold*.

—wrote verse epistle "My dear Mr. Murray".

Jan. 19—Sent MS. of *Beppo* to Murray.

Jan. 22—Met briefly the Countess Guiccioli at Albrizzi's *conversazione*.

Jan.—Feb.—Dissipation in the Carnival.

Feb. 28—*Beppo* published.

March—Liaison with Marianna Segati ended.

April 6—Lady Melbourne died.

April 28—Fourth Canto of *Childe Harold* published.

May 2—Allegra arrived in Venice with her nurse Elise.

May—Took three year lease of Palazzo Mocenigo on Grand Canal.

June ?—Giovanni Battista Falcieri ("Tita") became Byron's gondolier.

June—Swimming match with Alexander Scott and Angelo Mengaldo.

July 3—Began *Don Juan*.

July ?—Margarita Cogni became Byron's "housekeeper" in the Palazzo Mocenigo.

Aug. 22—Claire and Shelley arrived in Venice.

Aug. 23—Byron and Shelley rode on the Lido—(basis of Shelley's "Julian and Maddalo").

Aug.—Allegra sent to Villa at Este with Claire.

Sept. 19—First Canto of *Don Juan* finished.

Sept. 24-29—Byron visited by Shelley and Mary.

Nov. 11—Hanson arrived in Venice with Newstead papers.

Nov. 17—Signed Codicil to Will leaving £5000 to Allegra.

Dec. 13—Began second canto of *Don Juan*.

1819 Jan.—Deep in Carnival dissipations.

Feb. 16—Purchase money from Newstead sale finally paid.

Feb.—Arguments with English friends who objected to publication of *Don Juan*.

March—Resolved to publish *Don Juan* anonymously.

April 2–3—Met Countess Teresa Guiccioli at Countess Benzoni's *conversazione*.

April 13–Guicciolis left for Ravenna.

June 1—Byron left Venice to visit the Guicciolis in Ravenna.

June 3–4—at Ferrara.

June 5–8—at Bologna.

June 10—Arrived in Ravenna.

June—Wrote the *Prophecy of Dante*.

June 28—*Mazeppa* and *Ode on Venice* published.

June—July—In love with the Countess Guiccioli.

July—Visited the Cardinal Legate and made friends with his secretary, Count Alborghetti.

July 15—Cantos I and II of *Don Juan* published anonymously.

Aug. 9—Followed the Guicciolis to Bologna.

Aug.—Interested in emigrating to South America.

Aug.—Allegra arrived in Bologna.

Sept. 12—Teresa left Bologna for Venice, accompanied by Byron, to see Dr. Aglietti.

Sept.—Oct.—Teresa and Byron at La Mira.

Oct. 7—Thomas Moore arrived at La Mira.

Oct. 7–10—Byron with Moore in Venice.

Oct. 11—Gave Moore his Memoirs.

Oct. 28—Seized with a fever at Palazzo Mocenigo—cared for by Teresa.

Nov. 1—Count Guiccioli arrived at Palazzo Mocenigo to take his wife back to Ravenna.

Nov. 10?—Teresa, persuaded by Byron, left with her husband for Ravenna.

Nov.—Byron resolved to return to England.

—Delayed by Allegra's fever.

Dec.—Changed his mind and decided to return to Ravenna.

Dec. 21—Left for Ravenna.

Dec. 24—Arrived in Ravenna.

BYRON'S LETTERS AND JOURNALS

1.

My dear Mr. Murray,
You're in a damned hurry
To set up this ultimate Canto,
But (if they don't rob us)
You'll see Mr. Hobhouse
Will bring it safe in his portmanteau.—[1]

2.

For the Journal you hint of.[2]
As ready to print off;
No doubt you do right to commend it
But as yet I have writ off
The devil a bit of
Our "Beppo", when copied—I'll send it.—[3]

3.

In the mean time you've "Gally"[4]
Whose verses all tally,
Perhaps you may say he's a Ninny,
But if you abashed are
Because of "Alashtar"
He'll piddle another "Phrosine".—

4.

Then you've Sotheby's tour,[5]
No great things to be sure—
You could hardly begin with a less work,
For the pompous rascallion
Who don't speak Italian
Nor French, must have scribbled by guesswork.

---

[1] Hobhouse left Venice for England on January 8, carrying with him the manuscript of the fourth canto of *Childe Harold*.

[2] Murray had contemplated starting a new periodical of his own, and had suggested that Byron might contribute to it. He finally purchased a half-share in William Blackwood's *Edinburgh Monthly Magazine* (founded in 1817—Murray became half proprietor in August, 1818, but sold his share the following year).

[3] Byron finally copied and sent *Beppo* to Murray on January 19th. It was published on February 28th.

[4] Byron made sport of the Oriental verse tales of Henry Gally Knight. See his comments on *Alashtar* and *Phrosine* Sept. 4, 1817, to Murray, (Vol. 5, p. 262).

[5] Sotheby's *Farewell to Italy* was published in 1818. Byron started to write a skit on Sotheby's tour. See *LJ*, IV, 452–453.

5.

No doubt he's a rare man
Without knowing German
Translating his way up Parnassus,
And now still absurder
He meditates Murder
As you'll see in the trash he calls *Tasso's*

6.

But you've others his betters
The real men of letters—
Your Orators—critics—and wits—
And I'll bet that your Journal
(Pray is it diurnal?)
Will pay with your luckiest hits.—

7.

You can make any loss up—
With "Spence"[6] and his Gossip,
A work which must surely succeed,
Then Queen Mary's Epistle-craft,[7]
With the new "Fytte" of "Whistlecraft"[8]
Must make people purchase and read.—

8.

Then you've General Gordon[9]
Who "girded his sword on"
To serve with a Muscovite Master
And help him to polish
A ⟨people⟩ Nation so *owlish*,
They thought shaving their beards a disaster.

---

[6] *Observations, Anecdotes, and Characters of Books and Men*, by the Rev. Joseph Spence, arranged with notes by the late Edmund Malone, 1820.

[7] *The Life of Mary Queen of Scots*, by George Chalmers, 1819.

[8] John Hookham Frere's "Whistlecraft" was first published in 1817 and gave Byron a hint for the style of *Beppo*. Cantos III and IV were published in 1818.

[9] Thomas Gordon (1788–1841) had visited Ali Pasha shortly after Byron was there. He travelled extensively in the East and from 1813 to 1815 served in the Russian army. Byron must have assumed that Murray was negotiating with him for the publication of a book. He later served with Ipsilanti in the Greek war for independence and wrote a *History of the Greek Revolution* (1832).

For the man *"poor and shrewd"**
With whom you'd conclude
A Compact without more delay.
Perhaps some such pen is
      *(Vide your letter)
Still extant in Venice,
But ⟨pray⟩ please Sir to mention *your pay?*—

Now tell me some news
Of your friends and the Muse
Of the Bar,—or the Gown—or the House,
From Canning the tall wit
To Wilmot the small wit
Ward's creeping Companion and *Louse.*—

⟨He's⟩ Who's so damnably bit
With fashion and Wit
That ⟨still a⟩ he crawls on the surface like Vermin
But an Insect in both,—
By his Intellect's growth
Of what *size* you may quickly determine.

Now, I'll put out my taper
(I've finished my paper
For these stanzas you see on the *brink* stand)
There's a whore on my right
For I rhyme best at Night
When a C—t is tied close to *my Inkstand.*

It was Mahomet's notion   (See his life in
That comical motion   Gibbon's abstract)
Increased his "devotion in prayer"—
If that tenet holds good
In a Prophet, it should
In a poet be equally fair.—

For, in rhyme or in love
(Which both come from above)
I'll *stand* with our *"Tommy"* or *"Sammy"* ("Moore" and
    "Rogers")
But the Sopha and lady
Are both of them ready
And so, here's "Good Night to you dammee!"

[TO DOUGLAS KINNAIRD]   *Venice January 13th. 1818*

Dear Douglas—I have received both your letters, Hobhouse set
off last Thursday for England.—As my potestas of attorney you are
entitled and authorized—& further hereby desired to interfere in the
disposal of the purchase money for Newstead,[1]—of course, the debts
must be liquidated—the *Jew annuities* first—(saving the Massingberd
ones which may wait till the last as the others are more pressing) [.]
Hanson's bill must come in with the rest, & if the whole surplus of
money (after the settlement is fulfilled)—is not sufficient to settle the
claims—I must devote a portion of the income till they are so—&
what ⟨quantity⟩ annual sum, I have no objection to leave to the
discretion of my trustees & Creditors.—As you have been so lucky
with Newstead (which appears to have been very fairly sold) I wish
you would try at *Rochdale* too—I should be then quite clear—& have
some little to boot—which (as it is not settled) I could employ in the
purchase of an annuity for my life & for my sister's—supposing we
could get the Manor & minerals tolerably sold.——I am as you may
suppose very well pleased so far with regard to Newstead, it was &
will be a great relief to me—at least I hope so.——I hope it will not
be necessary for me to come to England to sign papers &c.—but if it
is—I must—but not before Autumn—I would rather have a Clerk
sent out. I don't want to go [to] England any more.——About Siri
& Willhalm—your people had first given me credit for a thousand
£—that was some *hundreds more* than was advanced in cash before
you came out in August—and since have sent me a clear account in a
letter to *me* but as they have not written to *Siri* &c. my *credit there*
falls rather short of the balance due (after all drafts up to this day)
according to the letter of Messrs Morlands—so I have sent their

[1] See Dec. 11, 1817, to Hanson, note 1, (Vol. 5, p. 277).

epistle to Siri's to warrant my drawing as far [as] it goes—I wish you to apply to Hanson for any balance from Newstead at Michaelmas— & also for Sir R. Noel's money now due—and Murray can or may advance a few hundred pounds of [on?] the copy of the coming canto, (as though I have nine hundred pounds in circular notes Morland & Hammersley included—I don't like to use them *here*—because if I travel—or have occasion to go home I wish to reserve them for my journey and expenses elsewhere—having no *letters* of *credit* but for Venice—only these reserved circulars)[.] I would not break in upon my purchase money principal on any account—besides which it will not be forthcoming till April—and the papers must be signed &c. &c. & so forth.—When you write don't write such damned scraps of letters. I owe you a grudge for the last (which was four lines) and you know how spiteful I am—I'll work you you dog you.——— Shelley (from Marlow) has written to me about my Daughter (the last bastard one) who it seems is a great beauty—& wants to know what he is to do about sending her—I think she had better remain till Spring—but will you think of some plan for remitting her here—or placing her in England—I shall acknowledge & breed her myself— giving her the name of *Biron* (to distinguish her from little Legiti- macy)—and mean to christen her Allegra—which is a Venetian name.—I hope Scrope is well and prepared to row H[obhouse] who has been a long time in setting off—I have transported my horses to the *Lido*—so that I get a gallop of some miles along the Adriatic beach daily—H[obhouse]'s notes are rather lengthy—and you are so damned sincere you will be telling him so—now *don't*—at least till I come—I have extended the Canto to *184* Stanzas.———

ever yrs
B

P.S.—My respects to Mrs. K. Whatever sum or sums however small may be advanced in future you had better send the credit to Siri's direct (or in circulars to me which perhaps may be best) as I don't like discussions & explanations with those kind of persons.—

[TO JOHN MURRAY]   *Venice. January 19th. 1818*

My dear Sir—I send you the story[1] (in three other separate covers) it won't do for your journal—being full of political allusions—*print alone—without name—alter nothing—*get a Scholar to see that the

[1] *Beppo.*

7

Italian phrases are correctly published—(your printing by the way always makes me ill with it's eternal blunders, which are incessant) & God speed you.—Hobhouse left V[enice] a fortnight ago saving two days.—I have heard nothing of or from him.——

[yrs. truly]
B

He has the whole of the M.S.S. So put up prayers in your back shop— or in the Printers' "Chapel".

[TO JOHN CAM HOBHOUSE]   *Venice. January 23d. 1818*

My dear H.—You should have looked in Bianchoni's *prose*—not his verse—for the Ariosto thunder & lightning.—I have made a Clerk copy out the extract[1]—because I hate the bore of writing—& because what I write is scarcely legible.—Here it is annexed & enclosed "communibus *sheetibus*".—I ran to our *Peterkin* & quoted your epistle—"I roared like thunder, he ran like lightning"[2] you know the rest.—I also went to M[adam]e Albrizzi—where there was Rizzo & Francesconi—& a lot of the learned (besides the prettiest girl I ever saw half Greek half French a foreigner from Padua for the Carnival) all of whom swore that Petrotini was a liar—& that there was no such thunder.——Petrotini heard of this—& brought me the *printed book* Chapter & verse—next day—from which I send the extract—& the honourable company with Rizzo at their head have since owned that "*aveva ragione quel diavolo*".—So put your trust in liars for the future —for Petrotini has proved that his falsehoods are well founded.—I write a few words (like that damned D[ougla]s K[innair]d) just to convey you this annotation—but I will write more at length before you can get home—Go on & prosper & believe me

ever yrs. most [truly]
B

[1] Hobhouse was writing notes for the 4th canto of *Childe Harold*. This refers to the first two lines of stanza 41:

"The lightning rent from Ariosto's bust
The iron crown of laurel's mimicked leaves"

Hobhouse explained in his note: "Before the remains of Ariosto were removed from the Benedictine church to the library of Ferrara, his bust, which surmounted the tomb, was struck by lightning, and a crown of iron laurels melted away. The event has been recorded by a writer of the last century." Byron wrote at the top of the Italian transcript: "Extract from the third Vol. (Milan Edition 1802) of Bianchoni's works—pages 176–177. 'Lettera al' Signor Guido Savini Arcifisio-critico Sull' Indole di un fulmine caduto in Dresda l'anno 1759.' "

[2] Unidentified

8

P.S.—I miss you damnably—there is no bad fun at the Ridotto &c. this Carnival—I have lately (as a resource to supply your loss) taken again to the Natives—Mrs. Hoppner has made a Son.—[On cover, addressed in care of John Murray] Mr. Murray—I sent you in 3 packets a copy of——the other day—have you got them? there was a letter besides.

[TO JOHN MURRAY]   *Venice—J[anuar]y 27th. 1818*

Dear Sir—My father—that is, not God the Father, but my father in God—my Armenian father Padre Pasquali[1] in the name of all the other fathers of our convent sends you the inclosed Greeting.— Inasmuch as it has pleased the translators of the long lost & lately found portions of the text of Eusebius to put forth the inclosed prospectus of which I send six copies—you are hereby implored to obtain Subscribers in the two Universities—& among the learned and the unlearned who would unlearn their ignorance;—this *they* (the Convent) request—*I* request—& *do you* request.—I sent you Beppo—some weeks agone—you had best publish it alone—it has politics & ferocity, & won't do for your Isthmus of a Journal.——Mr. Hobhouse—if the Alps have not broken his neck—is—or ought to be—swimming with my Commentaries & his own coat of Mail in his teeth & right hand— in a Cork jacket between Calais & Dover.—It is the height of the Carnival—and I am in the estrum & agonies of a new intrigue—with I don't know exactly whom or what—except that she is insatiate of love—& won't take money—& has light hair & blue eyes—which are not common here—& that I met her at the Masque—& that when her mask is off I am as wise as ever.——I shall make what I can of the remainder of my youth—& confess—that like Augustus—I would rather die *standing.*—

[yrs. truly?]

B

[TO THOMAS MOORE]   *Venice, February 2d, 1818*

Your letter of Dec. 8th arrived but this day, by some delay, common but inexplicable. Your domestic calamity is very grievous,[1] and I feel

---

[1] Father Pasquale Aucher, with whom Byron collaborated in writing an English-Armenian Grammar at the monastery of San Lazzaro.
[1] The death of Moore's daughter Barbara in September, 1817.

9

with you as much as I *dare* feel at all. Throughout life, your loss must be my loss, and your gain my gain; and, though my heart may ebb, there will always be a drop for you among the dregs.

I know how to feel with you, because (selfishness being always the substratum of our damnable clay) I am quite wrapt up in my children. Besides my little legitimate, I have made unto myself an *il*legitimate since (to say nothing of one before),[2] and I look forward to one of these as the pillars of my old age, supposing that I ever reach—which I hope I never shall—that desolating period. I have a great love for my little Ada, though perhaps she may torture me, like * * * * *
* * * * * * * * * * * * * * * *
Your offered address will be as acceptable as you can wish. I don't much care what the wretches of the world think of me—all *that's* past. But I do care a good deal what *you* think of me, and, so, say what you like. You *know* that I am not sullen; and, as to being *savage*, such things depend on circumstances. However, as to being in good-humour in *your* society, there is no great merit in that, because it would be an effort, or an insanity, to be otherwise.

I don't know what Murray may have been saying or quoting. I called Crabbe and Sam the fathers of present Poesy; and said, that I thought—except them—*all* of *"us youth"* were on a wrong tack.[3] But I never said that we did not sail well. Our fame will be hurt by *admiration* and *imitation.* When I say *our,* I mean *all* (Lakers included), except the postscript of the Augustans. The next generation (from the quantity and facility of imitation) will tumble and break their necks off our Pegasus, who runs away with us; but we keep the *saddle,* because we broke the rascal and can ride. But though easy to mount, he is the devil to guide; and the next fellows must go back to the riding-school and the manège, and learn to ride the "great horse."

Talking of horses, by the way, I have transported my own, four in number, to the Lido (*beach* in English), a strip of some ten miles along the Adriatic, a mile or two from the city; so that I not only get a row in my gondola, but a spanking gallop of some miles daily along a firm and solitary beach, from the fortress to Malamocco, the which contributes considerably to my health and spirits.

I have hardly had a wink of sleep this week past. We are in the agonies of the Carnival's last days, and I must be up all night again, as well as to-morrow. I have had some curious masking adventures this Carnival; but, as they are not yet over, I shall not say on. I will work

2 See Jan. 17, 1809, to Hanson, note 1 (Vol. 1, p. 189).
3 See Sept. 15, 1817, to Murray (Vol. 5, pp. 265–266).

the mine of my youth to the last veins of the ore, and then—good night. I have lived, and am content.

Hobhouse went away before the Carnival began, so that he had little or no fun. Besides, it requires some time to be thoroughgoing with the Venetians; but of all this anon in some other letter. * * * * *

* * * * * * * * * * * * * * *

I must dress for the evening. There is an opera and ridotto, and I know not what, besides balls; and so, ever and ever yours,

B

P.S.—I send this without revision, so excuse errors. I delight in the fame and fortune of Lalla, and again congratulate you on your well-merited success.

[TO JOHN MURRAY]   *Venice.—February 20th. 1818*

Dear Sir—I have to thank Mr. Croker[1] for the arrival—& you for the Continents of the Parcel which came last week—much quicker than any before—owing to Mr C[roker]'s kind attention, and the official exterior of the bags, and all safe—except much fraction amongst the Magnesia—of which only two bottles came entire—but it is all very well—and I am accordingly obliged to you.———The books I have read, or rather am reading—pray who may be the Sexagenarian[2]— whose Gossip is very amusing—many of his sketches I recognize— particularly Gifford — Mackintosh — Drummond — Dutens[3] — H. Walpole—Mrs. Inchbald—Opie &c. with the Scotts—Loughborough & most of the divines and lawyers—besides a few shorter hints of authors—& a few lines about a certain *"Noble Author"*[4] charac- terized as Malignant and Sceptical according to the good old story "as it was in the beginning—is now—*but not* always shall be"—do you know such a person Master Murray? eh? and pray of the Book- sellers which be you? the dry—the dirty—the honest—the opulent— the finical—the splendid, or the Coxcomb Bookseller?[5]—"Stap my

1 John Wilson Croker, a contributor to Murray's *Quarterly Review*, was a friend of Canning and Secretary to the Admiralty.

2 *The Sexagenarian, or Recollections of a Literary Life* was a posthumous publica- tion of the Rev. William Beloe (1756–1817), Keeper of Printed Books at the British Museum and editor of *The British Critic*.

3 Louis Dutens (1730–1812), French writer settled in England, published his *Memoirs of a Traveller* in 1806.

4 Beloe spoke of "the Noble Author" as "certainly possessed of great intellectual powers, and a peculiar turn for a certain line of poetry", but his "bad passions so perpetually insinuate themselves in every thing which he writes, that it is hardly possible to escape the injury of his venom. . . ." (*Sexagenarian*, II, 230.)

5 Murray was referred to as the "coxcomb" Bookseller (*Sexagenarian*, II, 253).

vitals"[6]—but the author grows scurrilous in his grand Climacteric.
——I remember to have seen Porson at Cambridge in the Hall of our College—and in private parties—but not frequently—and I never can recollect him except as drunk or brutal and generally both—I mean in an Evening for in the hall he dined at the Dean's table—& I at the Vice-Master's so that I was not near him, and he then & there appeared sober in his demeanour—nor did I ever hear of excess or outrage— on his part in public—Commons—college—or Chapel—but I have seen him in a private party of under-Graduates—many of them freshmen & strangers—take up a poker to one of them—& heard him use language as blackguard as his action; I have seen Sheridan drunk too with all the world, but his intoxication was that of Bacchus— & Porson's that of Silenus—of all the disgusting brutes—sulky— abusive—and intolerable—Porson was the most bestial as far as the few times that I saw him went—which were only at Wm. Bankes's (the Nubian Discoverer's) rooms—I saw him once go away in a rage —because nobody knew the name of the "Cobbler of Messina"[7] insulting their ignorance with the most vulgar terms of reprobation.— He was tolerated in this state amongst the young men—for his talents —as the Turks think a Madman—inspired—& bear with him;—he used to recite—or rather vomit pages of all languages—& could hiccup Greek like a Helot—& certainly Sparta never shocked her children with a grosser exhibition than this Man's intoxication.——I perceive in the book you sent me a long account of him—of Gilbert Wakefield's account of him which is very savage[.][8] I cannot judge as I never saw him sober—except in *Hall* or Combination room—& then I was never near enough to hear—& hardly to see him—of his drunken deportment I can be sure because I saw it.——With the Reviews I have been much entertained—it requires to be as far from England as I am—to relish a periodical paper properly—it is like Soda water in an Italian Summer—but what cruel work you make with Lady Morgan[9]— you should recollect that she is a woman—though to be sure they are now & then very provoking—still as authoresses they can do no great

---

[6] Byron frequently repeated this phrase of Lord Foppington in Vanbrugh's *The Relapse* (or Sheridan's adaptation of it, *The Trip to Scarborough*).

[7] Probably the shoemaker's apprentice mentioned by Juvenal in his 5th satire. He won wealth and power at the court of Nero by accusing the most distinguished men of the time and exposing corruption.

[8] The Sexagenarian defended Porson from the attacks of Gilbert Wakefield in his *Correspondence* with Charles James Fox (pp. 99–101).

[9] There was a severe critique of Lady Morgan's *France* in the *Quarterly Review*, Vol. XVII, page 260.

harm—and I think it a pity so much good invective should have been laid out upon her—when there is such a fine field of us Jacobin Gentlemen for you to work upon; it is perhaps as bitter a critique as ever was written—& enough to make sad work for Dr. Morgan— both as a husband and an Apothecary—unless she should say as Pope did—of some attack upon him—"that it is as good for her as a dose of *Hartshorn*".——I heard from Moore lately & was very sorry to be made aware of his domestic loss—thus it is—"Medio de fonte leporum" in the acme of his fame—& of his happiness comes a draw- back as usual.—His letter somehow or other was more than two months on the road—so that I could only answer it the other day.— What you tell me of R⟨ogers⟩ in your last letter is like him—but he had best let *us* that is one of us—if not both—alone—he cannot say that I have not been a sincere & a warm friend to him—till the black drop of his liver oozed through too palpably to be overlooked—now if I once catch him at any of his juggling with me or mine—let him look to it—for—if I spare him—then write me down a goodnatured gentleman; & the more that I have been deceived—the more that I once relied upon him—I don't mean his petty friendship (what is that to me?) but his *good* will—which I really tried to obtain thinking him at first a good fellow—the more will I pay off the balance—and so if he values his quiet—let him look to it—in three months I could restore him to the Catacombs.——Mr. Hoppner—whom I saw this morning—has been made the father of a very fine boy—Mother & Child doing very well indeed.—By this time Hobhouse should be with you—& also certain packets—letters—&c. of mine sent since his departure.——I am not at all well in health within this last eight days;—my remembrances to Gifford & all friends

yrs. [truly?]

B

P.S.—In the course of a Month or two, Hanson will have probably to send off a Clerk with conveyances to sign—(N[ewstea]d being sold in Novr. last for Ninety four thousand & five hundred pounds) in which case I supplicate supplies of articles as usual—for which desire Mr. Kinnaird to settle from funds in their bank—& deduct from my account with him.—

P.S.—Tomorrow night I am going to see '*Otello*" an opera from our "Othello"—and one of Rossini's best, it is said.—It will be curious to see in Venice—the Venetian story itself represented—besides to discover what they will make of Shakespeare in Music.—

My dear H.—Your arrival is gratifying (I hope to yourself) but I cannot approve of the menaced divorce between text & notes; of course Murray would be but too glad to make a separate publication[1] —(particularly if he is to give nothing for it) but I beg leave to say to him *that the text shall not* be published without the Notes—& that if this is contemplated—It shan't be published at all—& so I hope to hear no more of it—though I foresaw from your extreme soreness in all that regards all persons & things pertaining to the Quarterly—some such damned drawback—which makes me very uncomfortable. I sent you some weeks ago the extract from Bianchoni's *prose* works about the Lightning & Ariosto's bust;[2]—& as you say nothing of it's arrival—I enclose a duplicate.—They may say what they like of Petrotini's being a liar—but he has told me the only two truths that I have heard in Venice—the first—about the passage in Bianchoni—& it *is* in Bianchoni —& the second that a Girl (whom you don't know—Elena da Mosta —a Gentil Donna) was clapt—& she has clapt me—to be sure it was *gratis*, the first Gonorrhea I have not paid for.—I am getting better— the Carnival was short—but very lively—and there was good fun among the Masques. I write to you in haste & low spirits for your demurs about the notes—are provoking enough.—If you see Spooney[3] —tell him I had his late (his son's) letter—of course I wish to hear of Scrope & our learned brother the Honourable Doug.—When Spooney, sends out a Clerk in Spring with the writings it will be a very good time to send out my little *shild* (I mean the bastard) and I wish you would settle it in that way with Shelley—who has written to me frequently upon it—as for the legitimate I hear she is very well.—I wish you all kinds of welcome—& amusement—since you went—I have taken refuge amongst the Venetians—who are all very well

ever yrs.

B

P.S.—Will [you] tell Mr. Murray that in the line of Manfred
"Innumerable atoms;—and one desart,"
The punctuation is incorrect & should be
"Innumerable atoms, and one desart—"
The Semicolon makes nonsense of the whole passage.

[1] Some of Hobhouse's voluminous notes were retained in the publication of the fourth canto of *Childe Harold*, but Murray finally (reluctantly) published the bulk of them separately as *Historical Illustrations of the Fourth Canto of Childe Harold* (1818).
[2] See Jan. 23, 1818, to Hobhouse, note 1.
[3] See Vol. 4, p. 255, note 1.

Thanks—in a great hurry—but I hope that Mr. H[obhouse] will correct the proof of *Beppo* as well as t'other—else there will be deuce & all of blunders—In a few days I will write at large—at present I am not very well—I restore G[ifford]'s note which is highly gratifying.

Mind in *Beppo*.—I find a word left out which spoils an entire line—& drives me crazy.——

[TO RICHARD BELGRAVE HOPPNER]   *Venice, February 28, 1818*

My Dear Sir,—Our friend, il Conte M.,[1] threw me into a cold sweat last night, by telling me of a menaced version of Manfred (in Venetian, I hope, to complete the thing) by some Italian, who had sent it to you for correction, which is the reason why I take the liberty of troubling you on the subject. If you have any means of communication with the man, would you permit me to convey to him the offer of any price he may obtain or think to obtain for his project, provided he will throw his translation into the fire, and promise not to undertake any other of that or any other of *my* things: I will send his money immediately on this condition.[2]

As I did not write *to* the Italians, nor *for* the Italians, nor *of* the Italians, (except in a poem not yet published, where I have said all the good I know or do not know of them, and none of the harm), I confess I wish that they would let me alone, and not drag me into their arena as one of the gladiators, in a silly contest which I neither understand nor have ever interfered with, having kept clear of all their literary parties, both here and at Milan, and elsewhere.—I came into Italy to feel the climate and be quiet, if possible. Mossi's translation I would have prevented, if I had known it, or could have done so; and I trust that I shall yet be in time to stop this new gentleman, of whom I heard yesterday for the first time. He will only hurt himself, and do no good to his party, for in *party* the whole thing originates. Our modes of thinking and writing are so unutterably different, that I can conceive no greater absurdity than attempting to make any approach between the English and Italian poetry of the present day. I like the people very much, and their literature very much, but I am not the

1 Unidentified. [Michelli? See April 17, 1818, to Hobhouse]

2 Byron offered the translator 200 francs to give up his project and threatened to horsewhip him when he demurred. The man finally accepted the money and signed an agreement not to translate any other of Byron's works. (Moore, II, 165n.)

least ambitious of being the subject of their discussions literary and personal (which appear to be pretty much the same thing, as is the case in most countries); and if you can aid me in impeding this publication, you will add to much kindness already received from you by yours

Ever and truly,
BYRON

P.S.—How is *the* son, and mamma? Well, I dare say.

[TO JOHN CAM HOBHOUSE]   [*March? 1818*]

My dear Hobhouse—I hope that you or Mr. Gifford will do me the favour to cast an eye to the proof & press of this[1] as well as of "*Beppo*". I find some Italian words most damnably "*strappazzate*". I hate the sight of a proof—for God sake send me no more but correct at your own good pleasure—only *don't omit* for I want to be as tedious as need be—why leave out "*ould Apias Korkus*"[2] it was not restored when I wrote—and the Ministers may be damned for repealing it & spoiling my period.———

[TO SAMUEL ROGERS]   *Venice. March 3d. 1818*

My dear R.—I have not as you say "taken to wife the *Adriatic*" but if the Adriatic will take my wife—I shall be very glad to marry her instead;—in the mean time I have had wife enough as the Grammar has it "taedet vitae *pertaesum est conjugii*";[1] however the last part of this exquisite quotation only is applicable to my case—I like life very well in my own way.———I heard of Moore's loss from himself—in a letter which was delayed upon the road three months—I was sincerely sorry for it—but in such cases what are words?—The villa you speak of is one at Este, which Mr. Hoppner (Consul General here) has transferred to me;—I have taken it for two years as a place of Villeggiatura—the situation is very beautiful indeed, among the Euganean hills—& the house very fair;—the Vines are luxuriant to a great degree—and all the fruits of the earth abundant; it is close to the old Castle of

---

[1] This letter is written on the back of the proof sheets of the dedication (to Hobhouse) of the fourth canto of *Childe Harold*.

[2] In stanza 47 of *Beppo* Byron wrote "I like the Habeas Corpus (when we've got it)". The Tory government had suspended Habeas Corpus at a time when there was fear of popular uprisings.

[1] "Life is boring, marriage utterly so."

all the Estes—or Guelphs—and within a few miles of Arqua,—which I have visited twice—& hope to visit often.—Last Summer (except an excursion to Rome) I passed upon the Brenta; in Venice I winter, transporting my horses to the Lido bordering the Adriatic (where the fort is) so that I get a gallop of some miles daily along the strip of beach which reaches to Malamocco, when in health—but within these few weeks I have been unwell;—at present I am getting better.— The Carnival was short but a good one.—I don't go out much, except during the time of Masques,—but there are one or two Conversazioni—where I go regularly—just to keep up the system—as I had letters to their Givers—& they are particular on such points—& now & then—though very rarely—to the Governor's.——It is a very good place for women—I have a few like every one else. I like the dialect—& their manner very much—there is a naiveté about them which is very winning—& the romance of the place is a mighty adjunct; the "bel Sangue" is not however now amongst the "damé" or higher orders—but all under *"i fazzioli"* or kerchiefs a white kind of veil which the lower orders wear upon their heads;—the "Vesta Zendale" or old national female costume is no more.—The City however is decaying daily—& does not gain in population;—however I prefer it to any other in Italy—& here have I pitched my staff—& here do I purpose to reside for the remainder of my life,—unless events connected with business not to be transacted out of England, compel me to return for that purpose;—otherwise I have few regrets—& no desires to visit it again—for it's own sake.——I shall probably be obliged to do so to sign papers for my affairs; & a proxy for the whigs—& to see Mr. Waite—for I can't find a good dentist here—& every two or three years one ought to consult one.——About seeing my children I must take my chance;—one I shall have sent here—& I shall be very happy to see the legitimate one when God pleases— which he perhaps will, some day or other.—As for my mathematical Medea I am as well without her. Your account of your visit to F[onthill][2] is very striking.—Could you beg of *him* for *me* a copy in M.S.S. of the remaining *tales?* I think I deserve them as a strenuous & public admirer of the first one;—I will return it—when read—& make no ill use of the copy if granted—Murray would send me out any thing safely;—if ever I return to England I should like very much to see the author, with his permission;—in the mean time you could not oblige me more than by obtaining me the perusal I request—in French or English—all's one for that—though I prefer Italian to

2 Fonthill Abbey, the home of William Beckford, the author of *Vathek*.

either.—I have a french Copy of Vathek which I bought at Lausanne.
——I can read French with great pleasure & facility—though I
neither speak nor write it;—now Italian I *can* speak with some
fluency—& write sufficiently for my purposes—but I don't like their
modern prose at all—it is very heavy;—and so different from
Machiavelli.——They say Francis is Junius—I think it looks like it;—
I remember meeting him at Earl Grey's at dinner;—has not he lately
married a young woman?—& was not he Madame Talleyrand's
Cavalier servente in India—years ago?——I read my death in the
papers,—which was not true.—I see they are marrying the remaining
singleness of the royal family[3].—They have brought out Fazio[4] with
great & deserved success at Covent Garden—that's a good sign; I
tried during the directory to have it done at D[rury] L[ane] but was
overruled;—as also in an effort I made in favour of Sotheby's trash—
which I did to oblige the mountebank, who has since played me a
trick or two (I suspect)—which perhaps he may remember—as well as
his airs of patronage—which he affects with young writers—&
affected both to me and *of* me—many a good year;—he sent me
(unless the *handwriting* be a most extraordinary coincidental mistake)
an anonymous note at Rome about the "Poeshie" of Chillon &c.—I
can swear also to his phrases—particularly the word *"effulgence"*—
well—I say nothing.—If you think of coming into this country—you
will let me know perhaps beforehand;—I suppose Moore won't move.
Rose is here—& has made a "relazione" with a Venetian lady[5]—
rather in years—but not ugly—at least by Candle light—I saw them
the other night—at Madame Albrizzi's—He talks of returning in
May.—My love to the Hollands—

ever yrs. very truly & affectly.

BYRON

P.S.—They have been crucifying Othello into an Opera (*Otello* by
Rossini)—Music good but lugubrious—but as for the words!—all the
real scenes with Iago cut out—& the greatest nonsense instead—the
handkerchief turned into a billet doux, and the first Singer would not
black his face—for some exquisite reasons assigned in the preface.—
Scenery—dresses—& Music very good.—

[3] The Dukes of Clarence, Kent and Cambridge were all married in 1818. The
Duke of Kent became the father of Queen Victoria.

[4] A tragedy by Henry Hart Milman, better known later for his *History of the
Jews* (1830) and *History of Christianity* (1840). He was a frequent reviewer for the
Quarterly Review. His tragedy was acted at Covent Garden on February 5, 1818.

[5] William Stewart Rose married an Italian lady in 1818 and turned his attention
to Italian literature.

My dear H.—I have received & returned Murray's packets—& sent two stanzas for insertion near the end in another cover addressed to M[urray]. I think I may have made a slip of the pen in the last word which should be *"conceal"*.—Beppo was full of some gross omissions of words—which I hope will not go so before the public—as it spoils both sense & rhyme—though any body (if in his damned hurry he allowed any one to look at the proofs) might see where they occur *what* words ought then & there to come in.—Whether the error be of the M.S. or the printer—I know not—but they worry me cursedly with their nonsense at this distance—if other people are as sick of reading my late works as I have been—my Conscience may release M[urray] from his compact.—Petrotini is truth itself—it is *you* who are inaccurate—& have no memory which you know I told you *every day* for the Good of your soul—for many months bygone.—You have vexed me mightily about *your notes* on which I depended seriously—& was quite anxious—though you thought the contrary—however you must do as you like—only recollect that I *protest* against witholding the notes—& look upon myself as an ill used Gentleman.——I am glad to hear that Scrope is in repair—as for Kinnaird—since his letter I say nothing.——If Sir P. F. be Junius—I am glad for his sake—& sorry for that of Junius.——Now for Venice.—Hoppner has got a son—a fine child.—The Carnival was very merry.—Madame Albrizzi's Conversazioni are greatly improved, there have been some pretty women there lately.—San Benedetto has oratorios—Haydn & Handel —given by Andrea Erizzo.——My Whore-hold has been much extended since the Masquing began & closed—but I was a little taken aback by a Gonorrhea *gratis*—given by a Gentil-donna ycleped Elena da Mosta—a lady who has by no means the character of being disinterested—but from some whim or other—positively refused money or presents from *me* (you may suppose I did not then know she was ill) I presume for the novelty's sake;—it is the first of such maladies— which I believe not to have been purchased.——I have made (to supply your loss) several new acquaintances among the learned & noble of the land (or rather water) of this city,—and with one or two Inglesi—and an American—sensible people.—The Man of learning has been nearly bursten with an Indigestion and I was obliged to have an old Physician rooted out of his bed at three in the matina—& to beat up the "Pottecary"—they gave him a drench which would have cured a horse and did not kill him—to the great disappointment of his numerous foes—as he says all owing to his honesty—"he roared it like any Nightingale."—I have sent away Marietta—the housemaid, so that Stevens is obliged to get drunk alone.——She made mischief by tale-bearing & setting the fair & frail sex by the ears—one morning a new Maid—a *Caravaggiote* of the Segatis—who is about five ten in height & stout in proportion gave her a beating because she had attacked *"her honour"* (her very words for I asked her) by some piece of harlotry which she had attributed to her—this did some good—but I thought it best to give her her wage, & send her away.—I have not been riding lately at the Lido, but I hope to be well enough in a few days to resume Cavalkepsing—I met Rose and his relazione at Madame's the other night—he is a remarkably agreeable & accomplished man, apparently—but in a weak state of health.—I believe he moves homeward in Maggio.—I had fifty gossips to say—but am in haste & have forgotten them.—Is Scrope facetious? what does he? what says he? where dines he? what wins he? how is he?——How is Doug? "the *dog*, and Duck?" you know that's a sign—& the beginning of one of Jackson's songs besides.——"Ah Coquin! vare is my Shild?"[1] You must see Shelley about sending the illegitimate one with a Nurse —in the Spring.

yours alway
B

[TO JOHN CAM HOBHOUSE]   *Venice, March 5th. 1818*

My dear H—I wrote to you yesterday a long—& rather peevish letter—for the *Notes* not appearing—discomfited me sadly.—I must answer in great haste—the post pressing—one or two points of yrs. of the 17th—just received.—You are right—& I am right—*restore "the"* for *"some"*—which I had altered against my creed—to please G[ifford]—what other alterations I made according to his wish are I think properly made—as I am mostly of his opinion except as to *"some"*—& *"past Eternity"* which last I have not altered as I think with Polonius *"that's good"*—And recollect it is to be *"the Enchanters"* & not *"some Enchanters"*[.] I dare say G[ifford]'s objection was to the open vowel—but it can't be holpen.—I am however greatly obliged by G[ifford]'s suggestions which are well meant & generally well grounded—& surely good natured as can be—& one ought to attend to the opinions of a man—whose critical talents swept down a whole host

---

[1] Unidentified

of writers at once—I don't mean from *fear*—but real respect for the sense of his observations.—I can't give up Nemesis—my great favourite—I can't, I can't.——The wicked necessity of rhyming retains "lay"—in despite of sense & grammar.—But I bow to Scrope's alteration of the preface, and I request that it be adopted forthwith.——You do me too much honour in the association with the friends you mention—but I can't decline it, though useless—for I never will reside in England.—Thank them—& yourself.—Tell me how K[innair]d & his *Siora*—i.e. the *Dog* and *Duck*—do?—A Thousand thanks for yr. letter—& bumpers to Scrope;—more in a few days—

yrs. ever [& ever yrs?]
B

P.S.—The Post—The Post—The Post is just going out in the Padua Barca.—Pray correct *Beppo* there are *words* left out—either in the M.S.S. or by the printer.—

[TO JOHN MURRAY]   *Venice. March 9th. 1818*

Dear Sir/—If you have not yet printed,—or have an opportunity of reprinting "Beppo";—after the stanza which ends (I forget the Number) with

> "For most men till by losing rendered sager
> Will back their own opinions with a wager["]
> > *Insert this.*—
> 'Tis said that their last parting was pathetic,
>   As partings often are, or ought to be,
> And their presentiment was quite prophetic
>   That they should never more each other see,
>   (A sort of morbid feeling half poetic
>   Which I have known occur in two or three)
> When kneeling on the shore upon her sad knee
> He left this Adriatic Ariadne.—
> > yrs. [scrawl]

And After the stanza concluding with

> "*Or what becomes of damage and divorces?*"
> > *Insert.*—
> However—I still think with all due deference
> To the fair *single* part of the Creation

21

That married ladies should preserve the preference
 In téte a téte, or general conversation,—
And this I say without peculiar reference
 To England, France, or any other nation,
Because they know the world, & are at ease,
And being natural, naturally please.—

―――

'Tis true, your budding Miss is very charming,
 But shy, and awkward, at first coming out,
So much alarmed, that she is quite alarming,
 All Giggle, Blush;—half Pertness, and half Pout,
And glancing at *Mamma* for fear there's harm in
 What you, she, it, or they, may be about,
The Nursery still lisps out in all they utter,
Besides, they always smell of Bread and Butter.

yrs. [ever?]

The Line on Italy must run
 "With all *it's* sinful doings I must say" &c.
instead of "their" &c. as put at first.
These with speed.—

[TO JOHN MURRAY]   *March 11th. 1818*

Dr. Sir—To & In "Beppo" after ye stanza which concludes
                        "though Laughter
 Leaves us so doubly serious shortly after."
                Add & insert
Oh, Mirth and Innocence! Oh, Milk and Water!
 Ye happy mixtures of more happy days!
In these sad Centuries of sin & slaughter,
 Abominable Man no more allays
His thirst with such pure beverage.—No matter,
 I love you both, & both shall have my praise,
Oh! for old Saturn's reign of Sugar-candy!—
Meantime I drink to your return in Brandy.
This is the *4th* additional S[tanz]a I sent within ye. week—tell me if
you have received the others—*three* in one cover.

[scrawl for closing and signature]

22

My Dear Tom,—Since my last, which I hope that you have received, I have had a letter from our friend Samuel. He talks of Italy this summer—won't you come with him? I don't know whether you would like our Italian way of life or not. * * * * * *

* * * * * * * * * * * * * * *

They are an odd people. The other day I was telling a girl, "You must not come to-morrow, because Marguerita is coming at such a time,"—(they are both about five feet ten inches high, with great black eyes and fine figures—fit to breed gladiators from—and I had some difficulty to prevent a battle upon a rencontre once before),— ["]unless you promise to be friends, and"—the answer was an interruption, by a declaration of war against the other, which she said would be a "Guerra di Candia".[1] Is it not odd, that the lower order of Venetians should still allude proverbially to that famous contest, so glorious and so fatal to the Republic?

They have singular expressions, like all Italians. For example, "Viscere"—as we should say, "my love," or "my heart," as an expression of tenderness. Also, "I would go for you into the midst of a hundred *knives*."—"*Mazza ben.*" excessive attachment,—literally, "I wish you well even to killing." Then they say (instead of our way, "do you think I would do you such harm?") "do you think I would *assassinate* you in such a manner?"—"Tempo *perfido*," bad weather; "Strade *perfide*," bad roads,—with a thousand other allusions and metaphors, taken from the state of society and habits in the middle ages.

I am not so sure about *mazza*, whether it don't mean *massa*, i.e. a great deal, a *mass*, instead of the interpretation I have given it. But of the other phrases I am sure.

Three o'th'clock—I must "to bed, to bed, to bed,"[2] as mother S[iddons], (that tragical friend of the mathematical * * *) says,

* * * * * * * * * * * * * *

Have you ever seen—I forget what or whom—no matter. They tell me Lady Melbourne is very unwell. I shall be so sorry. She was my greatest *friend*, of the feminine gender:—when I say "friend," I mean *not* mistress, for that's the antipode. Tell me all about you and every

---

[1] Venice lost Candia (Crete) to Turkey September 29, 1669, after a 25-year siege. In Canto 4 of *Childe Harold* Byron refers to "Troy's rival, Candia!" (Stanza 14)

[2] *Macbeth*, Act V, scene 1.

body—how Sam is—how you like your neighbours, the Marquis[3] and Marchesa, &c. &c.

Ever, &c.

[TO JOHN MURRAY]   *Venice. March 25th. 1818*

Dear Sir—I have your letter with ye. account of "Beppo" for which I sent you 4 new Stanzas a fortnight ago—in case you print—or reprint.——As for the "amiable Man"[1] what "do the honest Man in my *Closet?*" why did the "amiable man" write me a scurvy *anonymous* letter at Rome?—(ask Mr. Hobhouse for it he has it with the book & his remarks) telling me that out of ten things—eight were good for nothing;—I dare say—the dog was right enough—but he should put his name to a note—a man may *print* anonymously—but not write letters so—it is contrary to all the courtesies of life & literature.——I had no prejudice against the pompous buffoon—I endured his acquaintance—I permitted his coxcombry—I endeavoured to advance his petty attempts at Celebrity;—I moved the Sub Committee & Kinnaird—& Kean & all the Aristocracy of Drury Lane—to bring out his play—whose insufferable Mediocrity gave it a great chance of success—I bore with him—the Bore—

> Bear witness all ye Gods of Rome & Greece!
> How willing I have been to keep the peace.

But he *would* begin—so he would—& see what he gets by it—it quite distresses me to be obliged to do such things—but Self Defence—you know—what can a man do?——Croker's is a good guess—but the style is not English—it is Italian—*Berni*[2] is the Original of *all.*— *Whistlecraft* was *my* immediate *model.* Rose's *Animali*[3]—I never saw till a few days ago—they are excellent—but—(as I said above) *Berni* is the father of that kind of writing—which I think suits our language too very well—we shall see by the experiment.—If it does —I'll send you a volume in a year or two—for I know the Italian way of life well—& in time may know it yet better—& as for the verse &

[3] Moore's cottage, Sloperton, was close to Bowood, the home of the Marquis of Lansdowne.

[1] William Sotheby.

[2] Francesco Berni (1490–1536) was the initiator of the Italian mock-heroic style in his adaptation of Boiardo's *Orlando Innamorato.*

[3] William Stewart Rose's *The Court and Parliament of Beasts, freely translated from the Animali Parlanti of Casti* was not published until 1819. Byron had seen the original work of Casti (1721–1803) as he told Pryse Gordon in 1816 (Pryse Gordon, *Personal Memoirs* II, 328).

the passions—I have them still in tolerable vigour.—If you think that it will do *you* or the work—or *works* any good—you may—or may not put my name to it—*but first consult the knowing ones*;—it will at any rate shew them—that I can write cheerfully, & repel the charge of monotony & mannerism.—

yrs. [ever?]
B

[TO JOHN CAM HOBHOUSE]   *Venice. March 25th. 1818*

My dear Hobhouse—I protest against the "pints" of your sober Association—not that my prospect of infringing the rule is very great—for I will not return to England as long as I can help it;—but as an honorary member—I use my privilege of protest—the restriction upon Scrope will of course have the usual effect of restrictions;—for my own part I have about the same conception of Scrope's company and a *pint* (of anything but brandy) that the close reflection of many years enables me to entertain of the Trinity; unless it be a Scotch pint—& even then it must be in the plural number.—I greatly fear that Scrope & I would very soon set up for ourselves—in case of my return like "Marius from banishment to power".[1]——You will have received by this time some letters—or letter—with ye. returned proofs.—I am anxious to hear from or of Spooney—in the hope of the conclusion of the New[stea]d Sale;—& I want you to spur him if possible into the like for *Rochdale*—a Clerk can bring the papers (& by the bye my *Shild* by Clare at the same time—pray—desire Shelley to pack it carefully) with *tooth powder red only*—Magnesia—Soda powders—*tooth brushes*—Diachylon plaster—and any new novels—good for any thing.——I have taken a Palazzo on the Grand Canal for two years[2]—so that you see I *won't* stir—so pray don't mention that any more—my old "relazione" is over—but I have got several new ones (and a Clap which is nearly well at present) with regard to the proxy I will renew it with pleasure if it can be done without dragging me to London for it[3]—otherwise *not* till I find it necessary to come on business;—there was no occasion for any body's name with Lord H[olland]—but

[1] The Roman, Caius Marius (157–86 B.C.), was banished and returned to power and his seventh consulship but died a few days later.

[2] This was a tentative agreement for the rental of the Gritti Palace, but he could not come to terms with Count Gritti, and finally leased one of the Mocenigo Palaces on the Grand Canal.

[3] Votes could then be given by proxy in the House of Lords.

undoubtedly your own would have greater weight with me than any other—had such been requisite—as for the Whigs *I* won't leave them though they will me—if ever they get anything to scramble for;—pray do you stand this ensuing election?——I wrote to Augusta the other day.——Remember me to Scrope—why don't he write? whenever you come out pray bring him—but I hope that you will turn parliament man—& stay at home,—I shall have great glee in seeing your speeches in the Venetian Gazette.—As for Doug. don't let him neglect his Potestas as At*tu*rney.—How came Scrope to kneel to his Duck—he who like Rollo[4] never kneels—except to *his* God.—

yrs [scrawl]

P.S.—The Man who makes your wig—says—that he sent the wig you made me order to *Geneva* to Hengo—who I suppose wears it himself—& be damned to him—*you* ought to pay Holmes—as it is all your doing.——I dined with Hoppner & Rose on Monday—all well. —With regard to my money matters—Murray may pay in his money to Morland's in regular order—as I cannot depend for the present on other remittances—& whether I could or not—I choose to have the cash tangible—the Sum is hardly considerable enough to turn into the annuity you proposed, besides I think I can spend the principal—& I like it.——*Spur Doug.* & *Spooney*—& never calculate on my return to England—which I may or may not but never willingly.——

[TO JOHN MURRAY]   *Venice. April 11th. 1818*

Dear Sir/—Will you send me by letter, packet, or parcel, half a dozen of the coloured prints from Holmes's Miniature (the latter done shortly before I left your country & the prints about a year ago). I shall be obliged to you as some people here have asked me for the like.——It is a picture of my upright Self—done for Scrope B. D[avie]s Esquire.—When you can reprint "Beppo"—instead of line

"Gorging the little Fame to get all raw"
insert—
Gorging the slightest slice of Flattery raw,—

because—we have the word "Fame" in the preceding Stanza—(also as a rhyme too)—perhaps the line is now a little weakened—because "*all raw*" expresses the Cormorant Cameleon's avidity for air—or inflation of his vicious vanity—but—ask Mr. Gifford—& Mr. Hobhouse—& as they think so let it be—for though repetition is only

4 First Duke of Normandy (860?–931?)

the "soul of Ballad singing" & best avoided in describing the Harlequin jacket of a Mountebank—yet anything is better than weakening an expression—or a thought.—I would rather be as bouncing as Nat Lee—than wishy-washy like—like—

He has twelve thousand pounds a year—
  I do not mean to rally
His Songs at sixpence would be dear
  So give them gratis—Gally.[1]
And if this statement should seem queer
  Or set down in a hurry
Go—ask (if he will be sincere)
  His Publisher—John Murray—
Come say—how Many have been sold?
  And don't stand shilly-shally,
Of bound & lettered red & gold
  Well printed works of Gally?

For Astley's Circus Upton[2] writes
  And also for the Surry—
Fitzgerald weekly (or *weakly*) still recites—
  Though grinning Critics worry—
Miss Holford's Peg—& Sotheby's Saul[3]
  In fame exactly tally—
From Stationer's Hall—to Grocer's [stall]
  They go—& so does Gally.—

He hath a Seat in Parliament—
  So fat, & passing wealthy—healthy
And surely he should be content
  With these—and being wealthy—
But Great Ambition will misrule
  Men at all risks to sally,—
Now makes a poet—now a fool
  And—*we* know *which*—of Gally.—

[1] Henry Gally Knight was the butt of Byron's jokes. He wrote two "ballads" on Knight in this letter to Murray.

[2] William Upton was the author of *Words of the most Favourite Songs, Duets . . . sung at the Royal Amphitheatre . . .*, which was dedicated to Mrs. Astley, [wife of?] Philip Astley, an equestrian performer who established a wooden circus at Westminster and a number of equestrian theatres.

[3] Miss Holford wrote *Margaret of Anjou*. Sotheby's poem *Saul* was published in 1817.

Between whom & Sotheby there is the difference of the foam of a washing tub from the froth of a Syllabub.—And *you* talk to me of sparing the Knight—because he probably is—but no matter—I was going to say a good customer—but you are above that—however *don't* I *spare* him?—do I molest him? I laugh at him in my letters to you—& that is all—& to these I would have confined myself with regard to t'other fellow—if *he* had not begun first—but in these at least I may say a coxcomb is a *coxcomb*—so allow me to expectorate the ineffable contempt I have for the genus—of that animal—do you ever find me attack the real men of merit—do I not delight in them?—But—

> Some in the playhouse like a *row*—
> Some with the Watch to battle—
> Exchanging many a midnight blow
> To music of the Rattle.
> Some folk like rowing on the Thames
> Some rowing in an Alley—
> But all the Row my fancy claims
> Is *rowing* of my Galley.

If you like the same chorus to another tune—of "Tally i.o. the Grinder."[4]

1.

> Mrs. Wilmot sate scribbling a play—
> Mr. Sotheby sate sweating behind her—
> But what are all three to the lay
> Of Gally i. o. the Grinder—
> Gally i.o. i.o.

2.

> I bought me some books t'other day
> And sent them down stairs to the binder,
> But the Pastry Cook carried away—
> My Gally i. o. the Grinder.—

3.

> I wanted to kindle my taper
> And called to the Maid to remind her,
> And what should she bring me for paper?
> But Gally i. o. the Grinder.—

---

[4] Probably a variant of Dibdin's song. *The Grinders.*

4.

Amongst my researches for *Ease*
I went where one's certain to find her—
The first thing by her throne that one sees
Is Gally i. o. the Grinder.—

Why have you not sent me an answer & list of Subscribers to the translation of the Armenian *Eusebius*—of which I sent you six copies of the printed prospectus (in French) two months ago.—Have you had this letter? I shall send you another—you must not neglect my Armenians.—Tooth powder—Magnesia—Tincture of Myrrh—tooth brushes—diachylon plaister.——and Peruvian Bark—are my personal demands.—

Strahan—Tonson—Lintot of the times
Patron and Publisher of rhymes
For thee the Bard up Pindus climbs—
        My Murray.—
To thee with hope & terror dumb—
The unfledged M.S. authors come—
Thou printest all—& sellest some—
        My Murray.—
Upon thy tables baize so green
The last new Quarterly is seen
But where is thy new Magazine—
        My Murray.—
Along thy sprucest bookshelves shine
The works thou deemest most divine—
The "Art of Cookery"[5] and Mine
        My Murray.—
Tours—Travels—Essays too—I wist—
And Sermons to thy Mill bring Grist—
And then thou hast the "Navy List"—
        My Murray.—
And Heaven forbid I should conclude
Without the "Board of Longitude"[6]
Although this narrow paper would—
        My Murray.—

[5] One of Murray's most successful books was Mrs. Rundell's *Domestic Cookery*, published in 1806.
[6] Byron was recalling the statement on the title page of the sixth edition of *Childe Harold* (1813): "printed by T. Davison, Whitefriars, for John Murray, Bookseller to the Admiralty, and to the Board of Longitude".

Dear Sir—This letter will be delivered by Signor Gio[rgion]e Bat[tist]a Missiaglia—proprietor of the Apollo library—and ye. principal publisher & bookseller now in Venice.—He sets out for London with a view to business and correspondence with the English Booksellers—& it is in the hope that it may be for your mutual advantage that I furnish him with this letter of introduction to you— if you can be of use to him either by recommendation to others, or by any personal attention on your own part—you will oblige him—& gratify me;—you may also perhaps both be able to derive advantage or establish some mode of literary communication pleasing to the public & beneficial to one another.—At any rate—be civil to him for my sake —as well as for the honour & glory of publishers & authors now & to come for evermore.—With him I also consign a great number of M.S.S. letters written in English—French—& Italian by various English established in Italy during the last Century—the names of the writers—Ld. Hervey—Lady M. W. Montague (hers are but few— some billets-doux in french to Algarotti[1]—& one letter in English-Italian—& all sorts of jargon to the same) Gray the poet—(one letter) Mason two or three—Garrick—Lord Chatham—David Hume —& many of lesser note all addressed to Count Algarotti.—Out of these I think with discretion an amusing Miscellaneous vol. of letters might be extracted—provided Israeli or some other good *Editor* were disposed to undertake the selection—& preface—& a few notes &c. ——The Proprietor of these is a friend of mine—*Dr. Aglietti*[2]—a great name in Italy—& if you are disposed to publish it will be for *his benefit*—& it is to & for him—that you will name a price—if you take upon you the work.—I would edite it myself—but am too far off—& too lazy to undertake it—but I wish that it could be done.—The letters of Ld. Hervey in Mr. Rose's opinion & mine are good—& the *Short* French love letters *certainly* are Lady M. W. Montague's— the *French* not good but the Sentiments beautiful—Gray's letter good & Mason's tolerable—the whole Correspondence must be *well weeded*——but this being done—a small & *pretty* popular volume might be made of it.—There are many Ministers letters—Gray the Ambassador at Naples—Horace Mann—& others of the same kind of

[1] Francesco Algarotti (1712–1764) was a voluminous and versatile Italian writer, a close friend of Frederick the Great and of Voltaire. His correspondents included some of the most distinguished people of the day.

[2] Francesco Aglietti (1757–1836), eminent medical doctor residing in Venice, had a turn for literature. He had edited the *Opere* of Algarotti (Venice, 1791–1794).

animal.—I thought of a preface—defending Ld. Hervey against Pope's attack—but Pope quoad Pope the poet against the world—in the unjustifiable attempts at depreciation begun by Warton—& carried on to & at this day by the new School of Critics & Scribblers who think themselves poets because they do *not* write like Pope.—I have no patience with such cursed humbug—& bad taste—your whole generation are not worth a Canto of the Rape of the Lock—or the Essay on Man—or the Dunciad—or "anything that is his" but it is three in the matin & I must go to bed.—

yrs. always
BYRON

[TO CHARLES HANSON]   *Venice. April 15th. 1818*

Dear Charles/—I have only time by the Post for five words—to say that *I can not* on any account whatever proceed to Geneva—& that the Messenger must be written to come on to *Venice* direct—I am unwell—& can't move.—Excuse haste the post is going out—but recollect that as I have said—so must it be—or not at all.—

yrs ever & truly
BYRON

[TO JOHN MURRAY]   *Venice. April 15th. 1818*

Dear Sir/—Two words in haste to deliver to Mr. Hanson,—or to my friend Mr. Hobhouse to convey to him.—I will *not* go to Geneva—not stir from Italy—(or Venice at present) for any human power or interest whatever.—It is as easy for the Messenger to proceed here as there—or for me to go there—and every step nearer England—would be to me disgusting.———Let this be said to H[anson] as my positive determination—

yrs in haste the Post just going
ever &c.

[TO JOHN CAM HOBHOUSE]   *Venice. April 17th. 1818*

Dear Hobhouse—I was paralyzed yesterday—or the day before—or Wednesday—by a letter from young Spooney containing the news of a Messenger for *Geneva*—& desiring me to repair *there*!!! if I stir from Venice—by anything but absolute force—may—but no matter for that.—Nothing but downright necessity—or destiny will ever make me to return to England—and there's an end.—I need hardly add that the Messenger should be directed to go to Venice—if not—he may go to Hell!—I won't meet him half way in either case.—It is easier & less expensive for him to proceed here—than for me to repair there—God damn that infernally stupid Chancery Lane & its inmates with their cursed Circumbendibus & Crinkum Crankum—as Mr. Sterling calls it.[1]——Pray stir up Spooney with a long pole—& don't let me be buffooned in this way with his "barbarous topography"—I dare say he thinks that Venice is in the valley of Chamouni.——In any case I repeat that I won't stir.—I would not for the best friend I have in the World (always bating Scrope who is not *my* friend—but "everybody's Huncamunca") far less for my own *in*convenience.—And now I wonder that *you* should allow such doings—you who know my way of thinking—

ever yrs very truly
BYRON

P.S.—I am sorry you left Venice because I have lately taken to going to the Benzone—& the Michelli—which is a variety—& there are people who would amuse you.——

[TO JOHN MURRAY] *Venice. April 17th. 1818*

Dear Sir—A few days ago I wrote to you a letter requesting you to desire Hanson to desire his Messenger to come on from Geneva to Venice—because I won't go from Venice to Geneva, & if this is not done—this Messenger may be damned, with him who missent him. Pray reiterate my request.——With the proofs returned I sent two additional stanzas for Canto 4th. did they arrive?——Your Monthly reviewer has made a mistake—*Cavaliere* alone is well enough—but *"Cavalier servente"* has always the *e* mute in conversation and omitted in writing—so that it is not for the sake of metre—& pray let Griffiths[1] know this with my compliments—I humbly conjecture that I know as much of Italian society and language as any of his people—but to make assurance doubly sure—I asked at the Countess Benzoni's last night the question of more than one person in *the office*—and of these "Cavalier*i* serventi" (in the plural recollect) I found that they all

[1] See Nov. 19, 1817, to Kinnaird, note 1 (Vol. 5, p. 274).
[1] Ralph Griffiths, founder and publisher of the *Monthly Review*.

accorded in pronouncing for Cavalier' Servente in the *singular* number.
—I wish Mr. Hodgson (or whoever Griffith's Scribbler may be)
would not talk of what *he* don't understand—such fellows are not fit to
be intrusted with Italian, even in a quotation.—Sotheby again!—he
had best be quiet—but no—ask him from *me* in so many words—did
he or did he not write an anonymous note at Rome accompanying a
copy of the "Castle of Chillon &c."—ask him from *me*? & let him be
confronted with the note now in the possession of Mr. Hobhouse! He
(Sotheby) is a vile—stupid—old Coxcomb—& if I do not weed him
from the surface of the society he infests & infects—may—may—but
I won't adjure a great power—for so scabby an object—as that
wretched leper of literature—that *Itch* of Scribbling personified—
Sotheby.
It is ten o'clock—& time to dress.——

[scrawl for closing and signature]

[TO JEAN ANTOINE GALIGNANI]   *Venise. 20 Avril 1818*

Je soussigné declare ceder à Mr. Jean Antoine Galignani Libraire à
Paris mes divers Ouvrages pour les rendre exclusivement en *France*
en toute proprieté et en tirer la nombre d'editions que lui conviendra.—

BYRON
Pair d'Angleterre

[TO DOUGLAS KINNAIRD]   *Venice. April 23d. 1818*

Dear Douglas/—I will *not* go to Geneva—and I look upon the
proposition as a very gross neglect on the part of Hanson and an
affront on that of my friends including you—Davies—Hobhouse &
every body else.—The Messenger must come here—is it not evident
that the expence and trouble must be less for the man & papers to
come to me than for me to go to the Man & papers?—At any rate, and
at any cost—I won't stir—and if anything occurs—it is all *your* faults
for not taking better care of my interests—besides wanting to drag
me a mile closer to your infernal country.——"Poor Maria" um!—I
do not understand the particulars—nor wish to hear them—all I
know is that she made your house very pleasant to your friends, and
as far as I know made no mischief—(which is saying infinitely for a
woman) and therefore whatever has or may happen—she has my good
will, go where she will;—I understand that you have provided for her

33

in the handsomest manner—which is your nature—& don't *surprize* me—as far as Prudence goes—you are right to dissolve such a connection—and as to provocation—doubtless you had sufficient—but I can't help being sorry for the woman—although she *did* tell you that I made love to her—which by the God of Scrope Davies! was not true—for I never dreamed of making love to any thing of yours except sixty pints of Brandy sixty years old—all or the greater part of which I consumed in your suppers.—God help me—I was very sorry when they were no more.—Now to business.—"Shylock, I must have monies"—so have at Spooney for Noel's & Newstead arrears—& have at Murray for coming copyrights—& let me have a credit forthwith;—I am in cash but I don't like to break in upon my *circular* notes—in case of a journey—or changing my residence—but look to my finance department—& above all *don't lecture me*—for I won't bear it & will run savage.—Make the *Messenger proceed* from Geneva—send him a letter therefor—that we may conclude the Newstead Sale—& if you can sell or settle a sale for Rochdale—do—Newstead has done well so far.——Do not suppose that I will be induced to return toward England for less than the most imperious motives—but believe me always

yrs.

[scrawl for signature]

P.S.—Don't mind Hobhouse—he would whistle me home—that is to *his* home—if he could—but *"thaut's impossible"* for the *son* & *heir* of Sir Wm. Meadows[1]——So look to it—& don't conspire against me —or my quiet.——

[TO JOHN MURRAY]   *Venice. April 23d. 1818*

Dear Sir—The time is past in which I could feel for the dead—or I should feel for the death of Lady Melbourne the best & kindest & ablest female I ever knew—old or young[1]—but "I have supped full of horrors"[2] & events of this kind leave only a kind of numbness worse than pain—like a violent blow on the elbow or on the head—there is one link the less between England & myself.——Now to business.— I presented you with "Beppo" as part of the contract for Canto fourth —considering the price you are to pay for the same—& intending it to

---

[1] See March 7, 1817, to Hobhouse, note 4 (Vol. 5, p. 182).
[1] Lady Melbourne died at Melbourne House on April 6, 1818.
[2] *Macbeth*, Act V, scene 5.

eke you out in case of public caprice or my own poetical failure—if you choose to suppress it entirely at Mr. Sotheby's suggestion—you may do as you please—but recollect that it is not to be published in a *garbled* or *mutilated state.*—I reserve to my friends & to myself the right of correcting the press—if the publication continues it is to continue in it's present form.——If Mr. S[otheby] fancies—or feels himself alluded to & injured by the allusion—he has his redress—by law—by reply—or by such other remedy personal or poetical as may seem good to himself or any person or persons acting for by or at his suggestion.³——My reasons for presuming Mr. S[otheby] to be ye. author of the anonymous note sent to me at Rome last Spring with a copy of "Chillon" &c. with marginal notes by the writer of the billet were—firstly—Similarity in the handwriting;—of which I could form a recollection from correspondence between Mr. S. & myself on the subject of "Ivan" a play offered to D[rury] L[ane] Theatre—2dly. the *Style*—more especially the word "Effulgence" a phrase which clinched my conjecture as decisively as any coincidence between Francis & Junius—3dly. the paucity of English *then* at Rome—& the circumstances of Mr. S[otheby]'s return from *Naples*— & the delivery of this note & book occurring at the same period—he having then & there arrived with a party of Blue-stocking Bi—women —I would say—of the same complexion whom he afterwards conveyed to the Abbate Morelli's at Venice—to view his Cameo—where they so tormented the poor old man (nearly twenty in number all with pencil & notebook in hand & questions in infamous Italian & villainous French) that it became the talk of Venice—as you may find by asking my friend Mr. Hoppner or others who were then at Venice— 4thly. my being aware of Mr. S[otheby]'s patronage & anxiety on such occasions which led me to the belief that with very good intentions —he might nevertheless blunder in his mode of giving as well as taking opinions—& 5thly. the Devil who made Mr. S[otheby] one author and me another.——As Mr. S says that he did not write this letter &c. I am ready to believe him—but for the firmness of my former persuasion—I refer to Mr. Hobhouse who can inform you how sincerely I erred on this point—he has also the note—or at least *had* it—for I gave it to him with my verbal comments thereupon. As to Beppo I will not alter or suppress a syllable for any man's pleasure but my own—if there are resemblances between Botherby & Sotheby or Sotheby and Botherby the fault is not mine—but in the person who

³ Byron feared that Murray would leave out his reference in *Beppo* to "bustling Botherby" (Stanza 72).

resembles—or the persons who trace a resemblance.—Who find out this resemblance?—Mr. S[otheby]'s *friends*—*who* go about moaning over him & laughing? Mr. S's *friends*—whatever allusions Mr. S. may imagine—or whatever may or may not really exist in the passages in question—I can assure him—that there is not a literary man or a pretender to Literature—or a reader of the day—in the World of London—who does not think & express more obnoxious opinions of his Blue-stocking Mummeries than are to be found in print—and I for one think and say that to the best of my knowledge & belief from past experience and present information Mr. Sotheby has made & makes himself highly ridiculous.—He may be an amiable man—a moral man —a good father—a good husband—a respectable & devout individual —I have nothing to say against all this—but I have something to say of Mr. S's literary foibles—and of the wretched affectations & systematized Sophistry of many men women & Children now extant & absurd in & about London & elsewhere;—which & whom in their false pretensions & nauseous attempts to make Learning a nuisance— & society a Bore—I consider as fair Game—to be brought down on all fair occasions—& I doubt not by the blessing of God on my honest purpose and the former example of Mr. Gifford & others my betters before my eyes—to extirpate—extinguish & eradicate such as come within the compass of my intention.———And this is my opinion—of which you will express as much or as little as you think proper. Did you receive two additional Stanzas to be inserted towards the close of Canto 4th.?—Respond—that (if not) they may be sent.—Tell Mr. Hobhouse & Mr Hanson that they may as well expect Geneva to come to me as that I should go to Geneva.—The Messenger may go on or return as he pleases—I won't *stir*—& I look upon it as a piece of singular absurdity, in those who know me imagining that I should— not to say *Malice,* in attempting unnecessary torture.—If on the occasion my interests should suffer—it is their neglect that is to blame—and they may all be damned together.—You may tell them this—and add that nothing but force—or necessity—shall stir me one step towards the places to which they would [wring?] me—I wonder particularly at Mr. Hobhouse (who is in possession of my opinions) sanctioning such a conspiracy against my tranquillity.—— If your literary matters prosper—let me know.—If Beppo pleases you shall have more in a year or two in the same mood.—And so "Good Morrow to you good Master Lieutenant."

yrs.
[Scrawl for signature]

Dear Hobhouse—I have written to Murray on Sotheby's affair—which response he will communicate—I suppose that you are in possession of the note and book—and I then & there told you my reasons for believing Sotheby the writer. I will not go to Geneva—and I look upon it as a great piece of ignorance & unfriendliness in those who have endeavoured to *trepan* me into such an infamous journey.—I would sooner perish than undertake it, at least upon such motives.—By this post I have written to Kinnaird on business;—I must have monies—and Hanson and Murray are to make some payments—or ought.—The cursed stupidity of sending me the Clerk & parchments to Geneva is beyond measure vexatious—but this comes of having friends—I wish they were all damned—from Pylades to the present day.——He must be eked on to Venice at any or all events—I will not stir—"no not for Venice" nor from Venice;—the expence must be much less for the fellow to come to me—than for me to be lugged over the Alps towards your country—which I hate as I do my mother in law.——Now I have sworn—and am easier.——Did not you get two additional stanzas for Canto 4th.? I sent them—if not arrived—tell me. Shelley has got to Milan with the bastard & it's mother—but won't send the shild—unless I will go & see the mother—I have sent a messenger for the Shild—but I can't leave my quarters—& have "sworn an oath"—between Attorneys,—Clerks—& Whores—& wives—& children—and friends—my life is made a burthen—and it is all owing to *your* negligence & "want of memory".——I can't help being sorry for D[ougla]s Kinnaird's piece—she gave me sixty bottles of brandy—the very best I ever drank—poor dear woman—she will be a great loss—I shall never see the like again.——I regret to hear of Scrope's not winning—such a man's destiny ought not to be in a dice box—or a horse's hoof—or a Gambler's hand. Venice is Venice.—I go now often to the Benzona's—the oddest & pleasantest of elderly ladies—& her Conversazione better than the Governor's or the Albrizzi's.—I have got a sty in my eye—Madame S[egati] has got an ague fever;—I have taken part of Gritti's palace for three years[1]—so don't think of dragging me over the Channel

yrs
[Scrawl for signature]

---

[1] See March 25, 1818, to Hobhouse, note 2.

Dear Sir—You are requested to procure Subscribers for the inclosed in the Universities or elsewhere[1]—this is the second bundle I have sent you of the same prospectus.—

yrs.
[Scrawl for signature]

[CONCERNING W. S. ROSE]   *Venice, May, 1818*

[At bottom of some rhymes by Rose]: These verses[1] were sent to me by W. S. Rose from Albaro, in the spring of 1818. They are good and true—and Rose is a fine fellow—and one of the few English who understand *Italy*—without which Italian is nothing.

[TO THE COUNTESS OF JERSEY]   *Venice. May 5th. 1818*

Dear Lady Jersey,—Il Cavaliere Vincenzo Peruzzi di Firenze—has been much recommended to me for letters of introduction to that Society in England—to which he has claim by birth & conduct.—In this point of view—I know not to whom I can introduce him with more propriety than to yourself—who unite so much that is powerful with all that is amiable.——You will do me a great favour by permitting the admission of this Gentleman into your Society—more especially as the Italians complain hitherto of English neglect—for which I feel the more remorse as I cannot retort the accusation—at least as far as my own slender experience goes.—In introducing him to your notice I give him a chance (or *certainty* if this recommendation has any weight) of seeing the best company which our English Circles can afford—and as far as I can recollect of all that I have ever seen there or elsewhere; the most agreeable.—With my best remembrances to Lord Jersey—I have the honour to be ever & truly dear Lady Jersey

yr. most obliged & faithful Sert.
BYRON

[1] See Jan. 27, 1818, to Murray.
[1] The verses begin:

Byron, while you make gay what circle fits ye,
    Bandy Venetian slang with the Benzon,
    Or play at company with the Albrizzi . . .
        (*LJ*, IV, 212n.)

My dear Hobhouse—By these presents you are recommended & requested to cherish, protect, and introduce to all fashionable people— the noble Cavaliere Vincenzo Peruzzi—born at Bologna—bred in Firenze.———"Give him Gruel—Give him *fuel*" the latter he will much want in our paese—if he comes in any month—but August.— Introduce him—& produce him—at Ld. Holland's—Lady Jersey's— and all such places as may give him an adequate notion of the English. Let him draw upon D[ougla]s K[innair]d & dine with every body—& tell Scrope to make him drunk—as he (Scrope) will make me when "we three meet again"

ever yrs.
BYRON

P.S.—My Bastard came three days ago[1]—very like—healthy— noisy—& capricious.—

Dear Hobhouse—That is right—row & spur Spooney;—& let Murray disburse—however I don't mean to pin him—if he feels losing I will let him down as many pounds as he likes—whether the Bulgars (the public) like the "poeshie" or no is no matter—the profit is the point—Let me know the facts—but don't let Murray be a loser—I threw in "Beppo" to eke him out in case of accidents—but let what is to be paid—be paid—readily—or steadily—because I see that Spooney dawdles—damn him—had I followed yr. advice—I should have now been hating myself at Geneva—waiting for his messenger—who was not there at the time—for I wrote to Hentsch the Banker—to kick his backside over the Simplon—& lo, he was not come.——I desire that Spooney may pay such balance of N[ewstea]d arrears into Dug's bank.—as may be received or cashable in whatever portions—great or small—when the man comes—I will sign all the papers of Sale & receipt proper to be signed—& Murray may as well be dating his bills;—I rejoice for the illustrations & the preface—but I wish you in Parliament—try—there is time 'twixt this & October.— Tell Ld. Kinnaird—that the lady to whom Vendiamini would not

---

[1] Byron's daughter Allegra by Claire Clairmont was sent from Milan, where Claire had arrived with the Shelleys, for him to rear. Allegra and her Swiss nurse Elise stayed with the Hoppners until Byron moved into the Palazzo Mocenigo at the beginning of June, and frequently thereafter.

introduce him—and to whom Rizzo[1] might have *introduced* him—(but I suppose shuffled also because he was an admirer) within the last ten days has become as far as a Cappricio—Roba mia;—I asked Rizzo to introduce me—who declined—for fear of an Austrian Colonel, nephew to Marechal Bianchi (who is her Cavalier Servente)—so I found a way by means of Soranzo another Venetian Noble and friend of mine—and have fucked her twice a day for the last six—today is the seventh—but no Sabbath day—for we meet at Midnight at her Milliner's—She is the prettiest Bacchante in the world—& a piece to perish *in.*—The Segati & I have been *off* these two months—or rather three.—I have a world of other harlotry—besides an offer of the daughter of the Arlechino of St. Luke's theatre—so that my hands are full——whatever my Seminal vessels may be—With regard to Arpalice Terucelli[2] (the Madcap above mentioned)—recollect there is no *liaison* only *fuff-fuff* and passades—& fair fucking—you may easily suppose I did not much heed her Austrian Dragon—who may do as he likes and be damned.—I have taken part of the Mocenigo Palace for three years—(on the Grand Canal) and have been much among the Natives since you went—particularly at the *Benzona's*—who is a kind of Venetian (late) Lady Melbourne.—Recollect my demands—*money*—*monies*—tooth powder—Magnesia—Soda powders —Spooney's papers—& good news of you & yours always & ever

B

[TO JOHN CAM HOBHOUSE]   *Venice. May 27th. 1818*

Dear Hobhouse—I write for my fee—"every man should have a proper regard for his fee".[1]—Douglas Kinnaird—(or in his absence) *you* as my deputy's deputy—are requested, & required, & besought— to extract payments (inas*much* as possible) from Spooney & Murray— the son of a Kinnaird never has written to me a syllable since one epistle about his late Mistress—let him at least dun Murray & Spooney if he will do nothing else.——Spooney writes to promise the writings for signature to *set* out for Venice the *end* of *this moon*—a pretty figure I should have cut at Geneva if I had set out at your former requisition —waiting for the Attorneo.—And let me beg of you & Douglas to keep an eye on Spooney's remittances and accounts of my Jew debts &c.

---

[1] Count Francesco Rizzo-Patarol, a *bon viveur* and man about town.
[2] Byron later spelled the name Tarruscelli and Taruscelli.
[1] Fielding, *Joseph Andrews*, Book IV, chap. 3: "Every man ought to have a proper value for his fee."

&c. at the period when the monies & discharges are in action—& let me have his *bill* surveyed by (what Mrs. Heidelberg calls)—"the Counsellors *at* law" and in short as you are my friend show yourself as *sich*—or why did I write a preface!—Talking of prefaces reminds me of the book which like "Gill comes tumbling after"—I have never heard of it since the day of publication & yr. letter two days after—which doth not answer so very splendidly for the publication—because had there been any thing good to tell you would have told it amongst you; —I don't much mind that—but I should like to have "my fee" and I desire that you will have a proper look out "for my fee." I desire money—and magnesia—and Soda powders—& any new publications —and tooth powder—& bark—and Diachylon plaister—& my love to every body—

yrs.
[Scrawl for signature]

P.S.—There must be some balance from Newstead & old Noel and whatever it may be let me have it—by the way old *Joe* must not be forgotten—I give Carte blanche about him—but *let him above all have all possible* comforts and requisites in any case—I can't write the prologue for F[rancesc]a²—"I'm not i' the vein"—but I wish you Joy & success.——My Bastard came a month ago—a very fine child— much admired in the gardens & on the Piazza—and greatly caressed by the Venetians from the Governatrice downwards.——Don't *forget my monies*—and let some be sent in *circular notes* in case I take to voyaging—for I don't like to be pinned only to one bank or banker. ——See if aught can be done for or with *Rochdale* also.——

[TO DOUGLAS KINNAIRD]   *Venice. May 27th. 1818*

Dear Douglas—Business.—I beg you to dun Spooney—there is or ought to be something (however trifling) from Newstead & old Noel the everlasting—no matter—let's have it.—Then there is Murray—I desire to have "my fee" or part of "my fee"—I desiderate monies—monies—"Shylock! I would have monies"—and pray *send me part in circulars* because I have been obliged to break into those I have—or rather had—and I don't like to be limited to Siri & Willhalm only—in case I should like to voyage.—I wrote to you a month ago

² Hobhouse had written a play called *Francesca*. See June 28, 1818, to Hobhouse.

and more—but you are as negligent as the rest—in the mean time I am & do very well being in good health & performance & very much

yrs. ever and Sincerely
BYRON

P.S.—*Keep an eye* on Spooney—& more particularly on his distribution *of the products of the Sale* when fulfilled—*spur* him about *Rochdale* also—and above all extract coin from him & Murray—and pray now don't forget—I hope you will *marry.*—*My* bastard came here a month ago—a very fine child—& much admired by the Venetian public.—Hobhouse can tell you her history.—I have broke my old liaison with la Segati—& have taken a dozen in stead;—all's well as yet.—

[TO MONSIEUR MICHELE LEONI[1]]   *Venice. May 30th. 1818*

Sir—I have been favoured through the medium of Madame Albrizzi, with yr. letter and translation with which you have honoured me; & return my thanks in my native language—that I may not do injustice to yours.—With the translation *I* have more reason to be satisfied than the *Public*, who will hardly forgive you for condescending (even for a moment) to lay aside Shakespeare—Milton—and Otway, to adorn the pages of a writer of the present day.—In common with every English reader of your language I feel highly indebted for the honour you have done to ours in your versions of the most Classical of our poets and I should be more gratified by your continuance to give *them* to Italy, than by any personal honour or advantage I could derive from the introduction of my own attempts (even under your auspices) to the foreign reader.—I have the honour to be, Sir,—

yr. obliged & very obedt. humble Servt.
BYRON

[TO CHARLES HANSON]   *Venice, May 31st. 1818*

Dear Charles—I have received your letter—and shall expect the Messenger.—On his return you will take the proper steps in conjunction with Mr. Kinnaird for the liquidation of the debts—settling however *all* the other claims prior to the Massingberd annuities—for

---

[1] Michele Leoni translated into Italian in 1818 Byron's *Lament of Tasso*, and in 1819 Canto 4 of *Childe Harold*. See May 8, 1820, to Murray.

which I conceive that terms less exorbitant may be made.——I also wish to have your father's bill;—and I could desire if possible that something definitive should be adjusted with regard to *Rochdale*—can't you sell it for me? You seem to have acted so well hitherto in the present Newstead purchase (as far as it has hitherto advanced) that it might encourage you to try a sale for *Rochdale* also.—I think you will agree with me that the Settlement with the Creditors will be more easily & readily made during my absence from England, than if I were upon the spot—make the best terms you can with them consistent with fairness of dealing to them & to myself.——I request that any balance due or received from Newstead or Sir R. Noel—may be paid in to my account at Morland's & the credit sent out by post immediately—if any such has been sent in by you—I have not received as yet the letter of advice from them.—For old Murray I leave you Carte blanche—& request you to deduct from remittances any sum requisite for his comfort & well doing—& the same half yearly. Recommending to you the above requests—particularly with regard to *Rochdale*—& desiring my best regards to you & yours believe me

ever & very truly yrs.
Byron

P.S.—It is the more requisite that you should act for me with all convenient speed & decision—as I am not in the present intention of quitting Venice for some years—having just taken a house in the city, & another in the country, for *three years*.——

[to james wedderburn webster] *Venice. May 31st. 1818*

Dear Webster—I [am] truly sorry to hear of yr. domestic misfortune —and as I know the inefficacy of words—shall turn from the subject. ——I was not even aware of yr. return to France—where I presume that you are a resident.——For my own part, after going down to Florence & Rome last year, I returned to Venice where I have since remained—& may probably continue to remain for some years—being partial to the people the language & the habits of life;—there are few English here—& those mostly birds of passage,—excepting one or two who are domesticated like myself.—I have the Palazzo Mocenigo on the Canal' Grande for three years to come—& a pretty Villa in the Euganean hills for the Summer for nearly the same term.——While I remain in the city itself—I keep my horses on an Island with a good beach, about half a mile from the town, so that I get a gallup of some miles along the shore of the Adriatic daily—the Stables belong to the Fortress—but are let on fair terms.—I was always very partial to Venice—and it has not hitherto disappointed me—but I am not sure that the English in general would like it—I am sure that I should not, if *they* did—but by the benevolence of God—they prefer Florence & Naples—and do not infest us greatly here.—In other respects it is very agreeable for Gentlemen of desultory habits—women—wine— and wassail being all extremely fair & reasonable—theatres &c. good —& Society (after a time—) as pleasant as anywhere else (at least to my mind) if you will live with them in their own way—which is different of course from the Ultramontane in some degree.—The Climate is Italian & that's enough—and the Gondolas &c. &c. & habits of the place make it like a romance—for it is by no means even now the most regular & correct *moral* city in the universe.—Young and old—pretty & ugly—high and low—are employed in the laudable practice of Lovemaking—and though most Beauty is found amongst the middling & lower classes—this of course only renders their amatory habits more universally diffused.—I shall be very glad to hear from or of you when you are so disposed—& with my best regards to Lady Frances—believe me

very truly yrs

B

P.S.—If ever you come this way—let me have a letter before hand —in case I can be of use.—

[TO JOHN CAM HOBHOUSE]   *Venice. June 1818*

Sir—With great grief I inform you of the death of my late dear Master[1]—my Lord—who died this morning at ten of the Clock of a rapid decline & slow fever—caused by anxiety—sea-bathing—women & riding in the Sun against my advice.—He is a dreadful loss to every body, mostly to me—who have lost a master and a place—also I hope you—Sir—will give me a charakter.—I saved in his service as you know several hundred pounds—God knows how—for I don't, nor my late master neither—and if my wage was not always paid to the day— still it was or is to be paid sometime & somehow—you—Sir—who are his executioner won't see a poor Servant wronged of his little all.—My dear Master had several phisicians and a Priest—he died a Papish [sic]

---

[1] In this letter Byron is pretending to be his valet William Fletcher.

but is to be buried among the Jews in the Jewish burying ground—
for my part I don't see why—he could not abide them when living nor
any other people—bating whores—who asked him for money.—He
suffered his illness with great patience—except that when in extremity
he twice damned his friends & said they were selfish rascals—you—
Sir—particularly & Mr. Kinnaird—who had never answered his
letters nor complied with his repeated requests.—He also said he
hoped that your new tragedy would be damned—God forgive him—I
hope that my master won't be damned like the tragedy.——His nine
whores are already provided for—& the other servants—but what is
to become of me—I have got his Cloathes & Carriages—& Cash—&
everything—but the Consul quite against law has clapt his seal &
taken an inven*tary* & swears that *he* must account to my Lord's heirs—
who they are—I don't know—but they ought to consider poor
Servants & above all his Vally de Sham. My Lord never grudged me
perquisites—my wage was the least I got by him—and if I did keep the
Countess (she is or ought to be a Countess although she is upon the
town) Marietta—Monetta—Piretta[2]—after passing my word to you
and my Lord that I would not never no more—still he was an indulgent
master—& only said I was a damned fool—& swore & forgot it
again.—What Could I do—she said as how she should die—or kill
herself if I did not go with her—& so I did—& kept her out of my
Lord's washing & ironing—& nobody can deny that although the
charge was high—the linen was well got up.—Hope you are well Sir—
am with tears in my eyes

yours faithfully to command
Wm. Fletcher

P.S.—If you know any Gentleman in want of a Wally—hope for a
charakter—I saw your late Swiss Servant in the Galleys at Leghorn for
robbing an Inn—he produced your recommendation at his trial.——

[TO THOMAS MOORE]
Palazzo Mocenigo, Canal Grande, Venice, June 1st. 1818

Your letter is almost the only news, as yet, of Canto 4th, and it has
by no means settled its fate—at least, does not tell me how the

---

[2] There is reference here to a real amorous adventure of Fletcher, and one which
lasted for some time, for when Byron was planning to return to England in
December, 1819, he wrote to Hoppner (Dec. 7, 1819): "pray beg Lancetti not to
give Fletcher's Tiretta passports for England."

"Poeshie" has been received by the public. But I suspect, no great things,—firstly, from Murray's "horrid stillness;" secondly, from what you say about the stanzas running into each other, which I take *not* to be *yours*, but a notion you have been dinned with among the Blues. The fact is, that the terza rima of the Italians, which always *runs* on and in, may have led me into experiments, and carelessness into conceit—or conceit into carelessness—in either of which events failure will be probable, and my fair woman, "superne," end in a fish;[1] so that Childe Harold will be like the mermaid, my family crest, with the Fourth Canto for a tail thereunto. I won't quarrel with the public, however, for the "Bulgars" are generally right; and if I miss now, I may hit another time:—and so, the "gods give us joy."[2]

You like *Beppo*, that's right. * * * * I have not had the Fudges[3] yet, but live in hopes. I need not say that your successes are mine. By the way, Lydia White[4] is here, and has just borrowed my copy of "Lalla Rookh."

* * * * * * * * * * * * * * *

Hunt's letter is probably the exact piece of vulgar coxcombry you might expect from his situation. He is a good man, with some poetical elements in his chaos; but spoilt by the Christ-Church Hospital and a Sunday newspaper,—to say nothing of the Surry Jail, which conceited him into a martyr. But he is a good man. When I saw "Rimini" in MSS., I told him that I deemed it good poetry at bottom, disfigured only by a strange style. His answer was, that his style was a system, or *upon system*, or some such cant; and, when a man talks of system, his case is hopeless: so I said no more to him, and very little to any one else.

He believes his trash of vulgar phrases tortured into compound barbarisms to be *old* English; and we may say of it as Aimwell says of Captain Gibbet's regiment, when the Captain calls it an "old corps." —"the *oldest* in Europe, if I may judge by your uniform,"[5] He sent out his "Foliage"[6] by Percy Shelley * * * , and, of all the ineffable Centaurs that were ever begotten by Selflove upon a Night-mare, I

---

[1] Horace, *Ars Poetica*, line 4: "Desinat in piscem mulier formosa superne". (Paints a woman above, a fish below.)

[2] *As You Like It*, Act III, scene 3.

[3] Moore's *The Fudge Family in Paris* (1818).

[4] See Vol. 3, p. 214, note 3.

[5] Farquhar, *The Beaux' Strategem*, Act III, scene 2:

   "Gibbet. A marching Regiment, Sir, an old Corps.
   Aimwell (aside). Very old, if your Coat be Regimental."

[6] Leigh Hunt's *Foliage, or Poems Original and Translated* (1818).

think this monstrous Sagittary[7] the most prodigious. *He* (Leigh H.)
is an honest Charlatan, who has persuaded himself into a belief of
his own impostures, and talks Punch in pure simplicity of heart,
taking himself (as poor Fitzgerald said of *him*self in the Morning
Post) for *Vates* in both senses, or nonsenses, of the word.[8] Did you
look at the translations of his own which he prefers to Pope and
Cowper, and says so?[9]—Did you read his skimble-skamble about
[Wordsworth] being at the head of his own *profession*, in the *eyes* of
those who followed it? I thought that Poetry was an *art*, or an *attribute*,
and not a *profession*;—but be it one, is that * * * * * at the head of
your profession in *your* eyes? I'll be curst if he is of *mine*, or ever shall
be. He is the only one of us (but of us he is not) whose coronation I
would oppose. Let them take Scott, Campbell, Crabbe, or you, or me,
or any of the living, and throne him;—but not this new Jacob Behmen,
this * * * * whose pride might have kept him true, even had his
principles turned as perverted as his *soi-disant* poetry.

But Leigh Hunt is a good man, and a good father—see his Odes to
all the Masters Hunt;—a good husband—see his Sonnet to Mrs.
Hunt;—a good friend—see his Epistles to different people;—and a
great coxcomb and a very vulgar person in every thing about him.
But that's not his fault, but of circumstances.

* * * * * * * * * * * * * *
* * * * * * * * * * * * * *

I do not know any good model for a life of Sheridan but that of
Savage. Recollect, however, that the life of such a man may be made
far more amusing than if he had been a Wilberforce;—and this
without offending the living, or insulting the dead. The Whigs abuse
him; however, he never left them, and such blunderers deserve neither
credit nor compassion. As for his creditors,—remember, Sheridan
never had a shilling, and was thrown, with great powers and passions,
into the thick of the world, and placed upon the pinnacle of success,
with no other external means to support him in his elevation. Did
Fox * * * *pay his* debts?—or did Sheridan take a subscription? Was
the Duke of Norfolk's drunkeness more excusable than his? Were his
intrigues more notorious than those of all his contemporaries? and is

---

[7] *Troilus and Cressida*, Act V, scene 5: "The dreadful Sagittary appals our
numbers".
[8] William Thomas Fitzgerald, who considered himself a kind of poet laureate,
was ridiculed by Byron in *English Bards and Scotch Reviewers*.
[9] Hunt said that Cowper's translation of Homer was spoiled by "over-timidity",
and he spoke of Pope's "elegant mistake . . . called Homer's *Iliad*". (Hunt's
Foliage, Preface, p. 31).

his memory to be blasted, and theirs respected? Don't let yourself be led away by clamour, but compare him with the coalitioner Fox, and the pensioner Burke, as a man of principle, and with ten hundred thousand in personal views, and with none in talent, for he beat them all *out* and *out*. Without means, without connexion, without character, (which might be false at first, and make him mad afterwards from desperation,) he beat them all, in all he ever attempted. But alas poor human nature! Good night—or, rather, morning. It is four, and the dawn gleams over the Grand Canal, and unshadows the Rialto. I must to bed; up all night—but, as George Philpot says, "it's life, though, damme it's life!"[10]

Ever yours,
B

Excuse errors—no time for revision. The post goes out at noon, and I shan't be up then. I will write again soon about your *plan* for a publication.

[TO DOUGLAS KINNAIRD]   *Venice. June 3d. 1818*

Dear Douglas—Though I wrote to you last week—I will refresh your memory with the present letter for fear of accidents.—My request is that you will apply to Hanson & Murray for *assetts*—monies—bills —or balances—great or small—as I must draw out my Conscription— for the year—the last having well nigh done it's duty.—Murray has published—so may begin to pay.—Hanson must have something in hand—no matter what—it is all Grist—& may be paid in with old Noel's balance—if not already paid.—It would be hard if with better prospects than last year's—having now sold Newstead, & M[urra]y having put forth his speculation—that I should find myself adry— which would however be the case—if *you* don't look sharp after those two worthies—who are neither of them the promptest at disbursement. —Let me have a few *Circulars* in case of travel—& the rest on Siri & Willhalm as usual.—Don't neglect these advices—& at any rate answer me—I answer you always by return of post;—I did not & will not go to Geneva—a pretty set of friends I have to advise me to such a step.—I have taken a Mocenigo palace furnished &c. on the Grand Canal—for *three* years—at four thousand eight hundred francs—(that

[10] Arthur Murphy, *The Citizen*, Act I, scene 2. Young George Philpot says, "Up all night—stripped of nine hundred pounds . . . cruel luck!—damn me, it's life though—this is life."

is two hundred Louis) per annum—it is a good situation—well furnished—every thing found me—& (they tell me) not dear, all things considered. The Segati & I are off.——

P.S.—Can anything be done about eternal Rochdale? I wish that it was settled—or rather sold—see what you can do with Spooney— (to whom I wrote the other day) with regard to it, & other affairs.— You must not mind Hobhouse—who wants to lug me back to England —which I never will revisit—unless from absolute necessity of health or business.—So don't conspire with the mountebanks who think of such things.——Hanson's man with the papers is to come out to Venice.

[TO DOUGLAS KINNAIRD]   *Venice June 8th. 1818*

Dear Douglas/—As a much longer period than usual has elapsed without my hearing at all from England—though I write repeatedly— I am under the necessity of troubling you (but too often) to apply to Hanson for any balance in his hands—and to Murray to make some payments and that speedily as my present funds here are drawing to a close.——The balance with Hanson should be paid—however trifling—& Murray by this time ought to have made some disbursements—I can only say that if these gentlemen neglect my requests— that I shall be put to inconvenience—without any just reason.— Whenever Wildman pays his money—(or the present interest) the interest should be remitted regularly half yearly—that is such portion of it as I may not direct for other purposes.—I must also add as the usual burthen of my song—that I hope that you will not forget to fillip Hanson about that eternal Rochdale.

ever yrs truly & affect.
BYRON

P.S.—Pray write.—

[TO JOHN CAM HOBHOUSE]   *June 8th. 1818*

Dear Hobhouse—Hearing nothing from you or anybody—makes me trouble you with five words—just to beg you to remind *Hanson— Kinnaird* & *Murray* the first & third—for *monies*—the second of my affairs—& to spur the others. I am in want of some remittances—& Hanson's balance however trifling *must* be paid—& Murray should be ready to disburse at least a portion of his bargain.—I have written lately (I think) and have only time to beg you not to forget this request & to believe me yrs. ever & truly.

BYRON

[TO CHARLES HANSON]   *Venice. June 10th. 1818*

Dear Charles—I am very much surprized indeed at not receiving any advice of the papers being forwarded—in preparation so long ago —& so far forward that you pressed me to go to Geneva to meet the bearer of them.—I trust that on receiving this letter you will let me have some tidings of the causes of the delay—if of nothing else.—I have lately written to you on this & other subjects—& will not trouble you further at present than to beg you will do your best in this matter & believe me

yours ever affectly.
BYRON

P.S.—My remembrances to your father & family.———I have written *twice* lately—on the N[ewstea]d papers—Rochdale—& requesting a remittance—& some information as to the time of the payments of the interest of the purchase-money.—I am now detained in Venice all the summer instead of going to the Country—waiting for yr. messenger.—

[TO JOHN CAM HOBHOUSE]   *Venice. June 12th. 1818*

Dear Hobhouse—As Post after post has elapsed for many weeks without any news from England—I repeat the trouble I have before given you—to remind Hanson & Murray to pay—& Kinnaird to receive as soon as possible otherwise I shall be put to considerable inconvenience—without any just reason—as those persons ought to have disbursed before now.———I never desire to trouble or hear from friends or acquaintance except on business—but on those occasions I could wish that they would write or cause others to write to the purpose—instead of giving me advice to take journeys to Geneva— without cause—or Christian charity;—you may suppose that I did better to stay at Venice—had I been at Geneva—I should have had to wait months for the ragamuffins.—Pray make those fellows *pay* any & all balances—& believe me

yrs [scrawl for signature]

Not a word since May 3d.—

Dear Hobhouse/—Still no letters.—My requests are the same—monies—Hanson & Murray—& Kinnaird—let the former pay all balances—& the latter send me credit for the same—or I shall be put to *immediate* & serious inconvenience.—I hope you are not dreaming of any plan for Murray's money—except spending, life is too precarious to buy annuities—& I want the whole directly.—In short whatever may be the case—you might write an answer from common civility.—About the first news I have had of Canto 4th, has been from Milan in a long & bitter letter against *you* from Di Breme (too long to send by post to England) in which he complains of very unfair representations on *your part* (in the notes) about the Italian *Romantici* & some stuff you have put in the illustrations besides about Foscolo[1]—who seems one of the Charlatans who usually have taken you in as far as I could *observe.*—I shall write him that as I never read the notes—he who wrote them may answer for himself, but he says he shall write to you himself immediately.——I have just been swimming from *Lido* to the *Riva* where the Gun-Brig lies—that is near the Piazzetta—so that you will excuse a little languor—I went in with Hoppner—Scott[2] (*not* the Vice Consul) and the Chevalier Mingaldo[3]—(a noted Italian swimmer who traversed the Danube in Napoleon's campaigns)—& I flatter myself gave them enough of it—for none of them went even *half* the distance (or even reached the Gardens)—but got back into their gondolas—& drest & were probably at dinner—before I had done my progress—Mingaldo seemed the best fish among them—but not in the true style—at least not bottom.—Hoppner & he both spewed when they got out into their boats.—

yrs. ever & truly

B

---

[1] Hobhouse, unknown to Byron, had engaged Ugo Foscolo, an Italian writer (Byron had admired his *Ultime Lettere di Jacopo Ortis,* a Werther-like novel) to write a section on Italian literature for his *Historical Illustrations of the Fourth Canto of Childe Harold.* This was not acknowledged as Foscolo's, and it caused a good deal of controversy in Italy because of his comments on contemporary writers.

[2] Alexander Scott. See biographical sketch in Appendix IV.

[3] The Cavalier Angelo Mengaldo (Byron frequently spelled it "Mingaldo") was a former soldier in Napoleon's army who boasted of his exploits, particularly of swimming the Beresina under fire. Byron first met him at Hoppner's on March 27, 1818, and was frequently associated with him and Alexander Scott during the spring and summer. Mengaldo was romantic and vain and often rubbed Byron the wrong way.

Dear Douglas—No letters—and my money is nearly expended.—
It is rather hard with a balance of some hundreds in Hanson's hands—
with two thousand five hundred guineas due from Murray—with the
prospects of half a year's interest of ninety five thousand pounds (in
three months in September, the half year then expiring) from the
Purchase of Newstead that I should be exposed to these anxieties—
& I may say neglect—from my correspondents—not a letter of any
sort since the first week in May—surely I might have an answer—
even were I writing to borrow it.—Murray is inexcusable—he has
never said one word—if he had any thing even disagreeable to say,
it would be better than suspence.—By this post I write to Hobhouse—
& by every post I must trouble him or you till I at least hear what I
have to expect.—Believe me ever

& truly yrs.

B

P.S.—Pray stir up Hanson & Murray—I do not want to hear of any
thing from *them* but business—& don't forget *Rochdale,*—I want *the
whole of Murray's money in a credit* and partly *circular notes* from your
house as usual—& also any balance from Hanson's & some there must
be even by *his own* account.——I have just swum from Lido to the
Gun brig which is anchored close to the Piazzetta.——that is within
pistol shot—I distanced three other swimmers.——

Dear Sir—Your last letter was dated the 28th of April—consequently a much longer period has elapsed than usual—without my
hearing from you—(or indeed from any one else) and considering all
things & the time you have chosen for this cessation—methinks it is
not well done.—If you have anything uncomfortable to say—recollect
it must come out at last—& had better be said at once than retained to
terminate a disagreeable suspence.——I have written repeatedly to
Mr. Hobhouse & Mr. Kinnaird—without the smallest effect—& am
fortunate in such friends & correspondents.—Most of my letters to
them & you required an answer.——The only thing Mr. H[obhouse]
has done has been to advise me to go to Geneva—which would have
been the cause of much useless expence & trouble to no purpose as the
Hanson Messenger is not yet arrived if even set out.—Tell Hobhouse

that I trust his tragedy will be damned—& that the Chevalier di Breme has written to me a long letter—attacking *him* (Hobhouse) for abusing the Italian *Romantici* in his notes—Mr. H[obhouse] will answer for himself—I never read the notes.—

yrs. very truly

B

P.S.—Mr. H[obhouse] & Ki[nnair]d will have something to say to you from me—at least, if they give themselves the trouble to comply with my request.—

[TO JOHN MURRAY]   *Venice. June 18th. 1818*

Dear Sir—Business and the utter and inexplicable silence of all my Correspondents renders me impatient & troublesome.—I wrote to Mr. Hanson for a balance which is (or ought to be) in his hands—no answer.—I expected the Messenger with the Newstead papers two months ago—& instead of him—I received a requisition to proceed to Geneva—which (from Hobhouse who knows my wishes & opinions about approaching England) could only be irony or insult.——I must therefore trouble *you* to pay into my Bankers *immediately* whatever "sum" or sums you can make it convenient to do on our agreement— otherwise I shall be put to the *severest* & most immediate inconvenience —& this at a time when by every rational prospect & calculation I ought to be in the receipt of considerable sums.——Pray do not neglect this—you have no idea to what inconvenience you will otherwise put me.—Hobhouse had some absurd notion about the disposal of this money in annuity (or God knows what) which I merely listened to when he was here to avoid squabbles & sermons—but I have occasion for the principal—& had never any serious idea of appropriating it otherwise than to answer my personal expences.— Hobhouse's wish is (if possible) to force me back to England—he will not succeed—& if he did I would not stay—I hate the Country—& like this—& all foolish opposition of course merely adds to the feeling. —*Your* silence makes me doubt the success of C[ant]o 4th.—if it has failed I will make such deduction as you think proper & fair from the original agreement—but I could wish whatever is to be paid—were remitted to me without delay through the usual Channel of course by post.—When I tell you that I have not heard a word from England since very early in May—I have made the eulogium of my friends—or the persons who call themselves so—since I have written so often & in the greatest anxiety—thank God—the longer I am absent the less cause I see for regretting the Country or it's living contents.——

I am yrs. ever & truly
BYRON

P.S.—Tell Mr. Hobhouse that he has greatly offended all his friends at Milan by some part or other of his illustrations—that I hope (as an author) he will be damned—and that I will never forgive him (or any body) the atrocity of their late neglect & silence at a time when I wished particularly to hear (for every reason) from my friends.—

[TO CHARLES HANSON]   *Venice June 18th. 1818*

Dear Charles,—Immediately on the receipt of this you will greatly oblige me by remitting whatever balance from Newstead may happen to be in your hands—as I shall otherwise be put to *much & severe immediate inconvenience.*—I have long expected your Messenger— when will he come—or even set out?—*Pray do not neglect my request— & pray desire Messrs Morland to send out the Credit for the sum directly—* as it is of great importance to me at present—however trifling the balance may be in itself.—I have had no account from *them* of Sir R. Noel's balance 271 £ (I think but am not sure) which you stated as paid some months ago. Don't forget *Rochdale*—try your best for me at a Sale—

yours & your father's ever truly
B

[TO JOHN CAM HOBHOUSE]   *Venice. June 25th. 1818*

Dear Hobhouse—I have received yrs. of the 5th.—& have had no letters from any one else—nor desire any—but *letters* of *Credit.*— Since my last I have had another *Swim* against Mingaldo—whom both Scott & I beat hollow—leaving him breathless & five hundred yards behind hand before we got from Lido to the entrance of the Grand Canal.—Scott went from Lido as far as the Rialto—& was then taken into his Gondola—I swam from Lido right to the end of the Grand Canal—including it's whole length—besides that space from Lido to the Canal's entrance (or exit) by the statue of Fortune—near the Palace—and coming out finally at the end opposite Fusina and Maestri—staying in half an hour &—I know not what distance more

54

than the other two—& swimming easy—the whole distance computed
by the Venetians at four and a half of Italian miles.—I was in the sea
from half past 4—till a quarter past 8—without touching or resting.—
I could not be much fatigued having had a *piece* in the forenoon—&
taking another in the evening at ten of the Clock—The Scott I
mention is not the vice-Consul—but a traveller—who lives much at
Venice—like My*sen*.—He got as far as the Rialto swimming well—
the Italian—miles behind & knocked up—hallooing for the boat.—
Pray—make Murray *pay*—& Spooney pay—& send the Messenger—
& with the other things the enclosed *Corn rubbers*.—As you are full
of politics I say nothing—except that I wish you more pleasure than
such trash could give to me.

yrs. very truly & affectly.
B

P.S.—*The wind & tide were both with me. Corn rubbers two dozen—*
recollect *they are light & may come in letters.*—

[TO JOHN MURRAY] *Venice. June 25th. 1818*

Dear Sir—The Post having arrived without any Answer to various
letters of mine to you & others—I continue my determination of
reminding you as usual that it might be as well to take some notice
of my request for a few lines of reply.—

I remain yrs &c.
B

P.S.—Your last letter was dated April 28th.—I wrote to you twice
last week on business.—

[TO JOHN MURRAY] *Venice. June 28th. 1818*

Dear Sir—As I perceive that it continues in vain for me to expect
any answer to my repeated letters—I shall write by next post to Mr.
Moore to propose from me some things which I have in view for next
year to the Messrs. Longman;—and as I think it fair not to do this without apprizing you of my intention—I hereby do apprize you and of the
cause thereof—which is the neglect of my correspondence lately
experienced—recollect that it is your own doing—& for any thing
that appears to ye. contrary may be your wish also;—I am

yours very truly
BYRON

Dear Hobhouse—Pray tell Murray to *pay* in *money, not* in bills—
I will have *ready* money—I am sure I always give him ready poetry—
& let him pay quickly.———No letters from him—& but one from you
of late.—I shall positively offer my next year to *Longman*—& I have
lots upon the anvil—& inform Master Murray that by next post I
shall write to Moore to propose to Longman for the time to come;—
I will teach the Admiralty Publisher a little attention to his correspondents.—Di Breme has written to me from Milan—to complain of
your notes for attacks upon God knows whom. My thanks to Dr.
Clarke &c. for his opinion "here are in all two worthy voices gained"[1]
—when do you come out with Francesca?—As you do not deserve
any kind—or *kind of* letter—I say no more but am yours as you behave
[Scrawl for signature]

P.S.—I shall be really put to very great inconvenience if Spooney
& Murray don't disburse—& that quickly.—Where is Spooney's
messenger?—*Geneva—Geneva*—pretty advice.—but you are all alike
—never had man such friends.———You say "why don't I come among
you?" I confess I don't see any great allurement—to you or yours for
the wish—& certainly none to me—besides as I have told you a
thousand times I prefer my present residence.—

Dear Hobhouse—When you can spare a moment from your political
aspirations—will you once more remind the worthies—Spooney &
Murray—that they have as yet sent neither—money—messengers—
nor letter even;—as to Murray—I will make him remember his
rudeness many a good day to come—one way or another—& so tell
him.———I hate boring you so—but what can I do—I am in the
greatest uneasiness & inconvenience about these cursed fellows—&
their insolent neglect.—

                              yrs ever & truly
                              BYRON

P.S.—Recollect I require *Cash* & *not bills* from Master Murray
Esquire.

---

[1] *Coriolanus*, Act II, scene 3: "There is in all two worthy voices begged."

Dear Charles—As I have immediate occasion for remittances—I must again remind you that I must require whatever balance you can get together—& that directly & *by post*.—It is high time that the Messenger also should set off—he is nearly three months already beyond the period which you mentioned—I wish also to know on *what day* Major W[ildman] was put in possession;—recollect that you deprecated the very delays which you appear to be indulging—& that I am prevented from going into the country at the best season—by waiting for these papers.—As I wrote lately I will not bother you further than by requesting an immediate answer.—

ever yrs. truly & affectly.

Byron

P.S.—My remembrances to all. What is to be done with Rochdale—Sell it—if possible.——

Dear Sir—I continue to remind you that I have received no letters from your quarter.—What your motives may have been for a neglect which has made me uneasy in one point of view—& has been of great inconvenience to me in another—I know not, but I tell you that I am not at all pleased with it—with the same sincerity which I used & will use with every one—One of my many letters was of recommendation to a Venetian now in London—I presume that he has delivered it—& imagine that it might have been acknowledged.—I am

yrs. very truly

B

P.S.—I will wait ten days longer—if by that time I do not hear from you—you will then receive the last letter to be addressed to you from me.—

My dear Count Albrizzi—I do not apologize to you for writing in English as you read the language.—Some time ago I was apprized

[1] Son of Countess Albrizzi.

partly by the Conte Rizzo[2]—& subsequently by your Mother the Countess Albrizzi[3] herself—that the Countess had done me the honour to compose, or write, a character of me—similar to those already written & published of many others with far better claims than mine to her good opinion, & such celebrity as may result from it.—This Character I have *never seen*—and as—I believe—I expressed both to Madame your Mother & to Conte Rizzo—I *never will*.—I have not the least idea of it's contents—nor have any reason to suppose them unfavourable—but I have no claims to be classed with the Italian & other worthies of the previous Collection—and to say the truth—am not particularly ambitious of appearing so publicly now, or at any future period, in their company.—You will therefore oblige me greatly by respectfully requesting the Countess your Mother to *deliver* to the *flames* this Character—(if still in existence) the publication or even circulation of which would be painful to me—at the same time assuring her that I am honoured by the kindness of her intention, ⟨at the same time that⟩ although I feel it my duty to decline it—& to beg that the sketch may be *destroyed*.——I have the honour to be

very truly your obliged & most obedt. devoted Sert.

BYRON

[TO JOHN MURRAY] *Venice July 10th. 1818*

Dear Sir—I have received your letter & the credit from Morland's &c. for whom I have also drawn upon you at sixty days sight for the remainder—according to your proposition.—I am still waiting in Venice in expectancy of the arrival of Hanson's Clerk—what can detain him I do not know—but I trust that Mr. Hobhouse & Mr. Kinnaird (when their political fit is ⟨sobered⟩ abated) will take the trouble to enquire & expedite him—as I have nearly a hundred thousand pounds depending upon the completion of the Sale & the Signature of the papers.——The draft on you—is drawn up by Siri & Willhalm—I hope that the form is correct.—I signed it two or three days ago—desiring them to forward it to Messrs. Morland & Ransom.—Your projected editions for November had better be postponed—as I have some things in project or preparation that may be of use to you—though not very important in themselves.—I have completed an Ode on Venice; and have two stories—one serious &

---

[2] Count Francesco Rizzo-Patarol. Iris Origo calls him a "well-known Venetian gossip."

[3] See biographical sketch in Vol. 5, Appendix IV.

one ludicrous (a la Beppo) not yet finished—& in no hurry to be so.[1] —You talk of the letter to Hobhouse[2] being much admired—& speak of prose—I think of writing (for your full edition) some memoirs of my life to prefix to them—upon the same model (though far enough I fear from reaching it) as that of Gifford—Hume—&c. and this without any intention of making disclosures or remarks upon living people which would be unpleasant to them[3]—but I think it might be done & well done—however this is to be considered.—I have *materials* in plenty—but the greater part of these could not be used by *me*—nor for three hundred years to come—however there is enough without these—and merely as a literary man—to make a preface for such an edition as you meditate—but this by the way—I have not made up my mind.——I enclose you a *note* on the subject of *"Parisina"*—which Hobhouse can digest for you—it is an extract of particulars from a history of Ferrara.——I trust that you have been attentive to Missiaglia—for the English have the character of neglecting the Italians at present—which I hope you will redeem.—

yrs. in haste

B

[TO DOUGLAS KINNAIRD]   *Venice. July 15th. 1818*

Dear Douglas—I hear wonders of your popular eloquence & speeches to the mobility—from all quarters—& I see by the papers that Captain Lew Chew[1] has been well nigh slain by a *potatoe*—so the Italian Gazettes have it—it serves him right—a fellow who has lost three ships—an Oran outang—a Boa Constrictor (they both died in the Passage)—and an Election—he be damned.—How came Burdett not to be at the head of the poll?——Murray's letters & the Credits are come—laud we the Gods!——If I did not know of old—Wildman to be Man of honour—& Spooney a damned tortoise in all his proceeds—I

[1] This seems to be the first indication that Byron was at work on *Don Juan*, which he had begun on July 3, 1818. The "serious" story may have been *Mazeppa*, which, however, was not finished by September, and was not published until the following year.

[2] The dedicatory letter to Hobhouse at the beginning of the fourth canto of *Childe Harold*.

[3] An early reference to the famous Memoirs which Byron gave to Moore the following year at La Mira.

[1] Captain Sir Murray Maxwell, the Tory candidate in the Westminster election, had explored the Loo-Choo Islands, an account of which was published in 1818. Kinnaird was nominated as a Reform candidate but withdrew and canvassed for Sir Francis Burdett, who was elected with Sir Samuel Romilly.

should suspect foul play—in this delay of the man and papers—now that your politics are a little subsided—for God his sake—row the man of law—spur him—kick him on the Crickle,—do something—any thing—you are my power of Attorney—and I thereby empower you to use it & abuse Hanson—till the fellow says or does something as a gentleman should do, I am staying in Venice—instead of summering it at Este—waiting for the Clerk & the conveyances—but "why tarry the wheels of his Chariot?"[2]——I hear of Scrope & his jests—& Holland & his toils;—I wish you all the pleasure such pursuits can afford—and as much success as usually attends them.——I have lately had a long swim (beating an Italian all to bubbles) of more than four miles—from Lido to the other end of the Grand Canal—that is the part which enters from Mestri—I won by a good three quarters of a mile—and as many quarters of an hour—knocking the Chevalier up—& coming in myself quite fresh—the fellow had swum the Beresina in the Bonaparte Campaign—& thought of coping with "us Youth"—but it would not do.——Give my love to Scrope & the rest of our ragamuffins & believe me

> yrs. [scrawl]
> B

Pray look very sharp after Spooney—I have my suspicions—my Suspicions—Sir—my Suspicions.—

[TO JOHN MURRAY]   *Venice. July 17th. 1818*

Dear Sir—I suppose that Aglietti will take whatever you offer[1]— but till his return from Vienna I can make him no proposal—nor indeed have you authorized me to do so.—The three French notes *are* by Lady Mary—also, another half-English French Italian—they are very pretty & passionate—it is a pity that a piece of one of them is lost.—Algarotti seems to have treated her ill—but she was much his Senior—and all women are used ill—or say so—whether they are or not.——I see the Mob have broken Lew Chew's head—it must have been but a foolish one to show itself on the hustings—I do not see how a voyage to China is to qualify a man to represent Westminster—& can not pity him—for stepping off his quarter deck,—first he loses a ship & then an election—and then nearly his life—he seems to be a rare fellow.——I shall be glad of yr. books & powders—I am still in waiting for Hanson's Clerk—but luckily not at Geneva—all my good

[2] *Judges*, 5:28.
[1] See April 12, 1818, to Murray.

60

friends wrote to me to hasten *there* to meet him—but not one had the good sense or the good nature to write afterwards to tell me that it would be time & a journey thrown away—as he could not set off for some months after the period appointed.—If I *had* taken the journey on the general suggestion—I never would have spoken again to one of you as long as I existed.———I have written to request Mr. Kinnaird when the foam of his politics is wiped away—to extract a positive answer from that knave or blockhead H[anso]n & not to keep me in a state of suspense upon the Subject.—I hope that Kinnaird who has my power of Attorney—keeps a look out upon the Gentleman—which is the more necessary—as I have a great dislike to the idea of coming over to look after him myself.———I have several things begun—verse and prose—but none in much forwardness.—I have written some six or seven sheets of a life—which I mean to continue—& send you when finished—it may perhaps serve for your projected editions.—If you would tell me exactly—(for I know nothing and have no correspondents except on business)—the state of the reception of our late publications & the feeling upon them—without consulting any delicacies—(I am too seasoned to require them) I should know how and in what manner to proceed,—I should not like to give them too much which may probably have been the case already—but as I tell you I know nothing.—I once wrote from the fullness of my mind—and the love of fame (not as an *end* but as a *means* to obtain that influence over men's minds—which is power in itself & in it's consequences) and now from habit—& from avarice—so that the effect may probably be as different as the inspiration; I have the same facility and indeed necessity of composition—to avoid idleness—(though idleness in a hot country is a pleasure—) but a much *greater* indifference to what is to become of it—after it has served my immediate purpose.—However I should on no account like to—but I won't go on like the Archbishop of Grenada—as I am very sure that you dread the fate of Gil Blas—& with good reason.—

yrs. [scrawl]

B

P.S.—I have written some very savage letters to Mr. Hobhouse—Kinnaird—to you—and to Hanson—because the silence of so long a time—made me tear off my remaining rags of patience.—I have seen one or two late English publications—which are no great things—except Rob Roy.—I shall be glad of Whistlecraft. Does the Coxcomb Wilmot get into parliament?—[2]

2 Robert Wilmot was elected for Newcastle-under-Lyme.

Dearest Augusta—I am not uncomfortable but have been obliged to scold Hobhouse &c. for not doing a thing or two for me in England in the way of business.—At present they are done and I am graciously appeased.—My little girl Allegra (the child I spoke to you of) has been with me these three months; she is very pretty—remarkably intelligent—and a great favourite with every body—but what is remarkable—much more like Lady Byron than her mother—so much so as to stupefy the learned Fletcher—and astonish me—is it not odd? I suppose she must also resemble her sister Ada—she has very blue eyes—and that singular forehead—fair curly hair—and a devil of a Spirit—but that is Papa's.——I am in health—& very much yrs.

B

I have just seen Lord Sidney Osborne[1] who was here a few days ago—very well & in high Spirits.——

Dear Sir—I beg you to forward ye. enclosed.—It is too hot and a Sirocco so that I cannot write at length.—Perhaps I shall have something for your November edition—about *20 sheets* of *long* & a few of letter paper—are already written of *"the* Life"[1] & I think of going through with it. We will see what sort of stuff it is & decide accordingly.——Tell young Hammond that his Dama—the Countess S[pined]a[2]—fell into my hands after his departure—that the consequence was a violent quarrel between her & the Tarruscelli[3]—who finding us out has been playing the devil—setting Fan*ni* by the ears with Melandri her Roman Admirer—and by means of espionage & anonymous letters doing a world of mischief—besides a row between herself & her Austrian—& finally between herself & me too.—She is gone to Padua by the blessing of the Gods.—The S[pined]a came back today from Treviso.—You won't understand all this—but Hammond will—so tell him of it.—

ever yrs
BYRON

[1] Lord Sydney Godolphin Osborne was the son of the 5th Duke of Leeds by his second wife, Catherine Anguish. The Duke and his children took an interest in Augusta, the daughter of his first wife by Captain Byron, father of the poet, with whom she eloped.

[1] The prose Memoirs.

[2] See Jan. 19, 1819, to Hobhouse and Kinnaird (*a*).

[3] See May 19, 1818, to Hobhouse.

Dear H[obhous]e—Now that my Monies are come you may scold as much as you please.—It is your turn now.—It was mine when I had neither answers to my letters—nor attention to my requests.—As for my "social qualities"—I will back them against yours or any of the Burdett Committee—(except Scrope) I will drink with you—laugh with you—or do any thing except *talk* with you—for any wager in wines you choose to name.—You Monster You!—I have heard of your "campaigning at the King of Bohemy" and your *speeches* which *seriously* I am told were very good ones—as well as Kinnaird's—throughout the election—but you don't shine as Purveyors—and you must have cut a queer figure spouting among the Decanters (most of them about the same height with yourself) in boots & spurs to appease the angry & famished ragamuffins who have been licking Lew-Chew and his Islanders for you.——Enclosed is Breme's scrawl—answer him if you like but I have given him a Siserana I promise you in mine already—I have no notion of his airs—he has brought all Italy into a squabble about his damned doctrines—(like the old stag of the Seicentisti & the previous Cruscan quarrels—poor devils—they are like *Moses* in the Vicar of W[akefield] too happy in being permitted to dispute about anything)—and then expect to be thanked for them by us Youth.—Row him—I say—he gives *you* devilish bitter words—and I long to see you by the ears—that I do.——I shall be very glad of the Corn rubbers—As to Spooney—I don't know what *he calls* expedition—but *you* always said he was a damned dawdle if not a rogue—& now you "snub me when I'm in Spirits" for coming over to your opinions.—

yrs. always
B

Dear Sir—You may go on with your edition—without calculating on the Memoir—which I shall not publish at present.—It is nearly finished—but will be too long—and there are so many things which out of regard to the living cannot be mentioned—that I have written with too much detail of that which interested me least—so that my autobiographical Essay would resemble the tragedy of Hamlet at the Country theatre—recited "with the part of Hamlet left out by particular desire."—I shall keep it among my papers—it will be a kind of Guide post in case of death—and prevent some of the lies which would otherwise be told—and destroy some which have been told already.—The tales also are in an unfinished state—and I can fix no time for their completion—they are also *not* in the best manner.— You must not therefore calculate upon any thing in time for this edition. The Memoir is already above forty four sheets of very large long paper—& will be about fifty or sixty, but I wish to go on leisurely—and when finished—although it might do a good deal for you at the time—I am not sure that it would serve any good purpose in the end to either—as it is full of many passions & prejudices of which it has been impossible for me to keep clear—I have not the patience.——Enclosed is a list of books which Dr. Aglietti would be glad to receive by way of price for his M. S. letters if you are disposed to purchase at the rate of fifty pounds sterling.—These he will be glad to have in part—and the rest *I* will give him in money—and you may carry it to the account of books &c. which is in balance against me ——deducting it accordingly.—So that the letters are yours if you like them at this rate—and he and I are going to hunt for more Lady Montague letters—which he thinks of finding.——I write in haste— thanks for the Article—and believe me

[Scrawl for closing and signature]

P.S.—I shall write again in a few days—having something to say. ——

[TO CAPTAIN BASIL HALL[1]]   *Venice. August 31st. 1818*

Dear Sir—Dr. Aglietti is the best Physician not only in Venice but in Italy—his residence is on the Grand Canal & easily found—I forget the number—but am probably the only person in Vencie who don't know it. There is no comparison between him & any of the other medical people here—I regret very much to hear of your indisposition —& shall do myself the honour of waiting upon you the moment I am up.—I write this in bed—& have only just received the letter & note— I beg you to believe that nothing but the extreme lateness of my hours would have prevented me from replying immediately or coming in person.—I have not been called a minute.—I have the honour to be

very truly yr. most obedt. Sert.

BYRON

[1] Captain Basil Hall, R. N. (1788–1844) was travelling on the Continent after a voyage to Canton and the eastern coast of Asia including the Loo-Choo Islands. He was taken ill with an ague in Venice. Byron sent Fletcher to watch over him during his fever, but Byron and Hall never met. (See *LJ*, IV, 252–53n.)

Dear Webster—[12 lines crossed out] It is not agreeable to me to hear that you are still in difficulties—but as every one has to go through a certain portion of sufferance in this world—the earlier it happens perhaps the better—and in all cases one is better able to battle up in one's youth than in the decline of life.——My own worldly affairs have had leisure to improve during my residence abroad—Newstead has been sold—& well sold I am given to understand—my debts are in the prospect of being paid—and I have still a large Capital from the residue—besides Rochdale—which ought to sell well—& my reversionary prospects which are considerable in the event of the death of Miss Milbanke's mother.—There is (as is usually said) a great advantage in getting the water between a man and his embarrassments—for things with time and a little prudence insensibly reestablish themselves—and I have spent less money—and had more for it—within the two years and a half since my absence from England —than I have ever done within the same time before—and my literary speculations allowed me to do it more easily—leaving my own property to liquidate some of the claims, till the Sale enables me to discharge the whole;—out of England I have no debts whatever.— —You ask about Venice;—I tell you as before that I do not think *you* would like it—at least few English do—& still fewer remain there— Florence & Naples are their Lazarettoes where they carry the infection of their society—indeed if there were as many of them in Venice as residents—as Lot begged might be permitted to be the Salvation of Sodom,—it would not be my abode a week longer—for the reverse of the proposition I should be sure that they would be the *damnation* of all pleasant or sensible society;—I never see any of them when I can avoid it—& when occasionally they arrive with letters of recommendation—I do what I can for them—if they are sick—and if they are well I return my card for theirs—but little more.——Venice is not an expensive residence—(unless a man chooses it) it has theatres— society—and profligacy rather more than enough—I keep four horses on one of the Islands where there is a beach of some miles along the Adriatic—so that I have daily exercise—I have my Gondola—about fourteen servants including the nurse (for a little girl—a natural daughter of mine) and I reside in one of the Mocenigo palaces on the Grand Canal—the rent of the *whole* house which is very *large* & *furnished* with linen &c. &c. inclusive is two hundred a year—(& I gave more than I need have done) in the two years I have been at

Venice—I have spent about *five* thousand pounds—& I needed not have spent one *third* of this—had it not been that I have a passion for women which is expensive in it's variety every where but less so in Venice than in other cities.——You may suppose that in *two years*—with a large establishment—horses—houses—box at the opera—Gondola—journeys—women—and Charity—(for I have not laid out all upon my pleasures—but have bought occasionally a shillings-worth of Salvation) villas in the country—another carriage & horses purchased for the country—books bought &c. &c.—in short every thing I wanted—& *more* than I ought to have wanted—that the sum of five thousand pounds sterling is no great deal—particularly when I tell you that more than half was laid out on the Sex—to be sure I have had plenty for the money—that's certain—I think at least two hundred of one sort or another—perhaps more—for I have not lately kept the recount.—— If you are disposed to come this way—you might live very comfortably—and even splendidly for less than a thousand a year—& find a palace for the rent of one hundred—that is to say—an Italian palace —you know that all houses with a particular front are called so—in short an enormous house,—but as I said—I do not think *you* would like it—or rather that Lady Frances would not—it is not so gay as it has been—and there is a monotony to many people in it's Canals & the comparative silence of it's streets—to me who have been always passionate for Venice—and delight in the dialect & naivete of the people—and the romance of it's old history & institutions & appearance all it's disadvantages are more than compensated by the sight of a single Gondola—The view of the Rialto—of the piazza—& the Chaunt of Tasso (though less frequent than of old) are to me worth all the cities on earth—save Rome & Athens.—Good even

yrs. ever & most truly

B

[TO THOMAS MOORE]   *Venice, September 19th, 1818*

An English newspaper here would be a prodigy, and an opposition one a monster; and except some extracts *from* extracts in the vile, garbled Paris gazettes, nothing of the kind reaches the Veneto-Lombard public, who are perhaps the most oppressed in Europe. My correspondencies with England are mostly on business, and chiefly with my [attorney], who has no very exalted notion, or extensive conception, of an author's attributes; for he once took up an Edinburgh Review, and, looking at it a minute, said to me, "So, I see you have got into the magazine,"—which is the only sentence I ever heard him utter upon literary matters, or the men thereof.

My first news of your Irish Apotheosis has, consequently, been from yourself.[1] But, as it will not be forgotten in a hurry, either by your friends or your enemies, I hope to have it more in detail from some of the former, and, in the mean time, I wish you joy with all my heart. Such a moment must have been a good deal better than Westminster-abbey,—besides being an assurance of *that* one day (many years hence, I trust), into the bargain.

I am sorry to perceive, however, by the close of your letter, that even *you* have not escaped the "surgit amari,"[2] &c., and that your damned deputy has been gathering such "dew from the still *vext* Bermoothes"[3]—or rather *vexatious*. Pray, give me some items of the affair, as you say it is a serious one; and, if it grows more so, you should make a trip over here for a few months, to see how things turn out. I suppose you are a violent admirer of England by your staying so long in it. For my own part, I have passed, between the age of one-and-twenty and thirty, half the intervenient years out of it without regretting any thing, except that I ever returned to it at all, and the gloomy prospect before me of business and parentage obliging me, one day, to return to it again,—at least, for the transaction of affairs, the signing of papers, and inspecting of children.

I have here my natural daughter, by name Allegra,—a pretty little girl enough, and reckoned like papa. Her mamma is English,—but it is a long story, and—there's an end. She is about twenty months old. * * * * * *

I have finished the First Canto (a long one, of about 180 octaves) of a poem in the style and manner of "Beppo," encouraged by the good success of the same.[4] It is called "Don Juan", and is meant to be a little quietly facetious upon every thing. But I doubt whether it is not —at least, as far as it has yet gone—too free for these very modest

[1] Because of his Irish National songs and his defence of Irish causes, Moore was made much of during his visit to Ireland.

[2] Lucretius, *De Rerum Natura*, IV, 1133:

> "Nequiquam, quoniam medio de fonte leporum
> surgit amari aliquid quod in issis floribus angat"

("All is vanity, since from the very fountain of enchantment rises a drop of bitterness to torment amongst all the flowers.")

[3] *Tempest*, Act I, scene 2. Moore had been appointed in 1803 Registrar to the Admiralty in Bermuda. He left the duties of the office to a deputy whose embezzlement left Moore liable for claims amounting to a thousand guineas.

[4] As usual Byron added stanzas and when it was published the following year the first canto had grown to 222 stanzas.

days. However, I shall try the experiment, anonymously, and if it don't take, it will be discontinued. It is dedicated to S[outhey] in good, simple, savage verse, upon the [Laureate's] politics, and the way he got them. But the bore of copying it out is intolerable; and if I had an amanuensis he would be of no use, as my writing is so difficult to decipher.

> My poem's Epic, and is meant to be
> Divided in twelve books, each book containing,
> With love and war, a heavy gale at sea—
> A list of ships, and captains, and kings reigning—
> New characters, &c. &c.

The above are two [sic] stanzas, which I send you as a brick of my Babel, and by which you can judge of the texture of the structure.

In writing the Life of Sheridan, never mind the angry lies of the humbug whigs. Recollect that he was an Irishman and a clever fellow, and that *we* have had some very pleasant days with him. Don't forget that he was at school at Harrow, where, in my time, we used to show his name—R. B. Sheridan, 1765,—as an honour to the walls. Remember * * * * * * *

* * * * * * * * * * * * * *

Depend upon it that there were worse folks going, of that gang, than ever Sheridan was.

What did Parr[5] mean by "haughtiness and coldness?" I listened to him with admiring ignorance, and respectful silence. What more could a talker for fame have?—they don't like to be answered. It was at Payne Knight's[6] I met him, where he gave me more Greek than I could carry away. But I certainly meant to (and *did*) treat him with the most respectful deference.

I wish you a good night, with a Venetian benediction, "Benedetto te, e la terra che ti fara!"—"May you be blessed, and the *earth* which you will *make*" is it not pretty? You would think it still prettier if you had heard it, as I did two hours ago, from the lips of a Venetian girl,[7] with large black eyes, a face like Faustina's, and the figure of a Juno—tall and energetic as a Pythoness, with eyes flashing, and her dark hair

---

[5] Samuel Parr (1747–1825), an assistant master at Harrow while Sheridan was there, was visited by Moore, then gathering material for a life of Sheridan. Parr had a reputation as a scholar which was probably inflated. He was called a Whig Dr. Johnson.

[6] Richard Payne Knight (1750–1824), numismatist and writer on ancient art. He was a collector of bronzes which he bequeathed to the British Museum.

[7] Probably Margarita Cogni, See Aug. 1, 1819, to Murray.

streaming in the moonlight—one of those women who may be made any thing. I am sure if I put a poniard into the hand of this one, she would plunge it where I told her,—and into *me*, if I offended her. I like this kind of animal, and am sure that I should have preferred Medea to any woman that ever breathed. You may, perhaps, wonder that I don't in that case. * * * * * * * *

* * * * * * * * * * * * * * *

I could have forgiven the dagger or the bowl, any thing, but the deliberate desolation piled upon me, when I stood alone upon my hearth, with my household gods shivered around me, * * * * * * * Do you suppose I have forgotten or forgiven it? It has comparatively swallowed up in me every other feeling, and I am only a spectator upon earth, till a tenfold opportunity offers. It may come yet. There are others more to be blamed than * * * *, and it is on these that my eyes are fixed unceasingly.

[TO AUGUSTA LEIGH]   *Venice. Septr. 21st. 1818*

Dearest Augusta—I particularly beg that you will contrive to get the enclosed letter safely delivered to Lady Frances—& if there is an answer to let me have it.—You can write to her first—& state that you have such a letter—at my request—for there is no occasion for any concealment at least with *her*—& pray oblige me so far—for many reasons.———If the Queen dies you are no more a Maid of Honour— is it not so?——Allegra is well—but her mother (whom the Devil confound) came prancing the other day over the Appenines—to see her *shild*—which threw my Venetian loves (who are none of the quietest) into great combustion—and I was in a pucker till I got her to the Euganean hills where she & the child now are—for the present—I declined seeing her for fear that the consequence might be an addition to the family;—she is to have the child a month with her and then to return herself to Lucca—or Naples where she was with her relatives (she is English you know) & to send Allegra to Venice again.—I lent her my house at Este for her maternal holidays.—As troubles don't come single—here is another confusion.—The chaste wife of a baker— having quarrelled with her tyrannical husband—has run away *to* me— (God knows without being invited) & resists all the tears & penitence & beg-pardons of her disconsolate Lord—and the threats of the police —and the priest of the parish besides—& swears she won't give up her unlawful love (myself) for any body—or anything—I assure you I have begged her in all possible ways too to go back to her husband—promising her all kinds of eternal fidelity into the bargain—but she only flies into a fury—and as she is a very tall and formidable Girl of three and twenty—with the large black eyes and handsome face of a pretty fiend—a correspondent figure—and a carriage as haughty as a Princess—with the violent passions & capacities for mischief of an Italian when they are roused—I am a little embarrassed with my unexpected acquisition;—however she keeps my household in rare order—and has already frightened the learned Fletcher out of his remnant of wits more than once—we have turned her into a house-keeper.———As the morals of this place are very lax—all the women commend her & say she has done right—especially her own relations. —You need not be alarmed—I know how to manage her—and can deal with anything but a cold blooded animal such as Miss Milbanke. ———The worst is that she won't let a woman come into the house—unless she is as old & frightful as possible—and has sent so many to the right about—that my former female acquaintances are equally frightened & angry.—She is extremely fond of the child—& is very cheerful & good-natured—when not jealous—but Othello himself was a fool to her in that respect—her soubriquet in her family—was *la Mora* from her colour—as she is very dark (though clear of complexion) which literally means *the Moor* so that I have "the Moor of Venice" in propria persona as part of my houshold—she has been here this month.———I had known her (and fifty others) more than a year—but did not anticipate this escapade which was the fault of her booby husband's treatment—who now runs about repenting & roaring like a bullcalf—I told him to take her in the devil's name—but she would not stir—& made him a long speech in the Venetian dialect which was more entertaining to anybody than to him to whom it was addressed. ———You see Goose—that there is no quiet in this world—so be a good woman—& repent of yr. sins.—

yrs [scrawl for signature]

[TO JOHN MURRAY] *Venice Septr. 24th. 1818*

Dear Sir—In the one hundredth and thirty-second stanza of Canto 4th.[1] the stanza runs in the Manuscript—

"*Left* the unbalanced scale—Great Nemesis ["]

and not "*lost*"—which is nonsense—as what *losing* a scale means—

[1] *Childe Harold.*

I know not—but *leaving* an unbalanced scale or a scale unbalanced is intelligible.—Correct this—I pray—not for the public or the poetry—but I do not choose to have blunders made in addressing any of the deities—so seriously as this is addressed.——

yrs [scrawl for signature]

P.S.—In the Translation from the Spanish[2]—alter

"In increasing Squadrons flew"   to
"To a mighty Squadron grew"

what does "thy waters *wasted* them" mean (in the Canto) *that is not me*. Consult the M.S. *always*. I have written the first Canto (180 octave stanzas) of a poem in the Style of Beppo—and have Mazeppa to finish besides.——In referring to the mistake made in stanza 132 I take the opportunity to desire that in future in all parts of my writings relating to religion you will be more careful—& not forget that it is possible that in addressing the deity a blunder may become a blasphemy —& I do not choose to suffer such infamous perversions of my words or of my intention.———I saw the Canto by accident.——

[TO JOHN HANSON]   *Venice. Septr. 30th. 1818*

Dear Sir—Many months ago I informed you of my determination not to quit Venice on the present business—that determination is unaltered and unalterable.—You therefore have the choice of three things;—1st. you can send on a proper person with the papers—2dly. you may come in person—or 3dly. you may return to England—as most assuredly I can not go to Geneva.—If the Sale is impeded—I cannot help it—it is no fault of mine—I told you my intention long ago—and I presume that in any case I shall have either the purchase money—or the property again.———You will decide as you please upon the journey——but in no case—in no circumstances—will I for such a purpose—be inclined to quit my residence—as I before said in the Spring of the present year.—

I am yrs. very truly & affectly.
BYRON

P.S.—Your best way will be to *send* a man—with instructions.

[2] "A Very Mournful Ballad on the Siege and Conquest of Alhama".

Dear Hobhouse/—Spooney writes that he will not advance beyond
Geneva.—I have answered that he may return—for I would not cross
to meet him—were it only to Fusina or Maestri.——I said so in the
Spring—and I repeat it now.—He hints possible delays—and in-
completion of the Sale—be it so—I gave him ample time—it is no
fault of mine—and if W[ildman] don't complete—I presume that I
shall at least have the property again.—But whatever may be the
consequence—my decision on that point—is what it was in Spring—
and would be in Secula Seculorum.—Pray tell him so on his return
from his fool's (or rogue's) errand and that I would see him and all
Chancery lane in Hell before I would cross a Canal for them—what am
I to be made the Polichinello of an Attorneo at thirty years of age?—
he may be damned—*they* may be damned—I have written to Douglas
Kinnaird & beg you to assist him with advice in a committee upon this
tedious mountebank's eternal dawdling.—Do what you can—& make
him do what you please—only recollect that I neither can nor will quit
home upon his call.—Why could he not send a Clerk?—I'm sure I
have no wish to see the original.——

                                    ever yrs. very truly & affectly.
                                                            BYRON

P.S.—I don't revise—and I write in a hurry—and in a passion—
so excuse errata—and remember that I *won't Stir*—Sunburn me if I
do!

P.S. 2d.—I saw the other day by accident your "Historical &c."—
the Essay is *perfect*[1]—and not exceeded by Johnson's Poets—which I
think the type of perfection.—I shall write again—but my rage at
present has made me quite unwell:—Excuse bother.——

Dear Douglas—I have received a letter from Hanson telling me
that he will *not* come further than *Geneva*.—I have written my answer
to say—that I will not quit Venice.—You will repeat this to him on
his return to England.—Pray try what you can as to my affairs—
which of course will be impeded by this man's delays—but be
assured—& assure *him*—that in no case & on no consideration will I

----

[1] It is ironic that Byron praised most in Hobhouse's *Historical Illustrations of the
Fourth Canto of Childe Harold* the essay on Italian literature, which was not written
by Hobhouse but by Ugo Foscolo.

swerve from my determination upon this subject—as I told him in the Spring.—Believe me

ever & truly yrs.
BYRON

P.S.—I have addressed my answer to H[anson] at *Geneva.*—My determination is definitive—if the Sale is not completed—I suppose that I shall have the estate again—but whether or no, neither he nor any one else shall make me the puppet of an Attorney.——

[TO JOHN HANSON] *Venice. Octr. 6th. 1818*

Dear Sir—I have received the duplicate of your letter—to which I have already answered.—I can only repeat that I apprized you six months ago that my leaving Venice was entirely out of the question—and—that nothing has occurred since to induce me to change my determination.——The parcel of books &c. which Mr. Murray will have consigned to your care—you had better send on by a proper person—& I will pay the expence.—On your return to England—your best way will be to send a Clerk with the papers—as he may have less pressing calls on his time and health;—the passage by the Simplon may be short—but that of Mont Cenis is open and easy at all periods—as may be ascertained.—For whatever delays may occur (or have occurred) *I* am not to blame—you were apprized already of my residence—and that I would not quit it—and it may suggest itself to you—that after two years and a half's absence from England—I may have business and connections here which would render it disagreeable for me to quit my family.—I should regret any inconvenience or interruptions in the completion of a desirable arrangement,—but having long ago expressed my definitive objections to quitting home, I have little to reproach myself with—whatever be the consequences.—It is not for the journey—which I have made before—(and many journeys ten times less easy) but I am settled where I am—& see neither motive—nor advantage in putting myself to expences and inconveniences which are quite superfluous.—A Clerk with the papers—and at any rate—a Courier with the books will be sufficient without travelling yourself more than you like—as for other matters—you & Mr. Kinnaird have Power of Attorney and my instructions already—

I am very truly yrs affectly. & [scrawl]
BYRON

Dear Colonel—I will so far avail myself . . . as to request you to take charge of the two enclosed miniatures . . . to convey them to my sister, Mrs. Col. Leigh, St. James's Palace, London, she is one of the Queen's—God knows what. I forget the style—but something in waiting—or bed chamber—it can't be Maid of Honour—for she has five children.

The one is a picture of a (natural) daughter of mine, and the other one of myself in which the Painter has endeavoured to make up in youth what it wants in likeness.

My remembrance to the illustrious Scrope. I am glad to hear of the recovery of his spirits and hope that they are not the only things which he has recovered, as I understand that he had been hit hard on the turf or at the table last year. . . .

[TO JOHN HANSON]   *Venice, October 13th, 1818*

Dear Hanson,—The season of the year being so advanced, I cannot possibly cross the Simplon now, and am astonished you should have deferred leaving England to so late a period. A letter I received from Hobhouse, as far back as August, stated that, on the part of Col. Wildman, he had heard from his Solicitor the deeds were ready for signature.

Monsieur Dejean, who knows me, will, by mentioning my name, furnish you with four horses and a Postilion, and convey you all to Mestri.[1] You will have to leave your carriage, and proceed by gondola from thence to Venice. The Hotel you had better come to in Venice is the *Grande Bretagne*, kept by Signora Boffini. I shall send Fletcher to engage apartments for you.

> I am, dear Hanson, your sincere
> BYRON

[TO COUNT GIUSEPPINO ALBRIZZI]   *Venice Novr. 2d. 1818*

Dear Count Albrizzi—Your letter would have been acknowledged sooner—(as it ought to have been—) but I have been unwell.—Mr.

---

[1] John Hanson and his son Newton and a Mr. Townsend, representing Major Wildman, left England on October 12th, and arrived at Dejean's Hotel in Sécheron near Geneva on the 21st. Instead of finding Byron there they found his letter of Oct. 6th. They reached the Grande Bretagne Hotel in Venice on Nov. 11th.

Hobhouse's address is "Whitton Park—Hounslow—near London—" where he resides with his father Sir Benjamin H[obhous]e *Baronet*—(which answers to *Cavaliere* in this Country.)—In mentioning your Mother amongst the few illustrious persons whom the Narrowness of my limits and of my Experience—permitted me to name as the present Lights of Italy[1]—I merely echoed the voice of her Country.—Your favourable opinion does me great honour, and affords me equal pleasure.——I beg my respects to the Countess your mother—& trust that you will always believe me most truly and affectionately

your obliged and faithful humble Sert.

BYRON

[TO CAPTAIN WESTON]   *Venice Novr. 5th. 1818*

Sir—I am truly obliged by your communication, though previously aware of it's substance.—The greater part of the notes—and amongst them the two in question were written by Mr. Hobhouse.—You may have perceived in the old pictures or prints of Venice—that the Gospel was placed in an upright position under the Lion's paw—and that it lies level at present and consequently is less visible—this may have been the occasion of the first mistake.[1]—With regard to the conversion of St. Luke's into a Lamp Warehouse—I am quite at a loss to conjecture what could have led Mr. H[obhouse] into this supposition. —I was too far from England to superintend the press—& saw no proofs except one of the text sent by post during the process of printing. —I had not read over my own M.S. with the care I ought—and Mr. H[obhouse]'s assumed a different form from that in which I saw it last—after his arrival in London.—Still however his general accuracy —and his anxiety to be accurate—have always been considerable— and his knowledge on the subjects which he has treated is far greater than I can in any shape pretend to.—I will take the earliest opportunity of repeating what has already been stated to him by Mr. Hoppner on the score of St. Mark's Lion—& St. Luke's Church.—You need hardly apprehend that your communication could be offensive;—I could not

---

[1] In his dedicatory letter to the fourth canto of *Childe Harold*, addressed to Hobhouse, Byron mentioned the Countess Albrizzi among the great names of Italy.

[1] In stanza 11 of the fourth Canto of *Childe Harold* Byron wrote: "St. Mark yet sees his Lion where he stood". Hobhouse began his note: "The Lion has lost nothing by his journey to the Invalides, but the gospel which supported the paw that is now on a level with the other foot."

but approve the kindness of your motive and acquiesce in the justice of your observations acknowledging myself very sincerely

> your obliged & very obedt. humble Sert.

> BYRON

Dear Hobhouse/—By the favour of Lord Lauderdale[1] (who tells me by the way that you have made some very good speeches—and are to turn out an Orator—*seriously*) I have sent an "Oeuvre" of "Poeshie" which will not arrive probably till some [time] after this letter—though they start together—as the letter is rather the youngest of the two.— It is addressed to you at Mr. Murray's.——I request you to read—& having read—and if possible approved to obtain the largest or (if large be undeserved—) the fairest price from him or any one else.— There are firstly—the first Canto of Don Juan—(in the style of Beppo —and Pulci—forgive me for putting Pulci second it is a slip—"Ego et Rex meus") containing two *hundred Octaves*—and a dedication in verse of a dozen to Bob Southey—bitter as necessary—I mean the dedication; I will tell you why.—The Son of a Bitch on his return from Switzerland two years ago—said that Shelley and I "had formed a League of Incest and practiced our precepts with &c."—he lied like a rascal—for they *were not Sisters*—*one* being Godwin's daughter by Mary Wollstonecraft—and the other the daughter of the present Mrs. G[odwin] by a *former* husband.—The Attack contains no allusion to the cause—but—some good verses—and all political & poetical.— He lied in another sense—for there was no promiscuous intercourse— my commerce being limited to the carnal knowledge of the Miss C[lairmont]—I had nothing to do with the offspring of Mary Wollstonecraft—which Mary was a former Love of Southey's—which might have taught him to respect the fame of her daughter.—— Besides this *"Pome"* there is "Mazeppa" and an Ode on Venice—the last not very intelligible—and you may omit it if you like—Don Juan—and Mazeppa are perhaps better—you will see.—The Whole consists of between two and three thousand lines—and you can consult Douglas K[innaird] about the price thereof and your own Judgment —& whose else you like about their merits.—As one of the poems is as free as La Fontaine—& bitter in politics—too—the damned Cant

---

[1] James Maitland, 8th Earl of Lauderdale (1759–1839). He held various governmental posts, but retired in 1807 and lived much of his life abroad.

and Toryism of the day may make Murray pause—in that case you will take any Bookseller who bids best;—when I say *free*—I mean that freedom—which Ariosto Boiardo and Voltaire—Pulci—Berni—all the best Italian & French—as well as Pope & Prior amongst the English permitted themselves;—but no improper words nor phrases—merely some situations—which are taken from life.—However you will see to all this—when the M. S. S. arrive.——I only request that you & Doug. will see to a fair price—"as the Players have had my Goods too cheap"—if Murray won't—another will.—I name no price—calculate by quantity—and quality—and do you and Doug. pronounce—always recollecting as impartial Judges—that you are my friends—and that he is my Banker.—Spooney arrived here today—but has left in Chancery Lane *all* my *books*—everything in short except a damned—(Something)-SCOPE.[2] I have broke the glass & cut a finger in ramming it together—and the *Cornrubbers* but I have given it him!—I have been blaspheming against Scrope's God—ever since his arrival. ——Only think—he has left every thing—every thing except his legal papers.—You must send off a Man on purpose with them on the receipt of this—I will pay anything within *three hundred pounds* for the expence of their transportation—but pray let them be sent without fail—and by a person on purpose—they are all in Chancery—(I mean the *Lane*—not the Court—for they would not come out of that in a hurry) with young Spooney[3]—extract them—and send a man by Chaise on purpose—never mind expence nor weight—I must have books & Magnesia—particularly "Tales of my Landlord".——I'll be revenged on Spooney—five men died of the Plague the other day—in the Lazaretto—I shall take him to ride at the Lido—he hath a reverend care & fear of his health—I will show him the Lazaretto which is not far off you know—& looks nearer than it is—I will tell him of the five men—I will tell him of my contact with Aglietti in whose presence they died—& who came into my Box at the (St. Benedetto's) Opera the same evening—& shook hands with me;—I will tell him all this —and as he is hypochondriac—perhaps it may kill him.——The Monster left my books—everything—my Magnesia—my tooth powder—&c. &c. and wanted me besides to go to Geneva——but I made him come.—He is a queer fish—the Customs House Officers wanted to examine or have money—he would not pay—they opened every thing.—"Ay—Ay—(said he) look away—*Carts Carts*" that was his phrase for *papers* with a strong English emphasis & accent on

2 Murray had sent a kaleidoscope.
3 Charles Hanson.

the *s* and he actually made them turn over all the Newstead & Rochdale
—& Jew—& Chancery papers exclaiming *"Carts Carts"* & came off
triumphant with paying a *Centime*—the Officers giving up the matter
in despair—finding nothing else—& not being able to translate what
they found.——But I have been in a damned passion for all that—for
this adventure nearly reconciled me to him.[4]—Pray remember the
man & books—and mind & make me a proper paction with Murray
or others—I submit the matter to you and Doug.—and you may show
the M. S. to Frere and William Rose—and Moore—& whoever you
please.—Forgive the Scrawl & the trouble—& write & believe me

ever & truly yrs.
[scrawl for signature]

P.S.—Lord Lauderdale set off today the 12th. Novr.—& means to
be in England in about a Month.—

[TO JOHN CAM HOBHOUSE AND DOUGLAS KINNAIRD (*a*)]
Venice Novr. 18th. 1818

Dear Hobhouse and Kinnaird—Enclosed is Mr. Hanson's statement
of my affairs.—You will perceive that Mr. Hanson is the largest
Creditor, and that without his bill there would be a Surplus of two or
three thousand pounds after paying all debts—Bond—Simple Contract
or whatsoever.—He states *his* bill roundly at *eight thousand pounds* up
to the period of partnership with his Son Charles.—The Bill *since* as
partners—at eleven hundred & seventy eight pounds—three shillings
—and one penny.—I have agreed to pay him *five thousand* pounds—but
on condition that his bill be *submitted* to *you twain*—and to such *person*
or *persons*—(legal or others—but probably Counsel) as you shall select
to examine—investigate—and advise upon the said account.—*You* will
also please to recollect that in the year 1813—he received the sum of
two thousand eight hundred pounds or thereabouts on account, for which

---

[4] The other side of the story is told by Newton Hanson in a manuscript account
quoted by Prothero. He said that Murray had left a wagonload of books at
Chancery Lane which they could not bring, that Byron was nervous and irritable
during their visit, that the reason his father had himself come on the voyage was
that he had hoped to effect a reconciliation between Byron and his wife, but that
Byron soon dispelled such hopes by a remark on the death of Romilly: "How strange
it is that one man will die for the loss of his partner, while another would die if they
were compelled to live together." Newton Hanson observed: "Lord Byron could
not have been more than 30, but he looked 40. His face had become pale, bloated,
and sallow. He had grown very fat, his shoulders broad and round, and the knuckles
of his hands were lost in fat." (*LJ*, IV, 266–267n.)

see his *Receipt* amongst my papers—now in the care of Mr. Hobhouse —who is hereby authorized to open any trunk or trunks—& search for the same in case of necessity—by applying to Messrs. Hoare's Bankers Fleet Street you will however ascertain the precise Sum which is not denied by Mr. John Hanson.—Of the principal of the purchase Money I request & direct that the Superflux (after Claims and Settlements) be applied to the payment of my debts—in such portion & manner as may seem best.———The settled part I wish to be invested either in Mortgage or other *Security*—provided the *Security* be such as may deserve the name.—The Interest accruing since last April in Major Wildman's purchase money—amounting to about two thousand eight hundred pounds or thereabouts according to the statement made to me—I request to be transmitted to me in letters of Credit and Circular notes—as being Income—which I wish to employ in my personal expences.—Of the principal—I devote all as far as the Surplus goes to the Creditors and I hope that you Hobhouse—& you Kinnaird—will understand me—& see that it is properly applied.— The Interest you will send to me as requested.———Mr. Hanson is to *receive* his *five thousand pounds*—the Bill Subject to strict Investigation. I have seen *no particulars*—though *often* asked for.—With regard to the other Creditors—You will hear Mr. Hanson—& consult your own Judgments—which Mr. Kinnaird can do more freely—being in Power as my Attorney.—If Lady Noel dies before Miss Milbanke or myself— I request that Sir Francis Burdett—Earl Grey—or Lord Grenville— be prayed to act as my Arbiters,—that is *one* of these,—I name *three* in case of refusal on the part of one of these—that the next may be applied to.———I am advised to proceed in the Rochdale Lawsuit—but Law Bills seem heavy—and if the expence is to exceed a thousand pounds—I think it should be paused upon—however in this as in all other things I am disposed to listen to such opinions as my *friends* (and you two among the first) think worthy of attention.———I am ever & truly—Dear H. and Dear K.—

yr. affectionate friend & obliged Sert.

BYRON

P.S.—*This Letter is private.*

[TO JOHN CAM HOBHOUSE AND DOUGLAS KINNAIRD (*b*)]

Venice. Novr. 18th. 1818

[In Hanson's hand] Respecting the Liquidation of Lord Byron's Simple Contract Debts I think under all the Circumstances the Cred[ito]rs may very fairly be required to accept a Composition in full and I recommend it to his Lordship to authorize such a Proposition to be made to them at least so far as an Abatement of one Third at the least.

John Hanson

[In Byron's hand] I have had a good deal of Conversation with Mr. Hanson upon this Subject—and being aware of the extent of the remaining funds after the deduction of the Annuity and Bond debts—and law expences—do not see any other present prospect of liquidating the Simple Contract debts—and submit to Mr. Hobhouse and Mr. Kinnaird how far this may be eligible.——

BYRON

[TO LADY BYRON]   *Venice. Novr. 18th. 1818*

Sir Samuel Romilly has cut his throat for the loss of his wife.—It is now nearly three years since he became in the face of his compact (by a retainer—previous and I believe general) the advocate of the measures and the Approver of the proceedings which deprived me of mine.—I would not exactly like Mr. Thwackum when Philosopher Square bit his own tongue—"saddle him with a Judgment"[1] but

> "this even-handed Justice
> Commends the ingredients of our poisoned Chalice
> To our own lips."[2]

This Man little thought when he was lacerating my heart according to law—while he was poisoning my life at it's sources—aiding and abetting in the blighting—branding—and Exile that was to be the result of his Counsels in their *indirect effects*—that in less than thirty six Moons—in the pride of his triumph as the highest Candidate for the representation of the Sister-City of the mightiest of Capitals—in the fullness of his professional Career—in the Greenness of a healthy old age—in the radiance of Fame—and the Complacency of self-earned Riches—that a domestic Affliction would lay him in the Earth —with the meanest of Malefactors—in a Cross road with the Stake in his body—if the Verdict of Insanity did not redeem his ashes from the sentence of the Laws he had lived by interpreting or misinterpreting, and died in violating.———The Man had eight Children—lately deprived of their Mother—could he not live?——Perhaps previous to his Annihilation he felt a portion of what he contributed his legal mite to make me feel,—but I have lived—lived to see him a Sexagenary

[1] *Tom Jones*, Book V, chapter 2.
[2] *Macbeth*, Act I, scene 7.

Suicide.——It was not in vain that I invoked Nemesis in the Midnight of Rome from the awfullest of her Ruins.———Fare you well.——

B

[TO MAJOR THOMAS WILDMAN]   *Venice. Novr. 18th. 1818*

My dear Wildman—Mr. Hanson is on the Eve of his return so that I have only time to return a few inadequate thanks for your very kind letter.——I should regret to trouble you with any requests of mine in regard to the preservation of any signs of my family which may still exist at Newstead—and leave every thing of that kind to your own feelings, present or future, upon the Subject. The portrait which you flatter me by desiring—would not be worth to you your trouble & expence of such an expedition—but you may rely upon your having the very first that may be painted—& which may seem worth your acceptance.——I trust that Newstead will, being yours—remain so—& that it may see you as happy, as I am very sure that you will make your dependents. With regard to myself—you may be sure that whether in the 4th.—5th.—or sixth form—at Harrow,—or in the fluctuations of after-life—I shall always remember with regard my old Schoolfellow —fellow Monitor—& friend;—and recognize with respect the gallant Soldier—who with all the advantages of fortune and allurements of youth to a life of pleasure—devoted himself to duties of a nobler order —and will receive his reward in the esteem and admiration of his Country.—

ever yours most truly & affectly.
BYRON

[TO JOHN CAM HOBHOUSE]   *Venezia. Novr. 23d. 1818*

Dear Hobhouse—You say Nobody knows nought of Luke Scalabrino the Magnificent Correspondent who went between Tasso and his Washerwoman. So the enclosed quotation!—You will wonder at my research—but it is not mine—but an English Gentleman's now here (Mr. Ingram of *Durham* "can anything good come out of *Nazareth*") who told me this—sent me the boke—I have caused a copy—and sent it by post.——Spooney is gone back with a long letter to *you* and *Kinnaird.*—Lord Lauderdale has a cargo of "poeshie" and is on his way too. So Sir S[amuel] R[omilly] has cut his throttle for the loss of his wife!—Mr. Thwackum "saddled Square with a Judgment" when he bit his tongue——when R. was legally mischief making between *my wife* & me three years agone or so—did he think that in less than thirty six moons *Nemesis* would level him in a cross road for a like ⟨self⟩ deprivation—See what comes of the Good old Gods—and remember how I always believed in & worshipped them—they wove my good stanzas.——

[Four Latin stanzas enclosed in another hand.]

The news arrived here the Night before Spooney's departure.— Spooney would not believe it was for the loss of his wife that Romilly "cut through both his Jugglers" (as Mr. Pyne said of poor Whitbread) but swore it must be because he "could not get the Seals"[.] He—Hanson—had no idea of not surviving one's wife—he said "it was a boyish trick" what said the Crowner? "Lunacy"—no doubt—be it so.——

[TO JOHN MURRAY]   *Venice, November 24th, 1818*

Dear Sir,—Mr. Hanson has been here a week and went five days ago; he brought nothing but his papers, some corn-rubbers, and a kaleidoscope. "For what we have received, the Lord make us thankful!" —for without his aid I shall not be so.

He—Hanson—left everything else in Chancery Lane whatever, except your copy-paper for the last canto, etc., which, being a degree of parchment, he brought with him.

You may imagine his reception; he swore the books were a "waggon-load." If they were, he should have come in a waggon—he would in that case have come quicker than he did.

Lord Lauderdale set off from hence twelve days ago, accompanied by a cargo of poesy directed to Mr. Hobhouse—all spick and span, and in MS. You will see what it is like. I have given it to Master Southey, and he shall have more before I have done with him. I understand the scoundrel said, on his return from Switzerland two years ago, that "Shelley and I were in a league of Incest, etc., etc." He is a burning liar! for the women to whom he alludes are not sisters—one being Godwin's daughter, by Mary Wollstonecraft, and the other daughter of the *present* (second) Mrs. G, by a *former* husband; and in the next place, if they had even been so, there was no *promiscuous intercourse* whatever.

82

You may make what I say here as public as you please—more particularly to Southey, whom I look upon, and will say as publicly, to be a dirty, lying rascal; and will prove it in ink—or in his blood, if I did not believe him to be too much of a poet to risk it. If he had forty reviews at his back—as he has the *Quarterly*—I would have at him in his scribbling capacity, now that he has begun with me; but I will do nothing underhand. Tell him what I say from *me*, and everyone else you please.

You will see what I have said if the parcel arrives safe. I understand *Coleridge* went about repeating Southey's lie with pleasure. I can believe it, for I had done him what is called a favour. I can understand Coleridge's abusing me, but how or why *Southey*—whom I had never obliged in any sort of way, or done him the remotest service—should go about fibbing and calumniating is more than I readily comprehend.

Does he think to put me down with his *canting*—not being able to do so with his poetry? We will try the question. I have read his review of Hunt,[1] where he has attacked Shelley in an oblique and shabby manner. Does he know what that review has done? I will tell you. It has *sold* an edition of the *Revolt of Islam*, which, otherwise, nobody would have thought of reading, and few who read can understand—I for one.

Southey would have attacked me, too, there, if he durst, further than by hints about Hunt's friends in general; and some outcry about an "Epicurean system," carried on by men of the most opposite habits, tastes, and opinions in life and poetry (I believe), that ever had their names in the same volume—Moore, Byron, Shelley, Hazlitt, Haydon, Leigh Hunt, Lamb—what resemblance do ye find among all or any of these men? and how could any sort of system or plan be carried on, or attempted amongst them? However, let Mr. Southey look to himself—since the wine is tapped, let him drink it.

I got some books a few weeks ago—many thanks; amongst them is *Israeli's* new edition. It was not fair in you to show him my copy of his former one, with all the marginal notes and nonsense made in Greece when I was not two-and-twenty, and which certainly were not meant for his perusal, or for that of his readers.[2] I have a great respect for

[1] The review of Hunt's *Foliage* in the *Quarterly Review*, Jan. 1818, pp. 324–335 (the issue appeared in June, 1818) was probably by John Taylor Coleridge and not by Southey as Byron supposed. (See Donald H. Reiman, *The Romantics Reviewed*, Part C, Vol. II, p. 758.)

[2] Byron had written some comments in the margins of a copy of Isaac D'Israeli's *The Literary Character*. This volume had been left with John Murray who showed it to D'Israeli, a close friend. The result was a new edition (1818) in the preface of which D'Israeli quoted Byron's remarks. The volume which Byron annotated is now in the Meyer Davis collection in the University of Pennsylvania Library.

Israeli and his talents, and have read his works over and over and over repeatedly, and have been amused by them greatly, and instructed often. Besides, I hate giving pain unless provoked; and he is an author, and must feel like his brethren; and although his liberality repaid my marginal flippancies with a compliment—the highest compliment—that don't reconcile me to myself, nor to *you*—it was a breach of confidence to do this without my leave. I don't know a living man's books I take up so often, or lay down more reluctantly, as *Israeli's*; and I never will forgive you—that is, for many weeks. If he had got out of humour I should have been less sorry, but even then, I should have been sorry; but, really, he has heaped his "coals of fire" so handsomely upon my head, that they burn unquenchably.

You ask me of the two reviews—I will tell you. Scott's is the review of one poet on another—his friend; and Wilson's the review of a poet, too, on another—his *idol*; for he likes me better than he chooses to avow to the public, with all his eulogy. I speak, judging only from the article, for I don't know him personally.

So Sir Samuel Romilly has cut his throat for the loss of his wife. Three years ago (nearly), when, after a long and general retainer, he deserted to Miss Milbanke, and did his best, or his worst, to destroy me, or make me destroy myself, did he dream that in less than thirty-six months a domestic deprivation would level him in a cross-road, but for a lying verdict of lunacy?

There would have been some excuse for such a fit at twenty-seven—but at sixty-four! Could not the dotard wait till his drivelling did it? You see that Nemesis is not yet extinct, for I had not forgot Sir S. in my imprecation, which involved many. I never will dissemble—it may be very fine to forgive—but I would not have forgiven him living, and I will not affect to pity him dead. There are others of that set (of course I except the women, who were mere instruments—all but one) who have throats; but whether they will be cut by their own hands, or no, is yet to be shown. There is much to be done; and you may yet see that what ought to be done upon those my enemies will be.

Here is a long letter—can you read it?

Yours ever,
Byron

[TO RICHARD BELGRAVE HOPPNER]   *Venice, Nov. 25th. 1818*

My dear Sir,—Many thanks for your kind note. Believe me I am truly grateful for attention so little deserved—you had no reason to be apprehensive that I should be displeased at your offer.—The remarks you make at the bottom of your letter cannot be more pertinent—we are all heirs to misfortune and disappointments—but *poets* especially seem to be a marked race—who has not heard of the blindness of *Milton*—the wretched life, and still more unhappy death of *Otway*—the long sufferings & unrequited services of *Cowley* and of *Butler*—the struggles against poverty & malice which occupied the life of *Dryden*—the constitutional infirmities which embittered the existence of *Pope*—the lamentable idiocy & madness of *Swift*—the almost unparalleled miseries and unhappy end of *Savage*—the frenzy of *Collins*—the indigence of *Goldsmith*—the morbid melancholy and sullen discontent of *Johnson*—the hypochondrianism of *Gray* and of *Beattie*—the tragical catastrophe of *Chatterton*—the disappointed hopes and premature death of *Burns*—and the sickness, despondency, and madness of *Cowper*?[1] To this deplorable list many additions might be made——Let me offer my most sincere wishes for your health and happiness—and allow me still to subscribe myself

> yours most sincerely
> BYRON

[TO JOHN MURRAY]   *Venice, December 7, 1818*

After *that stanza* in the first canto of *Don Juan* (sent by Lord Lauderdale) towards the *conclusion* of the canto—I speak of the stanza whose two last lines are—

> "The best is that in short-hand ta'en by Gurney,
> Who to Madrid on purpose made a journey,"

insert the following stanzas. "But Donna Inez," etc. [stanza 90. Byron's first intention had been to include seven stanzas after stanza 89, but these he withheld and substituted others (see *Poetry*, VI, 67–70n). The following "Character" was intended as a note to go with the stanzas on Brougham.]

---

[1] Byron had commented similarly on the madness of poets in a letter to Leigh Hunt (Nov. 4–6, 1815, Vol. 4, p. 332.)

⟨Doubted⟩ Distrusted by the democracy—disliked by the Whigs—
and detested by the Tories—too much of a lawyer for the people—and
too much of a demagogue for Parliament—a contestor of counties—
and a Candidate for cities—the refuse of half the electors of England—
and representative at last upon sufferance of the proprietor of some
rotten borough which it would have been more independent to have
purchased—a speaker upon all questions—and the outcast of all
parties—his support has become alike formidable to all his enemies—
(for he has no friends—) and his vote can be only valuable when
accompanied by his silence.—A disappointed man with a bad temper—
he is endowed with considerable but not first rate abilities—and has
blundered on through life—remarkable only for a fluency in which he
has many rivals at the bar and in the Senate and an eloquence in which
he has several superiors.—"Willing to wound and *not* afraid to strike"[2]
—till he receives a blow in return—he has not yet betrayed any illegal
ardour or Irish alacrity in accepting the [defiances?] and resenting the
disgraceful terms—which his proneness to evil speaking have brought
upon him.—In the cases of [Machinnes?] and Manners he sheltered
himself behind those parliamentary privileges which—Fox—Pitt—
Castlereagh—Canning—Tierney—Adam—Shelburne—Grattan—
[Cary?]—Curran—and Clare—disdained to adopt as their buckler.
——⟨In Italy after provoking Parliament⟩ The House of Commons
became the Asylum of his Slander—as the Churches of Rome were once
the Sanctuary of Assassins. His literary reputation (with the exception
of one work of his early career) rests upon some anonymous articles
imputed to him in a celebrated periodical work—but even these are
surpassed by the essays of others in the same Journal.——He has
tried every thing—& succeeded in nothing,—and he may perhaps
finish as a lawyer without practice as he has already been occasionally
an Orator without an audience,—if not soon cut short in his career.—

The above character is not written impartially—but by a man who has
had occasion to know the baser parts of it & regards him accordingly
with shuddering abhorrence and just as much fear as he deserves—in
him is to be dreaded the crawling of the Centipede and the Spring of

---

[1] Some time in 1816 or 1817 Byron heard, from Hobhouse or other English
friends, of the extent to which Brougham had spread rumours about him during
and after the separation. Byron did not then know that Brougham had been the
reviewer of *Hours of Idleness* in the *Edinburgh Review* in 1808.
[2] Pope, *Epistle to Dr. Arbuthnot*, line 208.

the tiger—the venom of the reptile and the strength of the animal—
the rancour of the miscreant not the courage of the man—
In case the prose or verse of the above should be actionable I put my
name that this man may rather proceed against me than the publisher
—not without the faint hope that the hand with which I blast him may
induce him however more tardily to a manlier revenge.—

Venice. Decr. 9th. 1818

Dear Douglas—You should have advised me before,—as my friend,
—my trustee, my Power of Attorney—and my Banker; because
although I always suspect a woman of being a whore—and generally a
man of being a rascal,———I do not set him down as an actual felon
(even although an Attorney)—without some overt Indications—or
at least previous hints;—and therefore you should have told me long
ago of Spooney.———The parchments which I have signed (to the best
of my recollection—and) according to what *they were* represented,—
were the Conveyances to Major Wildman—Releases (or whatever the
legal Cant may be) for the trustees—and answers for the Exchequer
relative to the Rochdale Cause,—but I cannot say that I *read over any*
of the parchments—nor *noted them*—so that you had better (and as my
Potestas you have the right) insist on a sight of all of them—Mr.
Townsend was witness for Major Wildman (a young man Clerk in
the Office of Wildman's Lawyer & Wildman's friend—Wildman will
give you his address) Hanson's son—Newton by name—& my Valet
the illustrious Fletcher—witnessed also,—you now know all that I
know.—I sent by Hanson a very long letter addressed to *you* &
Hobhouse jointly—upon the subject in general of my affairs, and as I trust
it will be safely delivered by Hanson—you will act upon it according to
your judgment and inclination, of the papers I have nothing but the
endorsements & signature—I should not have understood a syllable of
their Jargon had I read them, and till this moment I did not suspect
falsification or *Substitution,* but now do—because you say so—though
like all advice—it comes somewhat of the latest.—Hanson has been
gone this fortnight.—Lord Lauderdale—three weeks.—The former
conveys my papers—the Second my cargo of poesy, as both—have a
reference to finance—pray don't forget either—for money is power—
and pleasure—and I like it vastly.———I request that the *interest* due
on Wildman's purchase-money—from April till now—(about two
thousand seven or eight hundred pounds) be transmitted to my credit,

87

together with the purchase of Don Juan—& Mazeppa &c. which ought to bring a good price—there is more in quantity than my former cargos —and for the *quality* you will pronounce.——By the last two posts—I have sent some additions to the *"Poeshie"*.—You have put me in a fuss —as you always do—with your damned letters—because you never say any thing till after.—How was I to dream that any of those blasted parchments might be garbled—or falsified—? or that Hanson was so damned a rogue as you hint him?—at any rate there must be justice and law for me as well as another;—but I beg *you* will *scrutinize*—if not I can do nothing—you might at any rate have said all this before.—— Scrope's letter I have answered.——I cannot go to England.—I wish Hobhouse all possible Success—I am told that he speaks admirably well —and am sure that he will do wonders—win or lose.—But he will win.—I write in haste—& in no good humour—and am

yours very truly & affectly.

B

P.S.——In my letter to Scrope—my reasons are explained for not coming—in my letter to you and Hobhouse—my affairs are touched upon fully;—as for the rest the trustees should look to them and perhaps some of my friends may glance that way when they have leisure.—Hobhouse is right to stand at any rate—It will be a great step to have contested Westminster—and if he gains—it is every thing—You may depend upon it that Hobhouse has talents very much beyond his *present rate*—& even beyond his own opinion—he is too *fidgetty* but he has the elements of Greatness if he can but keep his nerves in order—I don't mean *courage but anxiety*.——Can you send me some of "Lardner's prepared Charcoal" (a toothpowder) and the Charcoal dentifrice? H[anso]n brought only his papers.—

[TO JOHN CAM HOBHOUSE] *Venice. Decr. 12th. 1818*

Dear Hobhouse—You do well to stand for Westminster[1]—the very Contest is an advantage—you show yourself & prove your talent for Eloquence—(which I can assure you I have heard from all hands to be very great) you have a fine field—& even if the tories should outnumber you the triumph will be yours in honour—honesty—& ability—and

---

[1] In November, 1818, Hobhouse entered the election to fill the seat for Westminster in the House of Commons that was made vacant by the death of Sir Samuel Romilly. He was supported by Kinnaird and other advocates of Reform, but was defeated in the following March by George Lamb.

what is the rest worth?——If you gain—you start with the greatest advantages—the Successor of Fox—as representative of one of the first of our cities—with good previous exercise for Oratory in the Senate by practice in the Forum—(during the election). I saw your late Speech in Galignani's newspaper—& with all the disfiguration & curtailment of the reporter—it was the best of the day.—You do not start a bit too late—you are thirty two—(I see they talked about *youth*—so much the better—be young as long as you can)—Burke was not in the house till thirty five years of age—Lord Mansfield—not till thirty seven—& have we ever had better? What have all these later younglings done?—what are Ward—& Mills—and W. Lambe—and Master Lambton?—*Peel* (my old Schoolfellow) is the best of all there but even he is a disappointed man—because not already minister.— Pitt's Exchequership at twenty three has been the ruin not only of his country but of all it's Coxcombs—they want to be Premiers at five & twenty and are ill used if they are not.——I see you have been in a devil of a hurry to give "a pledge" a *Cazzo*—why give it till they ask it?—the fact is they do not want *annual parliaments*—but *annual elections*—that I take to be the truth—but I see no harm in either—for assuredly till a great blow be struck—the present System will only conduct Castlereagh to his object.——A letter came to me from Scrope which I have answered—with my reasons for not returning at present to England—if I thought it would be of use to you—I would —but I think the contrary—& remain—to play Pomponius Atticus to your Cicero—or "Archias Poeta" if you like it better—by the Lord!— your Consulship (or rather Tribunate) should be written in Greek Hexameters.—You may be assured that if anything *serious* is ever required to be done—in which my insignificance can add an 0 to the Number—I will come over—& there "like little wanton boys we'll swim &c."[2] till Scrope despairs of the Republic.——The progress of your Contest will be to me extremely interesting—I had written to you by Hanson—& sent a packet by Lord Lauderdale (an Eulogist of your Speaking) &c. &c. but I knew not of your politicals—so pray— let all that stand—till you are chaired—which that you may be is the fairest hope & wish of yours

[Scrawl for signature]

P.S.—When you and I were cantering last year along the *Lido*— and I had all the difficulty possible to persuade you back to England—

[2] Adapted from *Henry VIII*, Act 3, scene 2.

what were the odds against Sir Romuel Samilly's election—against his cutting his throat—against the succeeding (& success) of yourself? —[As?] for the lawyer—he was one of Miss Milbanke's advisers—so much for Nemesis—I never would have forgiven him living & will not affect to pity him dead—I hate him still—as much as one can dislike dust.——I see the Queen is gone to join Semiramis & Zenobia;—the Princess last year—the Queen next—the tragedy of Tom Thumb is nothing to it.—

"Remember—Milor!—that delicaci ensure every Succes."

Thursday the 10th Inst. was Ada's birthday—a three year *old*—"Ah! Coquin—vhare is my Shild?"——

[MEMORANDUM FOR MR. KNOWLES[1]]   [*1819?*]

Tooth-powder—
Magnesia—
Macassar Oil—
Some Gunpowder from Manton's—
Military Sashes—
Tooth-brushes for the inside of the teeth particularly.
Apply to Mr. Murray, 50 Albemarle St., to Mr. Hobhouse—or the Honble. Douglas Kinnaird—who will have the goodness to commit the articles to the care of the bearer Mr. Knowles.

[TO COUNT GIUSEPPINO ALBRIZZI[1]]   *J[anuar]y 5th. 1819*

Dear Count Albrizzi—I have received the annexed copy of Mr. Hobhouse's letter to Mr. di Breme[2] which Mr. H. desires me to lay before Madame your mother the Countess Albrizzi.—It is his wish to make it as public as possible—& to have a translation inserted in the Gazettes, but I doubt whether some of the expressions are not too strong for the Censor.—

yrs. ever

B

---

[1] Unidentified.

[1] Son of the Countess Albrizzi, whose *conversazioni* Byron frequented in Venice.

[2] Ludivico di Breme, whom Byron and Hobhouse had met at Milan, took up the defence of the Italian writers who were criticised rather severely in Hobhouse's *Historical Illustrations of the Fourth Canto of Childe Harold*. An "Essay on the present Literature of Italy" in that volume, contributed anonymously by the exiled Italian writer Ugo Foscolo, brought a strongly worded protest from di Breme which Byron turned over to Hobhouse, who wanted his response published in Italy. Byron was still unaware that Hobhouse had not written the "Essay".

Dear H. and dear K.—I approve and sanction all your legal proceedings with regard to my affairs, and can only repeat my thanks & approbation—if you put off the payments of debts "till *after* Lady Noel's death"—it is well—if till *after* her damnation—better—for that will last forever—yet I hope not:—for her sake as well as the Creditors'—I am willing to believe in Purgatory.——With regard to the Poeshie—I will have no "cutting & slashing" as Perry calls it— you may omit the stanzas on Castlereagh[1]—indeed it is better—& the two "*Bobs*" at the end of the 3d. stanza of the dedication— which will leave "high" & "adry" good rhymes without any "*double* (or Single) Entendre*"[2]—but no more—I appeal—not "to Philip fasting" but to Alexander drunk—I appeal to Murray at his ledger—to the people—in short, Don Juan shall be an entire horse or none.—If the objection be to the indecency, the Age which applauds the "Bath Guide" & Little's poems—& reads Fielding & Smollett still—may bear with that;—if to the poetry—I will take my chance.— I will not give way to all the Cant of Christendom—I have been cloyed with applause & sickened with abuse;—at present—I care for little but the Copyright,—I have imbibed a great love for money—let me have it—if Murray loses this time—he won't the next—he will be cautious—and I shall learn the decline of his customers by his epistolary indications.——But in no case will I submit to have the poem mutilated.—There is another Canto written—but not copied—in two hundred & odd Stanzas,—if this succeeds—as to the prudery of the present day—what is it? are we more moral than when Prior wrote— is there anything in Don Juan so strong as in Ariosto—or Voltaire— or Chaucer?—Tell Hobhouse—his letter to De Breme has made a great Sensation—and is to be published in the Tuscan & other Gazettes—Count R[izzo][3] came to consult with me about it last Sunday—we think of Tuscany—for Florence and Milan are in literary war—but the Lombard league is headed by Monti[4]—& would make a

---

[1] In the Dedication (to Southey) of *Don Juan* Byron referred to "The intellectual eunuch Castlereagh", but since he published the first two cantos anonymously, he omitted the Dedication.

[2] The ribaldry of this couplet caused consternation among Byron's friends in England, to whom the *double entendre* was obvious. In Regency slang "a dry Bob" meant coition without emission.

[3] Count Francesco Rizzo-Patarol, a Venetian nobleman in the circle of the Countess Albrizzi.

[4] Vincenzo Monti, the Italian poet whom Byron and Hobhouse had met in Milan.

difficulty of insertion in the Lombard Gazettes—once published in the Pisan—it will find its way through Italy—by translation or reply.————So Lauderdale has been telling a story!—I suppose this is my reward for presenting him at Countess Benzone's—& shewing him—what attention I could.———Which "piece" does he mean?—since last year I have run the Gauntlet;—is it the Tarruscelli[5]—the Da Mosti[6]—the Spineda—the Lotti—the Rizzato—the Eleanora—the Carlotta—the Giulietta—the Alvisi—the Zambieri—The Eleanora da Bezzi—(who was the King of Naples' Gioaschino's mistress—at least one of them) the Theresina of Mazzurati—the Glettenheimer—& her Sister—the Luigia & her mother—the Fornaretta—the Santa—the Caligari—the Portiera [Vedova?]—the Bolognese figurante—the Tentora and her sister—cum multis aliis?—some of them are Countesses—& some of them Cobblers wives—some noble—some middling—some low—& all whores—which does the damned old "Ladro—& porco fottuto"[7] mean?—I have had them all & thrice as many to boot since 1817— Since *he* tells a story about me—I will tell one about him;—when he landed at the *Custom house* from *Corfu*—he called for *"Post horses— directly"*—he was told that there were no horses except mine nearer than the Lido—unless he wished for the four bronze Coursers of St. Mark—which were at his Service.—

I am yrs. ever—

Let me have H's Election immediately—I mention it *last* as being what I was least likely to forget.———

P.S.—Whatever Brain-money—you get on my account from Murray—pray remit me—I will never consent to pay away what I *earn*—that is *mine*—& what I get by my brains—I will spend on my b——ks—as long as I have a tester or a testicle remaining.—I shall not live long—& for that Reason—I must live while I can—so—let him disburse—& me receive—"for the Night cometh."———If I had but had twenty thousand a year I should not have been living now— but all men are not born with a silver or Gold Spoon in their mouths. ———My balance—also—my balance—& a Copyright—I have another Canto—too—ready—& then there will be my half year in June— recollect—*I* care for nothing but "monies".—January 20th. 1819.— You say nothing of Mazeppa—did it arrive—with one other—besides that you mention?———

5 See May 19, 1818, to Hobhouse.
6 See Feb. 23, 1818, to Hobhouse.
7 Fottuto = Fr. foutre, an epithet of disgust or disrespect.

P.S.—The Fornaretta has been restored to her husband some time[1]
—but not without an attempt with a knife—which was in the *Lamb*
style.—She then threw herself into the Grand Canal—and was fished
out without much damage except throwing Madame Mocenigo &
other spectators into fits—*all this* was for the *sake* of *effect* & not *real
stabbing* nor *drowning*—your *real Suicide* don't perform in public.—I
have quite given up Concubinage.—

My dear Hobhouse—I have written a *joint* letter to you & Kinnaird
—on affairs—with thanks & so forth—not to bother *you*—singly—
from your own—& better business.——I shall repeat no further what
I have said in that letter—except my best thanks;—that—I *won't*
have the *poeshie* curtailed or watered—except in the places indicated in
this same letter to you & K.—& that Lauderdale with his story is "a
son of a Bitch for all his laced Coat"—I have told a story in return
about him—which has the further advantage of being true.——I
rejoice in the perspective of your Success—it shall be like" Gordon's
Palates" while I trust that Maxwell's[1] pretensions will be "a wretched
attempt" like "Maclauren's *made* Dish.—"Take your fortune—take it
at the "flood"—now is your time—& remember that in your very
Start you have overtaken all whom you thought before you—above
all don't *diffide* in yourself—nor be nervous about your *health*—leave
that to poets & such fellows—& don't be afraid of your own talents—
I tell you as I have told others—that you think too humbly of them—
you have already shown yourself fit for very great things—"the
greatest is behind"—& once in the house—I hope to see you the best
heard in it—& first read out of it.——Above all recollect that it is all
Luck in this world—that all men have their time offered—that this
is yours—seize it.—Your letter to De Breme has greatly pleased
here—& we have had a consultation—about the best way of publishing
—some expressions are too strong for the Censure—& must be
softened—& Madame A[lbrizzi] is in a fuss about her "Serail" but I
have begged Count R[izzo] to intercede hard for the standing of the

---

1 See Aug. 1, 1819, to Murray.
1 See July 15, 1818, to Kinnaird, note 1.

Seraglio—it seems to me the Cream of the Correspondence.—Pray remember me to all friends—to the Scrope—& let me hear how you advance—I am ever & truly yours

B

Pray explain to Mr. M[urray]—the reason why I attacked S[outhey]— is it not sufficient?

[TO JOHN MURRAY]   *Venice. January 20th. 1819*

Dear Sir—I write two lines to say that if you publish Don Juan— I will only have the stanzas on Castlereagh *omitted*—and the two concluding words (Bob-Bob) of the two last lines of the third Stanza of the dedication to S[outhey]—I explained to Hobhouse why I have attacked that Scoundrel & request him to explain to you the reason. The opinions which I have asked of Mr. H. & others were with regard to the poetical merit—& not as to what they may think due to the Cant of the day—which still reads the Bath Guide[,] Little's poems— Prior—& Chaucer—to say nothing of Fielding & Smollett.—If published—publish entire—with the above mentioned exceptions— or you may publish anonymously—or *not* at *all*—in the latter event print 50 on my account for private distribution.—

Yours ever,

B

I have written by this post to Messrs. K[innaird] and H[obhouse] to desire that they will not erase more than I have stated. The second Canto of Don Juan is finished in 206 stanzas.

[TO JOHN MURRAY]   *Venice. January 25th. 1819*

Dear Sir—You will do me the favour to print privately—(for private distribution—) fifty copies of Don Juan—the list of the men to whom I wish it to be presented I will send hereafter.—The other two poems had best be added to the collective edition—I do not approve of *their* being published separately. *Print* Don Juan *entire* omitting of course the lines on Castlereagh as I am not on the spot to meet him.—I have a second Canto ready—which will be sent by & bye.—By this post I have written to Mr. Hobhouse—addressed to your care.

Yours ever truly

B

94

P.S.—I have acquiesced in the request—& representation—& having done so—it is idle to detail my arguments in favour of my own Self-love & "Poeshie;" but I *protest.*—If the poem has poetry—it would stand—if not—fall—the rest is "leather & prunella,"[1]—and has never yet affected any human production "pro or con."—Dullness is the only annihilator in such cases.—As to the Cant of the day—I despise it—as I have ever done all it's other finical fashions,—which become you as paint became the Antient Britons.—If you admit this prudery—you must omit half Ariosto—La Fontaine—Shakespeare—Beaumont—Fletcher—Massinger—Ford—all the Charles second writers—in short, *Something* of most who have written before Pope—and are worth reading—and much of Pope himself—*read him*—most of you *don't*—but *do*—& I will forgive you—though the inevitable consequence would be that you would burn all I have ever written, and all your other wretched Claudians of the day (except Scott & Crabbe) into the bargain.—I wrong Claudian who *was* a *poet* by naming him with such fellows—but he was the "ultimus Romanorum" the[2] tail of the Comet—and these persons are the tail of an old Gown cut into a waistcoat for Jackey—but being both *tails*—I have compared one with the other—though very unlike—like all Similies.—I write in a passion and a Sirocco—and was up till six this morning at the Carnival; but I *protest*—as I did in my former letter.

[TO JOHN CAM HOBHOUSE]   *Venice. January 25th. 1819*

My dear Hobhouse—The Most satisfactory answer to your letter is acquiescence—and I acquiesce in the *nan*-publication[1]—but I am a scribbler fond of his bantling—& you must let me *print fifty* privately —about a dozen of which I wish to be distributed—(& will send you the list of to *whom* hereafter) by Mr. Murray;—from *this* I cannot recede—& I hope it will seem to you enough.—The three letters I wrote to you—Kinnaird—& Murray the other day—dated 20th—of course go for nothing. About the bitch my wife—I differ from you entirely.—The other two poems[2] are not worth a separate publication —or any price that may be mentioned—Murray had best publish them in his next edition of all the poems as an adjunct—for I *will not* allow

---

[1] Pope's *Essay on Man*, Ep. IV, line 204.

[2] Last page of MS. missing. The end of the letter is in *LJ*, IV, 278.

[1] All Byron's friends in England counselled him not to publish *Don Juan* because of the satire on Lady Byron as Donna Inez, and the offence it might give to conventional moral codes.

[2] The other two poems, finally published together on June 28, 1819, were *Mazeppa* and *Ode on Venice*.

their separate appearance.—I have another Canto of Juan finished—which I will send by & bye—after the printing of the other;—the motto "domestica facta" merely meant—*common life*—which I presume was Horace's meaning;[3]—the *Julian* adventure detailed was none of mine—but one of an acquaintance of mine—(Parolini by name) which happened some years ago at Bassano with the Prefect's wife when he was a boy—and was the Subject of a long cause ending in a divorce or separation of the parties during the Italian Vice-royalty.— —If you suppose I don't mind the money—you are mistaken—I do mind it most damnably—it is the only thing I ever saw worth minding—for as *Dervish* told me it comprehends all the rest;—but Honour must be considered before it & friendship also—& it is sufficient for me that you disapprove of the publication, though I by no means approve of your disapproval.—But for the *printing*—I must stickle on account of my vanity—"nothing is more vain than Vanity" so says Strap in Roderick Random—and here you have a fresh example.— —Your answer to the Knight-Abbot has made the Devil's own row—and—great admiration of the composition & writer have been suscitated.—Breme is actually ill—& Monti frantic in consequence.[4]—I enclose you Countess Benzone's letter to me—for your Epistle has become the great desideratum of all the Conversazioni.—Publication is to follow—but you know the Italian custom—they *Canvas* FIRST.—The Albrizzi—the Michelli—the Benzone—all celebrated for literature—wit—and Gallantry for the last half Century—& for Beauty the other half—contested for the perusal.—I think the orthography of your name will please you.—The Chevalier Mingaldo a friend of mine came to me today to beg it for a poetical friend of his—& in short—you know Italy—& Venice—& may imagine—that such a thing is as likely to raise a new war—as ever the raption of the Sabines.— —Rizzo told me last night at the Opera that the letter was half-translated & they only waited it's recovery from the Benzone to traduct the other half.— —For my own opinion I think your answer a Capo d'opera—& this *not* because *every body* else thinks so—for you know *that* is not amongst *my* family of Vices.— —Wilberforce[5]—the

[3] The motto of *Don Juan* when it was published was "Difficile est propria communia dicere", from Horace's *Art of Poetry* (line 128); "It is difficult to speak of common things in an appropriate manner."

[4] See Jan. 5, 1819, to Count Albrizzi, note 2.

[5] William Wilberforce (1759–1833), the Evangelical whose missionary zeal was combined with political activity, was apparently contemplating running against Hobhouse for the Westminster seat in the House of Commons. From 1812, to 1825 he was M.P. for Bramber.

canting Ludro!—that son of a bitch must be beaten or one shall have the Abbey of Westminster turned into a Conventicle—and a cockeyed bust of Whitfield—of the Colossal size—occupying the space of the demolished monuments in poet's Corner.—Say this to your Constituents with my compliments.—

[At bottom of note from the Countess Benzone]:

Dear Hobhouse—This is the note of the Countess Benzone—who is a Venetian Lady Melbourne—and without having been one of the chastest—the best of her Sex.—a Great patroness of mine—& Admirer of you.——

yrs.

B

[TO JOHN CAM HOBHOUSE]   [*January 26, 1819*]

P.S.—Cazzo—Corpo—ed' anche &c.—Sangue di &c. O! Mar*ie*! Can' della Madonna tixe un Gran &c. &c. &c.[1]——all your compliments have not sweetened me a bit—& Scrope too![2] *that* is the unkindest cut of all—I meant to have added a *P.S.*—but I wish first to hear that you are *M. P.*—which is I may say—what I have most at heart—do not omit to report your progress.——I had some time ago a letter from Miss Boyce the actress[3]—it is full of Sentiment—and love—and the most sublime diction—but all of a sudden breaks off into "and the worst of all is that they want to cut down our Salaries." —Tell it to D. Kinnaird as this "cutting & slashing" is the result of his not tumbling down the trap-door, from which he was saved by Miss Tree, then Columbine,—and add that "I say ditto to Miss Boyce" the worst of all is the cutting down the Salary.—Capite? or in Venetian has tu Cap*io*?—

[TO DOUGLAS KINNAIRD]   *Venice. January 27th. 1819*

My dear Douglas—I have received a very clever letter from Hobhouse against the publication of Don Juan—in which I understand

---

[1] Venetian idiomatic profanity which Byron learned from his mistresses. See Aug. 1, 1819, to Murray.

[2] Byron was shocked that the profane Scrope Davies had joined with his other friends in England in the opinion that *Don Juan* should not be published.

[3] Susan Boyce, a minor actress at Drury Lane Theatre, with whom Byron had a brief affair before going abroad. See Marchand, II, 549–550.

you have acquiesced (you be damned)—I acquiesce too—but reluctantly.——This acquiescence is some thousands of pounds out of my
pocket—the very thought of which brings tears into my eyes—I
have imbibed such a love for money that I keep some Sequins in a
drawer to count, & cry over them once a week—and if it was not for a
turn for women—(which I hope will be soon worn out)—I think in
time that I should be able not only to clear off but to accumulate.——
God only knows how it rends my heart—to part with the idea of the
sum I should have received from a fair bargain of my recent "poeshie"
the Sequins are the great consideration—as for the applauses of
posterity—I would willingly sell the Reversion at a discount—even to
Mr. Southey—who seems fond of it—as if people's Grandchildren
were to be wiser than their forefathers—although no doubt the
simple Chances of change are in favour of the deuce-ace turning up at
last—just as in the overturn of a Coach the odds are that your arse
will be first out of the window.—I say—that as for fame and all that—
it is for such persons as Fortune chooses—and so is money.—And so
on account of this damned prudery—and the reviews—and an Outcry
and posterity—a Gentleman who has "a proper regard for his fee" is
to be curtailed of his "Darics," (I am reading about Greece & Persia)
this comes of consulting friends—I will see you all damned—before I
consult you again—what do you mean now by giving advice when you
are asked for it?—don't you know that it is like asking a man how he
does—and that the answer in both cases should always be *"Very well
I thank you"?——*

yrs. ever [scrawl]
B

P.S.—Give my love to Frere and tell him—he is right—but I
never will forgive him nor any of you.——"My fee—My fee"—"I
looked for a suit &c. &c. and you stop my mouth with &c. a whoreson
Achitophel—May he be damned like the Glutton."[1]——

[TO JOHN MURRAY]   *Venice. February 1st. 1819*

Dear Sir—After one of the concluding stanzas of the first Canto of
Don Juan—which ends with—(I forget the number)—

> To have ....
> ...... when the original is dust,
> A book, a d——d bad picture, & worse bust.

---

[1] Adapted from *Henry IV*, Part II, Act I, scene 2.

Insert the following stanza—

> What are the hopes of Man? Old Ægypt's King
> Cheops erected the first Pyramid
> And largest, thinking it was just the thing
> To keep his Memory whole, and Mummy hid,
> But Somebody or Other rummaging
> Burglariously broke his Coffin's lid,
> Let not a Monument give you or me hopes,
> Since not a pinch of dust is left of Cheops.—

I have written to you several letters—some with additions—& some upon the subject of the poem itself which my cursed puritanical committee have protested against publishing—but we will circumvent them on that point in the end. I have not yet begun to copy out the second Canto—which is finished;—from natural laziness—and the discouragement of the milk & water they have thrown upon the first.— I say all this to them as to you—that is for *you* to say to *them*—for I will have nothing underhand.—If they had told me the poetry was bad—I would have acquiesced—but they say the contrary—& then talk to me about morality—the first time I ever heard the word from any body who was not a rascal that used it for a purpose.—I maintain that it is the most moral of poems—but if people won't discover the moral that is their fault not mine.—I have already written to beg that in any case you will print *fifty* for private distribution. I will send you the list of persons to whom it is to be sent afterwards.—Within this last fortnight I have been rather indisposed with a rebellion of Stomach—which would retain nothing—(liver I suppose) and an inability or phantasy not to be able to eat of any thing with relish—but a kind of Adriatic fish called "Scampi" which happens to be the most indigestible of marine viands.—However within these last two days I am better and

> very truly yours
> [BYRON]

[TO JOHN MURRAY]   *Venice. Feb. 22d. 1819*

Dear Sir—Within these last two months or rather three—I have sent by letter at different times—several additions to "Don Juan" to be inserted in the places specified.—Have any or aught or none of these been received? I write in haste—it is the last day but one of the Carnival and I have not been in bed till seven or eight in the morning for these ten days past.———It is very probable that I shall decide on the publication of Don Juan—the second canto I have not yet begun to copy—but the first might proceed without.

yrs. [scrawl]
B

I *have written several times*—there was also a note in answer to Hazlitt[1]—to be placed with Mazeppa.—

Venice. February 22d. 1819

Dear Douglas—Hanson states the interest of the £66000 & £200 at £2525–5–0 & you at £2400—which is right? I shall be glad to know. —I can't say that I approve at all of the *funds* in which I have no faith whatever—& I wish to have the money either laid out on Mortgage— or at any rate in any thing rather than so precarious a tenure as I conceive the funds to be.—And pray why not in the 5 per cents instead of the *three* for the time being? I know nothing of the matters—but methinks you have "stricted me in my Singings" most damnably.— Tell Hobhouse that "Don Juan" must be published—the loss of the copyright would break my heart—all that he says may be very fine & very true—but my "regard for my fee" is the ruling passion and I must have it.—I have written to let him omit the two "bobs" high & dry and I think all the rest very decent.—Mr. Murray has not answered—although I have written very often with additions notes &c. —if that superb Gentleman don't mind his manners—I shall not trouble him further.—Yours in haste—it is the last but one of the Carnival days—and I have been up till eight in the morning for these ten days past.—Last month I was ill—had knocked up my stomach the people said by women—but I say by catching cold—however I was sick & could keep nothing upon it—but am now better.—

yours [scrawl]
B

[P.S.] Don't forget the rest of the Interest due on the year of the purchase-money-when paid.—

1 The note, not published in the first edition, but added by Murray in later editions of Byron's works, was appended to the second stanza of Canto I of *Don Juan*. It begins: "In the eighth and concluding lecture of Mr. Hazlitt's canons of criticism, delivered at the Surrey Institution, I am accused of having 'lauded Buonaparte to the skies in the hour of his success, and then peevishly wreaking my disappointment on the god of my idolatry.'" He then goes on to refute the charge of inconsistency, saying that he had been "impartial and discriminative". (See *Poetry*, VI, 12–13.)

My dear Douglas—You will pay Mr. Hanson the five thousand pounds—as they were promised—but at the same time you will express my surprize at his account being still undelivered.—As it was my intention & my word to advance this sum—it must be paid—but I desire particularly that the account be made out without further delay —you will also recollect that nearly three thousand pounds were paid to him late in 1813 or early in 14—for which the receipt is among my papers at Whitton—& which he will please to reckon in his account— it is also in my Banker's account then Messrs Hoares Fleet Street.——— After mature consideration I have determined to have Don Juan published (*anonymously*) and I Venture to request you will bargain with Mr. Murray for that—for Mazeppa—& for the Ode—& also for a *second* Canto of two hundred & six stanzas—which I have begun to copy out (it is finished)—& will send at leisure.—You will get what you think a fitting price.———Your opinion & that of the others is I dare say quite right—& that there will be a war of Criticism & Methodism in consequence—but "I have supped full of horrors" and it must be a "dismal treatise" that will make my "fell of hair stir & move" nowadays.—The poem has merit you all say—very well— leave the rest to the chances—and recollect that nothing would console me for the omission of the monies—I love money, so get what you can for the M.S. present & to come—the second Canto is more correct—but I think at least equal to the first in the whole—as fun & poetry.———The Cash & Credit transmitted is acceptable—but let Sir Jacob[1] pay his two hundred pounds———it looks well & goes far in *francs*—besides I like regularity—& money like "motley is the only wear".—I name no sum from Murray—but you may suppose that I shall greatly admire the largest possible.———Don't answer me with any more damned preachments from Hobhouse—about public opinion ———I never flattered that & I never will—& when the public leaves off reading what I write—the booksellers will tell us—& then I shall respect it more than ever I did yet—though I would not change a word to regain it even then—unless it had my own approbation.— Do you or anybody else suppose that I am to be lectured out of some thousand pounds more or less?—Sunburn me if I submit to it—& I wonder at you & Scrope—though not at Hobhouse—whose politics must naturally make him timbersome—for acquiescing in such

[1] Byron's nickname for Sir Ralph Noel. See Jan. 19, 1815, to Moore, note 5 (Vol. 4, p. 256).

nonsense—although no doubt H. is in the right as to the Consequences.
—Bargain with M[urra]y & let me know—there's a good fellow.——
Don't abate Claughton a centesimo—what does he mean?—not pay?—
"Rem quocunque modo—rem".[2]—Write by return of post with your
usual precision—accept thanks for all the good you have done—& all
you mean to do & believe me

yrs. ever
B

P.S.—If Murray comes down handsomely—let me know—&
although I am in cash that is no reason not to have more—particularly
as I have neither wish nor thought of going into your country while
I can avoid it.——

[TO DOUGLAS KINNAIRD] *Venice. March 9th. 1819*

Dear Douglas—I wrote to you by last post—desiring that Hanson
should have his money—but expressing my great *surprize* at *his bill
not* being sent in.—This letter—is ditto repeated.—A word more.—I
shall never rest while my property is in the English funds—do, for God
sake—let it be invested in *land* or *mortage* although at a present loss.—
I have no faith—but a dread & detestation of the funds—founded upon
the revealed religion of their utter worthlessness—& wretched
imposture.—Could not the Sum be vested on Sir Ralph N[oel]'s
estates (who wants money)—he giving mortgage—& paying fair &
lawful interest?—thus there might be an accommodation for both.—
But whether or no—do look out—& vest the £66,000—in some more
solid shape than this wretched phantom of your dead & buried
finances, which appears to me the Spider's web of all weak enough to
fly on "blest paper Credit."——Now—don't be facetious—but believe
me quite serious.—I should never sleep again—if I thought that your
damned Consols were to be what I were to trust to.—Land—mortgage
—anything but the nothing—to which for the present you have
annihilated the sum paid—by investing it in the debt of an insolvent
people & a swindling Government.———I requested you in my last
to barter—with that Coxcomb Murray—for the present & ensuing
Canto of Don Juan—if the puppy don't like to purchase—some other

[2] Horace: "Rem, facies rem;/Si possis recte, si non, quocunque modo rem."
("Get money; honestly if you can, if not, by any means get money.")

will—& you will tell me accordingly.—I have had no answer from him to any letter—for these three months—if the tradesman don't understand civility—change him—he is but a sort of intellectual tailor—& in taking measure of men's minds, would trust to his journeymen;—but if he or they don't make my suit in time—we'll take another.——I write in bad humour—Doug. my dear, but not with *you*—(the best of friends & bankers), but with myself & the funds— & the booksellers.—& Hobhouse (with his damned prudery about Don Juan) and I am always

[scrawl]

P.S.—I have written to Murray with some additions to "Don Juan" several times since Novr. without any answer—if the man is not civil—take another.——

Dear Sir—I wrote by last post to Mr. K[innaird] on the subject of the money to be advanced on account—desiring it to be so—but I am equally surprized with him—that there should be any difficulty in presenting the *bill*—which surely might have been ready by this time. —However—I shall keep *my word*—& have written accordingly.—I have no fault to find with any of the proceedings but *one*;—you know my *horror* & *dread* of the *funds*—the most unstable of all properties—I do beg & pray—request & require—that the settled property be invested in some other way—on land or mortgage—even at a discount —rather than continue my property on such precarious security, which I look upon in fact to be none at all; this being the case—I earnestly hope that you will lose no time in representing to the trustees my opinion upon the subject & taking measures accordingly. —Could not the sum be settled on some of Sir Ralph N.'s estates—he giving security—& lawful interest—if he wants money—and the interest can be secured—it would be an accommodation to both. I shall never rest while I think that my income depends on the English funds —& my property on that of a nation without any.—I pray you keep this in mind—& let me hear from you soon.

yrs. [scrawl]
BYRON

[Fragment]

... [Impostor?] to the name of Southey.

He is besides a notorious renegado of the same species as your own Kotzebue and deserving of the same kind of Criticism as that which was published by Sandt[2]—were he not too despicable for an honourable man's indignation—and too powerless to require a "vigour beyond the law" for his chastisement.—Kings and Conquerors might at times be thus swept from the earth over which they tyrannize—but it is a waste of life to forfeit it by shortening the days of a paltry Scribbler— and lending a lustre of compassion to his memory which ⟨elevates it from?⟩ [softens?] away the contempt due to his life.—

[TO JOHN MURRAY] *Venice, April 3, 1819*

Dear Sir,—You have had the second Canto of *Don Juan* which you will publish with the first, if it please you. But there shall be *no mutilations* in either, *nor omissions*, except such as I have already indicated in letters to which I have had no answer. I care nothing for what may be said, or thought, or written, on the Subject. If the poem is, or appears, dull, it will fail; if not, it will succeed. I have already written my opinion in former letters, and see no use of repetition. There are some words in the Address to the Scoundrel Southey which I requested Mr. H. to omit, and some stanzas about Castlereagh, which cannot decently appear as I am at too great a distance to answer the latter, if he wished it, personally; the former is as great a coward as he is a Renegade, and distance can make no odds in speaking of him—as he dare do nothing but scribble even to his next neighbour; but the other villain is at least a brave one, and I would not take advantage of the Alps and the Ocean to assail him when he could not revenge himself. As for the rest I will never flatter *Cant*, but, if you choose, I will publish a preface saying that you are all hostile to the publication. You may publish anonymously, or not, as you think best for any reasons of your own. Never mind me.

Yours,

B

You have never answered my letter asking if you had received the additions to Canto 1st. "Julia's letter," etc., etc.

[1] Similarity of the subject matter in this letter to that of April 3, 1819, to Murray suggests that this was written shortly before or after.

[2] Charles Sandt assassinated Kotzebue, whom he suspected of being a Russian spy, at Mannheim, March 23, 1819.

Books seem coming from all quarters—but none are come since the Ship *"Spartan"* (the least Laconic of the name—and be damned to her —for She was six months on her Voyage) Hanson's cargo I suppose *you* to be sending by various conveyances—but how?———

[TO JOHN MURRAY (*b*)]   *Venice April 6 1819*

Dear Sir—The Second Canto of Don Juan was sent on Saturday last by post in 4 packets—two of 4—& two of three sheets each—containing in all two hundred & seventeen stanzas octave measure.— But I will permit no curtailments except those mentioned about Castlereagh & the two *"Bobs"* in the introduction.—You sha'n't make *Canticles* of my Cantos. The poem will please if it is lively—if it is stupid it will fail—but I will have none of your damned cutting & slashing.—If you please you may publish *anonymously*[;] it will perhaps be better;—but I will battle my way against them all—like a Porcupine.—So you and Mr. Foscolo &c. want me to undertake what you call a "great work" an Epic poem I suppose or some such pyramid. —I'll try no such thing—I hate tasks—and then "seven or eight years!" God send us all well this day three months—let alone years— if one's years can't be better employed than in sweating poesy—a man had better be a ditcher.—And works too!—is Childe Harold nothing? you have so many *"divine"* poems, is it nothing to have written a *Human* one? without any of your worn out machinery.—Why—man— I could have spun the thought of the four cantos of that poem into twenty—had I wanted to book-make—& it's passion into as many modern tragedies—since you want *length* you shall have enough of *Juan* for I'll make 50 cantos.—And Foscolo too! why does *he* not do something more than the letters of Ortis—and a tragedy—and pamphlets—he has good fifteen years more at his command than I have—what has he done all that time?—proved his Genius doubtless —but not fixed it's fame—nor done his utmost.—Besides I mean to write my best work in *Italian*—& it will take me nine years more thoroughly to master the language—& then if my fancy exists & I exist too—I will try what I *can* do *really*.—As to the Estimation of the English which you talk of, let them calculate what it is worth—before they insult me with their insolent condescension.—I have not written

---

1 Written in the margin of a catalogue of contributors to a Medallion to Madam Fodor Mainvielle, enclosed with letter of April 6, 1819, to Murray.

for their pleasure;—if they are pleased—it is that they chose to be so, —I have never flattered their opinions—nor their pride—nor will I.— Neither will I make "Ladies books" "al dilettar le femine e la plebe"— I have written from the fullness of my mind, from passion—from impulse—from many motives—but not for their "sweet voices."[1]—I know the precise worth of popular applause—for few Scribblers have had more of it—and if I chose to swerve into their paths—I could retain it or resume it—or increase it—but I neither love ye—nor fear ye—and though I buy with ye—and sell with ye—and talk with ye—I will neither eat with ye—drink with ye—nor pray with ye.[2]—They made me without my search a species of popular Idol—they—without reason or judgement beyond the caprice of their Good pleasure—threw down the Image from it's pedestal—it was not broken with the fall— and they would it seems again replace it—but they shall not. You ask about my health—about the beginning of the year—I was in a state of great exhaustion—attended by such debility of Stomach—that nothing remained upon it—and I was obliged to reform my "way of life" which was conducting me from the "yellow leaf" to the Ground with all deliberate speed.—I am better in health and morals—and very much yrs. ever,

[scrawl]

P.S.—Tell Mrs. Leigh I never had "my Sashes" and I want some tooth-powder—the red—by all or any means.—

[TO JOHN CAM HOBHOUSE]   *Venice April 6. 1819*

My dear Hobhouse—I have not derived from the Scriptures of Rochfoucault that consolation which I expected "in the misfortunes of our best friends".[1]——I had much at heart your gaining the Election[2] —but from "the filthy puddle" into which your Patriotism had run you—I had like Croaker my bodings but like old "Currycomb" you make so "handsome a Corpse"[3]—that my wailing is changed into

---

[1] *Coriolanus*, Act II, scene 3.
[2] *Merchant of Venice*, Act I, scene 3.
[1] Rochefoucauld's *Maxim*: "There is something in the misfortunes of our best friends which does not displease us."
[2] Hobhouse lost the election to the House of Commons from Westminster to George Lamb.
[3] At the end of the first act of Goldsmith's *The Good-Natured Man*, Croaker says: "but come with me, and we shall see something that will give us a great deal of pleasure, I promise you; old Ruggins, the curry-comb maker, lying in state: I am told he makes a very handsome corpse. . . ."

admiration.—With the Burdettites divided—and the Whigs & Tories united—what else could be expected? If I had guessed at your *opponent*[4] —I would have made one among you Certes—and have f——d Caroline Lamb out of her "two hundred votes" although at the expence of a testicle.——I think I could have neutralized her zeal with a little management—but alas! who could have thought of that Cuckoldy family's ⟨sitting⟩ *standing* for a *member*—I suppose it is the first time that George Lamb ever *stood* for any thing—& William with his "Corni Cazzo da Seno!" (as we Venetians say—it means— Penis *in earnest*—a sad way of swearing) but that you who know them should have to con*cur* with such dogs—well—did I ever—no I never &c. &c. &c.——I have sent my second Canto—but I will have no gelding.——Murray has my order of the day.—Douglas Kinnaird with more than usual politeness writes me vivaciously that Hanson or I willed the *three per cents* instead of the five—as if I could prefer *three* to *five* per Cent!—death & fiends!—and then *he* lifts up his leg against the publication of Don Juan—et "tu *Brute*" (the *e mute* recollect) I shall certainly hitch our dear friend into some d——d story or other —"my dear Mr. Sneer—Mr. Sneer—my dear"——I must write again in a few days—it being now past four in the morning—it is Passion week—& rather dull.—I am dull too for I have fallen in love with a Romagnuola Countess from Ravenna[5]—who is nineteen years old & has a Count of fifty—whom She seems disposed to qualify the first year of marriage being just over.—I knew her a little last year at her starting, but they always wait a year—at least generally.—I met her first at the Albrizzi's, and this Spring at the Benzone's—and I have hopes Sir—hopes—but She wants me to come to Ravenna—& then to Bologna—now this would be all very well for certainties—but for mere hopes—if She should plant[6] me—and I should make a "fiasco" never could I show my face on the Piazza.——It is nothing that Money can do—for the Conte is awfully rich—& would be so even in England—but he is fifty and odd—has had two wives & children before this his third—(a pretty fair-haired Girl last year out of a Convent— now making her second tour of the Venetian Conversazioni—) and does not seem so jealous this year as he did last—when he stuck close to her side even at the Governor's.——She is pretty—but has no tact

[4] Lady Caroline Lamb electioneered for her brother-in-law George Lamb.

[5] This was Byron's first mention in a letter of the Countess Teresa Guiccioli whom he had met a few days before.

[6] This is Byron's literal translation of the Italian "piantare", to abandon, or leave in the lurch.

—answers aloud—when she should whisper—talks of age to old ladies who want to pass for young—and this blessed night horrified a correct company at the Benzona's—by calling out to me "Mio Byron" in an audible key during a dead Silence of pause in the other prattlers, who stared & whispered [to] their respective Serventi.—One of her preliminaries is that I must never leave Italy;—I have no desire to leave it—but I should not like to be frittered down into a regular Cicisbeo.—What shall I do! I am in love—and tired of promiscuous concubinage—& have now an opportunity of settling for life.—

[ever yours]

P.S.—We have had a fortnight ago the devil's own row with an Elephant who broke loose—ate up a fruitshop—killed his keeper—broke into a Church—and was at last killed by a Cannon Shot brought from the Arsenal.—I saw him the day he broke open his own house—he was standing in the *Riva* & his keepers trying to persuade him with *peck-loaves* to go on board a sort of Ark they had got.—I went close to him that afternoon in my Gondola—& he amused himself with flinging great beams that flew about over the water in all directions—he was then not *very* angry—but towards midnight he became furious —& displayed the most extraordinary strength—pulling down every thing before him.—All Musquetry proved in vain—& when he charged the Austrians threw down their musquets & ran.—At last they broke a hole & brought a field-piece the first shot missed the second entered behind—& came out *all but* the Skin at his Shoulder.—I saw him dead the next day—a stupendous fellow.—He went mad for want of a She it being the rutting month.—Fletcher is well.—I have got two monkeys, a fox—& two new mastiffs—Mutz is still in high old age.—The Monkeys are charming.—Last month I had a business about a Venetian Girl[7] who wanted to marry me—a circumstance prevented like Dr. Blifil's Espousals not only by my previous marriage—but by Mr. Allworthy's being acquainted with the existence of Mrs. Dr. Blifil.[8]——I was very honest and gave her no hopes—but there was a scene—I having been found at her window at Midnight and they sent me a Priest and a friend of the family's to talk with me next day both of whom I treated with Coffee.——

[7] The girl's name was Angelina and she was the daughter of a noble. Byron gave more details of the affair in a letter to Murray, May 18, 1819.
[8] Fielding, *Tom Jones*, Book I, Chap. 10.

Dear Douglas—Why do you lay the *"three* per Cents" on me?—it was Spooney and you—"you dour [Crandy?] eater" that did it—I wanted & expected 5 per cent & more, so I did. As for what you say about the five thousand pounds—I should like to keep them—but then I promised—however he maun send in his account.—As for the "Don Juan" you may talk till you are hoarse—I sent the second Canto & will have both published—all for the fee—what care I for the *"public attunement"* did I ever flatter the rascals?—never & I never will—let them like or not—I shall soon know by Murray's long or short face— and then I will plant the rogues—but till then I will have my monies.— Now pray Mr. Dougal—do something for Countess Giorgi's Son (now with Mr. Rose) whom I commended to your protection many moons ago—his Mother asks after him every day—and besides Rose is my friend—so do get a Clerkship for the lad who is a fine young man of a good family.—And mind you get me a mortgage—or the Cash transferred to the 5 per Cents—and recollect to make a good bargain with Murray—remember there are several thousand lines of poeshie besides "Mazeppa" & the Ode. Did he ever get the additions to Canto second, Julia's letter, &c. &c.?—I wish H. had not been so fiercely Burdetted—his losing his Election surprized us here a good deal. Sam Rogers's "Human Life" I have not Seen nor heard of except from you and Hobhouse—I am sorry for his failure (if it be a failure) and that's more than he would be for mine.—He is a "Cankered Carle," but a poet for all that.—I have been so long out of your Sphere as to have almost forgotten the taste of Scrope's jokes—but I am glad to get them even at second hand—the Dog never writes— which he should do—considering that in all probability we shall not meet again.—Tell Murray that I sent Canto second by last post— that I have written to H.—& to M. himself.—I want some tooth powder (*red*), some *Sashes* (red too) and any articles—Spooney brought nothing but a kaleidoscope and his papers.——

Health and Safety, yours ever

B

Carissimo il mio Bene—La tua carrissima arrivata oggi m'ha fatta provare il primo momento di piacere dopo la tua partenza.—Il sentimento espresso nella tua lettera è pur troppo corrisposto da parte mia,—ma sarà ben difficile per me rispondere nella tua bella lingua alle espressioni dolcissime che meritano una risposta piuttosto di fatti che di parole:—mi lusingo pero che il tuo Cuor saprà soggerire *cosa* e *quanto* il mio vorrebbe dirti.—Forse se ti amassi meno non mi costarebbe tanto a spiegare i pensieri miei, poiche adesso ho di superare la doppia difficolta di esprimere un' dolor' insopportabile in una lingua per me straniera.—Perdona ai miei spropositi, il più barbaro che sarà lo Stile mio più rassemiglierà al' mio Destin' lontano da te.—Tu che sei il mio unico ed ultimo Amor, tu—che sei il mio solo diletto, la delizia di mia vita—tu—che fosti la mia sola Speranza, tu—che fosti—almeno per un momento—tutto mio——tu sei partita —ed io resto isolato nella desolazione. Ecco in poche parole la 'storia nostra! è un caso commune il quale abbiamo di soffrire con' tanti altri poiche l'Amor non è mai felice, ma noi altri l'abbiamo di soffrire di più perche le tue circonstanze e le mie sono equalmente fuori del' ordinario—ma di queste non voglio pensare, amiamo

> "............. amiamo or quando
> Esser si puote riamato amando"

Quando l'Amor non è *Sovrano* del' Cuore, quando tutto non cede a lui, quando tutto non viene sacrificato per lui, allora è Amicizia— Stima—quel' che vuoi—ma non più *Amor*.—Tu mi giurasti la tua costanza,—ed io non ti giuro nulla, vedremmo chi di noi due sara più fedele—Ricordati quando arriva il momento che tu non sentirai più per me non avrai da ricevere rimproveri; è vero che soffrirò. ma in silenzio. —Conosco pur troppo il cuor dell'uomo, e forse anche un poco quello della donna, Conosco che il Sentimento non dipende da noi—ma che è la cosa più bella e fragile della nostra esistenza,—dunque—quando tu senti per un altro quel' che hai sentita per me—dimmi sinceramente— non cercaro annojarti—non ti vedro più—portero invidia all felicita di mio rivale,—ma non ti daro più disturbo.—Questo ti prometto pero— tu mi dici qualche volta che sono stato il tuo *primo* Amor vero, ed io t'assicuro che tu sarai l'ultima mia Passione.——Posso ben' sperare di non innamorarmi più—adesso tutto è divenuto indifferente per me,— prima di conoscerti—molte m'interessarono ma giammai una sola, ora amo a te, e per me non v'ha altra donna in terra.——Tu parli di pianti, e della tua infelicita; il mio dolor' è interno, io non verso lacrime, tu hai attaccata al' tuo braccio un' immagine—che non merita tanto; ma la tua è nel' mio cuor, è divenuta una parte di mia vita, della mia anima, e se vi fosse una vita dopo questa anche colà saresti mia,— senza di te dove sarebbe il Paradiso? piuttosto che il Cielo privo di te preferirei l'Inferno di quel' Grande sepolto in tua Città, basta che tu fosti meco come Francesca col'suo Amante.———Ben' mio dolcissimo— io tremo scrivendoti, siccome tremai nel vederti—ma non più—con quei soavi palpiti.—Ho mille cose a dirti, e non so come dirle, mille baci a mandarti—ed' Oimè! quanti Sospiri! Amami—non come *io* ti amo—perche questo sarebbe renderti troppo infelice, Amami—non come io merito perche questo sarebbe troppo poco,—ma come il tuo Cuor ti dirigerà.—Non dubitare di me—sono e sarò sempre il tuo più tenero Amante

BYRON

P.S.—Quanto piu beato di me sarà questo foglio! che tra pochi giorni sarà nelle tue mani—e forse anche potra essere portato vicino alle tue labbra,—con tale lusinga lo bacio prima che 'l parti.—Addio— Anima mia.—
Ap[ri]le 23. 4 ore—
In questo momento ricevo due altre lettere:—L'irregolarità della posta e stata la causa di dispiaceri a tutte due—ma ti prego—Amor mio—di non sospettarmi—quando non recevi delle nuove mie—credi che sono morto piuttosto che infedele ò ingrato. Risponderò presto alle tue carissime.—Adesso la posta parti.—Ti bacio 10000 volte.[1]
[On the cover in Byron's hand] Scritto 22 A[pri]le 1819.
Aprile 28. 1820. l'ho letto a Ravenna dopo un' anno di avventure singolarissime.

[TRANSLATION]   *Venice, April 22nd, 1819*

My dearest Love:—Your dearest letter came today and gave me my first moment of happiness since your departure.[1] My feelings correspond only too closely to the sentiments expressed in your letter, but it will be very difficult for me to reply in your beautiful language to your sweet expressions, which deserve an answer in deeds, rather than words. I flatter myself, however, that your heart will be able to suggest to you *what* and *how much* mine would like to

---

[1] For a discussion of the style and grammar of Byron's letters in Italian to the Countess Guiccioli, see Origo, p. 423. They are generally correct (except occasionally for spelling and accents) but often he uses not Italian idioms but English translated into Italian. He puts in extra (English) consonants as in "circonstanze" and omits accents. These errors have been left uncorrected.

[1] Byron's meeting with the Countess Guiccioli at the Countess Benzoni's must have been on the 2nd or 3rd of April. She left with her husband for Ravenna on the 12th or 13th.

say to you. Perhaps if I loved you less it would not cost me so much to express my thoughts, but now I have to overcome the double difficulty of expressing an unbearable suffering in a language foreign to me. Forgive my mistakes, the more barbarous my style, the more will it resemble my Fate away from you. You, who are my only and last love, who are my only joy, the delight of my life—you who are my only hope—you who were—at least for a moment—all mine—you have gone away—and I remain here alone and desolate. There, in a few words, is our story! It is a common experience, which we must bear like so many others, for love is never happy, but we two must suffer more, because your circumstances and mine are equally extraordinary. But I don't want to think of all this, let us love

> . . . let us love now
> When love to love can give an answering vow.

When *Love* is not *Sovereign* in a heart, when everything does not give way to him, when all is not sacrificed to him, then it is Friendship—esteem—what you will—but no longer *Love*.

You vowed to be true to me and I will make no vows to you; let us see which of us will be the more faithful. Remember that, when the time comes that you no longer feel anything for me, you will not have to put up with my reproaches; I shall suffer, it is true, but in silence. I know only too well what a man's heart is like, and also, a little, perhaps, a woman's; I know that Sentiment is not in our control, but is what is most beautiful and fragile in our existence. So, when you feel for another what you have felt for me, tell me so sincerely—I shall cease to annoy you—I shall not see you again—I shall envy the happiness of my rival, but shall trouble you no more. This however I promise you: You sometimes tell me that I have been your *first* real love—and I assure you that you shall be my last Passion. I may well hope not to fall in love again, now that everything has become indifferent to me. Before I knew you—I felt an interest in many women, but never in one only. Now I love *you*, there is no other woman in the world for me.

You talk of tears and of our unhappiness; my sorrow is within; I do not weep. You have fastened on your arm a likeness that does not deserve so highly; but yours is in my heart, it has become part of my life, of my soul; and were there another life after this one, there too you would be mine—without you where would Paradise be? Rather than Heaven without you, I should prefer the Inferno of that Great Man buried in your city, so long as you were with me, as Francesca was with her lover.

My sweetest treasure—I am trembling as I write to you, as I trembled when I saw you—but no longer—with such sweet heartbeats. I have a thousand things to say to you, and know not how to say them, a thousand kisses to send you—and, alas, how many Sighs! Love me—not as I love you—for that would make you too unhappy, love me not as I deserve, for that would be too little—but as your Heart commands. Do not doubt me—I am and always shall be your most tender lover.

BYRON

P.S.—How much happier than I is this letter: which in a few days will be in your hands—and perhaps may even be brought to your lips. With such a hope I am kissing it before it goes. Goodby—my soul.

April 23d., 4 o'clock

At this moment two other letters of yours have come! The irregularity of the post has been a great trouble to us both—but pray—my Love, do not lose faith in me. When you do not get news from me—believe that I am dead, rather than unfaithful or ungrateful. I will answer your dearest letters soon. Now the post is going—I kiss you ten thousand times.

> On the superscription is added, in Byron's hand:
> 'Written April 22nd, 1819.
>> April 28th, 1820. I have re-read it in Ravenna, after a year of most singular events.'

[TO DOUGLAS KINNAIRD] *Venice April 24th. 1819*

Dear Douglas—

> "When that the Captain comed for to know it,
> He very much applauded what she had done,"

and I only want the command "of the gallant Thunder Bomb" to make you my "first Lieutenant".—I meant "five thousand pounds" and never intend to have so much meaning again—in short—I refer you Gentlemen—to my original letter of instructions which by the blessing of God—seems to bear as many constructions as a Delphic Oracle;—I say I refer you to that when you are at a loss how to avoid paying my money away;—I hate paying—& you are quite right to encourage me.—As to Hanson & *Son*—I make no distinctions—it would be a sort of blasphemy—I should as soon think of untwisting the Trinity—what do they mean by separate bills?—With regard to the Rochdale suit—and the "large discretion" or Indiscretion of a thousand pounds—what could I do? I want to gain my suit—but I will be guided by you—if you think "punds Scottish" will do better—let me know—I am docile.—Pray what could make Farebrother[1] say that Seventeen thousand pounds had been bidden for the undisputed part of Rochdale manor?—it may be so—but I never heard of it before—not even from Spooney—if anybody bids—take it—& send it me by post—but don't pay away to those low people of tradesmen—they may survive Lady Noel—or me—and get it from the executors and heirs—but I don't approve of any living liquidations—a damned deal too much has been paid already—the fact is that the villains owe me money —& not I to them.—Damn *"the Vampire,"*[2]—what do I know of Vampires? it must be some bookselling imposture—contradict it in a solemn paragraph.—I sent off on April 3rd. the 2nd. Canto of "Don Juan" addressed to Murray—I hope it is arrived—by the Lord! it is a Capo d'Opera—so "full of pastime and prodigality"[3]—but you shan't decimate nor mutilate—no—"rather than that come Critics into the list—and champion me to the uttermost."[4]—Nor you nor that rugged rhinoceros Murray have ever told me in answer to fifty times the question—if he ever received the additions to Canto *first* entitled "Julia's letter" and also some four stanzas for the beginning.—I have fallen in love within the last month with a Romagnuola Countess from Ravenna—the Spouse of a year of Count Guiccioli—who is sixty —the Girl twenty—he has eighty thousand ducats of rent—and has had two wives before—but he is Sixty—he is the first of Ravenna Nobles—but he is sixty—She is fair as Sunrise—and warm as Noon— we had but ten days—to manage all our little matters in beginning middle and end. & we managed them;—and I have done my duty— with the proper consummation.—But She is young—and was not content with what she had done—unless it was to be turned to the advantage of the public—and so She made an eclat which rather astonished even the Venetians—and electrified the Conversazioni of the Benzone—the Albrizzi—& the Michelli—and made her ⟨Lord⟩

---

[1] Farebrother was the auctioneer who twice offered Newstead for sale, once in August, 1812, and again in the summer of 1815. Both times the bids were insufficient and it was withdrawn from sale.

[2] *The Vampyre*, written by Dr. Polidori, based on a tale Byron began at Diodati in 1816, was published anonymously in 1819. It was widely supposed to be Byron's work, and was ascribed to him in *Galignani's Messenger*.

[3] Unidentified.

[4] Unidentified.

husband look embarrassed.—They have been gone back to Ravenna—
some time—but they return in the Winter.—She is the queerest
woman I ever met with—for in general they cost one something in
one way or other—whereas by an odd combination of circumstances—I
have proved an expence to HER—which is not my custom,—but an
accident—however it don't matter.—She is a sort of an Italian
Caroline Lamb, except that She is much prettier, and not so savage.—
But She has the same red-hot head—the same noble dis*dain* of public
opinion—with the superstructure of all that Italy can add to such
natural dispositions.—To be sure they may go much further here with
impunity—as her husband's rank ensured their reception at all
societies including the Court—and as it was her first outbreak since
Marriage—the Sympathizing world was liberal.—She is also of the
Ravenna noblesse—educated in a convent—sacrifice to Wealth—
filial duty and all that.—I am damnably in love—but they are gone—
gone—for many months—and nothing but Hope—keeps me alive
seriously.

yrs. [scrawl]

[TO COUNTESS TERESA GUICCIOLI]   *Venezia, Addi 25 Aprile 1819*

Amor Mio—Spero che avrai ricevuta la mia in data li 22 ed
indirizzata alla persona in Ravenna già indicata da te prima di partire
da Venezia.—Tu mi fai rimproveri per non averti scritta in campagna
—ma come? Ben mio dolcissimo tu non m'hai data altro indirizzo che
quello di Ravenna,—Se tu sapesti quanto e quale è l'Amor che mi
anima non mi crederesti capace di dimenticarti per un solo istante;
impara a conoscermi meglio—saprai forse un giorno che quantunque
non ti merito—pur troppo ti amo. Vorresti sapere chi sia la persona
che vedo con maggior piacere dopo la tua partenza? Chi mi fa tremare
a sentire—non quello che tu sola puoi creare nella mia anima—ma
qualche cosa che lo rassomiglia?—Ebbene—ti dirò—è il *vecchio
facchino* mandato dalla Fanni coi tuoi biglietti quando tu fosti in
Venezia—e adesso il latore delle tue lettere sempre care, ma non care
come quelle che mi lusingarono colle speranza di vederti lo stesso
giorno alla solita ora.—Teresa mia dove sei? tutto costi mi fa ricordare
di te—tutto è lo stesso, ma tu non ci sei ed io ci sono.—Nei distacchi
chi parte soffre meno di chi reste.—La distrazione del viaggio, il
cangiar' del' Sito, la Campagna—il Moto, forse anche la lontananza
dissipa il pensier' ed allegerisce il cuore.—Ma Chi resta si trova
circondato dalle medesime cose, domani è come jeri—mancando

solamente quella che feceva dimenticare che domani potrebbe arrivare.
—Quando vado alla Conversazione, mi abbandono alla noja troppo
felice ad annojarmi piuttosto che soffrire. Vedo le medesime fisionomie
—sento le medesime voci—ma non oso guardare quel' Sofa dove non
ti vedrei piu—ma in vece qualche vecchiarda chi parirebbe essere la
Maldicenza in persona, Sento senza la minima emozione aprirsi quella
porta che io guardava con tanta ansieta quando mi ci trovai prima di
te sperando vederti entrare. Non ti parlerò *dei siti piu cari assai*; perche
la finche tu torni, non vado; io non ho altro piacere che pensare a te, ma
non so come—vedendo i luoghi dove siamo stati insieme—massima-
mente quelli piu consecrati al' amor nostro—mi farebbero morire di
dolor.—La fanni è adesso a Treviso—e Dio sa quando avro ancora delle
tue lettere—ma intanto ho ricevuto tre; tu sarai arrivata a Ravenna—
bramo di sentire di quel' tuo arrivo;—il mio destin dipende della tua
decisione.—La Fanni tornerà in qualche giorni—ma domani la mando
un biglietto per man' di un mio amico, di pregarla di non dimenticare
a mandarmi delle tue nuove, in caso che riceve delle lettere prima di
tornare a Venezia.———Ben Mio—la mia Vita è divenuta la più
monotona e trista—nè libri—nè la musica—nè *cavalli*—(cosa rara a
Venezia—ma tu sai che gli miei sono sul lido) nè cani—mi danno più
piacer;—la Società di donne non più mi alletta;—non parlo della
Sociata dei uomini;—perche gli ho sempre sprezzato.—Sono alcuni
anni ch'io cercava per Sistema di evitare le passioni forti avendo
sofferto troppo della tirannia d'Amor,—il *non ammirare*—ed' il
divertirmi senza metter troppa importanza nel' divertimento stesso—
l'Indifferenza per l'affari humani,—il disprezzo per molti,—ma l'odio
per nessuno, era le base della mia filosofia. [Non] voleva più amar—
nè sperava di esser' più riamato.—Tu hai messa in fuga tutte mie
risoluzioni,—adesso son tutto a te,—e diveniro quel' che tu vuoi—
forse felice nel' amor tuo—ma mai piu tranquillo.———To hai fatto
male nel' risvegliare il mio cuore—poiche—(almeno in mio paese)
l'amor mio è stato fatale a coloro che amai—ed a me stesso.—Ma
questi riflessi vengono troppo tardi, tu sei stata mia—e qualunque sia
l'esito—io sono e sarò eternamente tutto tuo.—Ti bacio mille volte
—ma—

> "Che giova a te, cor mio, l'esser amato?
> Che giova a me l'aver si cara amante?
> Perchè crudo destino—
> Ne disunisci tu, s'Amor ne stringe?"

Amami—come sempre il tuo più tenero e fedele

B

My Love,—I hope you have received my letter of the 22nd, addressed to the person in Ravenna of whom you told me, before leaving Venice.[1] You scold me for not having written to you in the country—but—how could I? My sweetest treasure, you gave me no other address but that of Ravenna. If you knew how great is the love I feel for you, you would not believe me capable of forgetting you for a single instant; you must become better acquainted with me—perhaps one day you will know that although I do not deserve you—I do indeed love you.

You want to know whom I most enjoy seeing, since you have gone away, who makes me tremble and feel—not what you alone can arouse in my soul—but something like it? Well, I will tell you—it is the *old porter* whom Fanny used to send with your notes when you were in Venice—and who now brings your letters—still dear, but not so dear as those which brought the hope of seeing you that same day at the usual time. My Teresa, where are you? Everything here reminds me of you—everything is the same, but you are not here and I still am. In separation the one who goes away suffers less than the one who stays behind. The distraction of the journey, the change of scene, the landscape, the movement, perhaps even the separation, distracts the mind and lightens the heart. But the one who stays behind is surrounded by the same things; tomorrow is like yesterday—while only She is lacking who made him forget that a tomorrow would ever come. When I go to the Conversazione, I give myself up to Tedium, too happy to suffer ennui rather than grief. I see the same faces—hear the same voices—but no longer dare to look towards the sofa where I shall not see *you* any more—but instead some old crone who might be Calumny personified. I hear, without the slightest emotion, the opening of that door which I used to watch with so much anxiety when I was there before you, hoping to see you come in. I will not speak of *much dearer* places still, for *there* I shall not go—*until* you return. I have no other pleasure than thinking of you, but I do not see how I could see again the places where we have been together—especially those most consecrated to our love—without dying of grief.

Fanny is now in Treviso—and God knows when I shall have any more letters from you—but meanwhile I have received three; you must by now have arrived in Ravenna—I long to hear of your arrival;

---

[1] Teresa had given Byron the name of an obliging priest, Don Gaspare Perelli, who would deliver messages and letters to her secretly.

my fate depends upon your decision. Fanny will be back in a few days—but tomorrow I shall send her a note by a friend's hand to ask her not to forget to send me your news, if she receives any letters before returning to Venice.

My Treasure—my life has become most monotonous and sad; neither books, nor music, nor *Horses* (rare things in Venice—but you know that mine are at the Lido)—nor dogs—give me any pleasure; the society of women does not attract me; I won't speak of the society of men, for that I have always despised. For some years I have been trying systematically to avoid strong passions, having suffered too much from the tyranny of Love. *Never to feel admiration*[2]—and to enjoy myself without giving too much importance to the enjoyment in itself—to feel indifference toward human affairs—contempt for many, but hatred for none,—this was the basis of my philosophy. I did not mean to love any more, nor did I hope to receive Love. You have put to flight all my resolutions—now I am all yours—I will become what you wish—perhaps happy in your love, but never at peace again. You should not have re-awakened my heart—for (at least in my own country) my love has been fatal to those I love—and to myself. But these reflections come too late. You have been mine—and whatever the outcome—I am, and eternally shall be, entirely yours. I kiss you a thousand and a thousand times—but—

> What does it profit you, my heart to be beloved?
> What good to me to have so dear a lover?
> Why should a cruel fate
> Separate those whom love has once united?[3]

Love me—as always your tender and faithful,

B

Venice. April 27th. 1819

Sir,—In various numbers of your Journal—I have seen mentioned a work entitled "the Vampire" with the addition of my name as that

---

[2] Byron had in mind Horace's dictum:
> "Nil admirari prope res est una, Numici,
> solaque quae possit facere et servare beatum."
> > *Epistulae*, vi, 1.
> ("Nought to admire is perhaps the one and only thing,
> Numicius, that can make a man happy and keep him so".)

[3] Guarini, *Il Pastor Fido*, Act III, scene 4.

118

of the Author.[1]—I am not the author and never heard of the work in question until now. In a more recent paper I perceive a formal annunciation of "the Vampire" with the addition of an account of my "residence in the Island of Mitylene" an Island which I have occasionally sailed by in the course of travelling some years ago through the Levant—and where I should have no objection to reside—but where I have never yet resided.—Neither of these performances are mine—and I presume that it is neither unjust nor ungracious to request that you will favour me by contradicting the advertisement to which I allude.—If the book is clever it would be base to deprive the real writer—whoever he may be—of his honours;—and if stupid—I desire the responsibility of nobody's dullness but my own.——You will excuse the trouble I give you,—the imputation is of no great importance,—and as long as it was confined to surmises and reports—I should have received it as I have received many others, in Silence.—But the formality of a public advertisement of a book I never wrote—and a residence where I never resided—is a little too much—particularly as I have no notion of the contents of the one—nor the incidents of the other.—I have besides a personal dislike to "Vampires" and the little acquaintance I have with them would by no means induce me to divulge their secrets.——You did me a much less injury by your paragraphs about "my devotion" and "abandonment of Society for the Sake of religion"—which appeared in your Messenger during last Lent;—all of which are not founded on fact——but You see I do not contradict them.——because they are merely personal—whereas the others in some degree concern the reader——You will oblige me by complying with my request of contradiction—I assure you that I know nothing of the work or works in question—and have the honour to be—(as the correspondents to Magazines say) "your constant reader" and very

obedt humble Sert
BYRON

[TO FANNY SILVESTRINI]   *3*⁰. M[aggi]o 1819

or ora/di casa

    La lettera di Teresa non mi dici niente della ricevuta delle *mie due lettere*—ed io sono nel' maggior turbamento.—Che sara di queste

1 Dr. Polidori acknowledged the authorship in a letter in the *Courier* (May 5, 1819), addressed to the editor of the the *New Monthly Magazine*, in which the tale first appeared.

119

lettere? Ti prego di scriverla ed assicurla che io non ò mancato alla mia promessa—nè ai miei doveri—e che l'amo assai—assai più della mia vita.—Forse le vostre saranno più fortunate—intanto ecco la mia *terza*—che potete mandare al' indirizzo solito.—Fatemi la somma grazia di venire da mè *alle quattro ore* per un' momento—non so cosa dire—o pensare—la lettera di T. è del' dato 26.—Perdonatemi questo e tanti altri disturbi.——

sempre vostro
B

[TRANSLATION¹]   *Venice, May 3rd, 1819*

Just now, at home.

Teresa's letter says nothing about having received my two letters, and I am in the greatest distress. What can have happened to these letters? Pray write to her and assure her that I have not failed to keep my promise, nor in my duty—and that I love her more, much more, than my life. Perhaps your letters will be more fortunate—meanwhile here is my *third*—which you can send to the same address. Do me the very great favour of coming to me *at four o'clock* for a minute. I don't know what to say—or think—T[eresa]'s letter is of the 26th.

Forgive me this and all the other trouble I have occasioned.

Ever yours
B

[TO COUNTESS TERESA GUICCIOLI]   *Venezia. 3 Mag[gi]o 1819*

Anima Mia—Questa volta l'amicizia ti preme più del' amor, e la Fanni è stata più fortunata di me nel' veder' i tuoi caratteri.—La tua carissima da Ravenna mi dava pero sommo dispiacere nel' dirmi che fosti ⟨avvortita⟩ ammalata, colla lusinga nonostante che non porterà ad altre conseguenze; e con' questa speranza scrivo di pregarti, delle informazioni più precise sul' stato della tua Salute.—Avrei attribuito la tua malattia al' andar' a cavallo—ma tu mi scrivi come se fosse qualche *altra causa*, e non me dici la vera cagione,—ti prego mettermi a giorno del' *mistero*, che non hai voluto dir' ai medici.—[four lines crossed out] La Fanni è già ritornata da Treviso. Io attendo il tuo

¹ Fanny Silvestrini was a confidante of the Countess Guiccioli, who carried messages back and forth between Byron and his mistress. After Teresa left Venice, she stayed on to receive messages and to forward Byron's letters.

riscontro per sapere quando entraprendere il viaggio—e come condurmi al' mio arrivo.—Ricordati che non avrò altro oggeto nel' fare questo viaggio che quello di vederti—e di amarti.—Io non cerco nè voglio divertimenti—presentazioni—Societa—cose per me piene di noja.—Mi andarebbe più a genio essere con te in un deserto che di esser senza di te nel' paradiso di Maometto, il quale valé qualche cosa più del' nostro.——Te—Te sola cercharò, se potrò vederti per alcuni momenti ogni giorno, saprò passare le altre ore colla tua immagine; se vi potrebbe esser' un' istante, in cui io non pensassi a te me parirebbe una infedeltà.—L'Amor nostro,—ed i miei pensieri—saranno i miei soli compagni,—i libri ed i cavalli la mia unica distrazione fuorchè il viagetto a *Rimini* per non mancare alla promessa fatta ad un mio amico in Inghilterra—tre anni sono—in caso mai che io vedessi quella città gli mandarai qualunque tradizione più di quella che si trova in Dante (se tale esistesse) sulla storia di Francesca.——Quella storia di amor funesto, che sempre m'interessava, adesso m'interessa doppiamente, dopo che Ravenna rinchiude il mio cuore—Sospiro di abbraciarti e lascio il resto al' destino, che non sarà crudele finche mi conserva l'amor tuo.—Ti bacio con tutta l'anima—mille e mille volte—e sono eternamente il tuo amante

B

P.S.—Questa è la mia *terza* lettera—al' *indirizzo indicato*—spero in Dio che nessuna avrà mancata.——

[TRANSLATION]   *Venice, May 3rd, 1819*

My Soul:—This time friendship has prevailed over love, and Fanny has been more fortunate than I in seeing your writing. Your very dear letter from Ravenna, however, caused me great grief by telling me that you have been ⟨miscarried⟩ *ill*,[1] although I still trust that this will not bring about other consequences; and it is in this hope that I am writing to ask you to send me more precise news about the state of your health. I attributed your illness to riding,—but you write as if there were *some other cause* and do not tell me the real reason—pray clear up the mystery, which you have not wanted to tell the doctors.

Fanny has already come back from Treviso. I am waiting for your answer to know when to undertake my journey and how to behave on my arrival. Remember that I have no other object in taking this

---

[1] Teresa apparently wrote the word "ammalata" (ill) over another word which Byron had written, probably "avvortita" (for "abortito"—miscarried).

journey but that of seeing you—and loving you. I neither seek nor want diversions—introductions—Society—all very tedious things. It would suit me better to be with you in a desert, rather than without you in Mahomet's paradise, which is considerably more agreeable than ours.

I shall seek you, you alone; if only I can see you for a few moments every day, I shall be able to spend the rest of the time with your image; if there were to be a minute in which I did not think of you, I would consider myself unfaithful. Our love and my thoughts will be my sole companions, books and horses my only distractions, except for a little trip to Rimini, in order not to break a promise made to a friend in England three years ago that, if ever I should see that city, I would send him any tradition about the story of Francesca[2] (if any such remain there) beside what is to be found in Dante. This story of a fatal love, which has always interested me, now interests me doubly, since Ravenna holds my heart.

I long to embrace you and leave the rest to fate, which cannot be cruel, so long as it leaves me your love. I kiss you with all my soul— a thousand and a thousand times—and am eternally your lover.

B

P.S.—This is my *third* letter—to the *address given*—I trust in God that none has gone wrong.

[TO JOHN MURRAY]   *Venice. May 6th. 1819*

Dear Sir—Yours of the 17th and 20th are arrived.—I recopy the "Julia's letter" as the former copy sent in Winter seems to have miscarried, by your account.—Let me hear of the arrival of the enclosed. There are also *three other* stanzas for insertion in Canto first —in the earlier part referring to the character of Donna Inez.—You seem in a fright—remember, you need not publish, if you don't like it.—I am sorry my letter seemed "Cynical." It was not meant so to *you* personally—as to my *general opinions*—they are the same.—I will not forget your request about Missiaglia and the books.—About the 20th I leave Venice—to take a Journey into Romagna—but shall probably return in a month.—Address to Venice as usual—and pray let me hear of the arrival of this packet.—Methinks I see you with a long face about "Don Juan" anticipating the outcry—and the Scalping

---

[2] Leigh Hunt's *Story of Rimini*, which Byron had seen in manuscript and which he encouraged Murray to publish in 1816.

reviews that will ensue;—*all that* is my affair—do you think I do not foresee all this as well as you?—Why—Man—it will be Nuts to all of them—they never had such an opportunity of being terrible;—but don't *you* be out of *sorts*.—I never vex you willfully—as you may imagine—but you sometimes touch a jarring string—as for instance one or two in your last letter.—You are right about publishing *anonymously*—but in that case we will *omit* the dedication to Southey—I won't attack the dog so fiercely without putting my name—that is reviewer's work—so you may publish the poem without the dedicatory stanzas.—With regard to Mazeppa and the Ode—you may join—or separate them—as you please from the two Cantos.—Don't suppose I want to put you out of humour—I have a great respect for your good & gentlemanly qualities—& return your personal friendship towards me—and although I think you a little spoilt by "villainous company" —Wits—persons of honour about town—authors—and fashionables— together with your "I am just going to call at Carlton House [;] are you walking that way?" I say notwithstanding your "pictures—taste— Shakespeare—and the musical glasses"[1]—you deserve and possess the esteem of those whose esteem is worth having—and of none more (however useless it may be) than

yrs. very truly

B

P.S.—Make my respects to Mr. G[iffor]d.—I am particularly aware that "Don Juan" must set us all by the ears—but that is my concern— & my beginning—there will be the "Edinburgh" and all too against it—so that like "Rob Roy"—I shall have my hands full.[2]——

[TO MAJOR SOMERVILLE[1]]   *Venice May 12th. 1819*

Sir—If you can make it convenient to call upon me at 4. o Clock tomorrow (Thursday) afternoon—I shall be happy to [re]ceive the

[1] *Vicar of Wakefield*, Chapter IX. The Vicar says that the two ladies from town "would talk of nothing but high life, and high-lived company; with other fashionable topics, such as pictures, taste, Shakespeare, and the musical glasses."
[2] *Rob Roy*, Chapter XXXV.
[1] David Bonnell Green, who first published this letter in the *Keats-Shelley Journal* (Vol. V, 1956, pp. 97–99) has given some interesting details about the life of Major William Clarke Somerville which have a bearing on Byron's eagerness in 1819 to go to South America, and particularly to Venezuela. Somerville was born in 1790 in Bloomsbury, Maryland. As a young man he took an interest in the struggle for independence of the South American states and joined the Venezuelan army where he rose to the rank of Major. It may well have been Somerville who first put the idea of emigration to Venezuela in Byron's mind.

honour of your visit.—I did not receive your letter till this moment which will excuse the delay of my answer. I have the honour to be

yr. obliged & very obedt. Sert

BYRON

[TO LORD KINNAIRD[1]]   *Venice May 15th. 1819*

My dear *Lord*—Three years & some months ago when you were reading "Bertram"[2] at your brother's—on my exclaiming in the words of Parson Adams to his Son—"Lege Dick—Lege" (on occasion of some interruption that had occurred) you replied to me—"my name is *not Richard*—my Lord"—thus converting my luckless quotation into an intentional liberty—and reproving me there*for*.—This was a hint to me to address you in future with all Aristocratical decorum—as becomes our birth, parentage, and education—and now I pay you back in your own coin—& say unto you—my dear Lord—"my name is *not Lady*" with which you commence your letter—which I am nevertheless as glad to receive—as I shall be to see the writer.——"Your Lordship will be right welcome back to Denmark"[3]—Your good nature to the chaste Arpalice[4] has been very serviceable to her—for without it She would have never rejoined her principal Performer.—I had a letter from her soon after her arrival at Milan—but have heard nothing since—she may probably write from Munich.—It was my intention to have left Venice tomorrow—on my journey to R[avenna] —but the Lady has miscarried—& her recovery seems more remote than was expected—being still in bed;—I have been ordered to come at all events:—but what the deuce should I do in the mean time without the possibility of seeing her—or at least of seeing her to any purpose in her present state—however—on the mere chance of seeing her only—I shall set out about the 20th and leave the rest to the protecting deities.——I hope that you will arrive in Venice before I set out—and would wait a day or two on purpose if you will let me know by return of post—where are you going?—To *Reggio*?—I should like

[1] Charles, 8th Lord Kinnaird, older brother of Byron's friend and banker Douglas Kinnaird, was a collector of pictures and lived much abroad. He was at this time residing in Milan. He and his brother had visited Byron in Venice in September, 1817.

[2] Maturin's play, which on Byron's recommendation, had been staged at Drury Lane.

[3] *Hamlet*, Act V, scene 2.

[4] Arpalisce Taruscelli, an opera singer, with whom Byron had a brief affair in Venice in 1818. See May 19, 1818, to Kinnaird.

greatly to see you on your route—and will lay to till you come within hail, if you will make the Signal,—but pray respond by the first ordinary.——There is the devil to do here at present—an Englishman —son of a Baronet—robbed a Baronet (Sir W. Drummond) at his "Hostel or Inn" of goods & monies and is like "to be troubled at *Size*" about it—the young man is a damned Rascal—& is to be treated accordingly—by being permitted to get off—at least I suppose so.[5]—Don't forget to answer & believe me dear Kinnaird

very truly & affectly. yrs.
BYRON

P.S.—If they open our letters at the post they will be edified by the correspondence, it is all hitherto about whores & rogues.——

[TO JOHN MURRAY]   *Venice. May 15th. 1819*

Dear Sir—I have received & return by this post under cover—the first proof of "Don Juan."—Before the second can arrive it is probable that I may have left Venice—and the length of my absence is so uncertain—that you had better proceed to the publication without boring me with more proofs—I sent by last post an addition—and a new copy of "Julia's letter," perceiving or supposing the former one in Winter did not arrive.—Mr. Hobhouse is at it again about indelicacy —there is *no indelicacy*—if he wants *that*, let him read Swift—his great Idol—but his Imagination must be a dunghill with a Viper's nest in the middle—to engender such a supposition about this poem.—For my part I think you are all crazed.—What does he mean about "G—d damn"—there is "*damn*" to be sure—but no "G—d" whatever.— And as to what he calls "a p—ss bucket"—it is nothing but simple water—as I am a Sinner—pray tell him so—& request him not "to put me in a phrenzy," as Sir Anthony Absolute says—"though he was not the indulgent father that I am."[1]—I have got yr. extract, & the "Vampire". I need not say it is *not mine*—there is a rule to go by— you are my publisher (till we quarrel) and what is not published by you is not written by me.—The Story of Shelley's agitation is true[2]—

---

[5] See May 17, 1819, to Hobhouse.

[1] *The Rivals*, Act II, scene 1.

[2] Dr. Polidori in the Preface to *The Vampyre* told of an evening at the Villa Diodati when Shelley was so agitated while ghost stories were being told that he rushed out of the room and later confessed that his imagination had been so stirred that he conceived that one of the ladies (Mary Godwin) had eyes in her breasts.

I can't tell what seized him—for he don't want courage. He was once with me in a Gale of Wind in a small boat right under the rocks between Meillerie & St. Gingo—we were five in the boat—a servant —two boatmen—& ourselves. The Sail was mismanaged & the boat was filling fast—he can't swim.—I stripped off my coat—made him strip off his—& take hold of an oar—telling him that I thought (being myself an expert swimmer) I could save him if he would not struggle when I took hold of him—unless we got smashed against the rocks which were high & sharp with an awkward Surf on them at that minute;—we were then about a hundred yards from shore—and the boat in peril.—He answered me with the greatest coolness—"that he had no notion of being saved—& that I would have enough to do to save myself, and begged not to trouble me".—Luckily the boat righted & baling [sic] we got round a point into St. Gingo—where the Inhabitants came down and embraced the boatmen on their escape— the Wind having been high enough to tear up some huge trees from the Alps above us as we saw next day.—And yet the same Shelley who was as cool as it was possible to be in such circumstances—(of which I am no judge myself as the chance of swimming naturally gives self-possession when near shore) certainly had the fit of phantasy which P[olidori] describes—though *not exactly* as he describes it. The story of the agreement to write the Ghost-books is true—but the ladies are *not Sisters*—one is Godwin's daughter by Mary Wolstonecraft—and the other the *present* Mrs. Godwin's daughter by a former husband. So much for Scoundrel Southey's Story of *"incest"*—neither was there *any promiscuous intercourse* whatever—both are an invention of the execrable villain Southey—whom I will term so as publicly as he deserves.— Mary Godwin (now Mrs. Shelley) wrote "Frankenstein"—which you have reviewed thinking it Shelley's—methinks it is a wonderful work for a Girl of nineteen—*not* nineteen indeed—at that time.—I enclose you the beginning of mine[3]—by which you will see how far it resembles Mr. Colburn's publication.—If you choose to publish it in the Edinburgh Magazine (*Wilsons* & *Blackwoods*) you may—*stating why*, & with such explanatory proem as you please.—I never went on with it—as you will perceive by the date.—I began it in an old account-book of Miss Milbanke's which I kept because it contains the word "*Household*" written by her twice on the inside blank page of the Covers— being the only two Scraps I have in the world in her writing, except her name to the deed of Separation.—Her letters I sent back—except

[3] This fragment of a story, begun at Diodati, which was the basis for Polidori's *Vampyre*, was published with *Mazeppa* and the *Ode on Venice*.

those of the quarrelling correspondence—and those being documents are placed in possession of a third person (Mr. Hobhouse) with copies of several of my own,—so that I have no kind of memorial whatever of her but these *two* words—and her actions. I have torn the leaves containing the part of the tale out of the book & enclose them with this sheet.—Next week—I set out for Romagna—at least in all probability.—You had better go on with the publications without waiting to hear farther—for I have other things in my head.— "Mazeppa" & "the Ode"—*separate*—what think you?—*Juan anonymous without the dedication*—for I won't be shabby—& attack Southey under Cloud of night.—What do you mean? first you seem hurt by my letter? & then in your next you talk of it's "power" & so forth— "this is a d—d blind Story Beck—but never mind—go on." You may be sure I said nothing *on purpose* to plague you—but if you will put me "in a phrenzy, I will never call you *Jack* again."[4]—I remember nothing of the epistle at present.—What do you mean by Polidori's *diary?*—why—I defy him to say any thing about me—but he is welcome—I have nothing to *reproach* me with on his score—and I am much mistaken if that is not his *own* opinion—but why publish the names of the two girls? & in such a manner?—what a blundering piece of exculpation!—*He* asked Pictet[5] &c. to dinner—and of course was left to entertain them.—I went into *Society solely* to present *him* (as I told him) that he might return into good company if he chose—it was the best thing for his youth & circumstances—for myself I had done with Society—& having presented him—withdrew to my own "way of life."—It is true that I returned without entering Lady Dalrymple Hamilton's[6]—because I saw it full.—It is true—that Mrs. Hervey[7] (She writes novels) fainted at my entrance into Coppet—& then came back again;—on her fainting—the Duchesse de Broglie[8] exclaimed: "This is *too much*—at Sixty five years of age!"—I never gave "the English" an opportunity of "avoiding" me—but I trust, that if ever I do, they will seize it.—

I am yrs. very truly
B

---

[4] *The Rivals*, Act II, scene 1.

[5] Marc-Auguste Pictet, a prominent literary and political figure of Geneva.

[6] Jane, eldest daughter of the first Viscount Duncan, married in 1800 Sir Hew Dalrymple Hamilton.

[7] There seems some doubt as to the identity of this Mrs. Hervey. Prothero identifies three who wrote novels. See *LJ*, IV, 300n.

[8] Madame de Staël's daughter.

Signora Contessina Pregiatissima—Appena ricevuta la obbligantissima di lei lettera. Sig[nor]a Contessina, mi fa' un dovere di ⟨rispondere⟩ riscontrarvela collo stesso mezza, e di ringraziarla per i generosi sentimenti ch'Ella nutre a mio riguardo, nonchè pure ringrazio il Sig[no]r Cavaliere di Lei Marito, assicurando entrambi, che mi crederei onorato se potessi offerirle i libri ch'Ella—Sig[no]ra Contessina, con tantà buona grazia mi chiede.—Debbo assicurla non tener io presso di me cosa veruna, di mia penna, nè a Venezia pure si trovano le mie opere, perchè in tal caso mi farei un pregio di servirla. accio avess' Ella ed il Sig[no]r Cav[alier]e una prova della mia obbedienza.——Non è fuor di proposito che dovendo io recarmi fra pochi giorni a Bologna non passi anche a vedere la bella Romagna ed in ispecie le celebri antichita di Ravenna, ed allora avrei il doppio piacere di baciarle rispettosamente la mano, e riverire il Sig[no]r Cavaliere— a cui la prego far aggrandire gl'ingenui sentimenti della mia Stima ed amicizia. Intanto ho l'onore di essere di Lei Sig[no]ra Contessina

obb[eddissi]mo ed umil[issi]mo Ser[vitor]e

BYRON

Most Esteemed Signora Contessina,[1]

Having just received your very obliging letter, Signora Contessina, I have a duty to reciprocate, and to thank you for the generous sentiments that You entertain towards me, and I also thank the Signor Cavaliere your Husband, assuring you both that I would consider myself honored if I might furnish you with the books that You—Signora Contessina, request with such good grace.—I must assure you that I do not have with me anything at all from my own pen, nor are my works available in Venice, because if they were I would be privileged to serve you, so that You and the Signor Cavaliere might have an instance of my loyalty.—It is not unlikely that since I must go to Bologna in a few days I may come also to see fair Romagna, and especially the celebrated antiquities of Ravenna, and then I would have the double pleasure of respectfully kissing your hand and of paying my respects to the Signor Cavaliere—to whom I

---

[1] This formal letter was intended for the eyes of Count Guiccioli and was meant to justify Byron's visit to Ravenna to see Teresa.

beg you to magnify the simple sentiments of my Esteem and friendship. Meanwhile I have the honor of being, Signora Contessina, your

very obedient and very humble servant

BYRON[2]

My dearest Love—I have been negligent in not writing, but what can I say[.] Three years absence—& the total change of scene and habit make such a difference—that we have now nothing in common but our affections & our relationship.—

But I have never ceased nor can cease to feel for a moment that perfect & boundless attachment which bound & binds me to you— which renders me utterly incapable of *real* love for any other human being—what could they be to me after *you?* My own XXXX [Short word crossed out] we may have been very wrong—but I repent of nothing except that cursed marriage—& your refusing to continue to love me as you had loved me—I can neither forget nor *quite forgive* you for that precious piece of reformation.—but I can never be other than I have been—and whenever I love anything it is because it reminds me in some way or other of yourself—for instance I not long ago attached myself to a Venetian for no earthly reason (although a pretty woman) but because she was called XXXX [short word crossed out] and she often remarked (without knowing the reason) how fond I was of the name.—It is heart-breaking to think of our long Separation—and I am sure more than punishment enough for all our sins—Dante is more humane in his "Hell" for he places his unfortunate lovers (Francesca of Rimini & Paolo whose case fell a good deal short of *ours*—though sufficiently naughty) in company— and though they suffer—it is at least together.—If ever I return to England—it will be to see you—and recollect that in all time—& place—and feelings—I have never ceased to be the same to you in heart—Circumstances may have ruffled my manner—& hardened my spirit—you may have seen me harsh & exasperated with all things around me; grieved & tortured with *your new resolution,*—& the soon after persecution of that infamous fiend who drove me from my Country & conspired against my life—by endeavouring to deprive me of all that could render it precious—but remember that even then *you* were the sole object that cost me a tear? and *what tears!* do you

---

[2] Translation by Professor Nancy Dersofi.

remember *our* parting? I have not spirits now to write to you upon other subjects—I am well in health—and have no cause of grief but the reflection that we are not together—When you write to me speak to me of yourself—& say that you love me—never mind common-place people & topics—which can be in no degree interesting—to me who see nothing in England but the country which holds *you*—or around it but the sea which divides us.—They say absence destroys weak passions—& confirms strong ones—Alas! *mine* for you is the union of all passions & of all affections—Has strengthened itself but will destroy me—I do not speak of *physical* destruction—for I have endured & can endure much—but of the annihilation of all thoughts feelings or hopes—which have not more or less a reference to you & to *our recollections—*

> Ever dearest
> [Signature erased]

[TO JOHN CAM HOBHOUSE]   *Venice—May 17th. 1819*

Dear Hobhouse—I return by this post the second proofs—the first went by the former post—if the Subsequent ones don't reach you by return of post—you need not wait for them but publish without—as I leave Venice next week—and have ordered my letters *not* to be sent after me—my stay being uncertain—as my plans are.—What you say may be all very right—but the die is cast—and I must (not figuratively —but *literally*) "pass the *Rubicon*"—you know I believe that it is in my way,—The Adventure is so far past preventing—that we had consummated our unlawful union with all the proper rites four days and daily—previously to *her* leaving Venice.—She was with child too —previous to this ingrafting——and to our connection but [three or four words crossed out] miscarried at Pomposa on the road to R[avenn]a in [sic] her return, and is now on her recovery.—For any thing I know the affair may terminate in some such way as you hint at —for they are liberal with the knife in It[ali]a and the Cavalier Conte G[uiccioli] her respected Lord—is shrewdly suspected of two assassinations already—one of a certain Mazzoni—who had been the cause of Count G[uiccioli]'s being put in the Castle of Saint Angelo—for some dispute or other—the which Mazzoni soon after G[uiccioli]'s release was stabbed going to the theatre and killed upon the Spot—nobody knows by *whom*—and the other of a Commissary who had interfered with him—these are but "dicerie" & may be true or no—it is a place where proof is not particularly in request.—But be that as it may—

every thing is to be risked for a woman one likes—and those are not the things I mind—but your miserable cutting—maiming—and robbing—where you are incommoded & ill used for the sake of paltry pence and baggage—on the highway—and forced to expose yourself & your life without any one of the motives which reconcile one to the chances of a conflict.—And then a man may not only lose his life but his tooth-brushes and dressing Case—and shirts—and other articles difficult to be replaced.———I have looked over the proofs—and *not* acquiesced in the Suggestions—by the way there is one line we will alter towards the close of Canto *1st.* instead of
"I thought of dying it the other day"
(i.e. *hair*) put—
"I thought about a Wig the other day"
What are you so anxious about Donna Inez for? She is not meant for Clytemnestra—and if She were—would you protect the fiend—of whom I may say like "Jacopo Rusticucci" in Dante—

"è certo
La *fiera Moglie più ch'altro mi Nuoce*".—

and was it not owing to that "Porca buzzerena" that they tried to expose me upon Earth to the same stigma—which the said Jacopo is saddled with in hell?[1]—What—is a ludicrous character of a tiresome woman in a burlesque poem to be suppressed or altered because a contemptible and hypocritical wretch may be supposed to be pointed at?—Do you suppose that I will ever forgive—or forget—or lose sight of her or hers—till I am nothing?——You will talk to me of prudence—and give me good reasons for "ones own sake" &c. &c.— you will have the satisfaction of giving good advice—and I that of not taking it.—Excuse my warmth—it is the cursed subject which puts me out of temper.———Neither you nor Murray say aught of *Canto second*—from whence I infer *your* disapprobation—and *his fear* to have *any opinion at all*—till he knows what the Public think—and the Douglas has not written to me about "the fee" why the devil don't he make the (not Social) Contract? Don't go to America—there are leagues enough between us already.———What is all this about Dr. Polidori?—who I perceive has got into "the Magazine"?[2]—you may at least thank me for finding you always something to be done;—I thought it was a French imposition—and wrote to Galignani's Editor—

1 Jacopo Rusticucci, who ascribed his errors to a shrewish wife (*Inferno*, Canto XVI, line 45) was consigned to the third ring of the seventh circle reserved for sodomites.
2 *The Vampyre* was first published in *The New Monthly Magazine*, April, 1819.

to beg of him to contradict "the Vampire" and "a residence in Mitylene"—Oons what is this residence?——I saw Sir William Drummond the other day;—the same evening he was robbed at an Inn by a Mr. Wraxall—(an English Gentleman) of Cash & trinkets—Wraxall has been taken and is "like to be troubled at Size" about it—he hath since confessed—but is still in Custody; he was in the army and wears a Waterloo ribbon—the theft was of various Coins—Napoleons &c. rings—jewels and what not—the young man is of amiable manners—excellent conduct and is son to a Baronet—he had previously cheated and lied a good deal in various cities—but this is his first overt attempt at the direct conversion of property.——There has been a splendid Opera lately at San Benedetto—by Rossini—who came in person to play the Harpsichord—the People followed him about—crowned him—cut off his hair "for memory"[;] he was Shouted and Sonnetted and feasted———and immortalized much more than either of the Emperors.—In the words of my Romagnola (speaking of Ravenna & the way of life there which is more licentious than most here) "Ciò ti mostri una Quadri morale del' Paese; e ti basta".—Think of a people frantic for a fiddler—or at least an inspirer of fiddles.——I doubt if they will do much in the Liberty line.—An Elephant went Mad here about two months ago—killed his keeper—knocked down a house—broke open a Church—dispersed all his assailants and was at last killed by a Shot in his *posteriore* from a field-piece brought from the *Arse*-nal on purpose.—I'll tell you a story which is beastly—but will make you laugh;—a young man at Ferrara detected his Sister amusing herself with a Bologna Sausage—he said nothing—but perceiving the same Sausage presented at table—he got up—made it a low bow—and exclaimed *"Vi riverisco mio Cognato."*[3]—Translate—and expound this to Scrope—and to "the Creature Dougal".—Tell the "Dougal Creature"[4] to write—and let me know about "the fee".——Write—whether I am to hear from you or no—write.—But don't wait for my further revision of proofs—I can't be gone for less than a moon—and it would be losing time.—Publish Juan anonymously—*without* the dedication—"Mazeppa" and "the Ode" as you like but don't send the proofs here.——I sent Murray—a second copy of "Julia's letter"—of which the first copy seems not to be arrived.—Perhaps this may be more fortunate.

yrs. ever
B

3 "I pay my respects, my brother-in-law."
4 See *Rob Roy*, Chapter 31.

Dear Sir—Yesterday I wrote to Mr. Hobhouse and returned the proof under cover to you. Tell Mr. Hobhouse that in the Ferrara story I told him, the phrase was *Vi riveresco Signor Cognato* and *not Cognato mio* as I stated yesterday by mistake. I write to you in haste and at past two in the morning—having besides had an accident. In going, about an hour and a half ago, to a rendezvous with a Venetian Girl (unmarried and the daughter of one of their nobles), I tumbled into the Grand Canal—and not choosing to miss my appointment by the delays of changing—I have been perched in a balcony with my wet clothes on ever since—till this minute that on my return I have slipped into my dressing gown. My foot slipped in getting into my Gondola to set out (owing to the cursed slippery steps of their palaces) and in I flounced like a Carp—and went dripping like a Triton to my Sea-nymph—and had to scramble up to a Grated window

> "Fenced with iron within and without
> Lest the Lover get in, or the Lady get out."

She is a very dear friend of mine—and I have undergone some trouble on her account—for last winter the truculent tyrant her flinty-hearted father—having been informed by an infernal German Countess Vorsperg (their next neighbour) of our meetings—they sent a priest to me—and a Commissary of police—and they locked the Girl up—and gave her prayers and bread and water—and our connection was cut off for some time—but the father hath lately been laid up—and the brother is at Milan—and the mother falls asleep—and the Servants are naturally on the wrong side of the question—and there is no Moon at Midnight just now—so that we have lately been able to recommence;—the fair one is eighteen—her name Angelina—the family name of course I don't tell you. She proposed to me to divorce my mathematical wife—and I told her that in England we can't divorce except for *female* infidelity—"and pray, (said she), how do you know what she may have been doing these last three years?"—I answered *that* I could not tell—but that the status of Cuckoldom was not quite so flourishing in Great Britain as with us here.—But—She said—"can't you get rid of her?"—"not more than is done already" (I answered) —"you would not have me *poison her*?"—would you believe it? She made me *no answer*—is not that a true and odd national trait?—it spoke more than a thousand words—and yet this is a little—pretty—sweet-tempered,—quiet, feminine being as ever you saw—but the Passions of a Sunny Soil are paramount to all other considerations;—

an unmarried Girl naturally wishes to be married—if she can marry & love at the same time it is well—but at any rate She must love;—I am not sure that my pretty paramour was herself fully aware of the inference to be drawn from her dead Silence—but even the unconsciousness of the latent idea was striking to an Observer of the Passions—and I never strike out a thought of another's or of my own—without trying to trace it to it's Source.—I wrote to Mr. H. pretty fully about our matters—in a few days I leave Venice for Romagna—excuse this scrawl—for I write in a state of shivering from having sat in my dripping drapery—and from some other little accessories which affect this husk of our immortal Kernel.——Tell Augusta that I wrote to her by yesterday's post—addressed to your care—let me know if you come out this Summer—that I may be in the way—and come to me —don't go to an Inn—I do not know that I can promise you any pleasure [;] "our way of life" is so different in these parts, but I insure to myself a great deal in seeing you, and in endeavouring (however vainly) to prove to you that I am

very truly yrs. ever
B

P.S.—I have read Parson Hodgson's "Friends"[1] in which he seems to display his knowledge of the Subject by a covert Attack or two on Some of his own. He probably wants another Living—at least I judge so by the prominence of his Piety—although he was always pious—even when he was kept by a Washerwoman on the New road. I have seen him cry over her picture which he generally wore under his left Armpit.—But he is a good man—and I have no doubt does his duties by his Parish.—As to the poetry of his new-fangled Stanza—I wish they would write the octave or the Spenser—we have no other legitimate measure of that kind.—He is right in defending *Pope*—against the bastard Pelicans of the poetical winter day—who add insult to their Parricide—by sucking the blood of the parent of English *real* poetry—poetry without a fault—and then spurning the bosom which fed them.—

[TO COUNTESS TERESA GUICCIOLI]   *Venezia. 20 Mag[gi]o 1819*

Amor Mio—Io ti aveva scritto una lettera per l'ordinario passato che non ho mandato perchè la tua arrivatami nello stesso giorno era in

---

[1] *The Friends: a Poem* by the Rev. Francis Hodgson, was published by Murray in 1818. It was dedicated to the Duke of Rutland, a son-in-law of Lord Carlisle, which may have accounted in part for the acerbity of Byron's comments.

fatto una risposta alle ricerche fatte da me sul' viaggio concertato.—
Spero che la Fanni ti avrà scritta come la pregai di fare.—La tua
malattia mi inquieta moltissimo, e mi pare che tu non ti sii ben decisa
se il mio arrivo in questo momento sarebbe convenevole; intanto
attendo ancora delle tue nuove per sapere s'io deggio partire o no.
—Mi ricordo che tu dicesti, che nel mese di Giugno faresti un viaggio a
Bologna, e pensando forse di tutte le tue circonstanze [sic] il nostro
incontro colà sarebbe più conveniente non soltanto per i riguardi—
ma anche per la nostra felicità.—Sicuramente saresti la meno esposta
alle dicerie che nel' tuo paese.—Ti scrivo in gran fretta e con molta
inquietudine—ma ti prego di credere che sono sempre lo stesso
verso di te; ti amo—non trovo parole per esprimere a qual' grado,—
ma il tempo proverà e tu stesso troverai, che tu sei divenuta l'unico
oggetto per cui respiro, e pel quale spirerei.——Le tue istruzioni,—
mio Bene, sono un poco intortigliate; nostro primo incontro *non*
dovrebbe aver luogo *"in teatro"*; e "la Padrona" del' Albergo—della
quale tu dici tante belle cose!!—Santi Anima Mia—se Ella è come
dici—bisognerebbe ch'io fecessi ⟨all' amore con⟩ la corte a lei—
si o *no*;—se la fo Ella avrà certi diritti di fare la *Spia*—e se *no*—la
farà per dispetto, poichè una donna di tal' Sorte non perdona mai al'
disprezzo.—Io non intendo nulla delle tue allusione alla Signora Z.
la quale non ho avuto l'onor di conoscere senochè di vista nel' Carnevale
—dunque come mai può quella donna entrare nelle nostre interesse?
io non la conosco—Ella non mi conosce,—come può o potrebbe essere
nel' poter' di colei di affliggerti? Eppure tu mi dici che tu sei afflitta per
cagione di lei senza spiegarmine il motivo.—Amor mio ti bacio con
tutta l'anima—pensa di me come eternamente il tuo più tenero e
fedele

B

[TRANSLATION]   *Venice, May 20th, 1819*

My Love:—I had written you a letter to go by the last post, which
I did not send because yours, which arrived on the same day, was in
fact an answer to my questions about the journey we had planned. I
hope that Fanny wrote to you, as I begged her to do. Your illness is
causing me great anxiety and it seems to me that you have not made
up your mind whether my arrival at such a moment would be quite
fitting. Meanwhile I am still awaiting your news, to know whether I
shall start or not. I remember you told me that in June you would be

going to Bologna,—and perhaps, in view of all circumstances, our meeting there would be more convenient, not only for appearances, but also for our own happiness. Certainly there you would be less exposed to gossip than in your own town. I am writing in a great hurry and in very great agitation—but pray believe that I am always the same towards you. I love you—I cannot find words to express to what degree,—but time will prove and you yourself will see, that you have become the only object for which I live and for which I would die.

Your instructions, my Treasure, are a little confused; our first meeting is *not* to take place "at the theatre", and "the landlady of the Inn"—of whom you say so many nice things!! Listen, my Soul, if she is as you say, it would be necessary for me to make love to her;—Yes or no? If I do, she will have a certain right to play the Spy on us—and if *not*, she will do it out of spite, for a woman of that sort never forgives being despised.

I do not at all understand your allusions to Signora Z[inanni] whom I have not the honour of knowing, except perhaps by sight during the Carnival. How then can that woman come into our affairs? I do not know her—she does not know me—how can or could it be in her power to distress you? Yet you say you are distressed about her, without explaining the reason.

My love, I kiss you with all my soul—think of me as eternally your most tender and faithful.

B

[TO DOUGLAS KINNAIRD]   *Venice. May 20th. 1819*

My dear Douglas—It would be difficult for me to comprehend precisely what *you deny*—as I have no recollection of that which *I asserted*, something it seems about the funds—oh—now I think on't—I wanted *five* per Cent instead of *three*—and have blundered—but never will I contradict my worldly "Pastor and Master"—my Potestas and Banker;—if *you deny*—and the late Miss Milbanke demurred about "the Investment" as I have a high opinion of your friendship—and the highest of her Arithmetic—you must be both right—Hanson is a rogue or a bad calculator—and your humble servant a damned fool, to all which I sincerely subscribe;—*three* per *Cent*—that cursed Spooney!——So Mr. Murray made no answer about "the fee" and *you—you*—the hot and fiery Douglas—took his silence. —Say this—he will either come to some agreement previous to publication—or you transfer the M.S. to the highest bidder—I fix no price—but leave that to you and my *friend* H. simply stating that *I think* the poems well written!—if you differ—I submit—but I will not permit *Mr. Murray* to deal with me in that cavalier manner—let him answer yes or no—and as he *does* betray some reluctance to the publication—try some other bookseller.—I have left *no terms* with Hobhouse—but I did expect that *some* would have been come to in answer to my repeated request.—You may tell H. and M. and all— that I will alter nothing more than I have altered—that I neither care whether they like the poetry—or no—I think it good—but have no sanguine ideas of it's success—and have no objections to make Murray's *treaty conditional*—*receiving nothing* in case of *nothing being received*—and so on in proportion.— — I know that I shall have your Quarterly and your Edinburgh too about my ears—and all your *reading world*—and your writing *other world*; be it so—if I am in Spirits next winter I'll answer them—and if I am not—I shall have the best of it without.— — I must repeat once for all—that I never will flatter the public;—if they are pleased it is their choice—and no obligation;—and if not it is my dullness—which is in itself a sufficient fardel for the Conscience;—the question is reduced to this—is the poem clever or not?—if not—burn it—if well-written, publish. I sent you a letter of confirmation some time ago about your refusal to advance more than the five thousand.—I was in great hopes you would not have advanced that—notwithstanding my order—as then the Sin would all have lighted on you "the Creature Dougal" "the Dougal Creature" and the advantage on me the Baillie Nicol Jarvie.[1] — —It would have pleased me that you could have made the Count a Clerk[2]—but you are to do as you like.— —I shall rejoice to see Mr. Murray—but "business must be minded" for all that.— —I know my dear Douglas you must find me a bore—but recollect that distance— and my little knowledge of business—are the causes—so pray forgive when I make you "a speech" as I have forgiven a good many of yours. —Believe me

always & truly & affecly

B

P.S.—Tell Mr. Murray to bring me some bottles of Macasser oil— or Russia oil in July—that is if he likes.—As for his advice—I wish he would reserve it for the Bookbinder.— —It must be *three years not two*

[1] In Scott's *Rob Roy*.
[2] See April 7, 1819, to Kinnaird.

the postponement of *Claims*—Rochdale must be sold.—As for Lady Noel so much Good would arise from her death that I have little doubt of her Immortality.—Malice will keep her alive, the bitch is but a bare Seventy and a mere Minor in longevity, I have no hopes of surviving her but if I should to be sure it would not be much amiss.—

[TO JOHN MURRAY]   *Venice, May 21st. 1819*

Dear Sir—I should be glad to know why Mr. Hobhouse has not yet seen the second Canto?—and why you took no notice—nor gave any answer to Mr. Kinnaird, when he read to you a passage from my letter to him—requesting *him* to adjust with you some business?—Let me know the *precise time* of your coming here that I may be in the way to receive you, and pray bring me some *"Macassar"* or *"Russia Oil"*, as I begin to get venerable.—You talk of "approximations to indelicacy" —this reminds me of George Lamb's quarrel at Cambridge with Scrope Davies—"Sir—said George—he *hinted at my illegitimacy.*" "Yes," said Scrope—"I called him a damned adulterous bastard"— the approximation and the hint are not unlike.—What think you of Canto second? *there's* a Gale of Wind for you! all nautical—and true to the vocabulary;—Ask the "Navy List".—

yrs. [scrawl]
B

[TO JOHN CAM HOBHOUSE]   *Venice. May 21st. 1819*

My dear Hobhouse—Kinnaird—"the Creature Dougal" says that Murray took no notice of *his hint* about *the fee*—I have but a few words to say on that topic—*some decision* must be come to directly;— the highest bidder will have the poems,—if Murray won't, another will.—I name no price—you and Dougal may settle that—and you can estimate as you like—but I won't stand Mr. M[urray]'s—nor any Mister's *"taking no notice"* as Douglas calls it——as Bill Tibbs says *"that's mechanical"*——you will have received a letter by last post.——I'll alter nothing.——I wish you would send me some of what Fletcher calls Massacre (Macassar) Oil.——Some *toothbrushes*— and powder—I want also two bull dogs—a terrier and a Newfoundland dog.—

138

Io sarei già partito Mercoledi se avessi avuto tue lettere; Essendone privo sono di pessimo umore e non altro desidero che di averne per potermi determinar alla partenza.—Io ti prego di scrivermi, ma in ogni modo partirò Sabbato—ti bacio mille volte di Cuore e sono eternamente il tuo più tenero e fedele Amante.

B

[Postscript to Fanny Silvestrini's letter] I should have started on Wednesday, if I had had your letters. Being without them, I am still in a very ill humour and desire nothing but to receive some so as to be able to decide to start. Pray write to me, but in any case I shall leave on Saturday.—I kiss you a thousand times with my whole Heart and am eternally your most tender and faithful Lover.

B

Dear Sir—I have received no proofs by the last post and shall probably have quitted Venice before the arrival of the next.—There wanted a few stanzas to the termination of Canto 1st. in the last proof;—the next will I presume contain them and the whole or a portion of Canto 2d.—but it will be idle to wait for further answers from me—as I have directed that my letters wait for my return (perhaps in a month and probably so)—therefore do not wait for further advice from me—you may as well talk to the Wind—and better for *it* will at least convey your accents a little further than they would otherwise have gone, whereas *I* shall neither echo nor acquiesce in your "exquisite reasons".—You may omit the *note* of reference to Hobhouse's travels in Canto second—and you will put as Motto the Whole;—

> "Difficile est proprie communia dicere"
>   Horace.

I have requested Mr. Kinnaird to settle with you—and whatever he may say is authorized by me.—I mention this as you took no notice when he spoke to you before.—I am also not a little surprized that Mr. Hobhouse has not yet seen Canto second.——A few days ago I sent you all I know of Polidori's Vampire;—he may do, say, or write what he pleases—but I wish he would not attribute to me his own compositions;—if he has anything of mine in his possession the M S. will put it beyond Controversy—but I scarcely think that any one who knows me would believe the thing in the Magazine to be mine—even if they saw it in my own hieroglyphics.——I write to you in the agonies of a *Sirocco* which annihilates me—and I have been fool enough to do four things since dinner which are as well omitted in very hot weather—1stly.—to take a woman—2ndly. to play at billiards from ten to twelve under the influence of lighted lamps that doubled the heat—3dly. to go afterwards into a red-hot Conversazione—of the Countess Benzone's—and 4thly to begin this letter, at three in the morning.——But being begun it must be finished.—

ever very truly & affectly. yrs.

B

P.S.—I petition for tooth-brushes—powder—Magnesia—Macassar oil—(or Russia) *the* Sashes—and Sir N[athanie]l Wraxall's memoirs of his own times[1]——I want besides a Bulldog—a terrier—and two Newfoundland dogs—and I want (is it Buck's?) a life of *Richard 3d.*[2] advertised by Longman *long long long* ago—I asked you for it at least three years since—See Longman's advertisements.——

[TO LORD KINNAIRD]   *Venice, May 26th. 1819*

My dear Kinnaird,—I saw in the papers the attack you mention, which is blackguard enough, but what you ought naturally to have expected as the consequence of having endeavoured to do a good action, by discovering a bad one.—You remember the Scotch proverb ''The Redder eye gets the worst lick o' the fray'' so the next time that anyone is to be shot—pray—don't interrupt them;—it appeared to have equally displeased the gentleman missed—the gentleman missing —and the un-gentleman prosecuting—who has lavished upon you such gratuitous and absurd calumny.—For my own part (so you were out of it) I feel no curiosity about the matter unless to know whether Julia [Fremont?] the Dalilah of that very bad Shot—(who missed a whole Coach & horses, we could have taught him better at Joe Manton's) was a good Piece. I have no patience for the rest of their

[1] *Historical Memoirs of My Own Times from 1772 to 1784,* by Sir Nathaniel Wraxall. It was first published in 1815; a third edition appeared in 1818.

[2] Sir George Buc's *Life and Reign of Richard III*, originally published in 1646 as the work of George Buck, Esq.

trash, and if you don't lose yours—the thing can do you no real harm, though it is hard enough to be sure—to be treated in such a manner for having wished to expose an Assassin,—and discover a conspiracy.— It is my intention to leave Venice on Saturday next—perhaps you had better address to me "ferma in posta—Bologna". I will do my best to meet you on my return—as I shall probably remain but a few days at Ravenna.—I leave you your choice of time—& place—&c, as a few posts in or out of the way will make no difference.—I mean to proceed to Ravenna and Rimini and to stay a few days at Bologna in my way back again to Venice.—You may be very sure that I shall have great pleasure in meeting you.—My departure would have taken place before but our abortion has not yet let us out of our chamber at Ravenna—except once—when we fell ill again;—I was still required to set out, but my instructions were a little confused—and though I am really very much in love—yet I see no great use in not adopting a little caution;—we had already terminated the *Essential* part of the business *four* continuous days previous to her setting out from V[enice] (the whole affair was of a Week), so that there is nothing very new before us.—I can't tell whether I was the involuntary Cause of the ⟨abortion⟩ miscarriage, but certes I was not the father of the foetus for She was three months advanced before our first Passade—and whether the Count was the parent or not I can't imagine—perhaps he might—they are but a year married—and she miscarried once before. ——Pray—let me have your news—I have heard of your "campaign-ing at the King of Bohemy" as Jerry Sneak says of Major Sturgeon;[1]— and of Reggio—and Turin also—I recollect seeing your charmer dance three years ago—but never saw her off the Stage. believe me, my dear K.

> every yrs. very truly & affectly.
> BYRON

[Venezia li 28 Maggio 1819]

[Interpolated in Fanny Silvestrini's letter] Amor mio.—Sento con massimo dispiacere il tuo male e tanto più quanto credeva coll' ordinario d'oggi, di sentire il tuo perfetto ristabilimento. Ad ogni modo malgrado quello che tu mi scrivi io partirò da di qui Sabbato 29 Cor. Andrò a Bologna e colà aspetterò la lettera che tu mi dici di scrivermi, e che la Fanny non mancherà di subito innoltrarmi.—

[1] Samuel Foote, *The Mayor of Garratt*, Act II.

Eguale al' tuo è il mio desiderio di vederti, di abbraciati—e di dirti mille volte ch'io ti amo.—Ti bacio con tutta l'anima e sono sempre tutto tuo

> [scrawl for signature]

[TRANSLATION]   [*Venice, May 28, 1819*]

[Interpolated in Fanny Silvestrini's letter] My Love—I hear with the greatest distress of your illness, and all the more because I had hoped to hear by today's post that you were completely recovered. However, in spite of what you write I shall leave here on Saturday the 29th. I shall go to Bologna and there wait for the letter which you say you are sending me, which Fanny will not fail to forward. My desire is equal to yours, to see you, to embrace you—and to say a thousand times that I love you. I kiss you with all my soul, and am always yours.

> [scrawl for signature]

[TO JOHN CAM HOBHOUSE]   *Venice. May 29th 1819*

Dear Hobhouse—Today (Saturday) I leave Venice counting to remain a month—during which I have ordered no letters to be sent after me.—You had best publish without further delay (anonymously) pray send no proofs of Mazeppa—or of the Ode.—Make Murray settle about the fee.——There is a report that the Stock-holders are to be called upon to sacrifice or give five & twenty per Cent [of] their principal—is this t[rue?] I have written to Douglas to enquire [if we] should, in course we shall have some "Sword & Gun-fighting" for one's money—and you will put me down in your corps.—It is the only thing would make me return into your swindling Sodom of a Country —to chew the bitter Apples growing by the dead Sea into which the Villains have sunk the National prosperity.——

> ever yrs.
>
> B

[TO DOUGLAS KINNAIRD]   *Venice. May 29th. 1819*

My Dear Douglas—Mr. Hoppner showed me a letter from a Mr. Dawkins[1] (Secretary of Something at Florence) in which he says

---

[1] Edward Dawkins was British Chargé d'Affaires at Florence when Byron appealed to him in April, 1823, for assistance in dealing with the Tuscan Government following the so-called "Pisan Affray."

142

that "the Stockholders are to be called upon to sacrifice five & twenty per Cent of their Capital".[2]—Is this possible?—I do not know what the *other* Stockholders think, but if such an event does take place—I shall pay you a visit—and if nobody else will—shoot Castlereagh—I will take that service upon myself.—I trust that we won't bear this sort of thing neither—and that I shall get "a Charge of Horse" in the ensuing struggle—or a Commission of some sort or other among the twenty five per Cent recusants—I'll make *one*—if there be "but ten righteous" in your swindling Sodom and bankrupt Gomorrah.—If this should be the case—it will be too late to send out "Power of Attorney" but it seems incredible—yet why incredible?—"five and twenty per Cent" "three thousand ducats—tis a Sum"—at any rate let us have the "pound of flesh nearest his HEART"—by the Lord—the Carrion rotten as it is were worth the money—and I'd pay it for the *first* cut— there should be no need of a second.——Pray give me some information on this subject and at any rate let me get out of the funds an' it be possible;—it would be much better to lose five and twenty lives than *one* per Cent.——I wrote last week to beg you to be peremptory about Murray's *fee*—pray be so—he shan't play his coquetry with me—no fee—no publication——Next June (I think it is the end of June) when the interest becomes due (if there be any interest) will you forward it in "Circular notes" rather than letters of Credit—letters are stationary—but notes are ambulatory—and in case I should feel loco-motive—I like circulars,—I take circular notes to be the nearest approach to "the Perpetual Motion" yet discovered.—Address as usual to Venice.—believe me

ever & truly yrs.
B

P.S.—When you have decided on "the fee" let it be made tangible— and "palpable to feeling as to sight".[3]—

[TO RICHARD BELGRAVE HOPPNER]   *Padua June 2d. 1819*

My dear Hoppner,—When you see that learned Clerk Edgecombe[1] —will you tell him in your most agreeable manner—that the

---

[2] This rumour contributed to Byron's uneasiness about the English "funds" in which his money from the sale of Newstead had been invested.

[3] Probably from *Macbeth*, Act II, scene 1: ". . . sensible to feeling as to sight." Byron used the phrase in another context and with another variation in his juvenile poem "To Mary" in *Fugitive Pieces*: "Grateful to feeling as to sight".

[1] Edgecombe was a clerk in the British Consulate in Venice whom Byron employed to look after his affairs when he left for Ravenna.

repairs of the Carriages which he stated to be so complete as to warrant him in paying one hundred francs above the agreement are very far from doing credit to him or to the Coach-maker here—the wheels of the Servants carriage had not *been touched*—the wheels of my own made rather worse than before—and so far from being *cleaned* they had not even wiped the *Glasses*;—will you hint to him that if I do not find my Palazzo and Casini—in town & country in rather better order at my ritorno than I found the carriages at setting out—I will remit him to be Supercargo to a Venetian fishing boat.—And now he may go home and beat Mrs. Edgecombe.——I am just setting off for Ferrara—Mengaldo gave me a letter to the Podesta Count Mosti—for which—I am grateful which is a troublesome sensation.——I am proceeding in no very good humour—for La G[uiccioli]'s instructions are rather calculated to produce an éclat—and perhaps a scene—than any decent iniquity;—I had a letter from her on Monday which merely repeated the directions she had given me before with the addition of something about her own house.—Now to go to cuckold a Papal Count, who like Candide—has already been "the death of two men, one of whom was a priest" in his own house is rather too much for my modesty—when there are several other places at least as good for the purpose.——She says they must go to Bologna in the middle of June—and why the devil then drag me to Ravenna?—However I shall determine nothing till I get to Bologna—and probably take some time to decide when I am there—so that—the Gods willing—you may probably see me again soon.—The Charmer forgets that a man may be whistled any where *before*—but that *after*—a Journey in an Italian June is a Conscription—and therefore She should have been less liberal in Venice—or less exigent at Ravenna.—If I was not the most constant of men—I should now be swimming from the Lido—instead of smoking in the dust of Padua.—Should there be letters from England—let them wait my return.—And do look at my house and (not lands but) Waters, and scold—and deal out the monies to Edgecombe with an air of reluctance—and a shake of the head—and put queer questions to him—and turn up your nose when he answers.——Make my respects to the Consuless—and to the Chevalier[2]—and to Scotin[3]—and to all the Counts & Countesses of my acquaintance—and believe me ever

yr. disconsolate & affecte.

B

[2] Angelo Mengaldo. See June 16, 1818, note 3.
[3] Alexander Scott. See biographical sketch, Appendix IV

My dear Hobhouse—I left Venice on the first of the moon with the intention of expatiating into Romagna as far as Rimini but whether I shall go on as far as that city and Ravenna—or *ferm* me in Bologna till the people I was going to see come there—such being their idea for about the middle of this month—is more than I can pretend to say —being quite undecided as usual.—I wrote to you by last three posts to beg you not to wait for further corrections of *"Don Juan"* as I have desired my letters to be kept back till my return—and my return is not fixed nor fixable—it may be soon or late—I don't know and I can't say.—Address to Venice.—My wrath with Murray is great for his shuffling about the fee—and the "Creature Dougal" ought to have "looked sharp at the Silver".——We have been in a taking at Venice (that is Fletcher and myself fundholders) at some accounts of the Stocks—and of an intention of *Peel's* to demand a sacrifice of twenty five per Cent of the monied interest.—I like Peel—he was my old Schoolfellow—he is a man of talent—and my early acquaintance— but I would *peel* him into a second Marsyas[1] and make Saint Bartholomew look like the Man in armour on Lord Mayor's day in comparison of his state after flaying and then line the Treasury Bench with his Skin— rather than give up *any* per Cent. Oons! five & twenty per Cent!— One would think he was Chancellor to the Exchequer of King Cambyses, for this is talking "in his Vein".[2]——In looking over the M.S. of Ariosto today—I found at the bottom of the page after the last stanza of Canto 44, Orlando Furioso ending with the line

"Mi serbo a farsi udie ne l'altro Canto"

the follow[ing] autograph in pencil of Alfieri's

"Vittorio Alfieri vide e venerò"

8 Giugno 1783.—

The Librarian told me that Alfieri wrote this marginal note by permission of the Superiors—and that *he* himself had seen Alfieri crying for hours over the M.S.—I asked the Librarian about the Tasso letters and he gave me an account—but as he did not recollect me I did not betray myself nor my acquaintance with *you*—"the English Milord" as he qualified you who had taken & since stampatoed the copies of the

[1] Marsyas, in the Greek myth, challenged Apollo to a contest of flute with lyre. Apollo was able to win only by adding his voice to the music of the strings. But he punished Marsyas for his presumption by flaying him alive.

[2] *Henry IV*, Part I, Act II, scene 4.

Epic-maker's washing list.——I have been interrupted since I began this letter by a visit from the Gonfaloniere of this city Count Mosti to whom I had an introductory letter.—He seems an agreeable young man—wellbred—travelled and well-disposed to travellers—has been in England—and seen Ireland—and the Tower of London—and the inside of Windsor Castle which *I* have never seen—but he has never seen *Rome* nor the inside (not out) of St. Peter's which *I have* seen—and never went into Tasso's Cell till the other day when the Emperor came here.——It is midnight—and I am a bed-going—tomorrow evening I am to go to Count Mosti's, I might have gone to a Conversazione this evening—but preferred finishing my letter to you which is a Conversation much more agreeable because one can't have an answer at least for some time—"You are a Wag Sam—but I don't understand your jokes."—[3]

yrs.

[scrawl for signature]

[TO RICHARD BELGRAVE HOPPNER]   *Bologna. June 6th. 1819*

Dear Hoppner—I am at length joined to Bologna—where I am settled like a Sausage—and shall be broiled like one if this weather continues.—Will you thank Mengaldo on my part for the Ferrara acquaintance—which was a very agreeable one—I staid two days at Ferrara—& was much pleased with the Count Mosti and the little the shortness of the time permitted me to see of his family.—I went to his Conversazione which is very far superior to anything of the kind at Venice—the women almost all young—several pretty—and the men courteous & cleanly; the Lady of the mansion who is young—lately married—and with child—appeared very pretty by Candle light (I did not see her by day) pleasing in her manners and very lady-like —or thorough-bred as we call it in England a kind of thing which reminds me of a racer—an Antelope—or an Italian Grey-hound—— She seems very fond of her husband who is amiable and accomplished— he has been in England two or three times—and is young.—The Sister—a Countess Somebody—I forget what—they are both Maffei by birth—and Veronese of course—is a lady of more display—she sings & plays divinely—but I thought She was a d—d long time about it——her likeness to Madame Flahaut—(Miss Mercer that was) is something quite extraordinary—I had but a bird's eye view of these

[3] Unidentified.

people and shall not probably see them again—but I am very much obliged to Mengaldo for letting me see them at all;—whenever I meet with any-thing agreeable in this world it surprizes me so much —and pleases me so much (when my passions are not interested one way or the other) that I go on wondering for a week to come.—I fell too in great admiration of the Cardinal Legate's red Stockings.—— I found too such a pretty epitaph in the Certosa Cimetery—or rather two—one was

> Martini Luigi
> *Implora pace.*

the other—

> Lucrezia Picini
> "Implora eterna quiete."

that was all—but it appears to me that these two and three words comprize and compress all that can be said on the subject—and then in Italian they are absolute Music.——They contain doubt—hope—and humility—nothing can be more pathetic than the "implora" and the modesty of the request—they have had enough of life—they want nothing but rest—they implore it—and "eterna quieta"—it is like a Greek inscription in some good old Heathen "City of the dead".— Pray— if I am shovelled into the Lido Church-yard—in your time— let me have the "implora pace" and nothing else for my epitaph—I never met with any antient or modern that pleased me a tenth part so much.——In about a day or two after you receive this letter I will thank you to desire Edgecombe to prepare for my return—I shall go back to Venice before I village on the Brenta.——I shall stay but a few days in Bologna, I am just going out to see sights, but shall not present my introductory letters for a day or two till I have run over again the place & pictures——nor perhaps at all if I find that I have books & sights enough to do without the inhabitants.——After that I shall return to Venice where you may expect me about the eleventh— or perhaps sooner—pray make my thanks acceptable to Mengaldo— my respects to the Consuless—and to Mr. Scott;—I hope my daughter is well—ever yrs

& truly
BYRON

P.S.—I went over the Ariosto M.S. &c. &c. again at Ferrara—with the Castle—and Cell—and House—&c. &c. &c. One of the Ferrarese asked me if I knew "Lord Byron" an acquaintance of his *now* at

Naples—I told him *No*—which was true both ways—for I know not the Impostor—and in the other—no one knows himself.—He stared when told that I was "the real Simon Pure."[1]—Another asked me if I had *not translated* "Tasso".—You see what *fame* is—how *accurate*—how *boundless*;—I don't know how others feel—but I am always the lighter and the better looked on when I have got rid of mine—it *sits* on me like armour on the Lord Mayor's Champion—and I got rid of all the husk of literature—and the attendant babble by answering that I had not translated Tasso.—but a namesake had—and by the blessing of Heaven I looked so little like a poet that every body believed me. ——I am just setting off for Ravenna.—June 8th 1819. I changed my mind this morning & decided to go on———

[TO JOHN MURRAY]   *Bologna. June 7th. 1819*

Dear Sir—Tell Mr. Hobhouse that I wrote to him a few days ago from Ferrara.—It will therefore be idle in him or you to wait for any further answers or returns of proofs from Venice—as I have directed that no English letters be sent after me. The publication can be proceeded in without, and I am already sick of your remarks—to which I think not the least attention ought to be paid. Tell Mr. Hobhouse that since I wrote to him—that I had availed myself of my Ferrara Letters & found the Society much younger and better there than at Venice. I was very much pleased with the little the shortness of my stay permitted me to see of the Gonfaloniere Count Mosti, and his family and friends in general.——I have been picture-gazing this morning at the famous Domenichino and Guido—both of which are superlative.—I afterwards went to the beautiful Cimetery of Bologna—beyond the Walls—and found besides the Superb Burial Ground—an original of a Custode who reminded me of the grave-digger in Hamlet.——He has a collection of Capuchins' Skulls labelled on the forehead—and taking down one of them—said "this was Brother Desiderio Berro who died at forty—one of my best friends—I begged his head of his Brethren after his decease and they gave it me—I put it in lime and then boiled it—here it is teeth and all in excellent preservation—He was the merriest—cleverest fellow I ever knew, whereever he went he brought joy, and when any one was melancholy the sight of him was enough to make him cheerful again—He walked so actively you might have taken him for a Dancer—he joked—he laughed—oh! he was such a

---

[1] Mrs. Susanna Centlivre, *A Bold Stroke for a Wife*.

Frate—as I never saw before nor ever shall again".—He told me that he had himself planted all the Cypresses in the Cimetery—that he had the greatest attachment to them and to his dead people—that since 1801—they had buried fifty three thousand persons.—In showing some older monuments, there was that of a Roman Girl of twenty—with a bust by Bernini[1] She was a Princess Barberini—dead two centuries ago —he said that on opening her Grave they had found her hair complete —and "as yellow as Gold." Some of the epitaphs at Ferrara pleased me more than the more splendid monuments of Bologna—for instance

> "Martini Luigi
>   Implora pace."
> "Lucrezia Picini
>   Implora eterna quiete."

Can any thing be more full of pathos! those few words say all that can be said or sought—the dead had had enough of life—all they wanted was rest—and this they *"implore."* there is all the helplessness—and humble hope and deathlike prayer that can arise from the Grave— *"implora pace."* I hope, whoever may survive me and shall see me put in the foreigners' burying-Ground at the Lido—within the fortress by the Adriatic—will see those two words and no more put over me[.] I trust they won't think of "pickling and bringing me home to Clod or Blunderbuss Hall[.]"[2] I am sure my Bones would not rest in an English grave—or my Clay mix with the earth of that Country:—I believe the thought would drive me mad on my death-bed could I suppose that any of my friends would be base enough to convey my carcase back to your soil—I would not even feed your worms—if I could help it.——So— as Shakespeare says of Mowbray the banished Duke of Norfolk—who died at Venice (see Richard 2d.) that he after fighting

> "Against black Pagans—Turks and Saracens
> And toil'd with works of war, retired himself
> To Italy; and there, at *Venice*, gave
> His body to that *pleasant* Country's Earth,
> And his pure Soul unto his Captain Christ
> Under whose colours he had fought so long."[3]

Before I left Venice—I had returned to you your late—and Mr. Hobhouse's sheets of Juan—don't wait for further answers from me—

---

[1] Giovanni Lorenzo Bernini (1598–1680), painter, sculptor, and architect.
[2] *The Rivals*, Act V, scene 3.
[3] *Richard II*, Act IV, scene 1.

but address yours to Venice as usual. I know nothing of my own movements—I may return there in a few days—or not for some time—all this depends on circumstances—I left Mr. Hoppner very well—as well as his son—and Mrs. Hoppner.—My daughter Allegra was well too and is growing pretty—her hair is growing darker and her eyes are blue.— Her temper and her ways Mr. Hoppner says are like mine—as well as her features.—She will make in that case a manageable young lady.

——I never hear anything of Ada—the little Electra of my Mycenae— the moral Clytemnestra is not very communicative of her tidings— but there will come a day of reckoning—even if I should not live to see it;—I have at least seen Romilly shivered—who was one of the assassins.——When that felon, or Lunatic—(take your choice—he must be one and might be both) was doing his worst to uproot my whole family tree, branch, and blossoms; when after taking my retainer he went over to them—when he was bringing desolation on my hearth—and destruction on my household Gods—did he think that in less than three years a natural event—a severe domestic—but an expected and common domestic Calamity would lay his Carcase in a Cross road or stamp his name in a Verdict of Lunacy?—Did he (who in his drivelling sexagenary dotage had not the courage to survive his Nurse—for what else was a wife to him at his time of life?—) reflect or consider what my feelings must have been—when wife—and child— and Sister—and name—and fame—and Country were to be my sacrifice on his legal altar—and this at a moment when my health was declining—my fortune embarrassed—and my Mind had been shaken by many kinds of disappointment—while I was yet young and might have reformed what might be wrong in my conduct—and retrieved what was perplexing in my affairs. But the wretch is in his grave,—I detested him living and I will not affect to pity him dead—I still loathe him as much as we can hate dust—but that is nothing. What a long letter I have scribbled[.]

yrs. [scrawl]
B

P.S.—Here as in Greece they strew flowers on the tombs—I saw a quantity of rose-leaves and entire roses scattered over the Graves at Ferrara—it has the most pleasing effect you can imagine.——

[TO ALEXANDER SCOTT]   *Ravenna. June 10th. 1819*

My dear Scott—The moment you get this letter—pray let *Augustine* be dispatched off to *Bologna* to wait for me at the Inn *Pelegrino*—with the remaining *Carriage*—the *Carriage horses*—and the two *Grey* saddle horses—let him bring my letters—& Papers;—he will apply to Mr. Hoppner or to Siri for money—but pray let him set off immediately and wait for me according to the above directions for Bologna—bringing with him the saddles—harness &c. he can hire a man to lead the saddle horses if necessary.—The post setting off no time for a word more.———Pray answer me by return of the same———

yrs ever
BYRON

P.S.—The G[uiccioli] has been very ill—still in bed but better— I have seen her—and *she* is as usual—I am in love with her—more in my next.

[TO COUNTESS TERESA GUICCIOLI (a)]   *Giugno 10. 1819*

Ben mio—Eccomi giunto a Ravenna.—Se puoi combinare a vedermi sarò felice—se no, in ogni modo—non ho mancato alla mia parola—e spero almeno sentire che tu stai meglio di Salute.—

Sempre
B

[TRANSLATION (a)]   *June 10th, 1819*

My Treasure—Here I am, in Ravenna. If you can arrange to see me I shall be happy—if not, I have at any rate not broken my word— and I hope at least to hear that your health is better.

Always
B

[TO COUNTESS TERESA GUICCIOLI (b)]   *Giugno 10. 1819*

Amor mio—Sono stato al teatro senza trovarti—e sentiva colla più viva dispiacenza che tu sei ancora in un stato di debolezza.—Il tuo marito e venuto trovarmi in palco e ha risposto cortesemente alle poche ricerche che osava fare in quel' momento.—Il Conte Z. è poi capitato e mi sollecitava tanto di andare in palco suo—che non avrei potuto evitare quella visita senza scortesia—ed in fatto sono stato

151

là per un' momento.—Anima mia dolcissima—credi che vivo per te sola—e non dubitare di me.——Mi tratterò qui finche so più precisamente il tuo desiderio;—e anche se tu non puoi combinare a vedermi—non mi allontanarò.—Ti imploro disporre di me come tutto ed eternamente tuo.—Sagrificarei tutta la mia speranza in questo mondo;—e tutto che si crede trovaro nel' altro—vederti felice.—Non posso pensare del' stato di tua Salute senza condoglio e lagrime.—Ahi mio Bene! quanto abbiamo passati—e quanto abbiamo a passare!—e tu cosi giovane—cosi bella—cosi buona—tu hai avuta di soffrire per causa mia—qual' pensier! Ti bacio mille mille mille volte con tutta l'anima—

B

P.S.—Ti mandai questa sera un' viglietto per mezzo di *P*. ma il latore non lo trovava prima di mezza Notte. Ti scrivo adesso dopo il teatro prima di andar' in letto—spero che tu riceverai ambedue

[TRANSLATION (*b*)]   *June 10th, 1819*

My Love:—I have been to the theatre without finding you—and was sorry to hear that you are still weak. Your husband came to see me in the box and replied courteously to the few inquiries I dared to make at that moment. Count Z[inanni] then turned up and was so insistent that I should go to his box that I could not avoid paying that call without being rude—and I did go there for a moment.

My sweetest Soul—believe that I live for you alone—and do not doubt me. I shall stay here until I know what your wishes really are: and even if you cannot arrange to see me I shall not go away. I beseech you to command me as entirely and eternally yours. I would sacrifice all my hopes for this world and all that we believe we may find in the other—to see you happy. I cannot think of the state of your health without sorrow and tears. Alas, my Treasure! How much we endured—and shall still have to endure! And you so young—so beautiful—so good—you have had to suffer through my fault—what a thought!

I kiss you a thousand thousand thousand times with all my soul.

P.S.—I sent you a note this evening by means of P[erelli]. But the bearer did not find him until midnight. I am writing now after the theatre before going to bed. I hope you will receive both.

Amor mio—Ti prego di istruirmi come debbo condurmi in queste circonstanze.——Io non sono a giorno di ciò che si convenerebbe fare.—Penso di fermarmi qui finche tu parti—ed allora trovare la maniera di riunirsi a Bologna—e poi a Ferrara.—Ma tutti questi progetti dipendono della tua volontà.—Io non vivo più senonchè per te. —La mia pace è perduta in ogni modo,—ma preferirei la morte a questa incertezza.—Ti prego perdonarmi e compatirmi. Ricordati che sono qui perchè tu mi comandasti—e che ogni momento in cui non—— ma è inutile che scrivo—io sento un' dolor' inesprimibile, ti vedo— ma in qual' maniera? e in qual' stato!!———Cercai a distrarmi con quella farsa del' antichità—per mi una noja la più insopportabile— ma in questo momento tutto il resto è equalmente disgustoso.—Il poco ehe mi interesserebbe, il sepolcro di Dante—e alcune cose nella biblioteca—ho già guardato con'un' indifferenza perdonabile al' stato di mio cuore.—Tu vedi che non vado in società—e che cerco solamente i mezzi di avvicinarti—ma come mai?—tu sei così circondata;—io son' forestiere in Italia—e ancora più forestiere in Ravenna—e naturalmente poco praticato nel' uso del paese—temo di com-prometterti—per mi stesso non ce più a temere,—il mio destino è già deciso.—E impossibile per mi vivere per lungo tempo in questa agitazione—ti scrivo colle lagrime—ed io non son' uomo a piangere facilmente—quando piango le mie lagrime vengono dal' cuor' e sono di sangue.——In questo punto—(mezzanotte) ricevo le tue lettere— e il fazzoletto—e son' un poco calmato.—Studierò a fare tutto ciò che tu comandi—Continuo questo viglietto senza cambiare una parola—per mostrarti cosa era lo stato di quel' inferno che portai in petto dopo il mio arrivo.—Se tu sapessi quanto mi costò a reggermi in tua presenza!——ma non dirò di più,—speriamo—che il tempo m'in-segnerà l'ipocrisia.—Tu parli di "Sacrifizii miei &c."—non dire di più—il mio cuor è già sacrificato—e dopo quella vittima non puo essere più sacrifizio— Basta un' tuo cenno a condurmi o man-darmi—non solamente a Bologna ma alla tomba.—Non dubitare di me—io non dubito di te—ma delle difficoltà di nostre circonstanze [sic]—vorrei sperare—ma—ma—sempre un' *Ma!*—intanto *tu* speri —e ciò basta.———Ti ringrazio—ti abbracio—ti bacio mille mille volte

B

P.S.—Perchè vuoi mandarmi il *mio* fazzoletto?—vedo dal' ciffro che è quello che ti detti la sera prima di tua partenza—io non ti darei *un'filo* di tuo (che tengo sempre presso a me) per ottenere un' impero.——

My Love:—Pray instruct me how I am to behave in these circumstances. I am not clear as to what it is best to do. I think of staying here until you go—and then finding a way of meeting in Bologna, and then in Ferrara. But all these plans depend upon your wishes. I have no life now, except in you. My peace is lost in any case—but I should prefer death to this uncertainty. Pray forgive and pity me. Remember that I am here because you ordered me to come—and that every moment in which I do not——but it is useless to write. I feel inexpressibly unhappy. I do see you—but how?—in what a state?

I have tried to distract myself with this farce of visiting antiquities—it seems quite intolerably tedious—but at the moment everything else is equally displeasing. The little that interests me—Dante's tomb and a few things in the library—I have already seen with an indifference made pardonable by the state of my heart. You see that I do not go into Society—and that I only seek ways of being near to you—but how? You are so surrounded: I am a foreigner in Italy—and still more a foreigner in Ravenna—and naturally little versed in the customs of the country—I am afraid of compromising you. For myself there is little more to fear—my fate is already decided. It is impossible for me to live long in this state of torment—I am writing to you in tears—and I am not a man who cries easily. When I cry my tears come from the heart, and are of blood.

At this point (midnight) I have received your letters and the handkerchief—and I am a little calmer. I shall study to do all that you command.

I am continuing this note without changing a word—to show you what sort of an inferno I have carried in my heart since my arrival.

If you knew what it costs me to control myself in your presence! But I will not say more—let us hope that time will teach me hypocrisy. You speak of "my sacrifices"—don't say any more—my heart is already sacrificed, and after that victim, I can offer no other. A sign from you will suffice to lead me or send me—not only to Bologna, but to the grave.

Do not mistrust me—I do not mistrust you—but the difficulties of our circumstances. I should like to hope—but—but—always a *But*—meanwhile *you* hope—and that is enough.

I thank you—I embrace you—I kiss you a thousand times.

P.S.—Why send me back the handkerchief?[1] I see from the mark

1 This handkerchief was kept by Teresa in a box with her other Byron relics. (Origo, p. 67n.)

that it is the one I gave you on the evening before your departure. I would not give you back a *thread* of yours (which I always keep by me) to obtain an empire.

Sbaglio forse—mio Bene—ma questa villeggiatura improvisa del' tuo Zio con *P*. mi da dei sospetti che siamo traditi—e che *P*. sia portato in campagna per troncare la corrispondenza.——La Passione mi fa temer' tutto e tutti.—Se ti perdo cosa sara di me?—Era questo viaggio premeditato prima del' mio venire—o no?—Se *no* sentirò dei grandi dubbi.——In ogni caso come faremo adesso per ricevere le nostre lettere?—come potrò consegnarti anche questa senza rischio di una scoperta trista per te—e per me fatale.—Nel' perdermi tu perdi poco—ma io difficilmente sopravviverci a un' distacco da te.—— Finora la frutta di mio viaggio è piuttosto amara—ma se tu sei contenta—non mi chiamerò pentito di ciò che soffro—poiche soffro per cause tua.—L'Amor ha i suoi martiri come la Religione—con' questa differenza—che le vittime del' Amor perdono il Paradiso in questo mondo senza recuperarlo nel' altro, mentre i devoti del' altro culto guadagnano dal' cambiamento.—Intanto—Amor mio—insegnami cosa debbo fare?—stare qui?—o tornare a B[ologna]?—Se nascono dei contrasti—c'è una sola rimedia efficace—cioè di andar' via insieme—e per questo bisogna del' gran Amor—e qualche coraggio—l'hai abbastanza?——Posso già anticipare la tua risposta—sarà lunga e scritta divinamente—ma terminerà col' negativo.——Ti bacio di Cuor 10000000 volte.

[scrawl for signature]

Perhaps I am mistaken—my Love—but this sudden country expedition of your uncle's with P[erelli] makes me afraid that we have been betrayed—and that P[erelli] has taken off to the country to interrupt our correspondence. Passion makes me fear everything and everyone. If I lose you, what will become of me? Was this journey planned before my arrival—or not? If *not*, I feel very suspicious. In any case, how shall we manage to get our letters? How shall I be able to get even this one to you, without risk of a discovery which would be sad for you—and for me, fatal. In losing me you lose very little,—but I am unlikely to survive a break with you. Until now the fruits of my journey have been rather bitter—but if you are pleased, I do not regret what I am suffering—for I am suffering for your sake.

Love has its martyrs like religion—with this difference—that the victims of love lose their Paradise in this world, without reaching it in the other, while the devout of the other faith gain by the change.

Meanwhile—my Love—tell me what I am to do? Remain here?—or return to Bologna? If trouble arises there is only one adequate remedy, that is, to go away together—and for this a great Love is necessary—and some courage. Have you enough?

I can already anticipate your answer. It will be long and divinely written—but it will end in a negative.[1]

I kiss you from my heart ten million times.

[TO COUNTESS TERESA GUICCIOLI (a)]   *Giugno 15. 1819*

Tu hai ragione—ma quando si *ragiona* assai non ce un' Amor capace dei grandi sacrifizi.—La risposta è quella che aspettai—non mi sorprende e ciò basta.—Ricordati che la proposizione non era fatta per *questo momento*—io soltanto domandai *in caso dell' alternativa cosa faresti?* tu hai risposta bene—e adesso so che partito debbo prendere.

——I pensieri sono giustissimi—solamente sono venuti un poco troppo tarde—poiche il più gran' torto a——era già fatto in Venezia.

—Il andare via sarebbe una somma imprudenza—ed una cosa che si sarebbe soltanto in caso d'una scoperta—e nell' alternativa di esser' obligata ad abbandonare *uno* dei due, ma perdonami se ti dico che—(adesso che parliamo della moralità) il più gran *torto* è l'inganno—e non l'abbandonamento—di un' uomo già nelle circonstanze della maggior parte dei mariti.—Per altro lo stimo moltissimo—e farei amicizia con lui ben volontiere—ad ogni costo.—Tornando all' *alternativa*—posso dirti che *io anche* perderei molto—ma preferendoti ad ogni interesse—amandoti—ma non parlerò più d'amor—adesso tu non puoi dubitare del' *mio*, vedende a qual' grado io son'stato capace a sacrificare tutto per te.——Intanto tu non hai risposta alla mia

[1] Teresa recorded in her manuscript "Vie de Lord Byron en Italie" (p. 134): "Letter of devotion after leaving me, a masterpiece of passion, devotion and generosity". Iris Origo comments: "Byron was right. Teresa's answer was long, poetic and full of numerous good reasons why she should not run away with him. Nor indeed did he yet grasp, perhaps, how unheard-of a thing he was asking. The essence of *serventismo*, as he was to realize later, was that the lady should *stay* with her husband." (Origo, p. 70.)

domanda— cioè se sarà più convenevole alle tue brame il fermarmi
qui—o il partire per B[ologna].———Ti bacio e sono sempre

B

[TRANSLATION (*a*)]   *June 15th, 1819*

You are right—but when one can *argue* a great deal, Love is not
capable of very great sacrifices. Your answer is what I expected, it
does not surprise me and that is enough. Remember that my proposal
was not made for the present time. I only asked, in case the alternative
arose, what would you do? You are right in your answer, and now I
know what my decision must be.

What you say is very true, only it has come a little too late—for the
greatest injury to———was already done in Venice. To go away would
be the height of imprudence—a thing only to be done if we were discovered—in case you were obliged to abandon *one* of us two. But
forgive me if I say (now that we are speaking of morals) that the
greatest injury is in the deception, not the desertion, of a man who is
already in the condition of a great number of husbands.

Besides, I esteem him very much—and would make friends with
him willingly—at any cost.

Returning to the *alternative*—I can tell you that I too should lose a
great deal, but I prefer you to anything else—for I love you. But I
will not speak any more of Love—now that you cannot doubt *mine*,
after I have shown you how completely I would sacrifice everything.

Meanwhile you have not answered my question—that is, whether I
shall meet your wishes by staying here—or by leaving for Bologna.

I kiss you and am always.

B

[TO COUNTESS TERESA GUICCIOLI (*b*)]   *Giugno 15. 1819*

Anima mia—Io parlo d'*Amor* e tu mi rispondi del' *"Tasso"*—
scrivo di *te* e tu mi domandi di *"Eleanora"* se vuoi farmi divenire
più pazzo di lui—ti assicuro che sei nel' caso di riuscire.—In fatto mia
Cara la tua ricerca mi pare superflua, tu conosci almeno in parte la
mia storia—e puoi anche senza questa immaginarti che per dipingere
le passioni forti bisogna averle provato.—Uno di questi giorni—(se
mai mai più occorrono ciò che dubito pur troppo) quando ci troviamo
soli—ti diro a voce se tua conghiettura sopra l'originale del' *ritratto* è

fondata o no sulla verità.——Se tu sai cosa è Amore—se tu ami—se tu senti—come puoi in questi momenti—vedendo lo stato in cui ci troviamo, pensare e parlare di cose ideali? non abbiamo pur' troppo la *realtà?*—Ti giuro che questi ultima giorni sono stati dei più infelici della mia vita—l'amor—il dubbio—l'incertezza—il timor di comprometterti quando ti vedo in presenza dei altri—l'impossibilta [sic] di vederti sola—l'idea di perderti per sempre—combinano a distruggere la poca speranza che finora mi animò.——La Società m'inquieta—la Solitudine mi spaventa.—La mia unica consolazione è il vederti rimessa in salute.——Attendo colla maggior' impazienza tua risposta alle mie due lettere cosa debbo fare?——Mi pare che il tuo Padre ti guarda con qualche *sospetto*—e che naturalmente non è troppo ben' disposto vedermi cosi vicino—e questo viaggio del' Zio—con *P.*—e l'improvvisa partenza del *amica* non sono dei presagi più felici per noi.——Intanto il mio venire a R[avenna] come previdi—in vece di accrescere la nostra corrispondenza—l'ha diminuito.—Ah! Venezia! —Venezia!—*là* siamo stati uniti almeno per alcune ore.

B

P.S.—Perdona se t'ho risposto troppo *Inglesamente* nelle prime parole di questo viglietto—ma io non son' venuto in Italia per parlare di me stesso e dei fatti miei—ma piuttosto a dimenticare la mia vita *oltramontana*——e sopra tutto—per *amarti—te*—la mia unica ed ultima delizia.—Ecco la ragione per quale m'impazientai nel' risponder' alla tua domanda se l'*E[leanora]*—fosse la &c. &c. &c.——

[TRANSLATION *(b)*]   *June 15th, 1819*

My Soul: I speak of *Love* and you answer me about *Tasso*. I write about *you*, and you ask me about "Eleanora". If you want to render me even more insane than he, I can assure you you are on the way to succeeding. In fact, my dear, your inquiries seem to me superfluous. You know, at least in part, my story, and even without it can imagine that, in order to depict strong passions, it is necessary to have experienced them. One of these days (if *ever, ever* they occur again, which I, alas, doubt) when we are alone,—I will tell you whether your conjectures as to the original of the portrait are founded on truth or not. If you know what love is—if you love me—if you feel—how can you at this moment—seeing the state in which we find ourselves—think or speak of imaginary things? Have we not only too much *reality*? I swear that these last few days have been among the most unhappy of my life. Love—doubt—uncertainty—the fear of compromising you when I see you in the presence of others—the impossibility of seeing you alone—the thought of losing you for ever—these combine to destroy the few hopes that inspired me until now.

Society disturbs me—solitude terrifies me. My only consolation is to see you recovered in health.

I am awaiting with the greatest impatience your answer to my two letters. What shall I do?

It seems to me that your father looks at you with some suspicion—and that naturally he does not much like to see me so near you—and that this journey of your uncle with Perelli and the sudden departure of your friend [amica] are not the happiest presages for us. Meanwhile my coming to Ravenna, as I foresaw, instead of increasing our understanding, has diminished it. Oh Venice—Venice—*there* we were united, at least for a few hours!

P.S.—Forgive me if my answer has been *too English* in the first lines of this note—but I have not come to Italy to speak of myself and my own doings—but rather to forget my life of *beyond the mountains*—and above all, to love you—*you*, my only and last delight. That is why I showed impatience in answering your question whether E[leanora] was the—etc. etc.—

[TO COUNTESS TERESA GUICCIOLI]   *Giugno 16. 1819*

Amor Mio—non ci parliamo più adesso sopra quel' argomento.—Basti che tu non puoi dubitare di me—vedendo di quanto sarei capace per causa tua.—In ogni modo e in tutte le circonstanze la tua felicita sarà il mio unico pensier.—Se arriva il tempo dei contrasti e dei affanni per causa del' amor nostro allora tu deciderai secondo il' sentimento tuo.—Io non cercarò a persuaderti, o ad influire la tua scelta.—I *miei "doveri"* Carissima Teresa—sono sempre li stessi—e mi pare che io dimostro tutta la premura possibile per adempirli.—Tutto dipende da te—la mia vita—il mio onor—il mio amor,—amami dunque—il mio sentimento per te merita di esser corrisposto:—io soffro tanto nel' amare—che cercai ad evitare le passioni forti—per i ultimi tre anni—ma invano come *ora* tu vedi—Il amarti è per me il *passagio* del' *Rubicone* e gia ha deciso il mio destino.———Non mancarò ad osservare tutto ciò che tu dici.—Ti bacio 100000 volte

B

My Love: Let us not talk about the subject any more now. It is enough that you cannot doubt me, knowing what I would be capable of doing for you. In any case and in all circumstances your happiness will be my only care. If a time comes of trouble and disturbance caused by our love, then you shall decide, according to your feelings. I shall not try to persuade you or to influence your choice. My *"duties"*, dearest Teresa, are always the same—and it seems to me I am showing every possible eagerness to fulfil them.

Everything depends on you—my life—my honour—my love. Love me, then—my feeling for you deserves to be returned: I suffer so much in loving, that I have tried to avoid strong passions in these last three years—but in vain, as you see now. To love you is my crossing of the Rubicon and has already decided my fate.

I shall not fail to carry out all that you say—I kiss you 100000 times.

B

[TO COUNTESS TERESA GUICCIOLI] *Giugno 17. 1819*

Si Amor mio—sono *"ben indifferente"*—ho fatto il viaggio da Venezia—sono stato cosi felice dopo il mio arrivo—i miei divertimenti sono frequentissimi—me ne trovo cosi allegro——si—tu hai ragione in questo come in tutto—non v'è dubbio della *mia indifferenza.*— Pensa un'poco—Ben mio—e poi sfidarò qualunque che sia a trovare nella mia condotta dopo che ti ho conosciuto—la minima cosa che merita un' tale rimprovero. Ti amai pur' troppo—ma in *Amor* il *troppo non basta.*—Cio mi sento anche io—poiche credo che tu non mi ami al' grado che sospiro;—e intanto sono sicurissimo che il mio cuore è più impegnato del' tuo—ma ciò dovrebbe essere—perche tu *meriti* un' amor il quale io non potrei nè sperare nè inspirare.—Tal' amor io ti porto—vuoi delle prove?——Tu mi dici—ch'io "e *non il cavalcare* vi hanno cagionato tanto male"—questo vuol' dire che la causa del' ⟨abortire⟩ [male]—è stata qualche colpa mia.—Questa è la prima volta che tu mi lo dici—ed essendo un' accusa piuttosto seria— e fatta seriamente—bramerei avere qualche spiegazione.—Se tu sapessi—ma—è inutile—ciò che scrivo—ciò che dico.——Amor mio— noi avremmo abbastanza del' infelicità senza perderci nei sospetti mal' fondati—e nei tormenti cagionati dal' amor proprio offeso forse senza ragione.——Un' schiavo non è più umile in presenza del' suo Padrone—che io sono nella tua,—ma non abusare del' potere perche

tu sei troppo potente.—Pensa soltanto se veramente merito i rimproveri di tuo ultima biglietto—e poi perdona—*te stessa*—se tu puoi.
——Credimi eternamente il tuo più immutabile ed amante

B

[TRANSLATION] *June 17th, 1819*

Yes—my Love—I am *very indifferent* to you. I have travelled here from Venice—I have been so happy after my arrival—my diversions have been so many—they cheer me so greatly—yes—you are right in this as in everything—there is no doubt as to my *indifference.* Think a little—my Treasure—and then I shall challenge anyone whatever to find in my conduct ever since I have know you the slightest thing that deserves such a reproach. I love you only too much, but in *Love, too much* is not enough. This I feel, too—for I believe that you do not love me to the degree that I long for;—and meanwhile I am very sure that my heart is more engaged than yours—but that should be so—for you deserve a love which I could neither hope for nor inspire. Such a love I feel for you—do you want proofs?

You tell me that I, and not *"riding"*, have done you so much harm— this means that the cause of the illness[1] was a fault of mine. This is the first time that you have said this to me—and being a rather serious accusation—and seriously made—I should like to have some explanation. If you only knew—but—it is useless—all I write, or say.

My Love—We have surely enough trouble without making ourselves unhappy by ill-founded suspicions and torments caused by wounded pride, perhaps unnecessarily. A slave is not more humble in the presence of his master—than I am in yours,—but do not abuse your power, for you have too much. Think only if I deserve the reproaches of your last note—and then forgive——*yourself* if you can.

Believe me eternally your most unchangeable and loving

B

[TO COUNTESS TERESA GUICCIOLI] *Giugno 20. 1819*

"E voi potreste"——cosa è che *non "potreste"*—Amor mio—se'l vuoi?——Non puo essere cosa più lusinghiera per me della speranza di fare "il viaggio insieme"——Il tuo bigliettino termina—o piuttosto

---

[1] Byron had written "abortire" (miscarriage) and Teresa crossed it out and wrote "male" (illness).

non termina,—quando mi dirai il resto?——Come ti dissi tante volte
—il mio destino è nelle mani tue; dove tu sei sarà la mia patria—e
ciò che tu dici è la mia legge.—Intanto sospiro l'ora di rivederti—e ti
bacio con tutta l'anima instancabilmente.—

B

[TRANSLATION]   *June 20th. 1819*

"*And you could*"—What is there that you could not, my Love, if
you wish it?

There can be nothing more delightful to me than the hope of
"travelling together".

Your little note ends—or rather does *not* end—when will you tell
me the rest?

As I have said to you many times, my fate is in your hands; where
you are is my country—and what you say, my law. Meanwhile I am
longing for the hour when I see you again—and I kiss you untiringly
with all my soul.

B

[TO ALEXANDER SCOTT]   *Ravenna. June 20th. 1819*

Martricus Scottin—I wrote to you nine days byegone—to solicit
you and Mr Hoppner to dispatch—Carriage—& Cattle—(two saddle
the Grey—& two Carriage horses) with Augustine, saddles, &
harness &c. &c. to *Bologna* directly—there to wait for me at the
Pelegrino—"my hostel or Inn."—I begged—& beg this—as also a
line by return of *Post to Ravenna.*—Hitherto all here has gone on very
well but I have no intention of returning to Venice for some time.—
I am in sad want of my horses.—There could surely be no difficulty—
Hoppner had money in his hands—and if expended—Siri & Willhalm
would furnish my Coachman on his Master's credit—for the journey.
——I allow him to take a man to lead the saddle horses.—It will be
very disagreeable if he is not set off by this time. I don't like to say
much by post—but all has gone on very well—here—as you may
suppose by my stay.—The Lady does whatever she pleases with me—
and luckily the same things please both.———She had really been very
ill—and is a good deal thinner—*She* is very popular here with the
inhabitants—who seem a good natured people—the reverse of the
Venetians.———But at present I shall enter no further in detail—though

there has been comedy enough for a long narrative.————He is the wealthiest of the district—and not so much liked—but they all—even the women—speak well of her.—————Do not I beseech thee forget to expedite my beasts & drivers.—Remember me to those who care—and believe me ever truly yours

Byron

P.S.—I wished Augustine to bring on my English letters to Bologna.

[TO RICHARD BELGRAVE HOPPNER]   *Ravenna. June 20th. 1819*

My dear Hoppner—I wrote to you a week ago (particularly begging a line in answer by return of post) to request you would send off Augustine with the two Grey saddle horses—and the Carriage & Carriage horses—saddles &c. to wait for me at the Pelegrino—(the Inn there) in *Bologna.*—To this letter & one of the same purport to Mr. Scott I have had no answer—which makes me uneasy as I shall probably not return to Venice for some time.—I wished my English letters also to be forwarded with Augustine to Bologna.—If there was any want of Money—Siri & Willhalm would equip him.——Pray write to me here (*Ravenna*) by next post—it will reach me in time,—and do not let Augustine delay a moment for the nonsense of that son of a b——h Edgecombe—who may probably be the cause of his dawdling. I wrote to you from Padua—and from Bologna—& since from Ravenna.——I find my situation very agreeable—but want my horses very much—there being good riding in the environs.—I can fix no time for my return to Venice—it may be soon or late—or not at all—it all depends on the *Dama,* whom I found very seriously in *bed* with a cough and spitting of blood &c.—all of which has subsided—and something else has recommenced.—Her miscarriage has made her a good deal thinner;—and I found all the people here firmly persuaded that she would never recover;—they were mistaken however.—My letters were useful as far as I employed them—and I like both the place and people—though I don't trouble the latter more than I can help.—*She* manages very well—though the *local*[*e*] is inconvenient—(no *bolts* and be d——d to them) and we run great risks—(were it not at sleeping hours—after dinner)—and *no* place—but the great Saloon of his own palace—so that if I come away with a Stiletto in my gizzard some fine afternoon—I shall not be astonished.—I can't make *him* out at all—he visits me frequently—and takes me out (like Whittington the Lord Mayor) in a coach and *six* horses—the fact appears to be

that he is completely *governed* by her—for that matter—so am I.—
The people here don't know what to make of us—as he had the
character of Jealousy with all his wives—this is the third.—He is the
richest of the Ravennese by their own account—but is not popular
among them.———By the aid of a Priest—a Chambermaid—a young
Negro-boy and a female friend—we are enabled to carry on our
unlawful loves as far as they can well go—though generally with
some peril—especially as the female friend and priest are at present
out of town for some days—so that some of the precautions devolve
upon the Maid and Negro.———Now do pray—send off Augustine—&
carriage—and cattle to Bologna without fail or delay—or I shall lose
my remaining Shred of senses.———Don't forget this.—My coming—
going—and every thing depends upon *her* entirely just as Mrs.
Hoppner—(to whom I remit my reverences) said, in the true spirit of
female prophecy.———You are but a shabby fellow not to have written
before—and I am truly

yours [scrawl]

P.S.—Address by return of Post to me—at *Ravenna*.

[TO RICHARD BELGRAVE HOPPNER]   *Ravenna, June 22d. 1819*

My dear Hoppner—I am commissioned to ask you a question and
a favour—which would be a favour to me in serving a person to whom
I have some obligations.—Can you make a Vice-Consul?—(*without*
salary of course and merely for his protection the person's principal
object) could you appoint one *here*—at *Ravenna?*—and if you can *will*
you?—Here is what I have to ask—& what I trust you will answer.—
The Applicant through me to you is a Roman subject—whom of course
it would be proper for you to know—before his appointment[1]—all this
I will tell you in time.—His object is to have a *British protection*—
he is *rich* & *independent*—but he does not trust to the arbitrary proceedings on this side the Po—and would wish to have a British
diploma in his favour—this would be obtained by a Vice-Consulate—
he desires nothing more—there is no great commerce here—he could
do no harm—& might do some good.———I wish to add that I should
have great pleasure if you could do this without inconvenience to
yourself—or if not—if you could obtain it of Stanley—or some other

---

[1] Count Alessandro Guiccioli had asked Byron to try to get him a British Vice-
consulate. When Hoppner was unable to arrange it, Byron applied to John Murray,
to see what could be done though his Government connections, but nothing came of
the proposal.

of your Consular Brethren.—It would be a favour to the person—and to me as the Mediator—always *providing first* that you *approve* of the person when named—as I shall be at liberty to name him—in case that you have the *power*—the *will* will be for you to decide afterwards. —I wrote to you twice from this place—to which I beg an answer by return of post.—

> ever yrs. very truly & [scrawl]
> BYRON

P.S.—My best compliments to Mrs. Hoppner.——

[TO JOHN CAM HOBHOUSE]   *Ravenna. June 26th. 1819*

Dear Hobhouse—I have been absent from Venice since the first of the month.—By the return of my Courier today (whom I had sent to Venice for some Peruvian Bark of mine for the Countess Guiccioli— who still continues very weak from her miscarriage) I expected some English letters—but—not one from anybody!—I wrote to you also from Ferrara.—Lord Kinnaird who is in waiting at Faenza on the Bianchi (the Danseuse of Milan) who is engaged for the theatre there —came over for a day or two to see [me] and is just gone back again to his station—he has been plagued and pamphlet-writing about Marinet's business.[1]——Of my concerns—which I explained to you before I set out—I shall add nothing at present on account of the Pontifical post-masters—who open letters.—You know that I came here on amatory business—and may suppose that I remain because it has prospered.— But you will address your answer to Venice as usual—that being still head-quarters.——To my great surprise we hear that you have been challenged by Antient Pistol Major Cartwright[2]—this seems to me mere Midsummer madness—what had you to do with those black-guard Reformers? who made you defy & leave the Whigs, and make you lose your Election—and then call you out as a reward for your

[1] Lord Kinnaird had warned the Chief of Staff of the Army of Occupation of a plot to assassinate the Duke of Wellington, but he refused to give the name of his informant. When this man, Marinet, was arrested, after having been given an assurance, as Kinnaird thought, of safe conduct to Paris, Lord Kinnaird sent a letter of protest to the French Peers, accusing the Government of breach of faith. This caused Kinnaird's expulsion from Paris. Byron referred to the matter in *Don Juan* (Canto 9, stanza 2).

[2] Major John Cartwright (1740–1824) in his eightieth year challenged Hob-house to a duel, in the belief that the younger man had not shown him proper respect. Hobhouse's explanation satisfied him. Byron's last speech in the House of Lords in 1813 had been in support of Cartwright's petition for the right to petition Parliament for the redress of grievances of the people.

trouble?—This is the damnedest piece of impudence I ever heard of.—
Sunburn me if it is not!—I am and have been for *reform* always—but
not for the *reformers*—I saw enough of them at the Hampden Club—
Burdett is the only one of them in whose company a Gentleman would
be seen unless at a Public meeting—or in a Public house.——"I shall
have to bail my old friend out of the Round-house" *"what a Coalition!"*
as "Davy" said of Johnson and Beauclerck.[3]——You were the founder
of the Whig-Club at Cambridge—if my memory serve me rightly.
——Of my own matters—I know not what to say—nor you—nor
Dougal K. nor Mr. Bookseller Murray have honoured me with further
intelligence of "the *pomes*" and what I was anxious about—the copyright of "Juan" none of you say a word—although I repeated my
request at least twenty times by letter.——If Mr. Murray plays me
those kind of tricks—he will run himself into a puddle.——On the
end of this moon—or the beginning of next—half a year's *fee* from the
funds becomes due—to the remittance of which—and also the sum for
the copy of D.J.—I look forward as the Conscription of the ensuing year
—but there was no reason why the Juan part should not have been done
long ago.——You see I am not pleased with Albemarle Street.——I
sent you the proofs received back with such alterations as were suitable
to my own notions.——The weather is hot—but in the evening I take
a ride or a drive to the Pineta—the scene of Boccaccio's tale—and
Dryden's fable.——Afterwards I visit—and ——believe me

Yours ever truly

B

June 29th.—I have just had some letters from England but none
from you.—

[TO ALEXANDER SCOTT]   *Ravenna. June 26th. 1819*

My dear Scott*in*—Lionardo[1] has just arrived—but *no English
letters*—it is impossible—(there is some blunder of *Siri's* &c.) that
there should be none from the first of the month and Paris Newspapers
there must be—Galignani's messenger &c.——I write in haste to
[snatch?] the Post—many thanks—I will write by & bye, more at
length.—Will you catechise Siri & W[illhal]m and ask why they did

[3] Boswell reported this remark of David Garrick (*Life of Johnson*, account of
events in 1752).
[1] Byron's courier whom he had sent to Venice for letters.

not send on my English letters?—address your answer to me *here* still —two lines will do just to mention & why & how.———

ever yrs. most truly
BYRON

Ravenna. June 29th. 1819

My dear Scott—I have sent again to Venice for Dr Aglietti—the Guiccioli is seriously ill & her state menaces consumption—I need hardly say how this occupies and distresses me.——If you can say anything to Dr Aglietti to persuade him to come in addition to what I have written—pray do—I have written at Count Guiccioli's own request and enclosed besides a long medical statement of her case;—— although there is no doubt on that score—yet you may tell Aglietti *that I myself* will be responsible for his time trouble and expence & being reimbursed and that his coming will be to me also a great personal favour—I can say no more—

ever & truly yrs.
BYRON

[TO JOHN MURRAY] *Ravenna. June 29th. 1819*

Dear Sir—The letters have been forwarded from Venice—but I trust that you will not have waited for further alterations—I will make none——You ask me to spare *"Romilly"*—ask the Worms.—His dust can suffer nothing from the truth being spoken—and if it *could*— how did he behave to *me*?——You may talk to the Wind—which will ⟨at least⟩ carry the sound—and to the Caves which will echo you —but *not* to me on the subject of a villain who wronged me—whether dead or alive.——I have no time to return you the proofs—publish without them.—I am glad you think the poesy good—and as to "thinking of the effect"—think *you* of the sale—and leave me to pluck the Porcupines who may point their quills at you.——I have been here (at *Ravenna*) these four weeks having left Venice a month ago;—I came to see my "amica" the Countess Guiccioli who has been—& still continues very unwell—after her miscarriage which occurred in May last at Pomposa on her way here from Lombardy.——She is only twenty years old, but not of a strong constitution and I fear that neither the medical remedies—nor some recent steps of our own to repair at least the miscarriage—have done her any great good—she has a perpetual cough—and an intermittent fever—but bears up most *gallantly* in every sense of the word.——Her husband (this is his third wife) is the richest Noble of Ravenna—& almost of Romagna— he is also *not* the youngest—being upwards of three score—but in good preservation.—All this will appear strange to you who do not understand the Meridian morality—nor our way of life in such respects, and I cannot at present expound the difference.—But you would find it much the same in these parts.—At Faenza—there is Lord Kinnaird with an Opera Girl.—and at the Inn in the same town is a Neapolitan Prince who serves the wife of the Gonfaloniere of that city.——I am on duty here—so you see "cosi fan tutt*i*" e tutt*e*——I have my horses here—*saddle* as well as Carriage—and ride or drive every day in the forest—the *Pineta* the scene of Boccaccio's novel and Dryden's fable of Honoria &c. &c. and I see my Dama every day at the proper (and improper) hours—but I feel seriously uneasy about her health which seems very precarious—in losing her I should lose a being who has run great risks on my account—and whom I have every reason to love— but I must not think this possible—I do not know what I *should* do—if She died—but I ought to blow my brains out—and I hope that I should.—Her husband is a very polite personage—but I wish he would not carry me out in his Coach and Six—like Whittington and his Cat.——You ask me if I mean to continue D[on] J[uan] &c. how should I know? what encouragement do you give me—all of you with your nonsensical prudery?—publish the two Cantos—and then you will see.——I desired Mr. Kinnaird to speak to you on a little matter of business—either he has not spoken or you have not answered.— You are a pretty pair—but I will be even with you both—I perceive that Mr. Hobhouse has been challenged by Major Cartwright—is the Major "so cunning of fence?"—why did not they fight?—they ought.

yrs. ever truly

B

Address your answer to *Venice* as usual.—

[TO COUNTESS TERESA GUICCIOLI (*a*)]   [*June–July? 1819*]

[Fragments of a letter] Vado in letto—e sarebbe meglio per me che il sonno mio (se pure sarà possibile che dormo) divenisse eterno.

* * * * * * * * * * * * * *

la maniera di farlo scordare a venire da voi. Forse questo è solamente un prologo—e finirete. . .

* * * * * * * * * * * * * *

ma vi amai—e dopo esser' stato un uomo riconsciuto per l'indepen-
denza e la forza dello suo animo—

* * * * * * * * * * * * * * * *

Disgraziamente per me ha perduto le sue ale.—Forse le ritroverà—
almeno lo spero.—Addio.—

* * * * * * * * * * * * * * * *

[TRANSLATION (*a*)]   [*June–July? 1819*]

[Fragments of a letter][1]

   I am going to bed—and it would be better for me if my sleep (if
indeed sleep is possible for me) could become eternal . . . . . . how to
make him forget to come to you . . . . . Perhaps this is only a prologue
—and you will . . . . but I loved you—
and after having been a man well-known for his independence and
strength of mind . . . . Unfortunately
for me he has lost his wings.—Perhaps he will find them again, at
least I hope so. Farewell.—

[TO COUNTESS TERESA GUICCIOLI (*b*)]   [*June–July? 1819*]

   "I miei pensieri in me dormir' non ponno" ebbi dunque ragione—
cosa fa quel' uomo ogni sera e tante ore al' vostro fianco in palco?—
"dunque siamo intesi"—belle parole!—*"siete intesi"* a cio che mi pare,—
ho veduto che ogni momento in quale io voltai la testa verso il palco
scenico voi voltaste gli occhi a guardare quella persona—e cio dopo
tutto che è passato oggi!——Ma non temete, dimane sera lo lasciarò il
campo libero.——Io non ho forza a sostenere ogni giorno un' tormento
nuovo—m'avete fatto divinire spreggevole nei miei proprii occhi e fra
poco forse anche in quelli dei altri.—Non avete veduto i martiri miei?
non l'avete compatita? vi perdono cio che mi fate soffrire—ma non
posso mai perdonare a me stesso la debolezza di cuore la quale m'im-
pedisce finora a prendere il solo partito onorevole in tali circostanze
—cio—di⟨dirti⟩ dirvi Addio—in eterno.——

Mezza notte——

   Ora di riposo per me prima di conoscervi.——Lasciami partire—è
meglio morire del' dolore della lontananza—piuttosto che del'

---

   [1] These fragments are cut out of a larger letter, which obviously referred to
some of the lovers' quarrels and jealousies. Teresa preserved what was flattering
to her.

tradimento—la mia vita adesso è un' agonia sempiterna—ho goduto della felicità unica ed ultima nelle tue braccia—ma—Oh Dio!—quanto mi costano quei momenti!—e *questi—questo!*—ora che ti scrivo—solo—solissimo;—io non ebbe che te nel' mondo—e adesso non avendoti più (senza il cuore cosa è il resto?] la solitudine è divenuta noiosa come la società—poiche quel' immagine che io figurava cosi pura, cosi cara—non è più che un' ombra perfida e minacciante,—e pure sempre la *tua.*——

[TRANSLATION (*b*)]   [*no date*] [*June–July 1819?*]

"My thoughts cannot find rest in me"[1]—I was right then: what is that man doing every evening for so long beside you in your box? "So we are agreed"—fine words! "*You* are agreed", it appears. I have noticed that every time I turned my head toward the stage you turned your eyes to look at that man—and this, after all that had happened today! But do not fear, tomorrow evening I shall leave the field clear to him.—I have no strength to bear a fresh torment every day—you have made me despicable in my own eyes—and perhaps soon in those of others.—Have you not seen my torments? Have you not pitied them? I forgive you what you have made me suffer—but I can never forgive myself the weakness of heart which has prevented me until now from taking the only honourable step in such circumstances —that of bidding you good-bye—for ever—

                                                          Midnight

My time for sleep before I knew you.

Let me go—it is better to die from the pain of separation, than from that of betrayal—my life now is a constant agony. I have enjoyed a unique and final happiness in your arms—but—oh God! how much more those moments are costing me!—and *they* [cost] *this!*—now that I am writing to you alone— completely alone. I had no one but you in the world—and now, not having you any more (without the heart, what is the rest?) solitude has become as tedious as society—for that image, which I pictured as so pure, so dear, is now nothing but a perfidious and menacing shadow,—and yet—always *yours.*[2]

[1] Tasso, *Gerusalemme Liberata*, Canto X⁰: "I suoi pensieri in lui dormir non ponno" ("His thoughts cannot find rest in him"). This was the motto at the beginning of *The Corsair.*

[2] Teresa wrote a note accompanying this letter in her collection: "Billet de jalousie *magnifique—passionné—sublime mais* tres injuste. Il ne me connaissait encore que depuis trop peu!!!"

Amor mio—Perche non dopo pranzo? Cosa m'importa della "passeggiata" e delle "prescrizioni"? tu sai bene *cosa* mi "piace"— — ogni giorno in quale non ci vediamo e *amiamo* in fatto come in cuore—è (per me almeno) la perdita più irreparabile, una felicità di meno.— —Dimmi il *quando*—

sempre e tutto tuo

B

[TRANSLATION (*c*)] [*June–July? 1819*]

My Love—Why not after dinner? What do I care about the "promenade" and the "prescription"? You well know *what* I "like"— every day in which we do not see and *love* each other, in deed as in our hearts, is (at least for me) the most irreparable of losses, one happiness the less.

Tell me *when*—ever and entirely thine

B

[TO AUGUSTA LEIGH] [*Ravenna July 1819?*][1]

Allegra is well at Venice— —There are also a fox—some dogs and two monkeys—all scratching—screaming and fighting—in the highest health and Spirits.—Fletcher is flourishing. Lady B. has refused a *character* to his wife—a little revenge of a-piece with *her own*. —You say nothing of Ada, how is she?—doubtless Lady Noel is as immortal as ever.—Her death would do too much good—for Providence to permit it in this state of sublunary things—if you see my Spouse—do pray tell her I wish to marry again—and as probably she may wish the same—is there no way in *Scotland*? without compromising HER immaculacy—cannot it be done there by the *husband* solely?

[TO COUNT GIUSEPPE ALBORGETTI[1]] *Ravenna. July 1st. 1819*

My dear Count—I am as you know but a retired sort of being (of late years) and have been at more Mahometan than Christian courts, besides which though I have invariably voted in Parliament for the

[1] Written on the back of a letter cover postmarked Aug. 12, 1819.
[1] See biographical sketch, Appendix IV.

Catholics I am but little conversant with Cardinals.———However—
if,—as a stranger who has been some time at Ravenna nobody knows
why—you think that I ought to pay my respects to his Eminence for
whom I entertain great esteem and reverence—I will go.———In that
case [there is] nobody more agreeable to me personally—or so proper
in other respects to be my introducer as yourself.———Perhaps you
will do me the honour to call on me tomorrow at three—and indicate
the time and manner.———I could wish the *hour* to be an *Evening* one
—for a noonday presentation in the month of an Italian July—in our
English scarlet uniform—would be an operation of active service not
necessary in time of Peace, to any one but a Field Marshal,—and not
to a Member of the Sacred College.———I congratulate you (or rather
myself) on your English—I am *not* "the greatest poet" &c. as you are
pleased to say—and if I were you need not be afraid as you have written
very good English prose—a better thing when well done than poetry
at any time.———I have the honour to be with full esteem

yr. most obliged & very faithful Servt.

BYRON

[TO MRS. MARIA GRAHAM[1]]   *Ravenna. July 2d. 1819*

Madam—Your letter of the 12th. of June followed me from Venice
to this city—but I did not receive it till yesterday.———I am honoured
by the intentions of your countryman—and any questions which he
may be disposed to ask—I will answer.———The personage whom he
is disposed to introduce into his landscape—was not a Moor—and the
epithet *"black"* which I do not remember (not having read the poem
since it's publication) is either a mistake of mine—or was intended in
the Highland sense of the words—Dhu-voy—or[beau?]—black—red

---

[1] Mrs. Maria Graham was the daughter of Rear-Admiral Dundas. She had
travelled with her father to India, where she met and married Captain Thomas
Graham, R.N. On her return to England she published an *Indian Journal* (1812),
and *Letters on India* (1814). She was preparing a travel book, published the
following year, when she wrote to Byron from Rome on behalf of Charles Eastlake,
the painter. The fact that she was a close friend of John Murray gave her a claim to
Byron's attention. She later became a friend of Ugo Foscolo in England. Her
husband died on a voyage to South America on which she was accompanying him,
and she spent some years in Chile and Brazil. After she returned to England in
1826 she married the painter Augustus Callcott, and under her new name wrote
Little Arthur's History of England (1835), a book that went into 70 editions and
sold over a million copies. Yet another edition was published in 1975 by John
Murray. (See E. R. Vincent, *Ugo Foscolo, An Italian in Regency England*, 1953)

—or white—by *comparison*—as an Asiatic by origin is more swarthy than an European——without meaning that he was precisely japanned with the best patent blacking.——Does the Painter know the place? it is the defile in Phocis where four mountain roads meet and not far from the spot which Pausanias describes as the scene of the meeting of Laius with Oedipus and the death of the former.—Mr. Eastlake[2] will probably recollect the road down toward Livadia—from the village of Arracavo[3] (I am not sure of my orthography by the way) it was about half way—between these two places.—I envy Mr. E. his late residence in Greece—to which I have always longed to return—but circumstances have occurred to detain me in Italy.——I have to thank you for the honour of your letter—and regret the trouble which it has occasioned you—believe me to be very truly

yr. obliged & very faithl. humble Sert.
BYRON

[TO JAMES WEDDERBURN WEBSTER] *Ravenna. July 2d. 1819*

Dear Webster—Your letter followed me to this city—where I have been some time.—A friend of mine—the young Countess Guiccioli—is very unwell—and I came down from Venice to see her about a month ago.—The poor Girl—who is but twenty years old—and has been married about fifteen months to a very rich nobleman of Ravenna —(she is his third wife—& he is sixty) has had a bad miscarriage—and her symptoms threaten Consumption—but I hope better.—If you write to me address to Venice—my letters will be forwarded.——I answered you before about the bond—and do not know that I need say more upon the subject—I presume nobody has called upon you on my part for payment.——Newstead was sold and the purchase-money paid.——I regret that the tone of your letter is so desponding—and my own spirits at this moment are not in a state to reply to you very cheerfully.—The accounts you have heard of the alteration which has taken place in my appearance may be true—it would be odd indeed if some change had not occurred.—Mine has not been the most regular —nor the most tranquil of lives.—At thirty I feel there is no more to

---

[2] (Sir) Charles Lock Eastlake (1793–1865) later President of the Royal Academy and Director of the National Gallery, was then a young man studying landscape painting in Rome. He had travelled in Greece and was contemplating a landscape based on Byron's poetry. The result was his well-known "Byron's Dream".

[3] Arachova between Livadia and Delphi.

look forward to.—With regard to the imputed "Corpulence"—my size is certainly increased considerably—but I am not aware that it amounts to that "stupendous" degree which you enquire after.—At eight and twenty I was as thin as most men—and I believe that hitherto I have not exceeded the decent standard—of my time of life.—However—my personal charms have by no means increased—my hair is half grey—and the Crow's-foot has been rather lavish of it's indelible steps.——My hair though not gone seems going—and my teeth remain by way of courtesy—but I suppose they will follow—having been too good to last.——I have now been as candid as anything but a too faithful Mirror can be—I shall not venture to look in mine—for fear of adding to the list of that which Time has [added]—and is adding.—I regret that you do not pass into Italy—for my sake—because we should meet—and for yours—because it must be better than a provincial town of France.—*Here* all the cities are capitals—and have not that provincial tone of the secondary towns of other kingdoms.—If you were on this side of the Alps I would go a good way to meet you.—Why don't you come?—I really wish that you would, or could.

> yrs. ever & truly
> B

Tomorrow I have to undergo a presentation to the Cardinal Legate of the district, and I am not fond of introductions.—

P.S.—My best remembrances to Lady Frances.—

[TO RICHARD BELGRAVE HOPPNER]   *Ravenna July 2d. 1819*

My dear Hoppner—Thanks for yr. letter and for Madame's.—I will answer it directly. Will you recollect whether I did not consign to you one or two receipts of Madame Mocenigo's for House rent—(I am not sure of this but think I did—if not they will be in my drawers) and will you desire Mr. Dorville[1] to have the goodness to see if Edgecombe has *receipts* to all payments hitherto made by him on my account—and that there are *no debts* at Venice—on your answer I shall send an order of further remittance to carry on my household expences.—as my present return to V[enice] is very problematical—and it may happen ⟨that⟩—but I can say nothing positive—every thing with me being indecisive and undecided—except the disgust which Venice excites

---

[1] Henry Dorville was British Vice-Consul in Venice under Hoppner.

when fairly compared with any other city in this part of Italy—when I say *Venice* I mean the *Venetians*—the City itself is superb as it's History—but the people are what—I never thought them till they taught me to think so.—The best way will be to leave Allegra with Antonio's spouse—till I can decide something about her and myself—but I thought that you would have had an answer from Mrs. Vavassour.[2]—You have had bore enough with me & mine already.—I greatly fear that the Guiccioli is going into a consumption—to which her constitution tends;—thus it is with every thing and every body for whom I feel anything like a real attachment—"War—death—or discord doth lay siege to them"[3]—I never even could keep alive a dog that I liked or that liked me.——Her symptoms are [an] obstinate cough of the lungs—and occasional fever—&c. &c. and there are latent causes of an eruption in the skin which she foolishly expelled into the system two years ago—but I made them send her case to Aglietti—and have begged him to come—if only for a day or two —to consult upon her state.—She bears up most *gallantly* in every sense of the word—but I sometimes fear that our *daily* interviews may not tend to weaken her—(I am sure they *don't strengthen me*) but it is not for me to hint this—and as to her she manifests a most laudable perseverance—in spite of the pain of her chest—and the dizziness which follows shortly afterwards.—If it would not bore Mr. Dorville—I wish he would keep an eye on Edgecombe,—and on my other ragamuffins—I may or might have more to say—but I am absorbed about La Gu[icciol]i and her illness—I cannot tell you the effect it has upon me.——The horses came—&c. &c. and I have been galloping through the Pine forests daily.—Believe me

ever yrs. most [truly]

B

P.S.—My Benediction on Mrs. Hoppner—a pleasant journey among the Bernese Tyrants——and safe return—you ought to bring back a Platonic Bernese for my reformation;—if anything happens to my present Amica—I have done with the Passion forever —it is my *last* Love.—And as to Libertinism—I have sickened myself of that as was natural in the way I went on—and I have at least

[2] Mrs. Vavassour was an English widow of considerable means who saw and admired Allegra at the Hoppners and offered to adopt her. Byron wanted to employ her to care for his daughter as nurse and governess, but nothing came of the proposal.

[3] *Midsummer Night's Dream*, Act I, scene 1: "War, death, or sickness did lay siege to it."

derived that advantage from the Vice—to *Love* in the better sense of the word—*this* will be my last adventure—I can hope no more to inspire attachment—and I trust never again to feel it.—Addio.——

My dear Kinnaird—The G[uiccioli] has been very unwell (not ill enough though to induce any amatory abstinence except that single day when the *Chat* awoke a little prematurely) and I persuaded *him* to have Aglietti from Venice—he came yesterday they have put on leeches—and prescribed a regimen—and say that She may be cured if she likes—will she like?—I doubt her liking any thing very long— except one thing and I presume she will soon arrive at varying even that—in which case I should be at liberty to repass the Po—and perhaps the Alps—but as yet I can say nothing.—I had a letter from W. Webster the other day—he is at Nantes Loire Nif——and I have half a mind to go back in search of *La Fanchette*[1]—but I know nothing of the geography of the place—where the devil is Nantes? and what is Loire Nif—a river I suppose—an't it?—La Geltruda[2] is gone to Bologna—after pinching her left thigh one evening—I was never permitted to set eyes on her *not no more.*—It is no fault of mine her not coming to Faenza—she did not set off till yesterday.—I have been exchanging visits with the Cardinal Legate who called on me today—he is a fine old fellow—Malvasia by name—and has been rather loose in his youth—without being much tighter in his age.— He and I took very kindly to each other.——How am I to get the books and to leave yours?—is the Bianchi[3] to be visible—or my *Aunt* only? of course you could not doubt the lady and still less your friend— but I suppose nevertheless I shall see my aunt only—well—it is hard— but I agree—only adding that my green carriage has lost much of it's splendour and consequently I am shorn of one of the principal seductive qualities of an accomplished gentleman. I am as I said in perfect indecision—depending upon the *will* of a woman who has none—and on whom I never calculate for more than twelve hours—she will do as she pleases—and then so will I—a young Italian—married to a rich old Patrician—with only one man besides for a lover—is not likely to embarrass either with a long Constancy—and in that case you

---

[1] Probably a reference to Fanny (Frances) Webster.
[2] Geltrude Vicari, a friend of Teresa Guiccioli, with whom Byron flirted to pay back Teresa for making him jealous.
[3] Lord Kinnaird's mistress, a danseuse.

know—there could be no great harm in my beginning the world again —or giving it up for good.—Will you tell me where this *Nantes* is? ——I can't find it in the road book.——Addio. I am just going to take a canter into the Pine forest with Ferdinando.[4]——

yrs. ever & truly

B

P.S.—I approve your intentions about the books and the *Sequins* also.——

[TO ALEXANDER SCOTT]   *July 7th. 1819*

Dear Scott,—Pray present my respects to *Marina*[1] and *Beppi*[2] and say that I am delighted with Ravenna and disgusted with Venice.—— She writes that Madame Demper[3] has carried you off to joke at [*Seaces?*]—and that she has thus lost both her English—(you being Scotch by the way.)—The G[uiccioli] is better—and will get well with prudence.—Our amatory business goes on *well* and *daily*—not at all interrupted by extraneous matters or the threatened consumption.

yrs. ever

Bn

Tell Edgecombe that he is a "f——d pig" and a boar (*bore*) besides. ——Compliments to Hoppner and the Chevalier of Mengaldo. Compliments to Missiaglia.[4]

[TO COUNT GIUSEPPE ALBORGHETTI]   *Ravenna 9th of July 1819*

My dear Count—I thought that I had sufficiently manifested my sincere respect for the Cardinal in paying him the first visit—and if there is any manner in which I can further testify my esteem personally, it shall be shown—But I am not a man of society nor Conversazioni— it is some years that I have given up both—with regard to the attentions necessary to be paid to the "Chief of a province" &c—it cannot of course be my wish nor my interest to offend him—and I presume that such offence could only be the consequence of Mis- conduct; and that his Eminence is of a character not to disquiet himself

[4] Ferdinando was Count Guiccioli's son by a previous marriage.
[1] Countess Marina Querini Benzoni.
[2] Giuseppe Rangone, the cavalier servente of the Countess Benzoni.
[3] Unidentified.
[4] Giovan Battista Missiaglia, proprietor of the Apollo Library and a publisher and bookseller in Venice. Byron had a cordial relationship with him.

for such trifles as the appearance or non-appearance of a foreigner at a conversation.—When at Venice last Winter—I twice declined the offer of an introduction to the Vice-roy and to the Arch-Duchess Maria Louisa[1]—made to me through the medium of the Prince of Hohenzollern and the English Consul-General. I did not find that I was supposed to have been guilty of any affront—and I am sure at least that I was far from intending it. As little do I think of displeasing his Eminence to whom I am grateful for his kindness—and for *his own proper conversation*—I decline going into extensive society, because for these last three years I am not in the practice;—indeed it distresses me—I am besides unwell—and expressed as much to you yesterday; if his Eminence thinks for a moment he must be aware that I can have no design to slight or to offend him—but the contrary —I [trust]? that you will do me the favour to represent as much to his Eminence and to believe me ever very truly

yr most obliged and obedt

Sert.

Byron P[ai]r d'A[ngleterr]e

P.S.—I did *not* know that the Conversation was *made for me*—and I did say that I was *unwell in health* both to you and afterward to Count Zinanni.

[TO ALEXANDER SCOTT]   *Ravenna. July 12th. 1819*

My dear Scott—I enclose you Hoppner's last letter—you will understand *why* on reading it through.—All his amiable bile is *gratis* —and *unasked*[1]—now I *ask you* and whatever you say on the subject disagreeable will not be your fault but mine.—I never supposed that the G[uiccioli] was to be a despairing Shepherdess—nor did I search very nicely into her motives—all I know is that *she* sought me—and that I have *had her*—*there* & *here* & *everywhere*—so that if there is any fool-making on the occasion—I humbly suspect that *two* can play at that—and that hitherto the parties have at least an equal chance.— I have no hesitation in repeating that I *love* her—but I have also *self-love* enough to be cured by the least change or trick in her part when I know it.—Pride is one's best friend on such occasions.—As to her

---

[1] Probably Maria Louise, Napoleon's second wife, who was Grand Duchess of Parma. Byron disapproved of her because she would not follow Napoleon into exile. (See Vol. 4, p. 101.)

[1] Hoppner's letter (Origo, pp. 89–90) was filled with moral advice and warnings that Teresa from vanity wanted to entrap Byron and then leave him.

"vanity" (I wish it ⟨were⟩ may[—] there is no passion so strong) in getting me as Hoppner says—*that* might be very well in an English woman—but I don't see how *English* poetical celebrity—or rank is to operate upon an Italian—besides which I have no permanent character to go upon personally—at least in Italy—if he had said *"interest"* I should have thought him nearer the mark though I have *no right hitherto* to assert even that.—As you are much more in the way of hearing the *real truth or lie* than H[oppner] perhaps you will tell me to what Gossip he alludes—at any rate you will tell it without *mystery* and *hints* and without *bile*—so pray do—I forgive whatever may be unpleasant in the intelligence—and it may be of use to me. Pray answer by return of *Post*—lest I should be off again.——I suppose this may possibly be some *cookery* between—H[oppner] and Minghaldo—if it should not—*you* are fifty times more likely to know than he is—what does he mean by *"avowedly"* does he suppose a woman is to go and *"avow"* her likings in the Piazza?——I should think her public *disavowal* the strongest proof—at least it is thought so in most women—what think you? She is getting well very fast—all the rest as usual—and I very truly yrs.

B

P.S.—Comp[limen]ts to Missiaglia.—
P.S.—What does H[oppner] mean by *"when she is sure of me"? how "sure?"* when a man has been for some time in the habit of *keying* a female—methinks it is his own fault if the being "left in the lurch" greatly incommodes him—because the woman can never forget that she has been "under his paunch"—and unless he is a sighing swain—⟨terms⟩ accounts at parting are at least equal—if the lady takes another caprice—Ebbene? can't we match her in that too think you? & then let her boast of her "betraying &c."—I congratulate you on your *"cows"* in the Plural—hitherto—I am faithful—but the slightest dereliction— (at least when aware of it) will give me liberty—So—*Corroborate* or *contradict* that Consular Diogenes.——You should give me notice in time that I may be the first to throw up the Cards.——There has been [no] public exhibition for I never go out with her—except twice or thrice in the Carriage—but I am *not in waiting*.——Give me but a proof—or a good tight *suspicious confirmation*—and I will rejoin you directly, and—we will village at the Mira—there is a bribe for you. Of course I was perfectly aware that there would be a grand Benzonian Controversy—and much evil said & thought on the occasion—but all this was not in Hoppner's precise department—so that I am

"rimasto!!!" remember *you* and *I* can say & hear any thing from one another—it is in *our line*—but I never gave him the right of *hinting* & teazing me out of temper.——You will think me a damned fool—but when she was supposed in danger—I was really & truly on the point of poisoning myself—and have got the drug still in my drawer. ——If Hoppner is *not* gone ask him in a friendly way from *me* what he means—but *don't* show him this letter.

Dear Scot—I have forgotten one thing which will make you laugh [—] the G[*uiccioli*]'s brother wrote from Rome to their father *here* (I saw the letter) a long dissuasion against any "relazione" with me—because (principally) I had for *"molti* anni" confined (incarcerato) my wife in *"un suo castello"* in England of mine out of revenge!!!—Tell this to Hoppner it is a good set off to his letter.—I suspect Mengaldo—& Rizzo in Hoppner's diatribe—but be that as it may—I will never forgive H[oppner] for his gratuitous—bilious—officious inter-meddling.—He might at least have waited till asked.——I translated the enclosed to her *today* (the 12th) you may imagine her answer—of course She would be at no loss for that—none of them are—She volunteered an elopement saying "then instead of being at my mercy—I shall be at yours—you have my letters in which I have not only exposed my feelings but my name—you have every proof that a man can have of my having been in earnest—and if you desire more—try me."——"Besides—what do they *know* of me at Venice? you should judge by what they say of me here—if you like hearsay better than experience.—["]All this you may say to Hoppner from me—with my sentiments on his conduct into the bargain;—He is really intolerable.

[TO LADY BYRON]   *Ravenna. July 20th. 1819*

I have received from Holstein (I believe) the annexed paper of the Baroness of Hohenhausen &c. and the inclosed letter of a Mr. Jacob (or Jacobsen) and as they "ardently wish it could reach you" I transmit it.——You will smile—as I have done—at the importance which they attach to such things—and the effect which they conceive capable of being produced by composition—but the Germans are still a young and a romantic people—and live in an ideal world.—Perhaps it may not offend you—however it may surprize—that the good people on the frontiers of Denmark have taken an interest in your domestic Affairs—which have now—I think—nearly made the tour of Europe—and been discussed in most of it's languages—to as little purpose as in our own.—If you like to retain the enclosed—you can do so—an indication to my Sister that you have received the letter will be a sufficient answer.——I will not close this sheet without a few words more.—Fletcher has complained to me of your declining to give his wife a character—on account of your "doubts of her veracity in some circumstances a short time before She left you"—if your doubts allude to her testimony on your case during the then discussion—*you* must or at least ought to be the best judge how far she spoke truth or not;—*I* can only say that She never had directly or indirectly—through me or mine—the slightest inducement to the contrary—nor am I indeed perfectly aware of what her Evidence was never having seen her nor communicated with her at that period nor since.——I presume that you will weigh well your justice before you deprive the woman of the means of obtaining her bread——no one can be more fully aware than I am of the utter inefficacy of any words of mine to you on this or on any other subject,—but I have discharged my duty to Truth in stating the above—and now do yours.——The date of my letter—indeed my letter itself—may surprize you—but I left Venice in the beginning of June, and came down into Romagna—there is the famous forest of Boccacio's Story—and Dryden's fable—hardby—the Adriatic not far distant—and the Sepulchre of Dante within the walls.—I am just going to take a Canter (for I have resumed my Tartar habits since I left England) in the cool of the Evening—and in the Shadow of the forest—till the Ave Maria.——I have got both my Saddle and Carriage horses with me—and don't spare them, in the cooler part of the day.—But I shall probably return to Venice in a short time.——Ravenna itself preserves perhaps more of the old Italian manners than any City in Italy—it is out of the way of travellers & armies—and thus they have retained more of their originality.—They make love a good deal,—and assassinate a little.—The department is governed by a Cardinal Legate (Alderoni was once legate here) to whom I have been presented and who told me some singular anecdotes of past times—of Alfieri &c. and others. I tried to discover for Leigh Hunt some traces of Francesca—but except her father Guido's tomb—and the mere notice of the fact in the Latin commentary of Benvenuto da Imola[1] in M.S. in the library—I could discover nothing for him.—He (Hunt) has made a sad mistake—about "old Ravenna's *clear-shewn towers* and *bay*" the city Lies so low that you must be close upon it before it is "shewn" at all—and the Sea had retired *four miles* at least, long before Francesca was born—and as far back as the Exarchs

[1] See July 30, 1819, to Hobhouse, note 4.

and Emperors.—They tell me that at Rimini they know as little about her now—as they do here—so I have not gone there—it lies in the way to Rome—but I was at Rome in 1817.—This is odd—for at Venice I found many traditions of the old Venetians—and at Ferrara a plentiful assortment of the House of Este—with the remains of the very Mirror—whose reflection cost at least a dozen lives—including those of Parisina and Ugo.——I was wrong in placing those two naughty people in a garden.——Parisina was a Malatesta of Rimini—and her daughter by Niccolo of Este—was also put to death by some Italian Chief her husband in nearly the same manner as her mother.—Her name was Ginevra.—So that including the alliance of Francesca with Launcelot Malatesta of Rimini—that same Malatesta family appears to have been but indifferently fortunate in their matrimonial speculations.——I have written to you thus much—because in writing to you at all, I may as well write much as little—I have not heard of Ada for many months—but they say "no news is good news" she must now be three years and almost eight months old.—You must let her be taught Italian as soon as she can be taught any language but her own—& *pray* let her be musical—that is if She has a turn that way. —I presume that Italian being a language of mine—will not prevent you from recollecting my request at the proper time.——

I am &c.

𝔅

Bologna. August 31st. 1819.

This letter was written as far back as July 20th at Ravenna—but I delayed putting it in the post till my return here which will account for the interval between the date and the arrival of the letter—*if* it arrives. —Pray—state to Augusta that you have received it—on account of the inclosures.—I want no other answer—I should like to have a picture of Miss Byron—when she can conveniently sit to Holmes or any other painter.—Addio.——

[On the cover] Mr. Murray is requested to have the goodness to forward this letter—the writer not knowing the address.——

[TO ALEXANDER SCOTT]   *Ravenna. July 24th. 1819*

My dear *Scottin*—I imparted as you will perceive by the enclosed *some* portion of yr. letter to the G[*uiccioli*] I say *some*—because (as you will perceive also) I omitted all that could offend *her own* self

love—such as the *"ridicola*[1] &c."—and translated to her merely some
parts referring to her conduct towards me—and the presumed motives
of it—and the prophecies of *plantation.*[2]—Thereupon She chose to
write the enclosed—which she desires me to transmit to you—I took
care to *tell her* that *you* took her part—and did *not* believe the asseverations.—You will judge for yourself—knowing the people—I make no
more pretensions to any kind of Judgement—satisfied that I am a
damned fool.——She has *"Milorded"* you—taking that for granted.—
The letter was written at the other end of the room—with several
persons talking all at once—so that you may make some allowance for
the difficulty of the situation to say nothing of that of the Subject.——
I write in haste—but I have much to say—*I authorize most fully Mr.
Dorville's superintendance and command over Edgecombe in my concerns—*
and trust that you will aid and abet him therein.——I have taken *my
part*—which is *not* to return to Venice.—The G[uiccioli]s have no
influence in this—for *they* do return in Winter to pass some time.——
You will oblige me by announcing this to Mr. Dorville—and request
him to take measures accordingly—to give my Servants warning and
to see that there are all accounts ready.—I know of *no debts* that there
ought to be.—My house-rents are paid a year in advance.—I wish that
Madame Mocenigo be asked to take back hers—I will give up *this*
year's Rent already paid (the term began in June) and restoring the
house in good condition—I hope that she will agree to cancel the
papers—and give up the year *1820.*—If not I must keep the house on.
—I will also give up the Casinos in town and at the Mira.—That of
the Mira taken for the year—is paid for nine months in advance.—
Will they take it back?—the money they have and may keep.——I
desired Messrs. Siri &c. to advance small sums on house-keeping
account to Mr. Dorville—and said that I would be responsible.——
Mr. Dorville will give Edgecombe and the Servants *all warning*——
my books and *my own* furniture and things I will send for—when I
have settled my precise abode—the Gondola will be to be sold—the
posts and fixtures [rest?] to Madame Mocenigo.—I shall send for my
daughter also.——The animals also will come—fox—monkies and
the other mastiff.—I will write again by next post—but in the mean
time will you acknowledge this?—Remember me to Missiaglia—if

<hr>

[1] Scott had said in his letter in reply to Byron's of July 12th that Teresa had been
considered "ridiculous" in Venice.

[2] Byron's literal translation of the Italian "piantare", to leave or abandon.
Teresa insisted on writing herself to Scott to tell him how wrong he was. "What a
wretch I should consider myself if I feared that, one day, so great a man would
blush to have loved me!" (Origo, p. 94.)

there is aught unpaid—let him give the items. Perhaps he will have the goodness to see my books packed.———My love to the Benzon—and Rangone—and health and thanks to all my acquaintance including the Albrizzi.———As to the "adoration" of the Venetians—you are of course laughing;—I have never courted their liking but have done them no harm—at least none intentionally.—You need make no secret of my intended removal;—but at the same time you may state the fact—which is—that the G's have nothing to do with it—as they are to be in Venice next winter—for a long time.———I write in haste—but will specify next time—believe me ever & truly

yrs.
BYRON

[TO WHOM IT MAY CONCERN] *Ravenna. July 25th. 1819*

The Bearer of this—John Dodd an Englishman by birth was landed from the Nancy transport (in consequence of a fall from the rigging) on the coast near Ravenna.—This occurred some years ago.—In this city he has remained ever since without finding any opportunity of returning to Great Britain—as few English travellers pass through the city—& fewer vessels of that nation touch at this part of the Coast. He has subsisted occasionally in service—& sometimes on Alms.———His account of himself has been confirmed by the Police (whose passport he has obtained) and by several Gentlemen—The Counts Rasponi—Guiccioli—and others of my acquaintance.———I have thought it my duty to obtain for him a passage to Trieste and to furnish him with a small sum for his expences in order to enable him at least to set out according to his desire—with the purpose of returning to his Country & relations. This paper is added that in case he should meet by accident with any acquaintance of mine, my recommendation may not be wanting.—In the course of his probable application to any of his Majesty's Consuls—it may also serve in confirmation of his story—and together with his passport—tend to prevent suspicion of his being an Impostor.———According to the best information I could obtain, his story is true—and his case a hard one.—I therefore recommend him as far as lies in my power—to the aid of his more fortunate fellow Citizens—as not unworthy of their assistance and protection in his journey homeward,—His object is to obtain a passage by Sea if possible from Trieste to his native place.

BYRON
(Peer of England.)

P.S.—I ought not to omit that the poor fellow had nearly forgotten his own language—but that at present he has resumed it with more fluency;—from practice with my English Servant—of the truth of his story no doubt can be entertained.—It is now two months that I have been at Ravenna—and every circumstance has tended to confirm his Accuracy.—

B

[TO AUGUSTA LEIGH]   *Ravenna. July 26th. 1819*

My dearest Augusta—I am at too great a distance to scold you—but I *will* ask you—whether *your* letter of the *1st.* July *is an answer* to the letter I wrote you before I quitted Venice?—What? is it come to *this?*—Have you no memory? or no heart?—You *had* both—and I *have* both—at least for *you.*——I write this presuming that you received *that* letter—is it that you fear? do not be afraid of the post—the World has it's own affairs without thinking of *ours* and you may write safely —if you do—address as usual to *Venice.*—My house is not in St. Marc's but on the Grand Canal—within sight of the Rialto Bridge.— —I do not like at all this pain in your side and always think of your mother's constitution—you must always be to me the first considera- tion in the World.—Shall I come to *you?*—or would a warm climate do you good?—if so say the word—and I will provide you & your whole family (including that precious baggage your Husband) with the means of making an agreeable journey—you need not fear about *me*—I am much altered—and should be little trouble to you—nor would I give you more of my company than you like.——I confess after three years and a half—and *such years!* and *such a year* as preceded those three years! it would be a relief to see you again—and if it would be so to you—I will come to you.——Pray—answer me—and recollect that I will do as you like in everything—even to returning to England— which is *not* the pleasantest of residences were *you* out of it.——I write from Ravenna—I came here on account of a Countess Guiccioli—a Girl of Twenty married to a very rich old man of Sixty—about a year ago;—with her last Winter I had a *liaison* according to the good old Italian custom—she miscarried in May—and sent for me here—and here I have been these two months.—She is pretty—a great Coquette— extremely vain—excessively affected—clever enough—without the smallest principle—with a good deal of imagination and some passion;—She had set her heart on carrying me off from Venice out of vanity—and succeeded—and having made herself the subject of

185

general conversation has greatly contributed to her recovery.—Her husband is one of the richest Nobles of Ravenna—threescore years of age—this is his third wife.——You may suppose what *esteem* I entertain for *her*—perhaps it is about equal on both sides.—I have my saddle-horses here and there is good riding in the forest—with these —and my carriage which is here also—and the Sea—and my books— and the lady—the time passes—I am very fond of riding and always *was out* of England—but I hate your Hyde Park—and your turnpike roads—& must have forests—downs—or deserts to expatiate in—I detest *knowing* the road—one is to go,—and being interrupted by your damned fingerposts, or a blackguard roaring for twopence at a turn-pike.——I send you a sonnet which this faithful Lady had made for the nuptials of one of her relations in which she swears the most *alarm-ing constancey* to her husband—is not this good? you may suppose my *face* when she showed it to me—I could not help laughing—one of *our* laughs.——All this is very absurd—but you see that I have good morals at bottom.——She is an Equestrian too—but a bore in her rides—for she can't guide her horse—and he runs after mine—and tries to bite him—and then she begins screaming in a high hat and Sky-blue habit—making a most absurd figure—and embarrassing me and both our grooms—who have the devil's own work to keep her from tumbling—or having her clothes torn off by the trees and thickets of the Pine forest.——I fell a little in love with her intimate friend— a certain Geltruda—(that is *Gertrude*) who is very young & seems very well disposed to be perfidious—but alas!—*her* husband is jealous— and the G. also detected me in an illicit squeezing of hands, the consequence of which was that the friend was whisked off to Bologna for a few days—and since her return I have never been able to see her but twice—with a dragon of a mother in law—and a barbarous husband by her side—besides my own dear precious *Amica* —who hates all flirting but her own.—But I have a Priest who be-friends me—and the Gertrude says a good deal with her great black eyes, so that perhaps—but Alas! I mean to give up these things alto-gether.——I have now given you some account of my present state— the Guide-book will tell you about Ravenna—I can't tell how long or short may be my stay—write to me—love me—as ever

yrs. most affectly.

B

P.S.—*This* affair is *not* in the least expensive—being all in the wealthy line—but troublesome—for the lady is imperious—and exigeante—however there are hopes that we may quarrel—when we do you shall hear

[In margin of printed sonnet enclosed]

Ask Hobhouse to translate this to you—and tell him the reason.———

[TO JOHN CAM HOBHOUSE]   *Ravenna. July 30th. 1819*

Dear Hobhouse—Your last letter was of the beginning of June— how is it with you? are you slain by Major Cartwright?—or ill of a quinsey? or are you writing a pamphlet in rejoinder to Erskine?[1] I understand that a tailor and you are amongst the most strenuous writers in favour of the *measures* taken by the reformers;—I some- times get a glimpse of your speeches with the names of the tavern and company—in a stray newspaper—Galignani—or the Lugano Gazette [—] there is Mr. *Bicker*-steth[2]—the man-midwife—and several other worthies of the like Calibre—"there never was a set of more amicable officers"—as Major Sturgeon says[3]—pray let me hear how you go on. —My Sister writes to me that "Scrope looks ill and out of Spirits" and has not his wonted air of Prosperity—and that she fears his pursuits have not had all their former success.—Is it even so? I suppose there is no knowing, and that the only way in which his friends will be apprized will be by some confounded thing or other happening to him.—He has not written to me since the Winter, in last year's last month,— what is he about!—The Dougal Creature has written to mention the pact with Murray—if *it* (i.e. D. J. fails) the Sum is too much, if it succeeds it is too little by five hundred guineas in coin or ingots.— Donny Johnny will either succeed greatly—or tumble flatly—there will be no medium—at least I think not.—Galignani announces Mazeppa as stamped—but I know nothing and hear nothing of it or of Juan, what is become of the ode to Venice? I am endeavouring here— to get a transcript of Benvenuto da Imola's Latin commentary on

---

[1] Hobhouse did actually write a pamphlet later against Lord Erskine which landed him in Newgate. See Jan. 2, 1820, to Moore.

[2] Henry Bickersteth, a barrister with advanced and liberal views, was one of Hobhouse's friends among the Radical Reformers. Byron, with little knowledge of the state of politics in England at the time, was inclined to judge him as he did the rabble-rouser "orator" Hunt and the "physical force" radicals like Arthur Thistlewood.

[3] Samuel Foote, *the Mayor of Garratt*, Act I: "there never was a set of more amiable officers."

Dante[4]—never yet stamped—quite "inedita";—They promise it me.
—I have been swimming in the Adriatic, and cantering through
Boccaccio's Pinery—it is a fine forest—"so full of pastime and
prodigality"[5]—and I have persuaded my Contessa to put a side-
saddle upon a pony of her Sposo's and we ride together—She in a hat
shaped like Punch's and the Merry Mrs. Ford's of Windsor—and a
Sky-blue tiffany riding habit—like the Ghost of Prologue's Grandmother;—I bought an English ⟨steed⟩ horse of Capt. Fyler some
time ago (which with my others is here) and he is a famous leaper, and
my amusement has been to make her Groom on a huge Coach-horse
follow me over certain ditches and drain-lets, an operation in which he
is considerably incommoded by a pair of Jack-boots—as well as by the
novelty of the ⟨operation⟩ undertaking.—You would like the forest—
it reaches from here to Rimini.—I have been here these two months—
and hitherto all hath *gone on well*—with the usual exception of some
"Gelosie" which are the fault of the climate and of the conjunction of
two such capricious people as the Guiccioli and the Inglese——but
here hath been no stabbing nor drugging of possets—the last person
assassinated here was the Commissary of Police three months ago—
they *kilt* him from an alley—one evening—but he is recovering from
the slugs with which they sprinkled him from an "Archibugia" that
shot him round a Corner—like the Irishman's Gun.—He—and
Manzoni who was stabbed dead—going to the theatre at Forli—not
long before—are the only recent instances.—But it is the custom of
the Country—and not much worse than duelling—where one under-
takes at a certain personal risk of a more open nature—to get rid of a
disagreeable person—who is injurious—or inconvenient, and if such
people become insupportable—what is to be done?—It is give and
take,—like every thing else—you run the same risk—and they run
the same risk;—it has the same object with duelling—but adopts a
different means.—As to the trash about *honour*—that is all stuff—a
man offends—you want to kill him—this is amiable and natural—but
how?—the natural mode is obvious—but the artificial varies according
to education.——I am taking the Generous side of the question—
seeing I am much more exposed here to become the patient than the
Agent of such an experiment;—I know but one man whom I should be

[4] Benevenuto Rambaldi of Imola (d. circa 1390), a disciple of Boccaccio, wrote
a popular Latin commentary on Dante's *Commedia* which was used as notes in
many MSS. Parts of it were printed in Muratori's *Antiquitates Italicae*, but the
whole of it was not published until 1887.
[5] Unidentified.

tempted to put to rest[6]—and he is not an Italian nor in Italy—and therefore I trust that he wont pass through Romagna during my sojourn—*because* 'gin he did—there is no saying what the fashionable facilities might induce a vindictive gentleman to meditate;—besides—there are injuries where the balance is so greatly against the offender—that you are not to risk a life—against his—(excepting always the *law* which is originally a convention) but to trample as [you] would on any other venomous animal.—To return to Dante (where you will find a pretty eulogy on revenge) his tomb is within fifty yards of my "locanda", the effigy & tombstone well preserved, but the outside is a mere modern Cupola.——The house flanking this house but divided by a street is said to have been inhabited by him—but that is mere *Say-so* as far as I can make out—it is old enough to have been inhabited by Honorius for that matter.—The Polentani his patrons are buried in a Church behind his Grave—but there are no tidings nor tradition of Francesca—here or at Rimini—except the mere fact—which to be sure is a thumper—as they were actually killed in it.—Hunt made a devil of a mistake about

"Old Ravenna's clear shown towers and bay"

there has been no bay nor Sea within five miles since long before the time of the Exarchs, and as to "clear-shown" the town lies so low that you must be close upon it before it is seen at all—and then there is no comprehensive view unless you climb the steeple.—I was introduced to the Cardinal Legate—a fine old boy,—and I might have known all the world—but I prefer a private life, and have lived almost entirely with my paramour—her husband—*his* son by a former marriage—and her father—with her Confidante "in white linen" a very pretty woman, noble also as her friend, called Gertrude Vicari—who has however a jealous husband—"a strange Centaur" as Gibbon calls a philosophical Theologian.—But he is a profane historian.—I also fell in love with a promised bride named Ursula—Something—one of the prettiest creatures I ever saw—but her barbarous mother—suspecting her of smiling from a window upon me—has watched her ever since—and she won't be married till September—so there be no hopes—however I am trying my best—with a priest (*not* to marry me you may believe) and others to bring about some-at.——A precious epistle of Gossip this is.——But these are all I can say of "fatti miei"—I have had the G[uiccioli] (whom I came for) in any case—and what more I can get

---

6 Henry Brougham.

I know not—but will try—it is much better for beauty than Lombardy.
——Canova is now in the Austrian states—

ever &c. very truly yrs.

B

P.S. July 31st.—Considerable *lusinghe* that Ursula will be obtained —*She* being well disposed.——Do you know what happened to Lord Kinnaird at Faenza?—when he went back to Milan—they stopped his Carriage to search for the Bianchi (the dancer he keeps) thinking she had broke her engagement for the *fair* of Sinigaglia to return into Lombardy—Lege Dick Lege, but it was not so—She is dancing at the Fair. An old Woman at Rome reading Boccaccio exclaimed "I wish to God that this was saying one's prayers."——

[TO ALEXANDER SCOTT]   *Ravenna. July 31st. 1819*

Dear Scottin,—You were right—I *will* consider first, but the truth is I *do* like Terra firma a little after the long absence from it—as to the G[uiccioli]—She has not much to do with my resolution—as I have something besides her on my hands—and in my eye—but I shall say nothing more now—till I am more sure.——There are better things in that line—in this part—of the world—than at Venice—besides— like the preserve of a Manor—this part has not yet been shot over. ——It would be very unpleasant to me that you should quit Venice without our meeting again—I would almost take a flight there again on purpose to see you—rather than this should be—and arrange my concerns in person—where do you think of going? how are the Cows? —You are wrong about H[oppner]'s letter.—There was nothing in it —to offend *her*—but me.—For instance telling her that *She* would be the *planter*—that *She* was voluble—what is all this?—if I had told her that she was called and thought an absurd woman (which I carefully avoided) *there* indeed I should have been truly Hoppnerian.——You may tell a man that he is thought libertine—profligate—a villain—but not that his nose want's blowing—or that his neckcloth is ill tied.— Suppose you were to say to that Coxcomb Mengaldo that he was dangerous—disaffected—a severe disciplinarian in his regiment—that he had ill used Carlotta Aglietti[1]—that he had been guilty of atrocities in his retreat from *Moscow* (*Moscow* would sweeten him) he would affect but feel nothing—but if you told him his father sold eggs not very

---

[1] Mengaldo's unsuccessful suit of Dr. Aglietti's daughter had driven him to distraction and had made him a little ridiculous.

fresh—he would be wroth to a degree.— —I do not know whether I made myself understood—but it is in the little nooks of Character— where your true tormentors play the Mosquito and the Gadfly—and where such fellows as M[engaldo] & H[oppner] distil their little drop of venom.—Now I do maintain that I have always avoided this— which is never necessary—unless in cases where your fame or fortunes may be seriously attacked.—I could have driven Hoppner mad—had I ever told him a 10000th. part of the things that I know—and the buffone Cavaliere little less so—but I resisted the pettiness of repaying them in kind.—In future I shall be less kind to them—and you may tell Mengaldo so—a little tittle tattle boasting parvenu—who never could forgive one's beating him in his own narrow field—as we did hollow besides in the wider one of waters.—I wish you had heard the account he had left at Ferrara of the Swimming-match—*you* were sunk & omit- ted altogether—and *he* had passed the Rialto—and was only beaten by me by some accident!—But we knew him to be a liar before—but would think the complete dressing we both gave him in the swimming-match would have silenced him on that score.— —I could [not?] help saying on hearing it—to his friends, "this story is Mengaldo all over." I enclose a letter which I beg you to forward to Siri & Willhalm—I wish them to remit the 23 francs to Genoa, as I know not how.— —I have as yet decided nothing—but have a general idea of quitting Venice altogether—particularly if I can get this other Girl.—But in the mean time the establishment may remain as it is—except that I wish they enquire on what terms the landlords of the houses would take them back again supposing me to be so disposed.— —Edgecombe may have a hint of my thoughts, and Mr. Dorville also.— —As to the "[baron?] fottuto"2—as he is not the only thing "fottuto" (by me) in his family— I overlook that for his wife's sake. What *can* he do—unless I buy or sell with him?—and I don't mean to do either—if *She plants*—let her. "There are as good fish in the Sea as ever came out of it." There is a Scotch proverb for you—hot as haggis.—By the way how many *ts* are there in "fottuto" one or two?—"fotuto"—eh? Continue to write— remember me to Missiaglia and *Peppi*—& Marina—and all the Conversazioners—I regret to have missed Canova—at Venice having missed him also at Rome—and in London.— —Believe me

ever & truly yrs. affectly.
Byron

2 *Fottuto*—French *foutre*, an epithet of disgust or of imprecation, as in "mondo fottuto", or "porco fottuto".

Address yr. answer to Venice however

Dear Sir—Don't be alarmed.—You will see me defend myself gaily—that is—if I happen to be in Spirits—and by *Spirits* I don't mean your meaning of the word—but the spirit of a bull-dog when pinched—or a bull when pinned—it is then that they make best sport—and as my Sensations under an attack are probably a happy compound of the united energies of those amiable animals—you may perhaps see what Marrall calls "rare sport"[1]—and some good tossing and goring in the course of the controversy.—But I must be in the right cue first —and I doubt I am almost too far off to be in a sufficient fury for the purpose—and then I have effeminated and enervated myself with love and the summer in these last two months.—I wrote to Mr. Hobhouse the other day—and foretold that Juan would either fall entirely or succeed completely—there will be no medium—appearances are not favourable—but as you write the day after publication—it can hardly be decided what opinion will predominate.—You seem in a fright— and doubtless with cause.—Come what may—I never will flatter the Million's canting in any shape—circumstances may or may not have placed me at times in a situation to lead the public opinion—but the public opinion—never led nor ever shall lead me.—I will not sit on "a degraded throne" so pray put Messrs. Southey—or Sotheby— or Tom Moore—or Horace Twiss upon it—they will all of them be transported with their coronation.———You have bought Harlow's drawings[2] of Margarita and me rather dear methinks—but since you desire the story of Margarita Cogni—you shall be told it—though it may be lengthy.———Her face is of the fine Venetian cast of the old Time—and her figure though perhaps too tall not less fine—taken altogether in the national dress.———In the summer of 1817, Hobhouse and myself were sauntering on horseback along the Brenta one evening—when amongst a group of peasants we remarked two girls as the prettiest we had seen for some time.—About this period there had been great distress in the country—and I had a little relieved some of the people.—Generosity makes a great figure at very little cost in Venetian livres—and mine had probably been exaggerated—as an

---

[1] When Sir Giles Overreach curses his daughter in Massinger's *New Way to Pay Old Debts* (Act V, scene 1), Marrall asks: "Is't not brave sport?"

[2] George Henry Harlow, who had painted a portrait of Byron in England in 1815, was in Venice in 1818, and made drawings of the poet and his mistress which Murray bought when the artist returned to England. Margarita Cogni looks very demure in her portrait. Harlow's drawing of Byron shows him with long hair.

Englishman's——Whether they remarked us looking at them or no—
I know not—but one of them called out to me in Venetian—"Why do
not you who relieve others—think of us also?"—I turned round and
answered her—"Cara—tu sei troppo bella e giovane per aver'
bisogno del' soccorso mio"—she answered—["] if you saw my hut and
my food—you would not say so["]—All this passed half jestingly—
and I saw no more of her for some days—A few evenings after—we
met with these two girls again—and they addressed us more seriously
—assuring us of the truth of their statement.—They were cousins—
Margarita married—the other single.—As I doubted still of the
circumstances—I took the business up in a different light—and made an
appointment with them for the next evening.—Hobhouse had taken a
fancy to the single lady—who was much shorter—in stature—but a
very pretty girl also.——They came attended by a third woman—
who was cursedly in the way—and Hobhouse's charmer took fright
(I don't mean at Hobhouse but at not being married—for here no
woman will do anything under adultery), and flew off—and mine made
some bother—at the propositions—and wished to consider of them.—
I told her "if you really are in want I will relieve you without any
conditions whatever—and you may make love with me or no just as
you please—*that* shall make no difference—but if you are not in
absolute necessity—this is naturally a rendezvous—and I presumed
that you understood this—when you made the appointment".——She
said that she had no objection to make love with me—as she was
married—and all married women did it—but that her husband (a
baker) was somewhat ferocious—and would do her a mischief.—In
short—in a few evenings we arranged our affairs—and for two years—
in the course of which I had ⟨almost two⟩ more women than I can
count or recount—she was the only one who preserved over me an
ascendancy—which was often disputed & never impaired.—As she
herself used to say publicly—"It don't matter—he may have five
hundred—but he will always come back to me".——The reasons of
this were firstly—her person—very dark—tall—the Venetian face—
very fine black eyes—and certain other qualities which need not be
mentioned.—She was two & twenty years old—and never having had
children—had not spoilt her figure—nor *anything else*—which is I
assure you—a great desideration in a hot climate where they grow
relaxed and doughy and *flumpity* in a short time after breeding.——
She was besides a thorough Venetian in her dialect—in her thoughts—
in her countenance—in every thing—with all their naïveté and
Pantaloon humour.—Besides she could neither read nor write—and

could not plague me with letters—except twice that she paid sixpence to a public scribe under the piazza—to make a letter for her—upon some occasion when I was ill and could not see her.——In other respects she was somewhat fierce and "prepotente" that is—overbearing—and used to walk in whenever it suited her—with no very great regard to time, place, nor persons—and if she found any women in her way she knocked them down.—When I first knew her I was in "relazione" (liaison) with la Signora Segati—who was silly enough one evening at Dolo—accompanied by some of her female friends—to threaten her—for the Gossips of the Villeggiatura—had already found out by the neighing of my horse one evening—that I used to "ride late in the night" to meet the Fornarina.——Margarita threw back her veil (fazziolo) and replied in very explicit Venetian—"*You* are *not* his *wife*: *I* am *not* his *wife*—*you* are his Donna—and *I* am his *donna*—*your* husband is a cuckold—and mine is another;—for the rest, what *right* have you to reproach me?—if he prefers what is mine—to what is yours—is it my fault? if you wish to secure him—tie him to your petticoat-string—but do not think to speak to me without a reply because you happen to be richer than I am."——Having delivered this pretty piece of eloquence (which I translate as it was related to me by a byestander) she went on her way—leaving a numerous audience with Madame Segati—to ponder at her leisure on the dialogue between them.—When I came to Venice for the Winter she followed:—I never had any regular *liaison* with her—but whenever she came I never allowed any other connection to interfere with her—and as she found herself out to be a favourite she came pretty often.—But She had inordinate Self-love—and was not tolerant of other women—except of the Segati—who was as she said my regular "Amica"—so that I being at that time somewhat promiscuous—there was great confusion—and demolition of head dresses and handkerchiefs—and sometimes my servants in "redding the fray"[3] between her and other feminine persons—received more knocks than acknowledgements for their peaceful endeavours.——At the "Cavalchina" the masqued ball on the last night of the Carnival—where all the World goes—she snatched off the mask of Madame Contarini—a lady noble by birth—and decent in conduct—for no other reason but because she happened to be leaning on my arm.—You may suppose what a cursed noise this made—but this is only one of her pranks.—At last she quarrelled with her husband—and one evening ran away to my house.—I told her this would not do—she said she would lie in the street but not go back to

[3] *Waverley*, Chapter LIV.

him—that he beat her (the gentle tigress) spent her money—and scandalously neglected his Oven. As it was Midnight—I let her stay—and next day there was no moving her at all.———Her husband came roaring & crying—& entreating her to come back, *not* She!—He then applied to the Police—and they applied to me—I told them and her husband to *take* her—I did not want her—she had come and I could not fling her out of the window—but they might conduct her through that or the door if they chose it———She went before the Commissary—but was obliged to return with that "becco Ettico" (consumptive cuckold), as she called the *poor* man who had a Ptisick.—In a few days she ran away again.—After a precious piece of work she fixed herself in my house—really & truly without my consent—but owing to my indolence —and not being able to keep my countenance—for if I began in a rage she always finished by making me laugh with some Venetian panta-loonery or other—and the Gipsy knew this well enough—as well as her other powers of persuasion—and exerted them with the usual tact and success of all She-things—high and low—they are all alike for that.—Madame Benzone also took her under her protection—and then her head turned.—She was always in extremes either crying or laughing—and so fierce when angered that she was the terror of men women and children—for she had the strength of an Amazon with the temper of Medea. She was a fine animal—but quite untameable. *I* was the only person that could at all keep her in any order—and when she saw me really angry—(which they tell me is rather a savage sight), she subsided.—But she had a thousand fooleries—in her fazziolo—the dress of the lower orders—she looked beautiful—but alas! she longed for a hat and feathers and all I could say or do (and I said much) could not prevent this travestie.—I put the first into the fire—but I got tired of burning them before she did of buying them—so that she made herself a figure—for they did not at all become her.—Then she would have her gowns with a *tail*—like a lady forsooth—nothing would serve her—but "l'abito colla *coua*", or *cua*, (that is the Venetian for "la *Coda*" the tail or train) and as her cursed pronunciation of the word made me laugh—there was an end of all controversy—and she dragged this diabolical tail after her every where.———In the mean time she beat the women—and stopped my letters.—I found her one day pondering over one—she used to try to find out by their shape whether they were feminine or no—and she used to lament her ignorance—and actually studied her Alphabet—on purpose (as she declared) to open all letters addressed to me and read their contents. ———I must not omit to do justice to her housekeeping qualities—after

195

she came into my house as "donna di governo" the expences were reduced to less than half—and every body did their duty better—the apartments were kept in order—and every thing and every body else except herself.——That she had a sufficient regard for me in her wild way I had many reasons to believe—I will mention one.——In the autumn one day going to the Lido with my Gondoliers—we were overtaken by a heavy Squall and the Gondola put in peril—hats blown away—boat filling—oar lost—tumbling sea—thunder—rain in torrents—night coming—& wind increasing.—On our return—after a tight struggle: I found her on the open steps of the Mocenigo palace on the Grand Canal—with her great black eyes flashing though her tears and the long dark hair which was streaming drenched with rain over her brows & breast;—she was perfectly exposed to the storm—and the wind blowing her hair & dress about her tall thin figure—and the lightning flashing round her—with the waves rolling at her feet—made her look like Medea alighted from her chariot—or the Sibyl of the tempest that was rolling around her—the only living thing within hail at that moment except ourselves.—On seeing me safe—she did not wait to greet me as might be expected—but calling out to me— "Ah! Can' della Madonna xe esto il tempo per andar' al' Lido?" (ah! Dog of the Virgin!—is this a time to go to Lido?) ran into the house— and solaced herself with scolding the boatmen for not foreseeing the "temporale".—I was told by the servants that she had only been prevented from coming in a boat to look after me—by the refusal of all the Gondoliers of the Canal to put out into the harbour in such a moment and that then she sate down on the steps in all the thickest of the Squall—and would neither be removed nor comforted. Her joy at seeing me again—was moderately mixed with ferocity—and gave me the idea of a tigress over her recovered Cubs.———But her reign drew near a close.—She became quite ungovernable some months after—and a concurrence of complaints some true and many false—"a favourite has no friend"—determined me to part with her.—I told her quietly that she must return home—(she had acquired a sufficient provision for herself and mother, &c. in my service,) and She refused to quit the house.—I was firm—and she went—threatening knives and revenge. —I told her—that I had seen knives drawn before her time—and that if she chose to begin—there was a knife—and fork also at her service on the table and that intimidation would not do.—The next day while I was at dinner—she walked in, (having broke open a glass door that led from the hall below to the staircase by way of prologue) and advancing strait up to the table snatched the knife from my hand—cutting me slightly in the thumb in the operation.—Whether she meant to use this against herself or me I know not—probably against neither—but Fletcher seized her by the arms—and disarmed her.—I then called my boatmen—and desired them to get the Gondola ready and conduct her to her own house again—seeing carefully that she did herself no mischief by the way.—She seemed quite quiet and walked down stairs. —I resumed my dinner.—We heard a great noise—I went out—and met them on the staircase—carrying her up stairs.—She had thrown herself into the Canal.—That she intended to destroy herself I do not believe—but when we consider the fear women and men who can't swim have of deep or even of shallow water—(and the Venetians in particular though they live on the waves) and that it was also night— and dark—& very cold—it shows that she had a devilish spirit of some sort within her.—They had got her out without much difficulty or damage except the salt water she had swallowed and the wetting she had undergone.—I foresaw her intention to refix herself, and sent for a Surgeon—enquiring how many hours it would require to restore her from her agitation, and he named the time.—I then said—"I give you that time—and more if you require it—but at the expiration of the prescribed period—if *She* does not leave the house—*I* will".———All my people were consternated—they had always been frightened at her —and were now paralyzed—they wanted me to apply to the police— to guard myself—&c. &c.—like a pack of sniveling servile boobies as they were———I did nothing of the kind—thinking that I might as well end that way as another—besides—I had been used to savage women and knew their ways.—I had her sent home quietly after her recovery —and never saw her since except twice at the opera—at a distance amongst the audience.—She made many attempts to return—but no more violent ones.—And this is the story of Margharita Cogni—as far as it belongs to me.—I forgot to mention that she was very devout —and would cross herself if she heard the prayer-time strike—some- times—when that ceremony did not appear to be much in unison with what she was then about.—She was quick in reply—as for instance;—one day when she had made me very angry with beating somebody or other—I called her a *Cow* (*Cow* in Italian is a sad affront and tantamount to the feminine of dog in English) I called her "Vacca" she turned round—curtsied—and answered "Vacca *tua*— 'Celenza" (i.e. Eccelenza) *your* Cow—please your Excellency.—In short—she was—as I said before—a very fine Animal—of considerable beauty and energy—with many good & several amusing qualities— but wild as a witch—and fierce as a demon.—She used to boast publicly of her ascendancy over me—contrasting it with that of other women—and assigning for it sundry reasons physical and moral which did more credit to her person than her modesty.——True it was that they all tried to get her away—and no one succeeded—till her own absurdity helped them.—Whenever there was a competition, and sometimes—one would be shut in one room and one in another—to prevent battle—she had generally the preference.——

yrs. very truly and affectly
B

P.S.—The Countess G[uiccioli] is much better than she was.—I sent you before leaving Venice—a letter containing the real original sketch—which gave rise to the "Vampire" &c. did you get it?—

[TO HENRY DORVILLE] *Bologna. Aug. 2[22?], 1819*

I wrote some time ago to Edgecombe desiring him to bring my daughter Allegra directly to me at Bologna, and informing him that you would authorize from *me* Messrs. Siri to furnish the necessary sum for her [journey?] . . .

[TO COUNTESS TERESA GUICCIOLI (*a*)]

Ravenna. Ag[ost]o 4º. 1819

Mio Bene,—Ricordati del' ritratto tuo, e del' cuor mio.—Addio.— Qual' momento!—Addio!—

BYRON

[TRANSLATION (*a*)]

Ravenna. August 4th. 1819

My Treasure—Remember your portrait and my heart.— Farewell. What a moment! Farewell![1]

BYRON

---

[1] Teresa was leaving with her husband for his estates near Forlì before going on to Bologna, where Byron was to join them.

Ravenna. 4? Ag[ost]o 1819

Mio Bene—Tu mi rimproveri ingiustamente;—Alessandro e il tuo papa essendo presenti—non potendo io più allora stringerti al mio cuore—ti baciava la mano e m'affretava andare via per non dimostrare un' dolore il quale pur troppo avrebbe manifestato tutta—tutta la verità.—Io ti giuro che ti amo mille volte più, che quando ti conobbi a V[enezia] [—] tu lo sai—tu lo senti,—*pensa*—Amor mio—di *quiei* momenti deliziosi—pericolosi—ma *felici*—in tutti i sensi—non solamente per il piacere più di estatico—che mi diedero, ma pel' pericolo (a cui tu eri esposta) fortunatamente evitato.——Quella sala! quelle camere! le porte aperte! la servitu cosi curiosa e vicina—Ferdinando! le visite!—&c.——quanti ostacoli! ma tutti vinti—è stato il vero trionfo del' Amor—cento volte Vincitore!—Addio—mio solo Bene—mia unica Speranza—Addio—ti bacio instancabilmente di cuore—e sono sempre il tuo

[scrawl for signature]

P.S.—Mandami il biglietto *della tomba di Dante* col' tuo nome sopra. —L'ho veduto sopra la tua tavolina jeri l'altro.—Amami come ti amo.——Per l'indirizzo tutto va bene come istabilito—in caso che io non arrivo a B[ologna] sul' giorno proposto.——Cosa vuole dire l'*a.a.a.*—in quel tuo carissimo libretto?—Non dimenticare mandare da *Imsom* avvisarli consegnare le miei lettere solamente nelle mani della persona che viene da te.——In questo punto ricevo il tuo + ti giuro di non baciare altro che *quella* memoria di te finche ti rivedo.—Addio!—

[TRANSLATION (b)]   *Ravenna, August 4th, 1819*

My Treasure: Your reproaches are unjust;—Alessandro and your father being present—and I not being able then to clasp you to my heart—I kissed your hand and hurried away, so as not to show my suffering, which would only too clearly have revealed the whole, whole truth! I vow that I love you a thousand times more than when I knew you in V[enice]. You know it—you feel it. *Think*, my love, of *those* moments—delicious—dangerous—but—*happy*, in every sense— not only for the pleasure, more than ecstatic, that you gave me, but for the danger (to which you were exposed) that we fortunately escaped. The hall! Those rooms! The open doors! The servants so curious and so near—Ferdinando—the visitors! how many obstacles! But all over-come—it has been the real triumph of Love—a hundred times Victor.

Farewell—my only Treasure—my one Hope. Farewell—I kiss you untiringly from my heart—and am ever yours.

P.S.—Send me the note about *Dante's tomb* with your name in it. I saw it on your little table the day before yesterday,—Love me as I love you.

The address will be as we agreed—in case I do not arrive in B[ologna] on the day suggested.

What does a.a.a. mean in your very dear booklet?

Do not forget to send someone to Imsom[1] to tell him to hand over my letters only to someone sent by you.

I have just received yours. I swear I will kiss nothing but *that* remembrance of you until I see you again. Farewell!

[TO JOHN CAM HOBHOUSE]   *Ravenna. August 4th. 1819*

My dear Hobhouse—I have received yours of the 15th. of July—by which I perceive that Juan is before the public[1]—and at the same time arrived an epistle from Murray of the 16th. in which he seems in a state of perturbation—and he had by his own account taken refuge at Wimbledon from the torrent which was in all its foam against "his little bark" and the larger vessel also—To be sure—*his* (Murray's) is no *Steam-boat*, it won't work against the stream.—Your next letters will probably tell me that the *"pome"* has gone to the devil—in imitation of the last scene of the pantomime of the same name.—*That* can't be holpen—and was to be expected—and had been prophesied by all in the secret—and anticipated by me—I have had my own way—in spite of everybody and am satisfied.——I am surprized and pleased with the news of Dougal's election[2]—and should have had no objection to some of that same "turtle" swallowed on his inauguration—together with the cold punch annexed.—I am glad that *"us* youth" have made our due noise in the world—you and the Dougal have turned out very promising politicians in the honesty line—as well as orators; William Bankes hath made a stupendous traveller—Michael Bruce too is a fine

[1] Christoforo Insom (not Imsom) was Byron's banker in Bologna.

[1] The first two cantos of *Don Juan* were published together by Murray on July 15, 1819, in a quarto edition without the author's or the publisher's name on the title page. Only Murray's printer, Thomas Davidson, attached his name.

[2] Douglas Kinnaird had been elected to Parliament for Bishop's Castle in Shropshire.

fellow—and then there is the "Poeshie du Roi vot' maitre[;]" in short we are a fine batch including Scrope—the most celebrated of the six in his line—in which I hope he flourishes—but of him you have not reported progress.—I wrote to you last week—and will continue now I am in the humour.—Your reception at the theatre must have been gratifying—particularly as it was the consequence and not the contrast of the "self-approving hour".—
September 4th. 1819 Bologna.

Dear Hobhouse—I began this letter a month ago and finish it now—I have heard nothing from you nor from any body since it's date.—

yrs. truly
B

P.S.—Make the Dougal read Spooney's letter and send me Murray's and any body else's money—it don't much matter who's—so that it comes into my lawful possession.—

[TO COUNT ALESSANDRO GUICCIOLI]   *Ravenna August 7th. 1819*

My dear Chevalier,—I write my answer in English to the letter, which I had the honour of receiving from you and your amiable consort, for fear of "*Spropositi*" in Italian. I am very sorry that it will not be in my power to be at Forlì tomorrow Evening—as I must wait for the Post of *Domenica*;—but on *Lunedì* I intend to set out for *Bologna*—where I shall try to discover your Palazzo "Savioli".—My auberge will be the Pellegrino.——I make no apology for troubling you in English which you understand better than I can write in Italian, and even if you did not—I would rather be unintelligible in my own tongue than in yours.——My time has passed in a melancholy manner since your departure.——Ferdinando and I have been riding as usual—and he told me a sad story of Madame's losses—*un' anello*—*una catena*—e *dei quattrini*[1] &c.——I regretted to hear that you had *sospetti* of *Fer*[*dinand*]*o*—about the Scudi which disappeared—surely *he* would be the last person to be guilty of such a thing.——I desire my best respects to the Countess your gentle Consort—and with many thanks for your kind invitation—and in the hope of seeing you at Bologna in a few days believe me to be

very gratefully and affectionately yours
BYRON

[1] A ring, a chain, and some money.

Ravenna. Addi(?) 7 Agosto, 1819

Mio Bene—Ho scritto una risposta in Inglese a *A[lessandro]*—Mi rincresce infinitamente il non rivederti a Forlì—ma ben presto (Lunedi o Martedi) spero esser' giunto a Bologna.—Ti scrivo con qualche timera del' esito di questo biglietto—poiche bisognà che lo fido col' mio Corriere.—Spero pure che la Fortuna non ci abandonerà due amanti in tal' punto.———Dunque tu hai perduto *l'anello*— senza dirmi una sola parola! questo è una diffidenza che mi sorprende e me duole, *io* non ho mai avuto dei misteri con *te*.———Non posso dirti più adesso.—Ti Amo+++++++ m'intendi?—Per noi—si debbono essere pocha croci più sante che queste.———Tu non puoi immaginarti quanto la tua lontananza mi affligge,—sospiro il rivederti,—ma trema credendomi sempre sul' punto di perderti—e ne dubito—poiche quella tua testa è un'enigma—e *cuore tu non hai*. Mi pare vederti nel' atto di leggere queste ultime parole—'*Oh Rabbia!*' come dice il tiranno di nostra comica compagnia—Oime! *non più comica* dopo la tua partenza.—Il teatro [è] divenuto un' deserto—non oso guardare il tuo palco.—Non pensare dunque che dico seriamente che tu non hai del' cuore—tu l'hai—(per gli abiti?) *questo* fu solamente una gentilezza Inglese!—un' scherzo tramontano;—*è la mia vendetta* —non—per *la perdita—del' anello* ma per avermi trattato con poca confidenza tacendo sul' fatto.—Addio——carissimo il mio *Male*—Addio —mio tormento—Addio mio *tutto*—(ma *non tutto* mio!) ti bacio più volte che ti ho mai baciato—e questo (se la Memoria non m'ingonna) dovrebbe essere un'bel' numero, contato dal' principio.—Intanto—tu puoi star sicura di me—del amor mio—e del' poter' tuo.—'Imploro pace.'———Amami—non come ti amo—ciò sarebbe troppo pel' tuo Cuor' gentile—ma come tu ami il tuo *Elmo!*——Addio.—— Ti bacio 1000000 volte di cuore, insaziabilmente.——

Ravenna. August 7th, 1819

My Treasure—I have written an answer in English to A[lessandro]. I am extremely sorry not to see you again in Forlì, but very soon (on Monday or Tuesday) I hope to arrive in Bologna. I am writing in some anxiety as to the fate of this letter—for I must trust it to my Courier. I hope however that Fortune will not forsake two lovers at such a point.

So you have lost the *ring*[1]—without saying a single word to me! This is a lack of trust which surprises and hurts me, who have never made any mysteries with *you*. I cannot say more now. I love you + + + + + + + + +[2] Do you understand me? For us there can be few crosses holier than these.

You cannot imagine how much our separation is distressing me. I long to see you again, but I tremble, believing myself always about to lose you—and I feel anxious—for that head of yours is an enigma—and *you have no heart*. I can see you reading these last words—*"Oh Fury!"* as the tyrant says in our comic plays. Alas! *no longer comic* since your departure. The theatre has become a desert—I dare not look at your box. Don't think that I am saying seriously that you have no heart. You have one—for dress? *This* was only an English compliment; an ultramontane joke. *It is my revenge*—not for the *loss of the ring*, but for showing me little trust, in keeping silence about it.

Farewell, my dearest *Evil*—farewell, my torment—farewell, my *all* (but *not all mine!*) I kiss you more often than I have ever kissed you—and this (if Memory does not deceive me) should be a fine number of times, counting from the beginning. Meanwhile,—you can be sure of me—of my love—and of your power. "I pray for peace". Love me—not as I love you—that would be too much for your kind heart—but as you love your *Elmò*.[3] Farewell. I kiss you 1000000 times with my whole heart, insatiably.

[TO HENRY DORVILLE]   *Ravenna. August 9th. 1819*

Sir—I shall take it as a favour if you will have the goodness to inform Mr. Edgecombe and the *Signorè* (my landladies) that I (having changed my mind) *do not intend quitting or giving up my houses and establishment at present*—and that they and the Servants will continue for the present on the former footing.———I have written to Messrs Siri and Willhalm to advance money for all necessary expences of my household affairs—at requisition authorized by you—during my absence.—I cannot fix a time for my return.—I give you full authority over Mr. Edgecombe—who will be no worse for being

[1] This was a ring which Byron had given to Teresa. To be able to wear it openly, she had contrived to have a priest offer it to Guiccioli as a bargain from a distressed family forced to sell it for a third of its value. The Count bought it for his wife.

[2] These are the same crosses that Byron and Augusta used in their letters to each other. They seem to be symbols of their physical love.

[3] Elmò was Teresa's dog.

203

looked after.—If he is impertinent send him to the right about.—
Excuse the trouble which I give—and may continue to give you—you
will oblige me infinitely by keeping a tight hand over my ragamuffins.
—They are a d—d bad set as ever I sailed with.——Will you address
your answer to me at *Bologna*—for which place I set out the day after
tomorrow. Believe me very truly

yr. obliged & very obedt. Sert.
Byron

P.S.—How is my daughter—? I think of sending for or coming for
her—has she the same Governante?—I hope another.——

[TO ALEXANDER SCOTT]   *Ravenna. August 9th. 1819*

My dear Scott—Either you have *not* received my last letter or you
have made a mistake.—In it you were requested to leave things
houses &c. *as they are*—that is to take no further steps for the present
with the *landladies* of the Palazzo & the Cassini.—I shall keep them on
[—] the Palazzi (not the ladies) and also the Servitors——Unless you
hear to the contrary from me—pray replace things on their former
footing.—I am delighted to hear that you remain at Venice—this is a
reason the more for me to return on purpose to see you.—Tomorrow I
set off for Bologna—address your answer to me there.—*My dama and
I* go on very well together hitherto—*they* are going to Bologna too.
——If there has been no convention made with the Foscarini[1]—& the
Mocenigo—tell them—that I *mean to stay on* (at least for the present)
I perhaps may take a run up for my daughter—but I don't intend to
village ⟨for the present⟩ until the autumn probably.——*I authorize
you to authorize Mr. Dorville to act for me in household affairs as Mr.
Hoppner did* during my *absence.* Need there be more said?——So you
keep a *Cow!! you* a keeper!!! "Cadimus signe vicem probamus frura
sagittis"[2]——I neither lecture nor scold—nor preach—but I *am*
surprized.—In short I can be glad of anything that will tend to
continue our Neighbourhood.——My love to Missiaglia—how is my
daughter Allegra?—

yrs. ever most afft.
Byron

---

[1] Byron's summer house at La Mira was leased from the Foscarini family.

[2] Persius, *Satire* IV, 42: "Caedimus inque vice praebemus crura sagittis."
("We keep smiting by turns and by turns presenting our own legs to the
arrow.")

P.S.—Address to Messrs. Imsom &c. *Bologna*. Pray beg Missiaglia to obtain the enclosed Unguent for *Corns* (I send the advertisement) for me from Paris—I am so plagued with them that I am resolved to try any remedy—quack or no.———

[TO JOHN MURRAY]   *Ravenna. August 9th. 1819*

Dear Sir,—I wrote a long letter in answer to yours of the 16th. July—the other giving you an account of Margharita Cogni—as you wished.—But I omitted to tell you her answer when I reproached her for snatching Madame Contarini's mask at the Cavalchina.—I represented to her that she was a lady of high birth—"una *dama*" &c. —She answered—"se Ella e dama *mi io* son' *Veneziana*"—"If she is a lady—I am a Venetian"—this would have been fine—a hundred years ago—the pride of the nation rising up against the pride of Aristocracy —but Alas! Venice—& her people—and her nobles are alike returning fast to the Ocean—and where there is no independence—there can be no real self-respect.———I believe that I mistook or mistated one of her phrases in my letter—it should have been—"Can' della Madonna— cosa vus' tu? esto non è tempo par andar' a Lido"—I do not remember how I had worded it in my letter—but have a general idea of having blundered.———Talking of blunders—reminds me of Ireland—Ireland of Moore—what is this I see in Galignani—about "Bermuda—Agent —deputy—appeal—attachment &c."[1]—what is the matter? is it anything in which his friends can be of use to him?—Pray inform me.—— Of Don Juan I hear nothing further from *you*—you chicken-hearted— silver-paper Stationer you?—But the papers don't seem so fierce as the letter you sent seemed to anticipate, by their extracts at least in Galignani's Messenger.—I never saw such a set of fellows as you are —and then the pains taken to exculpate the modest publisher—he had remonstrated forsooth!—I will write a preface that *shall* exculpate *you* and Hobhouse &c. *completely*—on that point—but at the same time I will cut you all up (& *you* in particular) like Gourds.—You have no more soul than the Count de Caylus[2] (who assured his friends on his death-bed—that he had none, and that *he* must know better than they— whether he had one or no) and no more blood than a Water-Melon.

[1] Moore was Registrar to the Admiralty in Bermuda. His deputy embezzled money which left Moore liable to claims of 1000 guineas.

[2] Byron had read the story of the Comte de Caylus (1692–1765), who had an aversion to doctors and priests, in Grimm's *Correspondance Littéraire* (Première Partie, tome V, Sept. 1765, p. 11).

——And I see there hath been asterisks—and what Perry used to call "*damned* cutting and slashing."——But—never mind.——I write in haste—tomorrow I set off for Bologna—I write to you with thunder —lighting &c. and all the winds of heaven whistling through my hair —and—the racket of preparation to boot.—My "Mistress dear" who hath "fed my heart upon smiles and wine"[3] for the last two months set off for Bologna with her husband this morning—and it seems that I follow him at three tomorrow morning.—I cannot tell how our romance will end—but it hath gone on hitherto most *erotically*—such perils—and escapes—Juan's are a child's play in comparison.—The fools think that all my *Poeshie* is always allusive to my *own* adventures —I have had at one time or another better—and more extraordinary —and perilous—and pleasant than those any day of the week—if I might tell them—but that must never be.—I hope Mrs. M. has accouched

yrs ever
[Scrawl]

[TO JOHN MURRAY]   *Bologna. August 12th. 1819*

Dear Sir—I do not know how far I may be able to reply to your letter—for I am not very well today.—Last night I went to the representation of Alfieri's Mirra[1]—the two last acts of which threw me into convulsions.—I do not mean by that word—a lady's hysterics— but the agony of reluctant tears—and the choaking shudder which I do not often undergo for fiction.—This is but the second time for anything under reality, the first was on seeing Kean's Sir Giles Overreach.[2] —The worst was that the "*dama*" in whose box I was—went off in the same way—I really believe more from fright—than any other sympathy—at least with the players—but she has been ill—and I have been ill and we are all languid & pathetic this morning—with great expenditure of Sal Volatile.—But to return to your letter of the 23d. of July.——You are right—Gifford is right—Crabbe is right—Hob- house is right—you are all right—and I am all wrong—but do pray let

<hr>

[3] A phrase from Moore's *Irish Melodies*.
[1] Alfieri's play was suggested by Ovid's *Metamorphoses* (Book 10) where Myrrha became the mother of Adonis by her father. The tragedy of Mirra is linked by Alfieri to the vengeance of Venus. Mirra's mother had said her daughter was more beautiful than the goddess, who then fated the daughter to love her father. On confessing her incestuous love Mirra killed herself.
[2] In *A New Way to Pay Old Debts*.

me have that pleasure.—Cut me up root and branch—quarter me in the Quarterly—send round my "disjecti membra poetae" like those of the Levite's Concubine—make—if you will—a spectacle to men and angels—but don't ask me to alter for I can't—I am obstinate and lazy —and there's the truth.—But nevertheless—I will answer your friend C. V.[3] who objects to the quick succession of fun and gravity—as if in that case the gravity did not (in intention at least) heighten the fun.— His metaphor is that "we are never scorched and drenched at the same time!"—Blessings on his experience!—Ask him these questions about "scorching and drenching".—Did he never play at Cricket or walk a mile in hot weather?—did he never spill a dish of tea over his testicles in handing the cup to his charmer to the great shame of his nankeen breeches?—did he never swim in the sea at Noonday with the Sun in his eyes and on his head—which all the foam of ocean could not cool? did he never draw his foot out of a tub of too hot water damning his eyes & his valet's? did he never inject for a Gonorrhea?—or make water through an ulcerated Urethra?—was he ever in a Turkish bath— that marble paradise of sherbet and sodomy?—was he ever in a cauldron of boiling oil like St. John?—or in the sulphureous waves of hell? (where he ought to be for his "scorching and drenching at the same time") did he never tumble into a river or lake fishing—and sit in his wet cloathes in the boat—or on the bank afterwards "scorched and drenched" like a true sportsman?——"Oh for breath to utter"[4] ——but make him my compliments—he is a clever fellow for all that —a very clever fellow.——You ask me for the plan of Donny Johnny —I *have* no plan—I *had* no plan—but I had or have materials—though if like Tony Lumpkin—I am "to be snubbed so when I am in spirits"[5] the poem will be naught—and the poet turn serious again.—If it don't take I will leave it off where it is with all due respect to the Public—but if continued it must be in my own way—you might as well make Hamlet (or Diggory)[6] "act mad" in a strait waistcoat—as trammel my buffoonery—if I am to be a buffoon—their gestures and

[3] Francis Cohen [why Byron used the initials C.V. is not clear], who later took the name of Palgrave, was a scholar specializing in Italian and medieval history. He was a frequent contributor to the *Quarterly Review* and the *Edinburgh Review*. He later translated a passage from the *Cronica* di Sanuto which Byron appended to *Marino Faliero* as historical background for his play.

[4] *Henry IV*, Part I, Act II, scene 4.

[5] *She stoops to Conquer*, Act II. Tony Lumpkin said: "I wish you'd let me and my good alone, then. Snubbing this way when I'm in spirits."

[6] Diggery is a stage-struck servant who proposes to take the part of a madman in Jackman's farce *All the World's a Stage*.

my thoughts would only be pitiably absurd—and ludicrously constrained.—Why Man the Soul of such writing is it's licence?—at least the *liberty* of that *licence* if one likes—*not* that one should abuse it —it is like trial by Jury and Peerage—and the Habeas Corpus—a very fine thing—but chiefly in the *reversion*—because no one wishes to be tried for the mere pleasure of proving his possession of the privilege. ——But a truce with these reflections;—you are too earnest and eager about a work never intended to be serious;—do you suppose that I could have any intention but to giggle and make giggle?—a playful satire with as little poetry as could be helped—was what I meant—and as to the indecency—do pray read in Boswell—what *Johnson* the sullen moralist—says of *Prior* and Paulo Purgante[7]—— Will you get a favour done for me?—*you* can by your Government friends—Croker—Canning—or my old Schoolfellow Peel—and I can't. —Here it is—will you ask them to appoint (*without salary or emolument*) a noble Italian (whom I will name afterwards) Consul or Vice Consul for Ravenna.[8]—He is a man of very large property—noble too—but he wishes to have a British protection in case of changes— Ravenna is near the Sea—he wants *no emolument* whatever;—that his office might be useful—I know—as I lately sent off from Ravenna to Trieste—a poor devil of an English Sailor—who had remained there sick sorry and penniless (having been set ashore in 1814) from the want of any accredited agent able or willing to help him homewards. —Will you get this done?—it will be the greatest favour to me?—if you do—I will then send his name and condition—subject of course to rejection if *not* approved—when known.——I know that in the Levant—you make consuls—and Vice Consuls perpetually—of foreigners—this man is a Patrician and has twelve thousand a year.— His motive is a British protection in case of new Invasions.——Don't you think Croker would do it for us? to be sure *my interest* is rare!!— but perhaps a brother-wit in the Tory line might do a good turn at the request of so harmless and long absent a Whig—particularly as there is no *salary* nor *burthen* of any sort to be annexed to the office.——I can assure you I should look upon it as a great obligation—but Alas! that very circumstance may very probably operate to the contrary— indeed it ought.—But I have at least been an honest and an open

[7] Johnson defended Prior as "a lady's book," when Boswell questioned whether "Paulo Purgante and his Wife" should have been included in Johnson's edition of the *English Poets*. "There is nothing in Prior that will excite to lewdness", Johnson said. (Boswell, *Life of Johnson*, ed. Hill, III, 192.)

[8] See June 22, 1819, to Hoppner, note 1.

enemy.——Amongst your many splendid Government Connections—could not you think you? get our Bibulus[9] made a Consul?—Or make me one that I may make him my Vice.—You may be assured that in case of accidents in Italy—he would be no feeble adjunct—as you would think if you knew his property.——What is all this about Tom Moore? but—why do I ask?—since the state of my own affairs would not permit me to be of use to him—although they are greatly improved since 1816,—and may be—with some more luck—and a little prudence become quite Clear.—It seems his Claimants are *American* merchants. —*There* goes *Nemesis*.—Moore abused America.—It is always thus in the long run.—Time the Avenger.—You have seen every trampler down in turn from Buonaparte to the simplest individuals.——You saw how some were avenged even upon my insignificance; and how in turn Romilly paid for his atrocity.—It is an odd World—but the Watch has its mainspring after all.——So the Prince has been repealing Lord Ed. Fitzgerald's forfeiture[10]—"Ecco un' Sonnetto!"—

To be the father of the fatherless
To stretch the hand from the throne's height and raise
His offspring, who expired in other days
To make thy Sire's Sway by a kingdom less,
This is to be a Monarch, and repress
Envy into unutterable praise,
Dismiss thy Guard, and trust thee to such traits,
For who would lift a hand except to bless?—
Were it not easy, Sir, and is't not sweet
To make thyself beloved? and to be
Omnipotent by Mercy's means? for thus
Thy Sovereignty would grow but more complete,
A Despot thou, and yet thy people free,
And by the Heart not Hand enslaving Us

There you dogs—there's a Sonnet for you—you won't have such as that in a hurray from Mr. Fitzgerald.[11]——You may publish it with my name—an' ye wool—He deserves all praise bad & good—it was a very noble piece of principality.—Would you like an Epigram? ⟨upon a female⟩ a translation.——

If for silver or for gold—
You could melt ten thousand pimples

9 Bibulus was Consul with Julius Caesar in 59 B.C.
10 See Vol. 3, p. 249, note 1.
11 William Thomas Fitzgerald, a poetaster whom Byron had ridiculed in *English Bards and Scotch Reviewers.*

Into half a dozen dimples
Then your face we might behold
Looking doubtless much more smugly
Yet even then 'twould be damned ugly.

This was written on some French-woman, by Rulhières—I believe.—
"And so good morrow t'ye—good Master lieutenant."——

yrs. [scrawl]

[TO DOUGLAS KINNAIRD]   *Bologna. August 19th. 1819*

My dear Douglas—When I left Venice yr. correspondents Siri &
Willhalm instead of giving me a letter of transfer of credit desiring
Messrs Imsom to cash my draughts on *your house* in Pall Mall—thought
proper to desire the drafts to be transmitted through them to England
—making me pay *double* commission—viz—1[st]ly to Imsom—and to
them Siri & Willhalm—without right or moderation.—I wrote to
remonstrate—and enclose their own damned despondent explanation
—in which you will perceive also what they say of your *circular notes*—
which as Sartorini (in your letter of Indication) is no more—have no
negociator here.——Address your answer to Venice—but pray
remedy the defect in some way otherwise I pay twice over for every
sixpence—1 per Cent to Siri—and 1 per Cent to any body else they
choose to appoint while I am junketting.—This seems to me a damned
borough-mongering—oligarchical transaction of Siri & Willhalm—
and I solicit from you as my legislational Attorney—a radical reform.
—Read their letter—it seems to me not respectful to your house.—
At any rate it is of import to me not to be taxed in this way.——If
you like to send me credit or circulars for Murray's note—do.—I hear
nothing of Don Juan—except in two letters from Murray, the first
timid—the second in better spirits.—I know where I am—but know
not whither I am going—and hardly where I have been.—Address to
Venice—which will be head quarters.——It is not impossible that I
may be among you next spring—to look after my childer.——Do you
think there will be a row? civil war or any thing in that line?—because
as how—why then I should make one amongst you—I am a little tired
of this effeminate way of life—and should like "to wink and hold out
mine iron"[1] as Corporal Nym says "thats the humour on't"—I
congratulate the borough of Bishops-castle—on it's return from
rottenness—you are the prepared Charcoal and anti-putrescent or

---

[1] *Henry V*, Act II, scene 1.

(more politely) anti-*septic* sweetener of this maggoty joint of the Borough dead body corporate—I would Hobhouse were as safely moored.—But there be new reformers—there is Sir Wolseley—and Mr. Hunt—and Major Cartwright[2] who hath challenged Hobhouse— who should have wafered him with Mantons.—And so they have shooted Birch of Stockport[3]—"and there never were known such troublesome times especially for *Constables*"———Ask Hobhouse to explain that historical quotation—it is I think in the memoirs of P. P. Clerk of this parish.[4]—Write soon to me.—

yrs. ever

[TO JOHN CAM HOBHOUSE] *Bologna. August 20th. 1819*

My dear Hobhouse—I have not lately had of your news—and shall not reproach you because I think that if you had good to send me you would be the first.—I wrote to you twice or thrice from Ravenna— and now I am at Bologna—address to me however at Venice.—My time has been passed viciously and agreeably—at thirty-one so few years months days hours or minutes remain that "Carpe *diem*" is not enough—I have been obliged to crop even the seconds—for who can trust to *tomorrow*? *tomorrow* quotha? *to—hour—to—minute*——I can *not* repent me (I try very often) so much of any thing I have done—as of any thing I have left undone—alas! I have been but idle—and have the prospect of early decay—without having seized every available instant of our pleasurable year.—This is a bitter thought—and it will be difficult for me ever to recover the despondency into which this idea naturally throws me.—Philosophy would be in vain—let us try action.——In England I see & read of reform "and there never were such troublesome times especially for *Constables*" [;] they have wafered Mr. Birch of Stockport.—There is much of Hunt and Harrison and Sir Charles (Linsey) Woolsey[1]—but we hear nothing of you & Burdett? —The "Venerable Cartwright" too—why did you not shorten that fellow's longevity? I do assure you (though that lust for duelling of which you used to accuse me in the Stevens's Coffeehouse days has

---

2 These were the Radical Reformers of whom Byron disapproved as rabble rousers.

3 Unidentified.

4 Not in Pope's *Memoirs of P. P. Clerk of this Parish.*

1 Sir Charles Wolseley, 7th Baronet (1769–1846) was one of the founders of the radical Hampden Club. He was imprisoned in 1820 on a charge of sedition and conspiracy for his activities as a radical reformer.

long subsided into a moderate desire of killing one's more personal enemies) that I would have Mantoned old Cartwright most readily— I have no notion of an old fool like that drivelling defiance and coughing a challenge at his youngers and his betters—*"solder him up"* as Francis said of his defunct wife.²—And now what do you think of doing? I have two notions—one to visit England in the Spring—the other to go to South America.———Europe is grown decrepit—besides it is all the same thing over again—those fellows are fresh as their world—and fierce as their earthquakes.———Besides I am enamoured of General Paer³—who has proved that my Grandfather spoke truth about the Patagonians⁴—with his Gigantic Country.—Would that the Dougal of Bishop's Castle, would find a purchaser for Rochdale—I would embark (with Fletcher as a breeding beast of burthen) and possess myself of the pinnacle of the Andes—or a spacious plain of unbounded extent in an elegible earthquake situation.—Will my wife always live? will her mother never die? is her father immortal? what are you about? married and settled in the country I suppose by your silence?—

yrs. [scrawl]

P.S.—I hear nothing of Don Juan but in two letters from Murray— the first very tremulous—the second in better spirits.———Of the fate of the "pome" I am quite uncertain, and [do] not anticipate much brilliancy from your silence.—But I do not care—I am as sure as the Archbishop of Grenada⁵—that I never wrote better—and I wish you all better taste—but will not send you any pistoles.——

[TO ALEXANDER SCOTT]   *Bologna. August 22d. 1819*

My dear Scott—When I left Venice my daughter had a Governante —of course I supposed that she had one still.—Let one be obtained

    2 Unidentified.
    3 Unidentified.
    4 Commodore John Byron recorded in his "Journal" (in Hawkesworth's *Voyages*, I, 28) that in passing through the Straits of Magellan they saw natives who were giants, seven to eight feet high. Since no one else (except some of Commodore Byron's companions) ever saw them, this account had been taken for a traveller's tall tale. But in *Blackwood's Edinburgh Magazine* (Vol. V, July, 1819, pp. 431–33), which Byron had undoubtedly seen, there was a note on Patagonia in which it was said that a lieutenant of the navy (unnamed) recently returned from a voyage there reported seeing some natives of enormous size, and particularly two chiefs who measured eight feet in height.
    5 In *Gil Blas*.

(but not [that?] foolish mad woman Mrs. Edgecombe on any account) and let Allegra be sent accompanied by Edgecombe the moment this is received.—You need not be alarmed about the "Dama"—I wish to see my child—& have her with *me*—now that Hoppner is no longer in Venice and her being with me will not prevent my return (sooner or later according to circumstances) for to return to Venice is of course my intention & indeed obligation, to take my effects and settle about my books &c.——I have received the enclosed letter from the Advocate Castelli—I desired Edgecombe long ago to make him take possession of Merryweather's effects[1]—and I desire him again to proceed in the proper legal manner.—The Scoundrel has had full time and deserves no compassion for his infamous ingratitude.——I send this by express—that Allegra may set out without loss of time—you can surely find a proper woman to accompany her.—And Edgecombe must come to[o].—Messrs Siri will advance the sum requisite—Mr. Dorville will receive also & pay Castelli—tell Siri I desired Imsom to remit by last post the receipt of the Circular note.—I write in great haste—we may probably meet again soon—do not be alarmed about the G[uiccioli]'s—there is no peril of them.——If there is any thing to send—it can be sent at the same time—anything from Missiaglia.—[four lines crossed out]

yrs. ever most truly
BYRON

P.S.—I hope all the drawers were *re*-locked—as I have papers and Cloathes &c. in them.——
Will you send a large bottle of *Magnesia* which Fletcher says *is on the table*—(that is *if* it be on the table)—I have not sent the key not wishing the drawers to be reopened.

[TO JOHN CAM HOBHOUSE]   *Bologna. August 23d. 1819*

My dear Hobhouse—I have received a letter from Murray containing the "British review's" eleventh article.[1]—Had you any

---

[1] Francis Merryweather, an Englishman with a produce shop in Venice, had served Byron in various ways (he had brought Allegra and her nurse from Milan to Venice in May, 1818). Byron had been generous with him and loaned him 600 lire when he was in trouble. But some unexplained "ingratitude" caused him to sue the tradesman and charge him with some criminal offence.

[1] The *British Review*, a periodical with Tory and Evangelical views, was edited by Willian Roberts (1767-1849). In reviewing *Don Juan*, Roberts had taken seriously Byron's playful accusation "I've bribed My Grandmother's Review,— the British!" (*Don Juan*, I, 209)

conception of a man's tumbling into such a trap as Roberts has done? why it is precisely what he was wished to do.—I have enclosed an epistle for publication with a queer signature (to Murray who should keep the anonymous still about D Juan) in answer to Roberts[2]— which pray approve if you can—it is written in an evening & morning in haste—with ill health & worse nerves.—I am so bilious—that I nearly lose my head—and so nervous that I cry for nothing—at least today I burst into tears all alone by myself over a cistern of Gold fishes—which are not pathetic animals.[3]—I can assure you it is not Mr. Roberts or any of his crew that can affect me;—but I have been excited—and agitated and exhausted mentally and bodily all this summer—till I really sometimes begin to think not only "that I shall die at top first"[4]—but that the moment is not very remote.—I have had no particular cause of grief—except the usual accompaniments of all unlawful passions;—I have to do with a woman rendered perfectly disinterested by her situation in life—and young and amiable and pretty—in short as good and at least as attractive as anything of the sex can be with all the advantages and disadvantages of being scarcely twenty years old—and only two out of her Romagnuolo Convent at Faenza.———But I feel & I feel it bitterly—that a man should not consume his life at the side and on the bosom—of a woman—and a stranger—that even the recompense and it is much—is not enough— and that this Cisisbean existence is to be condemned.—But I have neither the strength of mind to break my chain, nor the insensibility which would deaden it's weight.—I cannot tell what will become of me—to leave or to be left would at present drive me quite out of my senses—and yet to what have I conducted myself?—I have luckily or unluckily no ambition left—it would be better if I had—it would at least awake me—whereas at present I merely start in my sleep.——I think I wrote to you last week—but really (Like Lord Grizzle)[5] cannot positively tell.—Why don't you write, pray do—never mind "Don

2 Byron's "Letter to the Editor of 'My Grandmother's Review' ", signed "Wortley Clutterbuck", like Swift's Partridge-Bickerstaff papers, set out with mock seriousness to prove that Roberts had actually accepted a bribe and then had not praised Byron's work. The "Letter" was published in the first number of *The Liberal*.

3 Teresa had gone to the country for a few days with her husband and Byron was disconsolate.

4 Byron frequently quoted Swift's premonition.

5 In *Tom Thumb*, a burlesque Opera, altered from Fielding by Kane O'Hara, Act I, scene 3.

Juan"—let him tumble—and let me too—like Jack and Gill.——
Write—and believe me—as long as I can keep my sanity

ever yrs. most truly & affectly.

B

Bologna. August 23d. 1819

Dear Sir—I send you a letter to Roberts signed "Wortley Clutter-buck"—which you may publish in what form you please in answer to his article.—I have had many proofs of man's absurdity but he beats all, in folly.—Why the Wolf in sheep's cloathing has tumbled into the very trap.—We'll strip him.—The letter is written in great haste and amidst a thousand vexations.—[Your] letter only came yesterday—so that there is no time to polish—the post [goes] out tomorrow.—The date is "Little Pidlington"—Let Hobhouse correct the proofs—he knows & can read the handwriting.——Continue to keep the *anonymous* about "Juan"—it helps us to fight against overwhelming numbers.—I have a thousand distractions—at present—so excuse haste—and wonder I can act or write at all—answer by post as usual

yrs. [scrawl]

P.S.—If I had had time and been quieter & nearer—I would have cut him to hash—but as it is—you can judge for yourselves.—

[TO COUNTESS TERESA GUICCIOLI]   *Bologna. August 23d. 1819*

My dearest Teresa—I have read this book[1] in your garden;—my Love—you were absent—or I could not have read it.—It is a favourite book of yours—and the writer was a friend of mine.—You will not understand these English words—and *others* will not understand them —which is the reason I have not scribbled them in Italian—but you will recognize the hand-writing of him who passionately loved you— and you will divine that over a book which was yours—he could only think of love. In *that word* beautiful in all languages—but most so in yours—*Amor* mio—is comprized my existence here and hereafter.——

[1] The book was Madame de Staël's *Corinne* (in Italian), now in the Biblioteca Classense in Ravenna.

I feel that I exist here—and I fear that I shall exist hereafter—to *what* purpose—you will decide—my destiny rests with you—& you are a woman [nineteen?]² years of age—and two years out of a Convent.— —I wish that you had staid there with all my heart—or at least that I had never met you in your married state.—but all this is too late—I love you—and you love me—at least you *say* so—and act as if you *did* so—which last is a great consolation in all events.—But *I* more than love you—and cannot cease to love you.—Think of me sometimes when the Alps and the Ocean divide us—but they never will—unless you wish it.

BN

[TO JOHN MURRAY]   *Bologna. August 24th. 1819*

Dear Sir—I wrote to you by last post—enclosing a buffooning letter for publication addressed to the buffoon Roberts—who has thought proper to tie a cannister to his own tail.—It was written off hand—and in the midst of circumstances not very favourable to facetiousness—so that there may perhaps be more bitterness than enough for that sort of small acid punch.—You will tell me.—Keep the *anonymous* in every case—it helps what fun there may be—but if the matter grows serious about *Don Juan* and you feel *yourself* in a scrape—or *me* either—*own that I am the author*. I will never *shrink*— and if *you* do—I can always answer you in the question of Guatimozin to his minister—each being on his own coals.¹—I wish that I had been in better spirits, but I am out of sorts.—out of nerves—and now and then—(I begin to fear) out of my senses.———All this Italy has done for me—and not England—I defy all of you & your climate to boot to make me mad.———But if ever I do really become a Bedlamite—and wear a strait waistcoat—let me be brought back among you—your people will then be proper compagny.———I assure you what I here say and feel has nothing to do with England—either in a literary or personal point of view.—All my present pleasures or plagues are as Italian as the Opera.—And after all they are but trifles—for all this arises from my "dama's" being in the country for three days (at

---

² Teresa tried to change "[nineteen?] years" to "seventeen".
¹ Guatimozin, the Aztec chief, was being tortured along with one of his followers by Cortez to make them reveal the location of the royal treasure. When his companion was weakening, Guatimozin checked him by asking: "Am I now reposing on a bed of flowers?" (Robertson, *History of America*, II, 126–127)

Capo-fiume) but as I could never live for but one human being at a time (and I assure you *that one* has never yet been *myself*—as you may know by the consequences, for the *Selfish* are *successful* in life) I feel alone and unhappy.——I have sent for my daughter from Venice,— and I ride daily;—and walk in a Garden under a purple canopy of grapes—and sit by a fountain—and talk with the Gardener of his toils which seem greater than Adam's—and with his wife—and with his Son's wife—who is the youngest of the party and I think—talks best of the three.—Then I revisit the Campo Santo—and my old friend the Sexton has two but *one* the prettiest daughter imaginable—and I amuse myself with contrasting her beautiful and innocent face of fifteen—with the skulls with which he has peopled several cells—and particularly with that of one skull dated 1766—which was once covered (the tradition goes) by the most lovely features of Bologna—noble— and rich.—When I look at these—and at this girl—when I think of what *they were*—and what *she* must be—why then my dear Murray— I won't shock you by saying what I think.——It is little matter what becomes of us "bearded men" but I don't like the notion of a beautiful woman's lasting less than a beautiful tree—than her own picture— her own shadow—which won't change so to the Sun—as her face to the mirror.——I must leave off—for my head aches consumedly—I have never been quite well since the night of the representation of Alfieri's Mirra—a fortnight ago.—

yrs. ever
B

[TO DOUGLAS KINNAIRD] *Bologna [August 27?] postmark Sept. 7, 1819*

[Fragment]

Do let me know what there will be likely to be done—that one may lend a hand.—A revolutionary commission into Leicestershire would just suit me—the patriots should have a faithful account of Lady Noel's cattle—corn—and coach-horses—&c. &c. what colour is our cockade to be—and our uniform?—[If] mine be a "Charge of horse"[1] [I] shall rub up my broad-sword exercise—in which I was really a

---

[1] Compare *Henry IV*, Part 1, Act II, scene 4: "I'll procure the fat rogue a charge of foot."

proficient—ask *old Angelo*[2]—if I did not cut his arms and elbows about rarely? during our practice in Albany.—Pray write—and Address to Venice.—

yrs. [scrawl]

[TO ALEXANDER SCOTT]   *Bologna. August 28th. 1819*

My dear Scott—I sent an express last Sunday—to hasten my daughter's departure. Did he arrive?—I must have her sent immediately with or *without* a Governante or *Edgecombe* shall instantly quit my service.—Do not let him delay *one moment more*—as I may leave Bologna in ten days or twelve at furthest.—I return to Ravenna—for the present.——Send anything from Missiaglia that may be arrived for me—

yrs ever & truly in haste
BYRON

[TO HENRY DORVILLE]   *Bologna. August 28th. 1819*

Dear Sir,—I sent an express last week to hasten the arrival of Allegra—who is not yet come.—If Edgecombe does not bring her directly—with or *without* a Governante—for I can have no further delays—you will have the goodness to dismiss him from my service. ——I wish her here instantly—as I now return to Ravenna—shortly. ——Pray excuse haste and believe me

very truly yr. obliged & very obedt. Sert.
BYRON

P.S.—I really must have the Child sent instantly—it is now more than a fortnight since I transmitted the order.——

[TO JOHN MURRAY]   *Bologna. August 29th. 1819*

Dear Sir—I have been in a rage these two days and am still bilious therefrom.—You shall hear. A Captain of Dragoons—Ostheid—

---

[2] Henry Angelo, the fencing master, from whom Byron took lessons while he was at Cambridge and afterwards.

Hanoverian by birth—in the Papal troops at present—whom I had obliged by a loan when nobody would lend him a Paul—recommended a horse to me on sale by a Lieutenant Rossi—an officer who unites the sale of cattle to the purchase of men.——I bought it.—The next day on shoeing the horse—we discovered the *thrush*—the animal being warranted sound.—I sent to reclaim the contract, and the money— The Lieutenant desired to speak with me in person.—I consented.— He came.—It was his own particular request.——He began a story.— I asked him if he would return the money.—He said no—but he would exchange.—He asked an exorbitant price for his other horses.—I told him that he was a thief.—He said he was an *officer* & a man of honour —and pulled out a Parmesan passport signed by General Count Neipperg.[1]—I answered that as he was an officer I would treat him as such—and that as to his being a Gentleman—he might prove it by returning the money—as for his Parmesan passport—I should have valued it more if it had been a Parmesan Cheese.—He answered in high terms—and said that if it were in the *morning* (it was about eight o Clock in the evening) he would have *satisfaction*.—I then lost my temper.—As for *that* I replied you shall have it directly—it will be *mutual* satisfaction I can assure you—you are a thief and as you say an officer—my pistols are in the next room loaded—take one of the candles examine & make your choice of weapons.—He replied that *pistols* were *English weapons—he* always fought with the *Sword.*—I told him that I was able to accommodate him, having three regimental swords in a drawer near us—and he might take the longest and put himself on guard.—All this passed in presence of a third person.—— He then said *No* but tomorrow morning he would give me the meeting at any time or place.—I answered that it was not usual to appoint meetings in the presence of witnesses—and that we had best speak man to man—& fix time and instruments.—But as the Man present was leaving the room—the Lieutenant Rossi—before he could shut the door after him—ran out roaring "help and murder" most lustily and fell into a sort of hysteric in the arms of about fifty people, who all saw that I had no weapon of any sort or kind about me, and followed him asking what the devil was the matter with him.—Nothing would do—he ran away without his hat, & went to bed ill of the fright.—He then tried his complaint at the police—which dismissed it as frivolous.

[1] Adam Albert, Comte de Neipperg (1771–1828), distinguished himself in the Austrian service during the Napoleonic wars, and was later Austrian Ambassador at Stockholm.

————He is I believe gone away or going—the horse was warranted —but I believe so worded that the villain will not be obliged to refund according to law.————He endeavoured to raise up an indictment of assault and battery—but as it was in a public inn—in a frequented street—there were too many witnesses to the contrary—and as a military man—he has not cut a martial figure even in the opinion of the Priests.—He ran off in such a hurry that he left his hat and never missed it till he got to his hostel or inn.—The facts are as I tell you—I can assure you he began by "coming Captain Grand over me"—or I should never have thought of trying his "cunning in fence"—but what could I do?—he talked of "honour and satisfaction—and his com- mission"—he produced a military passport—there are severe punish- ments for *regular duels* on the continent, and trifling ones for *rencontres* —so that it is best to fight it out directly—he had robbed—and then wanted to insult me—what could I do?—my patience was gone—and the weapons at hand—fair and equal—besides it was just after dinner when my digestion is bad—& I don't like to be disturbed.—His friend Ostheid—is at Forlì—we shall meet on my way back to Ravenna —the Hanoverian seems the greater rogue of the two—and if my valour does not ooze away like Acres's—"Odds flints and triggers" if it should be a rainy morning and my stomach in disorder—there may be something for the obituary.————Now pray "Sir Lucius do not you look upon me as a very ill used *Gentleman*?["]² ———I send my Lieutenant to match Hobhouse's *Major Cartwright*—"and so good morrow to you good Master Lieutenant".—With regard to other things I will write soon but I have been f—————g incessantly for the last three months and Quarrelling—and fooling—till I can scribble no more.

yrs. [scrawl]

[TO COUNTESS TERESA GUICCIOLI]   [*Settembre, 1819*]

Ti prego non lasciarlo fuori delle mani tue.—Come tu non saprai aprirlo—ho messo il *padre* e il *figlio dentro* la scatola—la mamma è dove era prima.————Ti lo mando perche tu lo commandi—ma mal volentieri;—io non mi fido niente—a cui non conosco—ed assai poco a loro già conosciuti.—Ecco la frutta della esperienza. Addio.

[scrawl]

² *The Rivals*, Act III, scene 4.

I beg you do not let it out of your hands. As you will not know how to open it—I have put the *father* and the *son inside* the box—the mamma is where she was before.[1]——I am sending it to you because you order it—but unwillingly;—I do not trust anyone—whom I do not know—and those whom I already know I trust very little.—That is the fruit of experience. Addio.[2]

[scrawl]

Dear Douglas—It is some time since your Election has permitted you to attend to any concerns (of mine at least) on this side of the Moon.—But instead of a letter I receive *four bonds* to sign—all in good time—there is no hurry—it seems there must be an *English* witness—I know no English—and shall hardly make their acquaintance on purpose.—I enclose you a letter of long ago—from *Hanson & Son*—is it true? no doubt I should like to have been *cleared*—and they say that I might.—Read the letter carefully—and reply to me and to them.—I can't sign bonds for less than *three* years—the very idea gives me a constipation. I have marked the principal passages of Hanson & Spawn's letter.—Remit Murray's Don Juan *money*—it must be nigh due.—Of the Don himself I hear nothing.——Address to Venice—whither I am returning—and where expences incurred & accumulated during my absence may cause me to draw for cash somewhat heavily even at Bologna. Gather together always what monies you can in my name.—*That* is the great point—and any sort of information will be greatly comfortable and gladly received.—I never will write to you except about money.——You remitted me Circulars for twelve hundred last half year—in July—is it not two thousand *five hundred* and *fifteen* per annum?—then there remains fifty pounds—seven pounds ten shillings for half year, and then the Sir Ralph's one hundred & ninety pounds—does the old [two words crossed out] Gentleman pay it?—& where is it?—

yrs. ever
BYRON

---

[1] This was Byron's Napoleon snuff box. Teresa described it as having on the lid the portrait of the Empress Marie Louise, and inside, revealed by a hidden spring, a miniature of Napoleon and another of the little King of Rome. (Origo, p. 437n.)

[2] Translated by Professor Nancy Dersofi.

P.S.—Mem.—Can't sign bonds till I have farther instructions—and then what is to be done for a witness—an *English* witness—there are only forty thousand in Italy.———Read carefully Spooney's letter.—You will *not* pay Spooney any thing—recollect—till the Account is properly sent in.———Cannot Farebrother or you find this quiet purchaser for Rochdale? I am of decided opinion for the Sale of the ——manor.—even without waiting for the decision of the Suit.—

[TO DOUGLAS KINNAIRD]   *Bologna Septr. 5th. 1819*

Dear Douglas—I have marked on this paper many *names* of Creditors whom I do not know and deny them thrice.—There is no *Hopkinson* of Southwell—& if there were I owe him nothing.—*Mealey* is the greatest Scoundrel in the world.———Davey—why should he be paid?—If as Hanson says the whole might have been nearly cleared with the fund?—Why not let him clear? Read his letter carefully.[1]

yrs. ever

B

[In margin of account] Depend upon many of these having been paid before, or are originally impositions.—Many names are quite unknown.

[TO AUGUSTA LEIGH]   [*about Sept. 10, 1819; p.m. Sept. 23*]

[Second sheet of letter—first sheet missing in MS.]
... and worse of Blake.[1]—Who would have thought it? a Stage Coach?—was it a long Coach?—was he inside or out?—and is ...

---

[1] Accompanying this letter is a three-page list, made out by Hanson or his clerk, giving details of outstanding debts and of payments made from the purchase money from Newstead Abbey (£94,500). After the Marriage Settlement Trust of £60,000, Sawbridge's Annuity of £6,000, and "Mortgage for part of Lady Byron's fortune paid off and advanced to Lord Byron on the Mortgage", £6,200, were subtracted, there remained a surplus of £22,300 for the payment of debts. Hanson then lists the debts in one column and payments made in another and makes the following summaries: Byron's total debts came to £28,162. Of the surplus, £17,622 had been paid to creditors, leaving a balance of £4,677, but the debts still unpaid (including £3,000 to Hanson) amounted to £6,158, leaving a deficiency of £1,480. But Hanson maintained that £10,854 was still in Mr. Kinnaird's hands.

[1] Blake was a fashionable barber. See [1813] to Lady Melbourne (*a*), note 2 (Vol. 3, p. 3).

[section cut out of letter] . . . get re-married—what . . . he left? Pray tell Waite[2] to take a post-chaise—for if our Dentist follows our barber—there will be ne'er a tooth or hair left which people can depend upon for a half year's engagement.—I am truly sorry for Blake—but as you observe with great truth and novelty "we are none of us immortal. "—It were to be wished however that Coachmen did not help people over the Styx—*that* used to be waterman's work and fare.—You say nothing in favour of my return to England.—Very well—I will stay where I am—and you will never see me more.— [section cut out of letter]

yrs. ever
B

P.S.—I sent Lady Byron the other day a letter—enclosing some letters from Germany to me concerning her chiefly—& which the writer wished her to have.——Ask her by letter if she has received that letter—I want no answer but a mere acknowledgement to *you* or to Mr. Murray of the arrival of my letter.—I want also a picture of Ada—and my miniature (by Holmes) of *you*.——Address to Venice as usual.—Allegra is here with me—in good health—& very amiable and pretty at least thought so.—She is English—but speaks nothing but Venetian—"Bon *di* papa" &c. &c. she is very droll—and has a good deal of the Byron—can't articulate the letter *r* at all—frowns and pouts quite in our way—blue eyes—light hair growing *darker* daily— and a dimple in the chin—a scowl on the brow—white skin—sweet voice—and a particular liking of Music—and of her own way in every thing—is not that B. all over?——

[TO JOHN MURRAY]   *Bologna, Sept. 17* [12?], *1819*

Dear Sir,—I have received a small box consigned by you to a Mr. Allan with three portraits in it.[1] Whom am I to thank for this? You never alluded to it in any of your letters. I enclose you an advertisement of Cognac brandy from Galignani's Messenger; it runs—"in order to facilitate the consumption of that truly wholesome and agreeable

---

[2] Waite was a dentist of some reputation at 2, Old Burlington Street. Byron frequently asked his friends to send him Waite's red tooth-powder.
[1] See [Sept. 1819] to Teresa.

article." Is not this delightful? The gravity of the author; and the *truly* wholesome!

Yours ever truly,
B

[TO JOHN MURRAY] *Venice, Sept. 27th, 1819*

Dear Sir,—I enclose Roberts.[1] You will be glad to hear that I am well. I never knew that I had written to say I was ill in *health*. I had a bad head, and nerves, owing to heat, and exhaustion, and plague with the illness of another person, and other vexations at Bologna, but am right again now—at least for the present. These fits are the penalties of the life I have always led, and must be paid. I am not the less obliged by your and everybody's good-nature. Thank Hobhouse, and say I shall write soon at full.

I write now merely to return Roberts. You must not mind me when I say I am ill; it merely means low spirits—and folly.

Yours ever truly,
BYRON

[TO ALEXANDER SCOTT] *Mira. Octr. 2d. 1819*

My dear Scott—I regret truly to hear what you say of M[issiaglia?]'s affairs—as he is the one whom I esteem most of the few of his country-men whom I esteem at all.—But to assist him is not in my present power.—Within the present year since the month of January I have had to pay in England *twenty eight thousand pounds sterling*—including a lawyer's bill of *eight thousand pounds*—five thousand of which I have paid and demurred upon the other three but expect daily to be called upon the [to?] liquidate the remainder.—You may suppose that this has not left me any superfluous bullion in my sinking fund—and that [I have nothing?] except my income to answer all the necessary family expences—which are considerable——I am not in a situation to supply M. on this occasion—the more so as my ignorance of his affairs—and my absence from Venice since last Spring rendered the communication

---

[1] Byron's "Letter to the Editor of 'My Grandmother's Review'". See Aug. 23, 1819, to Hobhouse, notes 1 and 2.

equally unexpected and unpleasant to me as his well wisher.—After so disagreeable a thing as being obliged to say *No*—what can I add?— regrets are useless—and words might seem insulting.—The expression of feelings without the proof is a deplorable cant—which I would not accept myself—nor will offer to others—when it is the only thing that I can offer. Believe me ever & truly

yrs.

BYRON

P.S.—I do not leave these parts immediately—and am not sure that I shall leave them before Spring—being as undecided as when I saw you at Venice.—Perhaps I may come up soon for a day—and will let you know.—At any rate after Guiccioli's return (at the end of 8bre) we shall meet—I can't make him out—conjectures are useless—we shall see.—He ought to have been here last week, but delays a month longer.

[TO JOHN CAM HOBHOUSE]   *Venice. Octr. 3d. 1819*

Dear Hobhouse—I wrote to Murray last week and begged him to reassure you of my health and sanity—as far as I know at present.— At Bologna I was out of sorts—in health and spirits.—Here—I have health at least.—My South American project[1] of which I believe I spoke to you (as you mention it)—was this.——I perceived by the inclosed paragraphs that advantageous offers were—or are to be held out to settlers in the Venezuelan territory.—My affairs in England are nearly settled—or in prospect of settlement—in Italy I have no debts —and could leave it when I chose.—The Anglo-Americans are a little too coarse for me—and their climate too cold—and I should prefer the others.—I could soon grapple with the Spanish language.——Ellice[2] or others could get me letters to Boliver and his government—and if men of little or of no property are encouraged there—surely with present income—and if I could sell Rochdale—with some capital—I might be suffered as a landholder there—or at least a tenant—and if possible and legal—a Citizen.——I wish you would speak to *Perry* of

---

[1] See May 12, 1819, to Major Somerville, note 1.

[2] Hobhouse's friend Edward Ellice, M.P. for Coventry, had associations with the Hudson's Bay Company and knew many traders and merchants who had been in America.

the M[orning] C[hronicle] who is their *Gazetteer*—about this—and ask like Jeremy Diddler[3]—not for eighteen pence—but information on the subject.——I assure you that I am very *serious* in the idea—and that the notion has been about me for a long time as you will see by the worn state of the advertisement.—I should go there with my natural daughter Allegra—now nearly three years old—and with me here—and pitch my tent for good and all.—I am not tired of Italy—but a man must be a Cicisbeo and a singer in duets and a Connoisseur of operas—or nothing here—I have made some progress in all these accomplishments—but I can't say that I don't feel the degradation.— Better be a[n] unskilful planter—an awkward settler—better be a hunter—or anything than a flatterer of fiddlers—and a fan-carrier of a woman.—I like women—God he knows—but the more their system here developes upon me—the worse it seems—after Turkey too—here the *polygamy* is all on the female side.——I have been an intriguer, a husband, and now I am a Cavalier Servente.—by the holy! —it is a strange sensation.—After having belonged in my own and other countries—to the intriguing—the married—and the keeping— parts of the town—to be sure an honest arrangement is the best—and I have had that too—and have—but they expect it to be for *life*—thereby I presume—excluding longevity.—But let us be serious if possible. ——You must not talk to me of England—that is out of the question. —I had a house—and lands—and a wife and child—and a name there —once—but all these things are transmuted or sequestered.—Of the last & best ten years of my life—nearly six have been passed *out* of it. —I feel no love for the soil after the treatment I received before leaving it for the last time—but I do not hate it enough to wish to take a part in it's calamities—as on either side harm must be done before good can accrue—revolutions are not to be made with rose water.——My taste for revolution is abated—with my other passions.——Yet I want a country—and a home—and if possible—a free one—I am not yet thirty two years of age—I might still be a decent citizen and found a *house* and a family,—as good—or better than the former.——I could at all events occupy myself rationally—my hopes are not high—nor my ambition extensive—and when tens of thousands of our Countrymen are colonizing (like the Greeks of old in Sicily and Italy) from as many causes—does my notion seem visionary or irrational?——There is no

---

[3] Jeremy Diddler, a character in James Kenney's farce *Raising the Wind* (1803) had various ingenious ways of raising money.

freedom in Europe—that's certain—it is besides a worn out portion of the globe.—What I should be glad of is *information* as to the encouragement—the means required—and what is accorded & what would be my probable reception—Perry—or Ellice—or many merchants would be able to tell you this for me.—I won't go there to travel but to settle.———Do not laugh at me—you will—but I assure you I am quite in earnest if this thing be practicable. I do not want to have anything to do with the war projects—but to go there as a settler—and if as a Citizen—all the better—my own government would not I think refuse me permission—if they know their own interest—such fellows as I am—are no desideratum for Sidmouth[4] at present—I think.—Address to me at Venice.———I should of course come to Liverpool—or some town on your coast—to take my passage—and receive my credentials—believe me

ever yrs. most truly
BYRON

[TO JOHN MURRAY] *Venice. October 3d. 1819*

Should Mr. H[obhouse] not be in London, you may open and read the inclosed letter, as the information which I want, and which is therein requested, might possibly be obtained for me as well or better by you than by Mr. H. himself. Let me have an answer when convenient.

Yours, ever truly,
BYRON

P.S.—Perry (as the Gazetteer of the Independanta), or Mr. Ellice, or any other of our great merchants, would be the persons most likely to give the information required.

[TO JAMES WEDDERBURN WEBSTER] *Venice. Octr. 5th. 1819*

Dear Webster—[eleven lines crossed out] The latter part of your letter which I presume refers to some communication you may have held with Lady B's family—I do not quite understand;—if you imagine that there is any prospect of a reconciliation, you are deceived either by your own good wishes for such an event—or by some

---

[4] Henry Addington, 1st Viscount Sidmouth (1757–1844), the Tory minister who was known for the rigour of his repressive measures, was largely responsible for the "Peterloo Massacre" of 1819.

ambiguity in *their* expressions on the subject which must naturally be an awkward one.—I feel naturally curious to know what could have led you for a moment into such a notion—and I ask you from curiosity to tell me more explicitly.—Did you see my daughter—and how is she? —I have another here (by a different mother) who is three years old nearly—and a pretty child.—Whatever you have to say—you may speak out—it is a subject too public long ago—and too remote now— to require any delicacy between old acquaintance further than politeness requires.—I have some idea of going with my natural daughter Allegra to settle in South America—provided a colonizing plan which I have heard of—as about to be proposed by some Commissioners from Venezuela now on their way to England—be put in execution.— On this subject my last letter to Mr. Hobhouse has explained my ideas.—If you are in any communication with the Noel family or Lady B—I wish you would request them to aid me in getting my *settled* property—transferred from the *funds* to *other* & (what I think) *safer* security.—Mortgage or any thing would be preferable to the funds. ——Pray write soon—and believe me,

> yrs. very truly
> BYRON

[TO DOUGLAS KINNAIRD]   *Venice. Octr. 5th. 1819*

My dear Douglas—You have not written to me for many months.— I wrote from Bologna—last month.—I now beg to repeat my wishes about the transfer of my funded property—every day alarms me more on that account.—Have you nothing to say about Rochdale?—My last letter from Bologna—enclosed some letters and accounts of Hanson. ——Have you received that epistle?——I wrote last week to Hobhouse a long letter on another subject which he will communicate to you.——Pray get my property out of the funds—and then reform and riot as much as you please.—My letter to Hobhouse was about a *South* American scheme of mine

> yrs. ever
> BYRON

[TO AUGUSTA LEIGH]   *Venice, Octr. 15th. 1819*

. . . . If there is to be a scene in England to which all seems approaching —by the violence of the political parties—you will probably see me in

England in the next spring but I have not decided yet the part I ought to take. They say in Italy that "Che nasce Patrizio innora Patrizio" and I am not democrat enough to like a tyranny of blackguards—such fellows as Bristol Hunt—are a choice of evils with Castlereagh— except that a Gentleman scoundrel is always preferable to a vulgar one. To me it appears that you are on the eve of a revolution which won't be made with rose water however. If so I will be one. As Liston says, "I love a row."

[TO RICHARD BELGRAVE HOPPNER]   *Octr. 22d. 1819*

My dear Hoppner—I am glad to hear of your return,[1] but I do not know how to congratulate you—unless you think differently of Venice from what I think now, and you thought always.—I am besides about to renew your troubles by requesting you to be Judge between Mr. Edgecombe and myself in a small matter of imputed peculation and irregular accounts on the part of that Phoenix of secretaries.—As I knew that you had not parted friends—at the same time that *I* refused for my own part any judgment but *yours*—I offered him his choice [of any] person the *least* Scoundrel native to be found in Venice—as his own umpire—but he expressed himself so convinced of your impartiality—that he declined any but *you*.—This is in his favour.—The paper within will explain to you the default in his accounts—You will hear his explanation, and decide if it so please you—I shall not appeal from the decision.——As he complained that his salary was insufficient—I determined to have his accounts examined—and the enclosed was the result—It is all in black and white with documents, and—I have despatched Fletcher to explain—(or rather to perplex) the matter.——I have had much civility and kindness from Mr. Dorville during your journey—and I thank him accordingly.——Your letter reached me at your departure and displeased me very much—not that it might not be true in it's statement and kind in its intention—but you have lived long enough to know how useless all such representations ever are and must be in cases where the passions are concerned;—to reason with men in such a situation is like reasoning with a drunkard in his cups—the only answer you will get from him is that he is sober—and you are drunk.——Upon that subject we will (if you like) be silent—you might only say what would distress me without answering any purpose whatever—and I have too many

[1] Hoppner had been taking a holiday in Switzerland with his Swiss wife.

obligations to you to answer you in the same style—so that you should recollect that you have also that advantage over me.——I hope to see you soon.—I suppose you know that they said at Venice—that I was arrested at Bologna as a *Carbonaro*—a story about as true as their usual conversation.——Moore has been here—I lodged him in my house at Venice—and went to see him daily—but I could not at that time quit la Mira entirely.——You and I were not very far from meeting in Switzerland.[2]——with my best respects to Mrs. Hoppner believe me

ever and truly yrs.
BYRON

P.S.—Allegra is here in good health—and spirits—I shall keep her with me till I go to England—which will perhaps be in the Spring.——It has just occurred to me that you may not perhaps like to undertake the office of Judge between Mr. E. and your humble servant.—Of course as Mr. Liston (the Comedian not the Ambassador) says "it is all *hoptional*" but I have no other resource.—I do not wish to find him a rascal if it can be avoided—and would rather think him guilty of carelessness than cheating.—The case is this—can I or not give him a character for *honesty?*—It is not my intention to continue him in my service.——

[TO RICHARD BELGRAVE HOPPNER] *October 25th, 1819*

You need not have made any excuses about *the* letter;[1] I never said but you might, could, should, or would have reason. I merely described my own state of inaptitude to listen to it at that time, and in those circumstances. Besides, you did not speak from your *own* authority—but from what you said you had heard. Now my blood boils to hear an Italian speaking ill of another Italian, because, though they lie in particular, they speak truth in general by speaking ill at all—and although they know that they are trying and wishing to lie, they do not succeed, merely because they can say nothing so bad of each other, that it *may* not, and must not be true, from the atrocity of their long debased national character.

---

2 Byron probably refers to a contemplated elopement with the Countess Guiccioli while they were on their way to Venice from Bologna (her husband had been called back to Ravenna by business).

1 See July 12, 1819, to Alexander Scott.

With regard to E[dgecombe], you will perceive a most irregular, extravagant account, without proper documents to support it. He demanded an increase of salary, which made me suspect him; he supported an outrageous extravagance of expenditure, and did not like the dismission of the cook; he never complained of him—as in duty bound—at the time of his robberies. I can only say, that the house expense is now under *one half* of what it then was, as he himself admits. He charged for a comb *eighteen* francs,—the real price was *eight*. He charged a passage from Fusina for a person named Iambelli, who paid it *herself*, as she will prove, if necessary. He fancies, or asserts himself, the victim of a domestic complot against him;—accounts are accounts—prices are prices;—let him make out a fair detail. *I* am not prejudiced against him—on the contrary, I supported him against the complaints of his wife, and of his former master, at a time when I could have crushed him like an earwig, and if he is a scoundrel, he is the greatest of scoundrels, an ungrateful one. The truth is, probably, that he thought I was leaving Venice, and determined to make the most of it. At present he keeps bringing in *account after account*, though he had always money in hand—as I believe you know my system was never to allow longer than a week's bills to run. Pray read him this letter—I desire nothing to be concealed against which he may defend himself.

Pray how is your little boy? and how are you?—I shall be up in Venice very soon, and we will be bilious together. I hate the place and all that it inherits.

Yours, &c.

[TO DOUGLAS KINNAIRD]   *Venice. Octr. 26th. 1818 [1819]*

My dear Douglas—My late expenditure has arisen from living at a distance from Venice and being obliged to keep up two establishments, from frequent journeys—and buying some furniture and books as well as a horse or two—and not from any renewal of the EPICUREAN system as you suspect. I have been faithful to my honest liaison with Countess Guiccioli—and I can assure you that *She* has never cost me directly or indirectly a sixpence—indeed the circumstances of herself and family render this no merit.—I never offered her but one present—a broach of brilliants—and she sent it back to me with her *own hair* in it (I shall *not* say of *what part* but *that* is an Italian custom) and a note to say that she was not in the habit of receiving presents of that value—but hoped that I would not consider her sending it back as an affront—nor the value diminished by the enclosure.—I have not had a whore this half-year—confining myself to the strictest adultery.——Why should you prevent Hanson from making a *peer* if he likes it—I think the *"Garret-ting"* would be by far the best parliamentary privilege—I know of. ——Damn your delicacy.—It is a low commercial quality—and very unworthy a man who prefixes "honourable" to his nomenclature. If you say that I must sign the bonds—I suppose that I must—but it is very iniquitous to make me pay my debts—you have no idea of the pain it gives one.—Pray do three things—get my property out of the *funds*—get Rochdale sold—get me some information from Perry about *South America*—and 4thly. ask Lady Noel not to live so very long.—— As to Subscribing to Manchester—if I do that—I will write a letter to Burdett—for publication—to accompany the Subscription—which shall be more radical than anything yet rooted—but I feel lazy.—I have thought of this for some time—but alas! the air of this cursed Italy enervates—and disfranchises the thoughts of a man after nearly four years of respiration—to say nothing of emission.—As to "Don Juan" —confess—confess—you dog—and be candid—that it is the sublime of *that there* sort of writing—it may be bawdy—but is it not good English?—it may be profligate—but is it not *life*, is it not *the thing*?— Could any man have written it—who has not lived in the world?—and tooled in a post-chaise? in a hackney coach? in a Gondola? against a wall? in a court carriage? in a vis a vis?—on a table?—and under it?—I have written about a hundred stanzas of a third Canto—but it is damned modest—the outcry has frightened me.—I had such projects for the Don—but the *Cant* is so much stronger than *Cunt*—now a days, —that the benefit of experience in a man who had well weighed the worth of both monosyllables—must be lost to despairing posterity.— After all what stuff this outcry is—Lalla Rookh and Little—are more dangerous than my burlesque poem can be—Moore has been here— we got tipsy together—and were very amicable—he is gone on to Rome—I put my life (in M.S.) into his hands—(*not* for publication) you—or any body else may see it—at his return.—It only comes up to 1816.——He is a noble fellow—and looks quite fresh and poetical— nine years (the age of a poem's education) my Senior—he looks younger—this comes of marriage and being settled in the Country. I want to go to South America—I have written to Hobhouse all about it. —I wrote to my wife—three months ago—under care to Murray— has she got the letter—or is the letter got into Blackwood's magazine? ——You ask after my Christmas pye—Remit it any how—*Circulars* is

232

the best—you are right about *income*—I must have it all—how the devil do I know that I may live a year or a month?—I wish I knew that I might regulate my spending in more ways than one.—As it is one always thinks that there is but a span.—A man may as well break or be damned for a large sum as a small one—I should be loth to pay the devil or any other creditor more than sixpence in the pound.—

[scrawl for signature]

P.S.—I recollect nothing of "Davies's landlord"—but what ever Davies *says*—I will *swear* to—and *that's* more than *he* would.—So pray pay—has he a landlady too?—perhaps I may owe her something.——With regard to the bonds I will sign them but—it goes against the grain.——As to the rest—you *can't* err—so long as you *don't* pay.——Paying is executor's or executioner's work.——You may write somewhat oftener—Mr. Galignani's messenger gives the outline of your public affairs—but I see no results—you have no man yet—(always excepting Burdett—& you & H[obhouse] and the Gentlemanly leaven of your two-penny loaf of rebellion) don't forget however my charge of horse—and commission for the Midland Counties and by the holies!—You shall have your account in decimals.—Love to Hobby—but why leave the Whigs?——

[TO RICHARD BELGRAVE HOPPNER]   *Octr. 28th. 1819*

My dear Hoppner—I do not request you to *decide* upon Mr. Edgeworth's [sic] *character*—but his *accounts*—which as I can not understand them—I shall be glad to find any body who *can*.—You are taking a great deal of trouble on my account—and I shall not add the difficult responsibility of pronouncing upon this person's honesty—being resolved to do that myself according to the result of the examination—and of other circumstances.—I expect from Mr. Edgecombe—1stly—all *receipts* of bills paid &c. lists of furniture &c.—since his entrance into my service. 2dly.—that no bills of long standing should appear—he having had money always—and orders to pay *weekly* without fail or excuse—and 3dly. some sort of order in his arrangement of the bills.—For instance—there is a bill of twenty francs brought in by a Chymist here of *May last*—which Mr. Edgecombe in his way to Venice *last week*—called to say *he would pay*.—Why was this not paid before?—the money has been in his hands since the *Spring*.—I should be glad of an explanation from him *why* Merryweather has not been arrested—the cause having been decided six months ago. I suspect

Collusion between Mr. E[dgecombe] and Merryweather—and Castelli the Advocate.—When the whore Margarita was dismissed from my house—several unpaid bills were brought in—for all of which I had advanced money before to *Mr. Edgecombe*,—was it or was it not his duty to have seen them paid?——I expect that he will go over the list of the Mocenigo furniture—as also that of this Casino—(to say nothing of the other) and give me a list of articles wanting—and the expence of those to be replaced—before I pay him off—or give him a character—*this* he had the order to do *monthly*—and I do not find that it has been done.—There is the price of the bay mare sold—and the rent of the lodgers to whom he let part of the Casino to be accounted for—and above all—*all receipts* and proofs of the non-existence of any bills of more than a fortnight's date.—I shall cause an advertisement in Italian to be inserted in the public gazettes—calling upon all persons for their accounts (in case of any demur or doubt on his part) with my reasons for so doing at length—so tell him—that he may get his honesty brushed a little cleaner than it appears at present.—There is nothing in which I have been all along more particular at Venice than to *settle weekly*—and to furnish the funds for so doing—I beg you to ask him this—and dare him to deny it.———I have to thank you for yr. letter—and your compliment to Don Juan.———I said nothing to you about it—understanding that it is a sore subject with the moral reader—and has been the cause of a great row.—But I am glad you like it. —I will say nothing about the Shipwreck—except that I hope you think it is as *nautical* and *technical* as Verse could admit in the Octave measure.———The poem has *not sold well*—so Murray says—"but the best Judges &c. say &c." so says that worthy man.—I have never seen it in print.—The third Canto is in advance about 100 Stanzas—but the failure of the two first has weakened my *estro*—and it will neither be so good as the two former—nor completed unless I get a little more *riscaldato* in its behalf—I understand the outcry was beyond everything —pretty Cant for people who read Tom Jones—and Roderick Random —and the Bath Guide—and Ariosto—and Dryden—and Pope—to say nothing of Little's poems[1].—Of course I refer to the *morality* of these works and not to any pretension of mine to compete with them in any thing but decency.———I hope yours is the Paris Edition—and that you did not pay the London price.———I have seen neither except in the newspapers—nor Mazeppa—nor the Ode to that now empty Oyster Shell—the city of Venice.—Pray make my respects to Mrs. H[oppner] and take care of your little boy—all my household have the fever and

[1] Thomas Moore published his early poems under the name of Thomas Little.

Ague—except Fletcher—Allegra—and M*ysen* (as we used to say in Nottinghamshire) and the horses and Mutz—and Moretto.[2]—In the beginning of Novr.—perhaps sooner—I expect to have the pleasure of seeing you.—To day I got drenched by a thunder storm and my horse and Groom too and his horse all bemired up to the middle in a cross-road—it was summer at Noon—and at five we were be-wintered— but the lightning was sent perhaps to let us know that the summer was not yet over.—It is queer weather for the 27th Octr.—

yrs. ever most truly
BYRON

I have no books nor parcels from England since your expedition—but my library is at your service.—Edgecombe has the key—there are some additions to it since you saw it last.—

[TO JOHN MURRAY]   *Venice. Octr. 29th. 1819*

Dear Murray—Yours of the 15th. came yesterday. I am sorry that you do not mention a large letter addressed to *your care* for Lady Byron —from me at Bologna—two months ago. Pray tell me was this letter received and forwarded?——You say nothing of the Vice Consulate for the Ravenna patrician—from which it is to be inferred that the thing will not be done.——I had written about a hundred stanzas of a *third* Canto to Don Juan—but the reception of the two first is no encouragement to you nor me to proceed.——I had also written about 600 lines of a poem—the Vision (or Prophecy) of Dante—the subject a view of Italy in the ages down to the present—supposing Dante to speak in his own person—previous to his death—and embracing all topics in the way of prophecy—like Lycophron's Cassandra.[1] But this and the other are both at a standstill—for the present.——I gave Moore who is gone to Rome—my Life in M.S. in 78 folio sheets brought down to 1816.[2] ——But this I put into his hands for *his* care—as he has some other M.S.S. of mine—a journal kept in 1814—&c.—Neither are for publication during my life—but when I am cold—you may do what you please.

[2] Mutz was a mongrel bought in Switzerland for a watchdog because he was mean; Moretto was a bulldog.

[1] The *Cassandra* of Lycophron, an Alexandrian poet (c. 284 B.C.) is a long poem prophesying events in Greek history.

[2] Byron added more to his Memoirs later and sent the additions to Moore who sold the whole for posthumous publication to John Murray for 2,000 guineas. The MS. was burned, together with a copy, at 50 Albemarle Street on May 17, 1824, three days after the news of Byron's death reached England. See *The Late Lord Byron* by Doris Langley Moore for the full account.

————In the mean time—if you like to read them—you may—and show them to any body you like—I care not.————The life is *Memoranda*— and not *Confessions*—I have left out all my *loves* (except in a general way) and many other of the most important things—(because I must not compromise other people) so that it is like the play of Hamlet— "the part of Hamlet omitted by particular desire".————But you will find many opinions—and some fun—with a detailed account of my marriage and it's consequences—as true as a party concerned can make such accounts—for I suppose we are all prejudiced.————I have never read over this life since it was written—so that I know not exactly what it may repeat—or contain.————Moore and I passed some merry days together—but so far from "seducing me to England" as you suppose —the account he gave of me and mine—was of any thing but a nature to make me wish to return;—it is not such opinions of the public that would weigh with me one way or the other—but I think they should weigh with others of my friends before they ask me to return to a place for which I have no great inclination.————I probably must return for business—or in my way to America—pray—did you get a letter for Hobhouse—who will have told you the contents.—I understood that the Venezuelan commissioners had orders to treat with emigrants— now I want to go there—I should not make a bad South-American planter, and I should take my natural daughter Allegra with me and settle.————I wrote at length to Hobhouse to get information from Perry who I suppose is the best topographer and trumpeter of the new Republicans. Pray write—

yrs. ever

[Scrawl]

P.S.—Moore and I did nothing but laugh—he will tell you of "my whereabouts" and all my proceedings at this present—they are as usual.————You should not let those fellows publish false "Don Juans"³—but do not put *my name* because I mean to cut Roberts up like a gourd—in the ⟨anonymous⟩ preface—if I continue the poem.

[TO RICHARD BELGRAVE HOPPNER]   *October 29th. 1819*

My dear Hoppner—The Ferrara Story is of a piece with all the rest of the Venetian manufacture—you may judge.—I only changed horses

³ The first two cantos of *Don Juan* were published together in a quarto on July 15, 1819. Four days later William Hone's *Don Juan, Canto the Third* appeared. Murray was handicapped in his attempt to prevent piracies and forgeries because Byron's poem had appeared without the name of either the author or the publisher.

there since I wrote to you after my visit in June last.—*"Convent"*—
and *"carry off"* quotha!—and *"girl"*———I should like to know *who* has
been carried off—except poor dear *me*—I have been more ravished
myself than anybody since the Trojan war—but as to the arrest and
it's causes—one is as true as the other—and I can account for the
invention of neither.—I suppose it is some confusion of the tale of the
For[narina]—and of M[adam]e Guiccioli—and half a dozen more—but
it is useless to unravel the web—when one has only to brush it away.—
I shall settle with Master Edgecombe who looks very blue at your indecision—and swears that he is the best arithmatician in Europe—and
so I think also—for he makes out two and two to be five.———You may
see me next week—I have a horse or two more (five in all) and I shall
repossess myself of Lido—and I will rise earlier—and we will go and
shake our livers over the beach as heretofore—if you like—and we will
make the Adriatic roar again with our hatred of that now empty
Oyster shell—without it's pearl—the city of Venice.—Murray sent me
a letter yesterday—the impostors have published—*two* new *third*
Cantos of *Don Juan*—the devil take the impudence of some blackguard
bookseller or other there*for*.—Perhaps I did not make myself understood—he told me the sale had not been great—1200 out of 1500
quarto I believe (which is nothing after selling 13000 of the Corsair
in one day) but that the "best Judges &c." had said it was very fine
and clever and particularly good English & poetry and all those
consolatory things which are not however worth a single copy to a
bookseller—and as to the author—of course I am in a damned passion
at the bad taste of the times—and swear there is nothing like posterity
—who of course must know more of the matter than their Grand-
fathers.—There has been an eleventh commandment to the women not
to read it—and what is still more extraordinary they seem not to have
broken it.———But that can be of little import to them poor things—
for the reading or non-reading a book—will never keep down a single
petticoat;—but it is of import to Murray—who will be in scandal for
his aiding as publisher.———He is bold howsomedever—wanting two
more cantos against the winter—I think that he had better not—for
by the larkins!—it will only make a new row for him.—Edgecombe is
gone to Venice today—to consign my chattels to t'other fellow.———
Count G[uiccioli] comes to Venice next week and I am requested to
consign his wife to him, which shall be done—with all her linen.—
What you say of the long evenings at the Mira—or Venice—reminds
me of what Curran said to Moore—"so—I hear—you have married a
pretty woman—and a very good creature too—an excellent creature

—pray—*how do you pass your evenings?*[''] it is a devil of a question that—and perhaps as easy to answer with a wife as with a mistress—but surely they are longer than the nights. I am all for morality now—and shall confine myself henceforward to the strictest adultery—which you will please to recollect is all that that virtuous wife of mine has left me.——If you go to Milan—pray leave at least a *Vice*-Consul—the only Vice that will ever be wanting in Venice.—Dorville is a good fellow.——But you should go to England in the Spring with me—and plant Mrs. Hoppner at Berne with her relations for a few months. —I wish you had been here (at Venice—I mean not the Mira) when Moore was here—we were very merry and tipsy—he *hated* Venice by the way—and swore it was a sad place.——So—Madame Albrizzi's death is in danger—poor woman.——Saranzo—is of course in the ⟨doleful⟩ crazy recollection of their rancid amours. ——Moore told me that at Geneva they had made a devil of a story of the Fornaretta—"young lady seduced—subsequent abandonment—leap into the Grand Canal—her being in the hospital of *fous* in consequence"—I should like to know who was nearest being made *"fou"* and be damned to them.——Don't you think me in the interesting character of a very ill used gentleman?—I hope your little boy is well —Allegrina is flourishing like a pome-granate blossom.—

yrs. ever
BYRON

[TO JOHN MURRAY]   *Venice. Novr. 8th. 1819*

Dear Murray—Mr. Hoppner has lent me a copy of "Don Juan" Paris Edition—which he tells me is read in Switzerland by Clergymen and ladies with considerable approbation.——In the second Canto you must alter the 49th. Stanza to

> "Twas twilight, and the sunless day went down
>   Over the waste of waters like a veil
> Which if withdrawn would but disclose the frown
>   Of one whose hate is masked but to assail,
> Thus to their hopeless eyes the Night was shown
>   And grimly darkled o'er their faces pale
> And the dim desolate deep; twelve days had fear
> Been their familiar, and now Death was here."

And in Stanza 208—of the same *canto* make the sixth line run

> "newly a—
> Strong palpitation rises, 'tis her boon,—"

otherwise there is a syllable too few.——On referring to the M.S. I found that I had stupidly blundered all the rhymes of the 49th. stanza,—such as they are printed.—Cast your eye over [;] you will perceive the necessity of the alteration.——I have been ill these eight days with a tertian fever—caught in the country on horseback in a thunderstorm—yesterday I had the fourth attack—The two last were very smart—the first day—as well as the last being preceded by vomiting.——It is the fever of the place—and the Season.—I feel weakened but not unwell in the intervals—except headache and lassitude. Count G[uiccioli] has arrived in Venice—and has presented his Spouse (who had preceded him two months for her health and the prescriptions of Dr. Aglietti) with a paper of conditions—regulations —of hours and conduct and morals—&c. &c. which he insists on her accepting—and She persists in refusing.—I am expressly it should seem excluded by this treaty—as an indispensible preliminary; so that they are in high discussion—and what the result may be I know not— particularly—as they are consulting friends.——Tonight as Countess G[uiccioli] observed me poring over "Don Juan" she stumbled by mere chance on the 138th. Stanza of the first Canto—and asked me what it meant—I told her—nothing but "your husband is coming" as I said this in Italian with some emphasis—she started up in a fright —and said "*Oh My God—is* he *coming*?" thinking it was *her own* who either was or ought to have been at the theatre.——You may suppose we laughed when she found out the mistake.——You will be amused as I was—it happened not three hours ago.——I wrote to you last week—but have added nothing to the third Canto—since my fever nor to "the Prophecy of Dante—" Of the former there are about 110 octaves done—of the latter about five hundred lines—perhaps more.— Moore saw the third Juan—as far as it then went.—I do not know if my fever will let me go on—with either—and the tertian lasts they say a good while.—I had it in Malta in my way home—and the Malaria fever in Greece the year before that.—The Venetian is not very fierce—but I was delirious one of the nights with it for an hour or two—and on my senses coming back—found Fletcher sobbing on one side of the bed—and la Contessa G. weeping on the other—so that I had no want of attendance.—I have not yet taken any physician— because though I think they may relieve in Chronic disorders such as

Gout and the like &c. &c. &c. (though they can't cure them) just as Surgeons are necessary to set bones—and tend wounds—yet I think fevers quite out of their reach—and remediable only by diet and Nature.——I don't like the taste of bark[1]—but I suppose that I must take it soon.—Tell Rose—that somebody at Milan—(an Austrian Mr. Hoppner says) is answering his book.[2]——William Bankes is in quarantine at Trieste.——I have not lately heard from you—excuse this paper—it is long paper shortened for the occasion.——what folly is this of Carlile's trial?[3]—why let him have the honours of a martyr? it will only advertise the books in question.——

yrs. ever

B

P.S.—As I tell you—that the Guiccioli business is on the eve of exploding in one way or the other—I will just add that without attempting to influence the decision of the Contessa—a good deal depends upon it.——If she and her husband make it up—you will perhaps see me in England sooner than you expect—if not—I shall retire with her to France or America—change my name and lead a quiet provincial life.—All this may seem odd—but I have got the girl into a scrape—and as neither her birth nor her rank nor her connections by birth or marriage are inferior to my own—I am in honour bound to support her through—besides she is a very pretty woman—ask Moore—and not yet one and twenty.——If she gets over this—and I get over my tertian I will perhaps look in at Albemarle Street some of these days en passant to Bolivar.—

[TO DOUGLAS KINNAIRD]   *Venice. Novr. 16th. 1819*

Dear Douglas—A few weeks ago I wrote to you to explain in answer to your letter—that my expenditure at Bologna &c. had arisen from various journeys—and some purchases of horses and furniture—as well as the keeping up two establishments for the time being—one at Venice—and the other in Romagna—besides living at hotels.—

1 The so-called Peruvian Bark, commonly used as a remedy for fevers, particularly malaria, was the bark of the cinchona tree from which quinine is derived.

2 William Stewart Rose published in 1819 his *Letters from the North of Italy to Henry Hallam.*

3 Richard Carlile (1790–1843) was a martyr to the fight for the freedom of the press. He had been a shoemaker and a tinman who set up as a printer espousing radical and unpopular causes. In 1818 he republished Paine's *Age of Reason.* For this and other "offences" he was imprisoned and fined in 1819. He remained in prison until 1825, and issued a periodical called *The Republican* from the Dorchester Gaol.

Your conjecture of my\having "been voluptuous" was wrong in *your* sense of the word—I have not for now a year—touched or disbursed a sixpence to any harlotry.—My "honnete arrangement"—answered all purposes much better—and cost me nothing—unless you calculate my expences in changing my residence.—I had every reason to be satisfied with my lot in all respects—but that is all over now—and I now write to apprize you that in a few weeks you will see me probably in England.

——I have for this reason drawn on Siri & Willhalm to pay off my *rents* here and to furnish for my journey.—My daughter will accompany me.——The causes are these.——In Septr. Countess Guiccioli—my Sovereign—was ordered to Venice for her health to consult Dr. Aglietti again.—Her husband went to Ravenna on business.—We travelled together—and lived together in the Country till her husband's arrival in Novr.——On the road, by the way—we were very near going off together—from Padua—for France and America—but as I had more prudence—and more experience—and know that the time would come when both might repent—I paused—& prevailed on her to pause also.——At last the Cavalier-Conte Guiccioli came to Venice—where he found his wife considerably improved in health, but hating him so cordially—that they quarrelled *violently*.—He had said nothing before—but at last on finding this to be the case—he gave her the alternative—*him*—or *me*—she decided instantly for *me*—not being allowed to have both—and the lover generally having the preference.—But he had also given her a paper of rules to which he wished her to assent—all of them—establishing *his* authority.——Her friends and relatives of Ravenna were in the meantime in despair—as an *elopement* in Italy is the devil—worse even than with *us*—because it is *super*erogation—and shows a headlong character.——What could I do?—on one hand to sacrifice a woman whom I loved for life—leaving her destitute and divided from all ties in case of my death—on the other hand to give up an "amicizia" which had been my pleasure my pride and my passion.—At twenty I should have taken her away—at thirty with the experience of *ten such years!*—I sacrificed myself only—and counselled—and persuaded her with the greatest difficulty to return with her husband to Ravenna—not absolutely denying—that I might come there again—else she refused to go.——But I shall quit Italy—I have done my duty—but the Country has become sad to me,—I feel alone in it—and as I left England on account of my own wife—I now quit Italy for the wife of another.——I shall make my way to Calais—as I can without going through Paris.—I do not come to England for pleasure—but I know not where to go unless to America—tell *Scrope* Davies—I must see *him* immediately—I shall write to him from Calais—perhaps to join me there—(he will pardon me the trouble) as there is a matter which has been upon my mind these three years (ever since I knew it) that I must settle immediately on my arrival.[1]—He will understand me—and so perhaps may you—but you are both too much men of honour (as well as Hobhouse from whom I have no secrets) to let it go further.—I have been very unwell with an Intermittent fever—which is leaving—but has not yet quite left me —but I trust that it will—as it is better—or rather I am better of it.— I return to England with a heavier heart than when I left it—with no prospects of pleasure or comfort—and indifferent to every thing—but that which it is my duty to do—& which I could wish done with all proper speed.—I shall bring my little daughter Allegra with me—but I know not where to go—I have nobody to receive me—but my sister —and I must conform to my circumstances—and live accordingly,— that is meanly in London & difficultly—on that which affords splendour & ease in Italy.———But I hope to get out to America—if I don't take a much longer voyage.———I should prefer Spanish America.—Pray make my remembrances to all our friends and believe me

yrs. ever & truly

B

P.S.—The enclosed papers will explain to you the close of the Ravenna romance—and confirm this letter;—Hobhouse will translate them to you—"A." means "Alessandro" the name of Count Guiccioli —pray—tell Hobhouse to take care of them for me & not lose them— let me find a line poste restante—Calais.———Novr. 17th. Since I wrote yesterday—I have had another attack of the tertian not violent —but very tiresome.—My daughter and her nurse are also fallen ill— so that I cannot fix any precise day for my setting out;—it would not be just on second thoughts to expect Scrope to take a winter journey to Calais to see me—but I hope to find him in town on my arrival—I will write to you both [whenever?] I am near at hand.———I write to you chiefly to account for my having drawn on Siri—as my rent for houses & bills & journey require it.—I am not much worse in body for my illness—but in very low spirits—for that and other reasons——pray excuse incoherencies and scrawling.———

---

[1] Byron intended to challenge Henry Brougham to a duel before he reached England.

Venice. Novr. 20th. 1819

My dear Bankes—A tertian ague which has troubled me for some time—and the indisposition of my daughter have prevented me from replying before to your welcome letter.——I have not been ignorant of your progress nor of your discoveries and I trust that you are no worse in health from your labours;—you may rely upon finding every body in England eager to reap the fruits of them—and as you have done more than other men—I hope you will not limit yourself to saying less than may do justice to the talents and time you have bestowed on your perilous researches.[1]——The first sentence of my letter will have explained to you why I cannot join you at Trieste;—I was on the point of setting out for England—(before I knew of your arrival) when my child's illness had made her & me dependent on a Venetian Proto-Medico.——It is now seven years since you and I met;—which time you have employed better for others & more honourably for yourself than I have done.—In England you will find considerable changes public & private—you will see some of our old College Contemporaries turned into lords of the treasury—admiralty and the like—others—become Reformers and orators—many settled in life—as it is called—and others settled in death—among the latter—(by the way *not* our fellow Collegians) Sheridan—Curran—Lady Melbourne—Monk Lewis—Frederick Douglas[2]—&c. &c. &c. but you will still find Mr. Sotheby living and all his family—as also Samuel Rogers who declares that one day at Epping he took off his hat to a fantastical carved rural chair in Sotheby's Grotto—mistaking it for Miss Sotheby.——Should you come up this way—and I am still here—you need not be assured how glad I shall be to see you;—I long to hear some part from you—of that which I [expect] in no long time to *see*—at length—You have had better fortune than any traveller of equal enterprise—(except Humboldt) in returning safe—and after the

---

[1] William John Bankes, who was at Cambridge with Byron and was there the "father of all mischief", had been in Parliament for two years before he set out on his Eastern travels, which were much more extensive than Byron's. He later represented Cambridge in Parliament.

[2] The Hon. Frederick Sylvester North Douglas, M.P. for Banbury, was the only son of Lord Glenbervie, who was an intimate friend of Byron during his years of fame in England. Douglas died in 1819 at the age of 29. He had published in 1813 an *Essay on Certain Points of Resemblance between the Ancient and Modern Greeks.*

fate of the Brownes—and the Parkes—and the Burckhardts[3]—it is hardly a less surprize than satisfaction to get you back again.———Believe me

ever & very affectionately yours
BYRON

Venice. Novr. 20th. 1819

My dear Hobhouse—A few days ago I wrote to Douglas K[innaird] to apprize him & my friends of my probable arrival near England in no very long period.—The cause I have detailed at some length in my letter to Douglas.—Il Conte Guiccioli at length discovering that his lady was estranged from him—gave her (like Mr. Croaker in the Goodnatured man) "a mutual choice"[1] that is the husband or the lover—him or me—one but not both.—The lady was for leaving him —and eloping—or separating—and so should I had I been twenty instead of thirty and one years of age—for I loved her—but I knew the event would for her be irreparable—and that all her family [,] her sisters particularly and father[,] would be plunged into despair for the reputation of the rest of the girls—and prevailed on her with great difficulty to return to Ravenna with her husband—who promised forgetfulness if she would give me up.—He actually came to *me* crying about it—and I told him "if you abandon your wife—I will take her undoubtedly—it is my duty—it is also my inclination in case of such extremity—but if as you say—you are really disposed to live with & like her as before—I will not only not carry further disturbance into your family—but even repass the Alps—for I have no hesitation in saying that Italy will be now to me insupportable."—After ten days of such things—during which I had (& have still) the tertian ague— She agreed to go back with him—but *I* feel so wretched and low— and lonely—that I will leave the country reluctantly indeed—but I will do it—for otherwise if I formed a new liaison she would cut the figure of a woman *planted*—and I never will willingly hurt her Self-love.—I *can have* no other motive for *here nobody fights*—and as to assassination

3 "William George Browne (1768–1813), the Oriental traveller, was murdered between Tabriz and Teheran, as it appeared, by banditti. Mungo Park (1771–1806), the African explorer, was killed by the natives on the Niger between Timbuctoo and Boussa. John Lewis Burckhardt (1784–1817), the Oriental traveller, died of dysentery at Alexandria while preparing an expedition to the Niger." Prothero (*LJ*, IV, 379, note 1)
1 Goldsmith, *The Good-Natured Man*, Act I.

—I have risked it many a good time for *her* at Ravenna—and should hardly shrink now;—I will say no more—except that it has been as bitter a cut up for me—as that of leaving England.—Guiccioli's lord intercepted a letter of her father (Count Ruggiero Gamba Ghiselli— there is the name at length) giving her some prudent advice to smooth the husband—& this blew up the whole affair [,] besides some awkward evidence about sleeping together—and doors locked— which like a Goose had been locked—& then afterwards forgotten to be re-opened—so that he knocked his horns against the door of his own drawing room.——There is packing and preparation going on— and I mean to plod through the Tyrol with my little "shild"— Allegrina—who however is not very well—and half the house have brought the tertian from the Mira—it made me delirious during one attack.——A German of the name of Simon—with your brother's recommendation from Trieste—has asked me to take him to England —and I will do so—with the permission of God.—William Bankes is at Trieste and has written to me.

Novr. 21st.

I have a little plague and some [little trouble] with the present state of my household of whom *five* including myself have the intermittent fever more or less—Dr. Aglietti has this moment informed me that Allegra has the "doppia terzana"—a febrile doubloon which it seems renders my departure from hence quite uncertain—(as I will not & can not go without her) it means that the poor child has the fever *daily*—& her nurse has it—besides a cameriere and barcariola—my own has diminished—at first it was violent to a degree of temporary delirium —but has subsided in the third week to a slight attack—but has left my mind very weak—and unintellectual.—All these things put together prevent me from entering upon any of my purposes—and indeed make me postpone from day to day my departure—for the Doctor will say nothing decided of my daughter and I dare not remove her till her journey is pronounced ⟨proper⟩ innocent.———I had things to say to Scrope.—There are things to say to you—and to Douglas— but Alas! here I am in a gloomy Venetian palace—never *more* alone than when alone—unhappy in the retrospect—& at least as much so in the prospect—and at the moment when I trusted to set out—taken aback by this indisposition of my child—which however—thank God —as far as I can learn, is not dangerous—but very tiresome & tedious.—At present all my plans of revenge first—and emigration afterwards—in case of arriving & surviving near your coasts—are lulled upon the feverish pillow of a sick infant.——I began this letter yesterday—and within the twenty four hours only was I made aware of the full extent of Allegra's malady.—But my former letter to Kinnaird is neutralized by this event—except in case of her speedy recovery;—in Italy I will not remain a moment longer than enables me to quit it.—I mean or meant to go by the Tyrol &c. &c. &c. and to write to you on my arrival at Calais.——You have never answered my letter of South American *enquiries*—I must go there, or to [the] Cape—anything but stay near England—that is to say if I accomplish what I ought to do—in approaching it near enough—and if I do not—succeed in my intention—I shall have no further need to accomplish anything. —I allude to more private business—but have no leisure—or rather too much—and too few spirits to explain further—at present.

yours ever & truly

B

[TO COUNTESS TERESA GUICCIOLI]

Venezia. addi [November] 25. 1819

Mio solo Bene—Tu sei e sarai sempre mio primo pensier'—ma in questo momento sono in un' stato orribile non sapendo cosa decidere; temendo, da una parte[,] comprometterti in eterno col' mio ritorno a Ravenna—e colle sue consequenze; e dal'altra—perderti—e me stesso—e tutto quel' che ho conosciuto o gustato di felicità, nel' non rivederti più.——Ti prego—ti supplico calmarti—e credere che non posso cessare ad' amarti che colla vita.—Non son' sortito di casa dopo la tua partenza—non vedo anima virante di questo paese e non lo desidero.—In ogni modo, rivedendoti o no—tu sei il mio destino—la più cara—la più amata di donne—di esseri—per me. Perdonami non so cosa dico.—*In Venezia* non resterò dopo che la' mia figlia è risanita—ma dove dirigerò i passi miei—e pur troppo incerto.—Ma ti amo—ti adoro—e ben tu lo sai. + + + + + + + + +

B

P.S.—L'Allegrina e la governante hanno tutte due la *doppia terzana*—e stanno molto male—la mia febbre e sparita.—Addio.— La Fanni ti ha scritto per ogni ordinario—e dovresti aver' ricevuto una lettera da lei col' piccolo ritrattino—il quale io ho ritrovato e mandato subito per consegnarti.—Saluta tutti i signori Papa—Rasponi &c. ed anche Allessandro—e non dimenticando Perelli—e Sandri—e tutti i nostri.——Ti scriverò quando sono più calmo—e *sempre* se tu mi permetti—mia unica ed ultima ed amatissima amica.

My only Treasure—You are and will always be my first thought—but at this moment I am in a terrible state of not knowing what to decide; I am afraid on the one hand of compromising you forever by my return to Ravenna—and its consequences; and on the other hand of losing you—and myself—and all that I have known or tasted of happiness by not seeing you ever again. I beg you—I supplicate you to be calm—and to believe that I cannot cease loving you so long as I live.—I have not gone out of the house since you left—I do not see a living soul of this land, nor do I desire it. In any case, whether I see you again or not—you are my destiny—the dearest—most loved of women—of beings—for me.—Forgive me—I do not know what I say. I shall not remain *in Venice* after my daughter has recovered her health—but where I shall direct my steps is, alas, uncertain.—But I love you—I adore you—and you know it well.

B

P.S.—Allegrina and her governess both have double tertian [fever] —they are very ill—my fever has vanished—Addio.—Fanny has written to you by every mail delivery—and you should have received a letter from her with a tiny little portrait—which I found and sent immediately for delivery to you. Greet all the Signori: Papa—Rasponi[1] &c. and also Alessandro—; do not forget Perelli[2]—and Sandri—and all our people.—
I will write you when I am more calm—and *always* if you permit me—my only and last and best loved friend.[3]

My dearest Augusta—Yours of the 11th. came today—many thanks.—I may be wrong—and right or wrong—have lived long enough not to defend opinions—but my doubts of the funds were Douglas Kinnaird's who also told me that at the investment—Lady B[yron] or her agents had demurred—I know nothing of England but through Douglas & Hobhouse who are alarming reformers—and the Paris papers which are full of bank perplexities.—The Stake concerns you and your children who are in part my heirs—and Lady B[yron]

---

[1] Count Giulio Rasponi was a member of the aristocratic circle in Ravenna who had extended courtesies to Byron while he was there.

[2] Gaspare Perelli was the accommodating priest who carried confidential messages and letters to Teresa from Byron.

[3] Translation by Professor Nancy Dersofi.

and her child who have a jointure and all that to come out of it—She may do as she pleases—I merely suggest—it is all your affair as much as mine.——Since I wrote to you last I have had with all my household & family a sharp tertian fever—I have got *well* but Allegra is still laid up though convalescent—and her nurse—and half my ragamuffins—Gondoliers, Nurses—cook—footmen &c.—I cured myself without bark—but all the others are taking it like trees.—— I have also had another hot [crater?]—in the shape of a scene with Count Guiccioli who quarrelled with his wife—who refused to go back to him—and wanted to stay with me—and elope—and be as good as married—at last they made it up—but there was a dreadful scene;—— if I had not loved her better than myself—I could not have resisted her wish—but at thirty one years—as I have—and *such years* as they have been—you may be sure—knowing the world that I would rather sacrifice myself ten times over—than the girl—who did not know the extent of the step she was so eager to take.——He behaved well enough—saying—"take your lover or retain me—but you shan't have both"—the lady would have taken her lover as in duty bound—not to do—but on representing to her the destruction it would bring on her family (five unmarried sisters) and all the probable consequences— she had the reluctant good grace to acquiesce and return with him to Ravenna.——But this business has rendered Italy hateful to me— and as I left England on account of my own wife—I leave Italy— because of another's.—You need not be frightened there was no fighting—nobody fights here—they sometimes assassinate—but generally by proxy—and as to intrigue, it is the only employment— but elopements and separations are still more serious than even with us—being so uncommon—and indeed needless—as excepting an occasionally jealous old gentleman—every body lets their spouses have a man or two—provided he be taken with decency.—But the Guiccioli was romantic—and had read "*Corinna*"—in short she was a kind of Italian Caroline Lamb—but very pretty and gentle—at least to me—for I never knew so docile a creature as far as we lived together —except that she had a great desire to leave her husband who is sixty years old—and not pleasant. There was the deuce—for her father's family (a very noble one of Ravenna) were furious against the *husband* —(not against me) for his unreasonable ways.——You must not dislike *her*—for she was a great admirer of *you*—and used to collect and seal up all *your letters* to me as they came that they might not be lost or mixed with other papers——and she was a very amiable and accomplished woman—with however some of the drawbacks of the

Italian character now corrupted for ages.——All this—and my fever —have made me low and ill—but the moment Allegra is better—we shall set off over the Tyrolese Alps, and find our way to England as we can, to the great solace of Mr. Fletcher—who may perhaps find his family not less increased than his fortune during his absence.——I cannot fix any day for departure or arrival—so much depending on circumstances—but we are to be in voyage—as soon as it can be undertaken with safety to the child's health.—As to the Countess G[uiccioli] if I had been single—and could have married her [by] getting her divorced—she would [proba]bly have been of the party—but this being out of the question—though *she* was as "all for love or the world well lost"—I who know what "love" and "the world" both are —persuaded her to keep her station in society.——Pray let Ada's picture be *portable* as I am likely to see more of the portrait than of the original.—Excuse this scrawl—think that within this month I have had a *fever*—an *Italian husband and wife quarrelling;—a sick family—* and *the preparation for a December journey over the mountains of the Tyrol all brewing at once in my cauldron.—*

yrs.
[scrawl]

P.S.—I enclose you *her* last letter to me by which you may judge for yourself—that it was a serious business.—I have felt it such, but it was my duty to do as I did as her husband offered to forgive every thing if she would return with him to Ravenna and give up her liaison.—— I will talk to you of my American scheme when I see you.

La mia partenza è indecisa ancora per la Stagione—scrivetemi se avete più piacere che venga o no.—Subito—Salutatemi Alessandro—

LORD BYRON

[Note from Byron to Teresa Guiccioli, not in Byron's hand, following short note of Fanny Silvestrini]

My leaving is still undecided because of the season—Write to me to say whether you wish me to come or not.—As soon as possible. Greet Alexander for me.[1]

LORD BYRON

[1] Editor's translation.

Amor Mio—Io parto per *salvarti*; e lascio un paese divenuto insopportabile senza di te.—Le tue lettere alla Fanni—ed anche a mi stesso—fanno torto ai miei motivi; ma col' tempo tu vedrai la tua ingiustizia.—Tu parli del'dolor—io lo sento—ma mi mancano le parole.——Non posso scriverti—ma se tu vedessi il mio cuore come tu lo vedevi quando eravamo insieme—non mi diresti delle ingiuriè così crudeli.——Non basta—lasciarti per dei motivi dei quali tu eri persuasa (non molto tempo fa) non basta partire dall' Italia col' cuore lacerato—dopo aver passato tutti i miei giorni dopo la tua partenza nella solitudine—ammalato di corpo e di anima—ma ho anche a sopportare i tuoi rimproveri—senza replicarti—e senza meritarli.——Addio—in quella parola—è compresa la morte di mia felicità—ma in ogni modo—lascia che ti ama ancora—lascia che penso di te come l'unico—ultimo oggetto di tante speranze—e di tanta passione;—colla quale ho passato dei momenti troppo dolci—ma— forse—un' giorno tornaremo abbraciarci—tornaremo essere + + +— ciò che siamo stati—ma—se no—[sappi] che nessuna donna sara amata in vece di te.——Ciò si dice al' principio di una relazione—io lo dico —al' fine.—Ti amo più che i primi giorni—del' amor nostro—e tu lo sai—anche del' sacrifizio che ora faccio—per il tuo ben essere.— Pensa di A[*lessandro*]—Pensa di tutto che egli ha fatto o voluto fare— allora tu non puoi biasimarmi.—Addio—Addio—Amami.—

B

P.S.—Tu avrai delle mie nuove nel' viaggio—e di più al' ritorno di Valeriani—che io mandero al mio arrivo.——Il mio indirizzo—è L.B.—

aux Soins de Messieurs Ransom
  Banquiers—Pall Mall. Londres Angleterre
Se ti conviene più—indirezzate le lettere
  presso i Signori Siri & Willhalm Banchieri *Venezia*

My Love—I am going away in order *to save you*; and I leave a land that has become unbearable without you. Your letters to Fanny—and also to myself—do wrong to my motives; but in time you will realize your injustice. You speak of pain—I feel it—but words fail me. I cannot write you—but if you could see my heart as you saw it when we were together—you would not speak to me of such cruel abuses. It is not enough—to leave you for motives of which you were convinced (not very long ago). It is not enough to depart from Italy with a heart that is rent—after having passed all my days since your departure in solitude—sick in body and in spirit—but I must also endure your reproaches—without answering you—and without deserving them. — —Addio—that word contains the death of my happiness—but even so—let me love you still—let me think of you as the single—ultimate object of so many hopes—and of so much passion;—with whom I have spent moments too sweet—but—perhaps—one day we will again embrace one another—we will again be + + +—what we have been—but—if not—know that no woman will be loved in your stead. That is said at the beginning of a relationship—I say it at the end. I love you more than in the first days of our love—and you know it—even by the sacrifice that I now am making—for your welfare. Think of A[lexander] —Think of all that he has done or wanted to do—then you cannot blame me.—Addio—Addio—Love me.

P.S.—You will hear from me during my trip—and again when Valeriani returns—I will send him upon my arrival. My address is care of Messrs. Ransom
Bankers—Pall Mall. London England
If it is more convenient for you—address your letters care of the Messrs Siri and Willhalm Bankers *Venice*[1]

[TO AUGUSTA LEIGH]   *Venice. Decr. 4th. 1819*

My dearest Augusta—The enclosed letter is from Douglas Kinnaird.—You can send it to Ly. B[yron] & hear what she says—if they,—that is the trustees—approve—I can have no objection.—I wish you too to express *your own* opinion—as—in case of my not marrying again & having a son—you & yours must eventually be my heirs according to my ⟨present⟩ Will—made 5 years ago—since the marriage.——You need not answer to this place—as I expect to be in or near England by the new year.—We propose setting out [in] a few days.—I wrote to you a long letter about ten days ago—explaining why &c. &c. I think of leaving Italy so soon—if you address a line to Calais it will I trust ⟨not miss⟩ be met by

yrs. ever most affctly.
B

[1] Translation by Professor Nancy Dersofi.

251

My dear Douglas—If the Securities be worthy of the name—the trustees accordant—and L[ad]y B[yron] acquiescent—you may suppose that I shall not refuse my consent.—I presume that all proper investigation & enquiry whether there are any *previous incumbrances*—and how far it may be safe & eligible to take *Irish* securities—will be made —the Interest seems large for the times—almost *suspiciously* so—but you will doubtless see to all this—or at least that it is seen to.—You will have received a long letter from me some days ago—stating my intention—& reasons there*for*—of proceeding to England—direct & directly—a letter will I trust meet me at Calais—I presume however that you have the full power of acting for me by Attorneyship during my absence in case a speedy arrangement should be necessary—for the Athlone[1] proposition. Believe me

ever & very truly yrs.

BYRON

My dear Murray—You may do as you please—but you are about an hopeless experiment—Eldon will decide against you[1]—were it only that my name is in the record.———You will also recollect that if the publication is pronounced against on the grounds you mention as *indecent & blasphemous* that *I* lose all right in my daughter's *guardianship* and *education*—in short all paternal authority—and every thing concerning her—except the pleasure I may have chanced to have had in begetting her.—It was so decided in Shelley's case—because he had written—Queen Mab[2]—&c. &c. however you can ask the lawyers— and do as you like—I do not inhibit you trying the question—I merely state one of the consequences to me.———With regard to the Copyright—it is hard that you should pay for a non-entity:———I will therefore refund it—which I can very well do—not having spent it— nor begun upon it—and so we will be quits on that score—it lies at

[1] Kinnaird had proposed, in view of Byron's distrust of the "Funds", an Irish mortgage on the property of the Earl of Athlone, but it was not followed through.

[1] Murray had applied in Chancery for an injunction to prevent the piracy of *Don Juan*. Despite Byron's fears it was obtained.

[2] John Westbrook, father of Shelley's first wife, had filed a Bill of Complaint to the Lord Chancellor, Lord Eldon, who delivered a judgment on March 27, 1817, which deprived Shelley of exclusive parental right over his children by Harriet. The decision was based on Shelley's atheistical writing (*Queen Mab*), his views on marriage, and his conduct.

my banker's.[3]——Of the Chancellor's law—I am no judge—but take
up Tom Jones & read him [—] Mrs. Waters and Molly Seagrim—or
Prior's Hans Carvel—& Paulo Purganti[4]—Smollett's Roderick Random
—the chapter of Lord Strutwell—& many others;—Peregrine Pickle
the scene of the Beggar Girl——Johnson's *London* for *coarse* expressions—for instance the word *"Clap"* & *"gropes his breeches* with *a
monarch's air"*—Anstey's Bath guide—the "Hearken Lady Betty
Hearken"—take up in short—Pope—Prior—Congreve—Dryden—
Fielding—Smollett—& let the Counsel select passages—and what
becomes of *their* copyright if his Wat Tyler—decision is to pass into
a precedent?[5]——I have nothing more to say—you must judge for
yourselves——I wrote to you some time ago—I have had a tertian
ague—my daughter Allegra has been ill also—and I have been almost
obliged to run away with a married woman.—But with some difficulty
—& many internal struggles—I reconciled the lady with her lord—&
cured the fever of the Child with bark—& my own with cold water.
——I think of setting out for England by the Tyrol in a few days—so
that I could wish you to direct yr. next letter to Calais.—Excuse my
writing in great haste—and late in the morning or night—whichever
you please to call it.—The third Canto of "Don Juan" is completed in
about two hundred stanzas—very decent—I believe—but do not
know—& it is useless to discuss until it can be ascertained if [it] may
or may not be a property.——My present determination to quit
Italy was unlooked for—but I have explained the reasons in letters to
my Sister & Douglas K[innaird]—a week or two ago.—My progress
will depend upon the snows of the Tyrol—& the health of my child who
is at present quite recovered—but I hope to get on well & am

yrs. ever & truly

B

P.S.—Many thanks for yr. letters to which you are not to consider
this as an answer—but an acknowledgement.—

[3] *Don Juan* was not a financial failure but had done very well, and there is no
evidence that Murray accepted Byron's offer to return the money he had received
for the copyright.
[4] Prior's Rabelaisian verse tales.
[5] Southey's *Wat Tyler*, written when he was a young man inspired by French
Revolutionary ideas, was printed by a pirating publisher in 1817. Southey, then a
Tory and Poet Laureate, tried to get an injunction, but it was denied by Eldon on
the ground that as it was seditious it was not subject to copyright.

[Venezia li 6 9bre 1819] *[10bre?]*

[postscript to a letter of Fanny Silvestrini to Teresa Guiccioli]

Amor mio—In questo momento—è impossibile per me scriverti in detaglio—ma col'tempo tu riconoscerai che sono e sarò sempre tuo.

+B

[TRANSLATION]   *[Venice, Dec.? 6, 1819]*[1]

[Postscript to a letter of Fanny Silvestrini to Teresa Guiccioli]

My Love—At the moment—it is impossible for me to write in detail—but in time you will realize that I am and always shall be yours.

+B

[TO RICHARD BELGRAVE HOPPNER]   *Venice. Decr. 7th. 1819*

My dear Hoppner—Partings are but bitter work at best—so that I shall not venture on a second with you.—Pray make my best respects to Mrs. H. and assure her of my unalterable reverence for the singular goodness of her disposition, which is not without it's reward even in this world—for even those who are no great believers in human virtues—would discover enough in her to give them a better opinion of their fellow creatures—and what is still more difficult—of themselves—as being of the same species—however inferior in approaching it's nobler models. And make what excuses you can for my omission of the ceremony of leavetaking—if we all meet again—I will make my humblest apology—and if not—why recollect that I wished you all well and—if you can—forget—that I have given you a great deal of trouble.—I enclose you a note of Siri & Will[halm] by which you will perceive the balance—to be 7416—*francs*—out of which two hundred Louis are to come for Mother Mocenigo's rent—the rest is to disburse according to Contingencies.—I *leave all Clear else*, as far as I know, except two months more (*when due*) of Sr. Lega's salary—(160 francs per month) and Castelli's bill & lawsuits.——*Half* Castelli's bill I shall pay.——The rest I keep to quicken him.——Should any

---

1 This letter was misdated Nov. 6, 1819, by Fanny. The context of her letter shows that it was written after Byron's letter of Nov. 25. 1819, stating his determination to leave Italy.

thing occur beyond—draw [several lines cut from manuscript] I
enclose you—the draft—on Siri &c.——Mr. Gnoatto—and Advocate
Castelli's account.——Don't give up the house till further letters
from me—on the subject ;—⟨and⟩ but sell *my chattels*—of which I send
you a list.—and carry the cash to account—there is my *Gondola*—my
water-posts—books—bed—two Silver Coffee pots & silver—and
sugar basin—Chairs—tables—dog—monkeys—and fox—old woman
&c.——A word more—pray beg Lancetti not to give Fletcher's
Tiretta passports for England.[1]——

[TO COUNTESS TERESA GUICCIOLI]
Venezia—li 9. 10bre [Dec. 9 1819]

[at end of letter of Fanny Silvestrini to Teresa Guiccioli]

Mia Carissima Amica—La tua ultima lettera [mi] ha fatto
sospendere il mio viaggio.—Io ti amo—ti amerò pur troppo—e per
sempre.—Disponi di me—tu hai tutti i diritti—[io] debbo la passata
felicità a te—e tu puoi disporre della [futura?] mia vita—basta—che
tu *non ti* [*penti?*] qualunque siano le consequenze.—Io credevo
salvarti col' partire—ma vedendo che tu pensi diversamente—attendo
il tuo cenno per tornare in R[avenna].—Riguardo ad *A.* farò ciò che
tu vuoi.—+ + + + +

[TRANSLATION]
Venice—Dec. 9, 1819

[at the end of Fanny Silvestrini's letter]

My Dearest Friend—Your last letter caused me to give up my
journey.—I love you—I shall love you, alas,—forever. Command me
—you can arrange my future life—It is enough that you do not repent,
whatever the consequences may be. I thought to save you by leaving—
but seeing that you think differently—I await your signal to return to
Ravenna.—Regarding A[llesandro] I will do as you wish.—
+ + + + +[1]

[TO DOUGLAS KINNAIRD]
Venice. Decr. 10th. 1819

My dear Douglas—The Winter has set in hard—& my daughter
not being well reestablished I have put off my intended voyage till the

[1] See June, 1818, to Hobhouse, note 2.
[1] Translation by Professor Nancy Dersofi.

Spring—or perhaps to the Greek Calends.——You can therefore write to me *addressed to this place* as usual (though I do not mean to remain in *it*) telling me of the Irish mortgage—and remitting the dividends of January when you please.——Murray it seems wishes to try a question of copyright of Don Juan—and bring *in my* name—I would rather pay him back the money;—as he will be sure to lose— the Chancellor would decide against him as he decided on Wat Tyler —as the cry is at present up with that fool Carlile and his trash in such a manner—that they would re-crucify Christ himself if he re-appeared in his old humble accoutrements—and had only his own word for his credentials.——Inform H[obhouse] & all friends—as well as my Sister of this variation in my compass—which need surprize nobody.— I have finished a third Canto of Don Juan—very *decent*—but *dull*— damned dull—and until I hear from you—I shall hardly venture him to sea again—I have read a collection of reviews which Murray sent me—there hath been "a cry of women"[1] and of old women—it should seem—but we shall see.——Murray should recollect one thing—if he tries his copy question and loses it—on the ground of the work being called licentious or irreligious—I lose all right legal & paternal to the guardianship or a portion of guardianship of my legitimate daughter Ada.——I would rather refund his purchase—as is fair.—So pray propose and let me know something about this. I do not mean to stay at Venice—I shall go again to Ravenna—anything better than England —it is better to be with a woman whom I love at the risk of assassina- tion than in a country where I neither like nor am liked—and where my first duty & intention is to cut the throat of a scoundrel.——But for all that we shall or may meet in the Spring.——Pray write

yrs. [scrawl]

Address to Venice

[TO JOHN MURRAY]   *Venice. 10th. 10bre. 1819*

Dear Murray—Since I last wrote I have changed my mind & shall not come to England—the more I contemplate—the more I dislike the place & the prospect.——You may therefore address to me as usual *here*—though—I mean to go to another city.——I have finished the third Canto of D[on] J[uan]—but the things I have read & heard dis- courage all further publication—at least for the present.——You may try the copy question—but you'll lose it—the cry is up—and cant is up—I should have no objection to return the price of the copyright— & have written to Mr Kin[nair]d by this post on the subject.——Talk

[1] *Macbeth*, Act V, scene 5.

with him.—I have not the patience—nor do I feel interest enough in the question, to contend with the fellows in their own slang,——but I perceive Mr. Blackwood Magazine and one or two others of your missives—have been hyperbolical in their praise—and diabolical in their abuse.——I like & admire Wilson[1]—and *he* should not have indulged himself in such outrageous license—it is overdone and defeats itself—what would he say to the grossness without passion—and the misanthropy without feeling of Gulliver's travels?—when he talks of Lady Byron's business—he talks of what he knows nothing about—and you may tell him that no one can more desire a public investigation of that affair than I do.——I sent home by Moore—(*for* Moore only who has my journal too) my memoir written up to 1816—and I gave him leave to show it to whom he pleased—but *not to publish* on any account.—You may read it—and you may let Wilson read it—if he likes—not for his *public* opinion—but his private—for I like the man—and care very little about his magazine.——And I could wish Lady B[yron] herself to read it—that she may have it in her power to mark anything mistaken or misstated—as it will probably appear after my extinction, and it would be but fair she should see it—that is to say —herself willing.——Perhaps I may take a journey to you in the Spring—but I *have* been ill—and *am* indolent—and indecisive because few things interest me.——These fellows first abused me for being gloomy—and now they are wroth but I am or attempted to be facetious. ——I have got such a cold and headache that I can hardly see what I scrawl—the winters here are as sharp as needles.—Some time ago I wrote to you rather fully about my Italian ⟨liaisons⟩ affairs—at present I can say no more—except that you shall know further by and bye.— Your Blackwood accuses me of treating women harshly—it may be so —but I have been their martyr.—My whole life has been sacrificed *to* them & *by* them.—I mean to leave Venice in a few days—but you will address your letters *here* as usual.—When I fix elsewhere you shall know.

yrs
[scrawl]

[1] *Blackwood's Edinburgh Magazine* for August, 1819, had a scathing review of *Don Juan.* Although the writer acknowledged that Byron "has never written any thing more decisively and triumphantly expressive of the greatness of his genius," he attacked the poem on moral grounds and particularly for its satire on Lady Byron. It is still a question as to whether John Wilson wrote the review, but it was apparently written at the behest of William Blackwood himself. (See Alan Lang Strout, *John Bull's Letter to Lord Byron,* 1947, pp. 84–87.) The personal attack on his life and character rankled and the following year Byron wrote a lengthy reply, which was not published until 1833.

P.S.—Pray let my Sister be informed that I am not coming as I intended—I have not the courage to tell her so myself—[at] least as yet—but I will soon—*with the reasons*—pray tell her so.——

Mia Carissima Amica—La Fanni ti avrà detta colla sua *solita sublimità*—che l'Amor ha vinto.——Io non ho potuto trovare forza di anima per lasciare il paese dove tu sei—senza vederti almeno un' altra volta—forse dipenderà da *te*—se mai ti lascio più.—Per il resto —parleremmo—tu dovresti adesso sapere cosa sarà più convenevola al' tuo ben essere—la mia presenza—o la mia lontananza.—Io sono Cittadino del' Mondo—tutti i paese sono eguali per me;—tu sei stata sempre (adesso che ci siamo conosciuti) l'unico oggetto di miei pensieri.——Credeva che il miglior partito per la pace tua—e la pace di tua famiglia fosse il mio partire—e andare ben' *lontano*— poichè stare vicino—e *non* avvicinarti sarebbe per me impossibile.— Ma tu hai decisa che io debbo ritornare a R[avenna]—tornarò—e farò—e *sarò* ciò che tu vuoi.—Non posso dirti di più.—La Fanni sarà assai più brillante—e probabilmente è in questo momento in tutti gli dolori della composizione—al' gran' dispendio del' povero dizionario. ——Ti prego salutare rispettosamente della parte mia—Papa—il Cavaliere—e tutti quanti che saranno disposti ricevere i miei rispetti. ——Spero che il tuo papa non avrà dispiacere—e che *A*[*lessandro*] sia come *tu lo dici*—in tua carissima del' ultimo ordinario.—In ogni modo —informarmi di tutto—per la mia noma. Ti bacio 10000+volte di cuore——

[scrawl]

P.S.—Dopo la tua partenza—non sono sortito ci casa—ed appena di camera—e non sortirò se non sia—per venire da te—o partire del' Italia.——Tu puoi informarti dagli altri della mia condotta—son' sicuro che sarai contenta.——

My Dearest Friend—Fanny will have told you, with her *usual sublimity*, that Love has won. I have not been able to find enough resolution to leave the country where you are, without seeing you at least once more:—perhaps it will depend on *you* whether I ever again shall leave you. Of the rest we shall speak. You should now know what is more conducive to your welfare, my presence or my absence. I am a citizen of the world—all countries are alike to me. You have always been (since we met) *the only object of my thoughts*. I believed that the best course, both for your peace and for that of your family, was for me to leave, and to go *very far away*, for to remain near and *not* approach you, would have been impossible for me. But you have decided that I am to return to Ravenna. I shall return—and do—and be—what you wish. I cannot say more. Fanny will be much more brilliant—and is probably at this moment in the throes of composition—at great expense to the poor dictionary. I pray you greet respectfully on my behalf—Papa—the Cavaliere—and all who may be glad to have my regards. I hope that your Papa will not be displeased—and that A[lexander] is *as you say*—in your very dear letter by the last post. In any case inform me of everything—for my guidance. I kiss you 10000 + times from my heart——

P.S.—Since your departure—I have not gone out of the house— and scarcely out of my room—nor shall I go out unless it be—to come to you or to leave Italy. You can learn from others of my conduct—I am sure you will be satisfied.[1]

[TO AUGUSTA LEIGH]   *Bologna, Decr. 23d. 1819*

Dearest Augusta—The health of my daughter Allegra—the cold Season—and the length of the journey—induce me to postpone for some time a purpose (never very willing on my part) to revisit Great Britain.——You can address to me at Venice as usual. Wherever I may be in Italy the letter will be forwarded.——I enclose to you—all that *long hair*—on account [of] which you would not go to see my picture.[1] ——You will see that it was not so very long.——I curtailed it yesterday—my head & hair being weakly after my tertian.——I wrote to you not very long ago—and as I do not know that I could [add] anything satisfactory to that letter—I may as well finish this.——In a letter to Murray—I requested him to apprize you that my journey was postponed——but here—there and every where know me

yours ever & very truly

B

[1] Translation by Professor Nancy Dersofi.
[1] This was the drawing by Harlow, made in Venice in 1818, which shows Byron's hair grown down below his collar. (See Frontispiece to this volume.)

Dear Douglas—You do not require long letters, nor do I write them.———I wrote some weeks ago to say that I had put off my coming —and it is well I did for my daughter has been very unwell—& would hardly have got over the Alps in this weather.———You can remit my half year either in circulars—or letter to Longhi of Bologna & Siri— Venice—or as many bankers as you please.———Circulars are perhaps bettermost.———Information about the transfer—and the proposed Irish Investment will be acceptable.—I have cured my fever and that of my *shild* & family and am

yrs
[scrawl]

Any thing—like or unlike—copy or original will be welcome— I can make no comparison and find no fault—it is enough for me to have something to remind me of what is yours and mine—and which— whatever may be mine—will—I hope be yours while you breathe.— It is my wish to give you as little further trouble as can be helped— the time—and the mode of sending the picture you can choose;—I have been taught waiting if not patience. The wretchedness of the past should be sufficient for you and me without adding wittingly to the future more bitterness than that of which time and eternity are pregnant.———While we do not approximate we may be gentle—and feel at a distance what we once felt without mutual or self reproach. ———This time five years—(the fault is not mine but of Augusta's letter 10th. Decr.—which arrived to day) I was on my way to our funeral marriage.—I hardly thought then that your bridegroom as an exile would one day address you as a stranger, and that Lady and Lord Byron would become bye words of division.—This time four years I suspected it as little.—I speak to you from another country—and as it were from another world—for this city of Italy is out of the track of armies and travellers and is more of the old time.—That I think of you is but too obvious—for three hours have not passed—since in society where I ought not to think of you—though Italian customs and Italian—perhaps even English—passions attach more importance and duty to such liaisons than to any nuptial engagement—the principal person concerned said to me—"tu pensi di tua moglie"—it was—so

260

right a conjecture that I started and answered why do you think so? the answer was—"because you are so serious—and she is the woman whom I believe tu ami più ed ami sempre."—If this had been said in a moment of anger or of playfulness—I should have thought it the consequence of ill humour or curiosity—but it was said without any such prologue—in a time of indifferent things and much good company —Countesses and Marchionesses and all the noble blood of the descendants of Guido di Polenta's contemporaries—with names eloquent of the middle ages.——I was nearly on the point of setting out for England—in November—but a fever the epidemic of the Season stopped me with other reasons——Augusta can tell you all about me & mine if you think either worth the enquiry.——But the object of my writing is to come.——It is this—I saw Moore three months ago and gave to his care—a long Memoir written up to the Summer of 1816, of my life—which I had been writing since I left England.—It will not be published till after my death—and in fact it is a "Memoir" and not "confessions" [.] I have omitted the most important & decisive events and passions of my existence not to compromise others.—But it is not so with the part you occupy—which is long and minute—and I could wish you to see, read and mark any part or parts that do not appear to coincide with the truth.—The truth I have always stated—but there are two ways of looking at it—and your way may be not mine.—I have never revised the papers since they were written.—You may read them—and mark what you please —I wish you to know what I think and say of you & yours.—You will find nothing to flatter you—nothing to lead you to the most remote supposition that we could ever have been—or be happy together.— But I do not choose to give to another generation statements which we cannot arise from the dust to prove or disprove—without letting you see fairly & fully what I look upon you to have been—and what I depict you as being.—If seeing this—you can detect what is false—or answer what is charged—do so—*your mark* shall not be erased.—— You will perhaps say *why* write my life?—Alas! I say so too—but they who have traduced it & blasted it—and branded me—should know— that it is they—and not I—are the cause.—It is no great pleasure to have lived—and less to live over again the details of existence—but the last becomes sometimes a necessity and even a duty.——If you choose to see this you may—if you do not—you have at least had the option.

[scrawl]

January 1st.

My dear Hoppner—Will you have the goodness to ask or cause to be asked of Siri and Willhalm—if they have not *three* sabres of mine in custody according to the enclosed note—if not they must have lost two—for they never sent them back.——And will you desire Missiaglia to subscribe for and send me the *Minerva* a Paris paper—as well as Galignani.—I have been here this week—and was obliged to put on my armour and go the night after my arrival to the Marquis Cavalli's[1]—where there were between two and three hundred of the best company I have seen in Italy—more beauty, more youth and more diamonds among the women than have been seen these fifty years in the Sea-Sodom.—I never saw such a difference between two places of the same latitude—(or *p*latitude—it is all one) music—dancing—and play all in the same Sal[l]e.—The G[uiccioli]'s object appeared to be to parade her foreign lover as much as possible—and faith—if she seemed to glory in the Scandal—it was not for me to be ashamed of it —nobody seemed surprized—all the women on the contrary were as it were delighted with the excellent example—the Vice-legate[2]—and all the other Vices were as polite as could be;—and I who had acted on the reserve—was fairly obliged to take the lady under my arm—and look as much like a Cicisbeo as I could on so short a notice, to say nothing of the embarrassment of a cocked hat and sword much more formidable to me than ever it will be to the enemy.——I write in great haste—do you answer as hastily.—I can understand nothing of all this—but it seems as if the G[uiccioli] had been presumed to be *planted* and was determined to show that she was not—*plantation* in this hemisphere being the greatest moral misfortune.—But this is mere conjecture—for I know nothing about it—except [that] every body are very kind to her—and not discourteous to me.—Fathers—and all relations quite agreeable.—

yrs. ever & truly
B

P.S.—Best respects to Mrs. H[oppner] I would send the *compliments* of the Season—but the Season itself is so little complimentary with snow and rain that I wait for Sunshine.—

---

1 The Marchese Antonio Cavalli was Teresa's cousin.
2 Count Giuseppe Alborghetti.

LIST OF LETTERS AND SOURCES

Date	Recipient	Source of Text	Page
		1818 (continued)	
June 8	John Cam Hobhouse	MS. British Museum (Add. 42093)	49
June 10	Charles Hanson	MS. Murray	50
June 12	John Cam Hobhouse	MS. British Museum (Add. 42093)	50
June 15 or 16	John Cam Hobhouse	MS. British Museum (Add. 42093)	51
June 16	Douglas Kinnaird	MS. British Museum (Add. 42093)	52
June 16	John Murray	MS. Murray	52
June 18	John Murray	MS. Murray	53
June 18	Charles Hanson	MS. Murray	54
June 25	John Cam Hobhouse	MS. British Museum (Add. 42093)	54
June 25	John Murray	MS. Murray	55
June 28	John Murray	MS. Murray	55
June 28	John Cam Hobhouse	MS. British Museum (Add. 42093)	56
June 30	John Cam Hobhouse	MS. British Museum (Add. 42093)	56
June 30	Charles Hanson	MS. Murray	57
June 30	John Murray	MS. Murray	57
July 1	Count Albrizzi	MS. Biblioteca Nazionale Centrale, Florence	57
July 10	John Murray	MS. Murray	58
July 15	Douglas Kinnaird	MS. Lord Kinnaird	59
July 17	John Murray	MS. Murray	60
Aug. 3	Augusta Leigh	MS. Murray	62
Aug. 3	John Murray	MS. Murray	62
Aug. 3	John Cam Hobhouse	MS. British Museum (Add. 42093)	63
Aug. 26	John Murray	MS. Murray	63
Aug. 31	Capt. Basil Hall	MS. Fac. Myers and Co. Cat.	64
Sept. 8	J. W. Webster	MS. Murray	65
Sept. 19	Thomas Moore	Text: Moore, II, 197–200	66
Sept. 21	Augusta Leigh	MS. The Earl of Lytton	69
Sept. 24	John Murray	MS. Murray	70
Sept. 30	John Hanson	MS. Murray	71

Date	Recipient	Source of Text	Page
		1819 (continued)	
Jan. 19	John Cam Hobhouse & Douglas Kinnaird (a)	MS. Murray	91
[Jan. 19?]	[Hobhouse & Kinnaird?] (b)	MS. Murray	93
Jan. 19	John Cam Hobhouse	MS. Murray	93
Jan. 20	John Murray	MS. Murray	94
Jan. 25	John Murray	MS. Murray	94
Jan. 25	John Cam Hobhouse	MS. Murray	95
Jan. 26	John Cam Hobhouse	MS. Murray	97
Jan. 27	Douglas Kinnaird	MS. Murray	97
Feb. 1	John Murray	MS. Murray	98
Feb. 22	John Murray	MS. Murray	99
Feb. 22	Douglas Kinnaird	MS. Murray	100
March 6	Douglas Kinnaird	MS. Murray	101
March 9	Douglas Kinnaird	MS. Murray	102
March 9	John Hanson	MS. Murray	103
[April?]	John Murray	MS. Murray	104
April 3	John Murray	Text: *LJ*, IV, 281	104
[April 6?]	John Murray (a)	MS. Murray	105
April 6	John Murray (b)	MS. Murray	105
April 6	John Cam Hobhouse	MS. Murray	106
April 7	Douglas Kinnaird	MS. Murray	109
April 22	Teresa Guiccioli	MS. Biblioteca Classense, Ravenna	109
April 24	Douglas Kinnaird	MS. Murray	113
April 25	Teresa Guiccioli	MS. Biblioteca Classense, Ravenna	115
April 27	Editor of Galignani's Messenger	MS. Facsimile, *Works of Lord Byron*, Published by A and W Galignani, Paris, 1826.	118
May 3	Fanny Silvestrini	MS. Biblioteca Classense, Ravenna	119
May 3	Teresa Guiccioli	MS. Biblioteca Classense, Ravenna	120
May 6	John Murray	MS. Murray	122
May 12	[To Major Somerville]	MS. Historical Society of Pennsylvania	123

FORGERIES OF BYRON'S LETTERS

Jan. 18, 1818: To J. Hoppner. Schultess-Young, Letter XXXIII, 136–37.

March, 1818: written in copy of Martial. Hansel Galleries, Chicago. Sale Sept. 23–24, 1973.

March 28, 1818: To Henry[?] Webster. Lettres Autographes (Noel Charaway), 52e année No. 293, Fev. 1899.

June 12, 1818: [To ?]: MS. Bodleian, MS. Montagu, d. 17 ff. 28–29.

Nov. 28, 1818: To J. Hoppner. Schultess-Young, XXVII, 199–200.

[1819 w.m]: To J. Perry. MS. Carl H. Pforzheimer Library.

Jan. 1819: To Douglas Kinnaird. MS. Murray Collection.

March, 1819: To Douglas Kinnaird. MS. Murray Collection

April 9, 1819: [To ?] MS. Berg Collection, New York Public Library.

June 28, 1819: To Capt. Hay. MS. Murray Collection.

Sept. ?, 1819: To Capt. Hay. From copy made at Nantes, 1925, in Murray Collection.

Nov. 9, 1819: To J. Wedderburn Webster. Schultess-Young, VII, 164–165.

Nov. 28, 1819: To Douglas Kinnaird (*a*). Maggs, Cat. 780, 1949.

Nov. 28, 1819: To Douglas Kinnaird (*b*). MS. Houghton Library, Harvard University.

Nov. 28, 1819: To Douglas Kinnaird (*c*). *Poems and Letters of Lord Byron*. Ed. from the Original Manuscripts in the possession of W. K. Bixby . . . Society of Dofobs. Chicago, 1912.

Dec. 5, 1819: To Douglas Kinnaird. Schultess-Young, VIII, 174–176.

Dec. 29, 1819: To Lord Holland, Schultess-Young, XXXI, 206–208.

BIBLIOGRAPHY FOR VOLUME 6

(Principal short title or abbreviated references)

Astarte—Lovelace, Ralph Milbanke, Earl of: *Astarte*: *A Fragment of Truth Concerning George Gordon Byron, Sixth Lord Byron.* Recorded by his grandson. New Edition by Mary Countess of Lovelace, London, 1921.

Bixby—*Poems and Letters of Lord Byron*, Ed. from the Original Manuscripts in the possession of W. K. Bixby of St. Louis by W. N. C. Carlton, M.A. Published for the Society of Dofobs, Chicago, 1912.

Dictionary of National Biography.

Elwin, Malcolm: *Lord Byron's Wife*, London, 1963.

LBC—*Lord Byron's Correspondence*, ed. John Murray. 2 vols., London, 1922.

LJ—*The Works of Lord Byron. A New, Revised and Enlarged Edition. Letters and Journals*, ed. Rowland E. Prothero, 6 vols., London, 1898–1901.

Marchand, Leslie A.: *Byron: A Biography*, 3 vols., New York, 1957; London, 1958.

Mayne, Ethel Colburn: *The Life and Letters of Anne Isabella Lady Noel Byron*, London, 1929.

Moore, Doris Langley: *Lord Byron: Accounts Rendered*, London, 1974.

Moore, Thomas: *Letters and Journals of Lord Byron: with Notices of His Life*, 2 vols., London, 1830.

Origo, Iris: *The Last Attachment*, London, 1949.

Poetry—*The Works of Lord Byron. A New, Revised and Enlarged Edition. Poetry*, ed. Ernest Hartley Coleridge, 7 vols., London, 1898–1904.

Smiles, Samuel: *A Publisher and His Friends: Memoir and Correspondence of the Late John Murray*, 2 vols. London, 1891.

BIOGRAPHICAL SKETCHES

OF PRINCIPAL CORRESPONDENTS AND PERSONS FREQUENTLY MENTIONED

(See also Sketches in earlier volumes)

COUNT GIUSEPPE ALBORGHETTI

When Byron arrived in Ravenna on June 10th, 1819, he carried a letter of introduction to Count Giuseppe Alborghetti, General Secretary to the Papal Legate of the Lower Romagna, a man with a taste for poetry and some knowledge of English. Born in Rome in 1776, he was trained in physical and material sciences but had a greater interest in literature. During his first residence in Ravenna, Byron was too much absorbed in his love for the Countess Guiccioli to pay much attention to Count Alborghetti, who introduced him to the Cardinal Legate and, impressed by his poetic fame, made every effort to be useful to him. Later when Byron was more at ease in his situation as the Cavalier Servente of the Countess Guiccioli, he became more intimate with Alborghetti, loaned him books and corresponded with him on political matters. The Count was apparently much attached to him and served him in various ways. He exercised some delicate diplomatic skill in getting the release of one of Byron's servants who had been arrested for a squabble with a soldier of the Cardinal. He even furnished him with secrets from the Cardinal's mail bag at a time when it might have been considered near treason, for he knew that Byron was connected, through Teresa Guiccioli's father and brother, with the revolutionary Carbonari organization. After the failure of the uprising and the exile of the Gambas, Count Alborghetti furnished the information that Teresa was threatened with being shut up in a convent if she did not follow her father and brother into exile but stayed behind with Byron as she wanted to do. And when Byron finally left Ravenna to join Teresa and the Gambas in Pisa, Count Alborghetti was desolated at the departure of the man for whom he had "great esteem and friendship".

The Countess Benzoni, plump and sixty when Byron frequented her salon or "conversazione" in Venice in 1818, had been a free spirit in her youth. She and Ugo Foscolo had danced about a liberty tree in the piazza at a fête inspired by the French Revolution. Her costume was an Athenian petticoat open along the flanks and a vest which left her bosom free. Lamberti had made her the heroine of a popular ballad "La Biondina in Gondoletta" (the blonde in the gondola). Her Cavalier Servente for thirty years Giuseppe Rangone ("Beppe") "still considered her as a divinity". Though she was faithful to him, she could not help making some amorous advances to the handsome young English poet. Byron found her "conversazioni" more relaxed and less formal than those of the Countess Albrizzi. Besides, he told Hobhouse, he found some pretty women there. He spoke of her as "a kind of Venetian Lady Melbourne". It was at her conversazione that he began his liaison with Countess Teresa Guiccioli.

COUNT ALESSANDRO GUICCIOLI

Count Guiccioli, a large land-holder and one of the richest men in the Romagna, was fifty-seven when he married as his third wife the Countess Teresa Gamba, then eighteen, in 1818. He had been a friend of the Italian dramatist Alfieri and had a passionate interest in the theatre. He was intelligent and agreeable in conversation and manners, but he was something of an enigma and seductive but tyrannical with his wives. He was also shrewd and calculating. He was an opportunist, who during the French occupation preferred "putting himself at the head of the canaille to losing his head to them". With the fall of Napoleon, he made himself agreeable to the Cardinal Legate and the Papal regime, but he was suspect, for he had in his third marriage allied himself with Count Gamba, one of the most ardent of the aristocratic "patriots". His first marriage to the Contessa Placidia Zinanni, much older but rich, was the foundation of his fortune. During this marriage one of his housemaids, Angelica Galliani, bore him six illegitimate children, and when his wife died, after making her will in his favour, he married Angelica. The evening that she died in 1817, he went to the theatre as usual. A year later he married the young daughter of Count Gamba, and during the first year of marriage, before she met Byron, they seemed to be very happy. When Byron first went to Ravenna, Count Guiccioli was very cordial, took him for

[1] Byron spelled the name variously: Benzon, Benzone, Benzona, Benzoni.

rides in his coach and six horses, and appeared either to be ignorant of or indifferent to the liaison with his wife. Byron admitted that he couldn't make him out and was darkly suspicious of his motives. He was puzzled further when the Count sought to borrow a thousand pounds from him and asked him to try to get him appointed a British Vice-consul in Ravenna. He allowed Teresa to accompany Byron to Venice, ostensibly for medical treatment, and to remain there with him until he (Guiccioli) came to get her several weeks later. When Teresa refused to go, it was Byron who persuaded her for the sake of her family to return to Ravenna with her husband. After Byron came back at the urging of Teresa and her father, Count Guiccioli rented him an apartment in his palace and appeared to be indifferent to his wife's easily arranged meetings with her lover, until he caught them *"quasi in the fact"*. After Teresa received a separation decree from the Pope and went to live with her father, Byron continued to live in the palace until he followed Teresa to Pisa some months later. Guiccioli seemed most concerned with the 100 scudi a month he was forced to pay his wife by the Papal decree, and when he learned that she was living alone with Byron in Pisa, he got the allowance stopped.

COUNTESS TERESA GUICCIOLI

Born Teresa Gamba Ghiselli, eldest daughter of Count Ruggero Gamba, of an old aristocratic family of Ravenna, she was only three months out of the convent school of Santa Chiara in Faenza when she was given in marriage in 1818 to the wealthy and eccentric Count Alessandro Guiccioli, nearly forty years her senior. Shortly after their marriage they were in Venice and Byron met them briefly at the Countess Albrizzi's. The next year (April, 1819) he saw her again at the Countess Benzoni's and after a few minutes' conversation a spark was lighted which changed both their lives. Within ten days he had fallen desperately in love with her and she with him, and, as he wrote to his friends in England, they had consummated their "unlawful union" four days and daily before she returned to Ravenna. When Byron followed her to Ravenna in June, she was ill and he had to see her in the presence of others and the tension mounted, but when she was better and they could ride in the Pineta, the affair became idyllic. Still Byron resisted becoming a regular shawl-carrying Cavalier Servente and wanted an elopement and a romance "in the Anglo fashion", but she declined and there were misunderstandings and jealousies, but Byron's loyalty and devotion were unfaltering. On Teresa's insistence he followed the Guicciolis to Bologna and then with her husband's consent accompanied her to Venice in September, where she remained until Count Guiccioli called for her in November. She refused to return until Byron finally persuaded her, not ruling out the possibility of his following her later. Frantic love letters passed between them while Byron considered returning to England or emigrating to South America. Teresa finally persuaded her father to invite Byron to Ravenna. At the beginning of 1820 he had returned and accepted his position as her Cavalier Servente. Teresa arranged for him to rent an apartment in the Guiccioli palace, where with the connivance of servants they carried on their love affair until the Count suddenly became obstreperous and Teresa's father managed a separation decree from the Pope. She then went to live with her family and Byron visited her there, being in the good graces of her father and brother. When the Gambas were exiled, and Teresa joined them in Florence and later Pisa, Byron eventually followed. His attachment was not so hectic as in the early days of their liaison but was as loyal and as strong as that of most marriages. He wrote: "I can say that, without being so *furiously* in love as at first, I am more attached to her than I thought it possible to be to any woman after three years. . . ." He did not tire of her, but of the excessive emotional demands of that attachment. His desire to escape the life he was leading was one motive for his final voyage to Greece.

Teresa's attachment to Byron was the one great event of her life, and she never forgot him. After Byron's death, she went back to her husband, but soon left him again. She flirted with Lamartine, who had a great interest in Byron, and with Henry Fox, son of Lord Holland, who like Byron was lame. She made a sentimental voyage to England in 1832, where she met many of Byron's friends and his sister Augusta, "the *nearest* and *dearest* relative of him—whom I have rather *worshipped* than loved. . . ." After Count Guiccioli's death she lived much in Paris and married (a bride of forty-seven) the Count de Boissy, who was equally fond of Byron's memory, and who used to introduce her as "Ma femme, ancienne maîtresse de Byron". In 1868 she published her *Lord Byron, Jugé par les Témoins de sa Vie* and in her last years she composed in loquacious but imperfect French her "Vie de Lord Byron en Italie" (still unpublished). She lived on her memories until 1879.

ALEXANDER SCOTT

Byron probably came to know Scott, a Scottish bachelor of independent means who lived in Venice, through the English Consul Hoppner.

Scott joined Byron and the Consul in their daily rides on the Lido. As a bachelor, Byron found him a congenial companion with whom he could discuss his amorous adventures more frankly than with Hoppner. They established a man-of-the-world camaraderie. He joined Byron in a swimming contest with Angelo Mengaldo, a Cavalier who had been in Napoleon's army and who boasted of having swum the Beresina River during the retreat from Moscow. Byron and Scott both left Mengaldo far behind in the swimming race from the Lido to the Grand Canal. Both Hoppner and Scott thought Byron was making a fool of himself in his infatuation for the Countess Guiccioli and tried to dissuade him from following her to Ravenna. In Byron's letters to Scott from Ravenna he took a cynical man-of-the-world tone in an attempt to conceal the depth and seriousness of his involvement.

INDEX OF PROPER NAMES

*Page numbers in italics indicate main references and Biographical Sketches in the
Appendix. Such main biographical references in earlier volumes are included in this index
and are in square brackets.*

Brougham, Henry (later Baron Brougham and Vaux), [*Vol. 1, 255n*], 189 and n; B.'s 'character' of, 86–7; writes for *Edinburgh Review*, 86n; B. to challenge him to a duel, 242 and n

Browne, William George, 244 and n

Bruce, Michael, 200–1

Buc, Sir George, *Richard III*, 140 and n

Buonaparte, Napoleon, 100n, 279; B.'s snuffbox, 221 and n

Burckhardt, John Lewis, 244n

Burdett, Sir Francis, [*Vol. 1, 186 and n*], 79, 166; elected to Parliament, 59 and n

Burke, Edmund, 48, 89

Burns, Robert, 85

Butler, Samuel, 85

Byron, Lady (née Annabella Milbanke), [*Vol. 2, 284*], 70, 78n, 90, 133; satirized as Donna Inez in *Don Juan*, 95n, 257n; correspondence with B., 126–7; 'the Investment', 136; refuses to give Fletcher's wife a character, 171; B.'s wish for a divorce, 171; her jointure, 247–8

Byron, Augusta Ada, d. of B. and Annabella, 10, 62, 90, 150, 171; B. hopes she will learn Italian, 182; he asks Lady Byron for her picture, 260

Byron, George Gordon, sixth Baron: Works:

Beppo, 4n, 46; publication, 3n; sent to Murray, 7–8; to be published alone, 9; misprints, 15 16, 19; insertions, 21–2; alterations, 26; B.'s conditions of publication, 35

Childe Harold (Canto IV), 3n, 46, 75n, 105; notes by Hobhouse, 7, 8 and n, 14 and n, 20, 51 and n; dedicated to him, 16n, 59 and n, 75n; reference to Candia, 23 and n; Italian translation, 42n; B.'s anxiety about its success, 53; corrections, 70–1

The Corsair, motto, 170n

Don Juan (Cantos I and II), 59n, 67 and n, 68, 76, 94, 96, 100; additions, 85, 98–9; omissions, 91, 94, 132; varying decisions on publication, 95, 100, 101, 132; satirizes Lady Byron, 95n, 257n; B.'s instructions, 104, 105, 109, 114, 122, 123, 125, 131; B. defends it against charges of indelicacy, 125, 207–8; payment for, 137–8, 139, 143, 187; reference to Kinnaird, 165n; copyright, 166, 252; publication, 200 and n, 236; to remain anonymous, 215, 236n; B. praises its poetry, 232; admired by Hoppner, 234; not well received, 234, 237; sales, 237; Paris edition, 238; alterations, 238–9; does well financially, 252–3, 253n; reviewed by *British Review*, 213 and n, 214

Don Juan (Canto III), 232; affected by reception of I and II, 234, 235 Hone's piracy, 236n; other impostures, 237; completion, 253, 256

English Bards and Scotch Reviewers, ridicules Fitzgerald, 209 and n

Fugitive Pieces, 'To Mary', 153n

Hours of Idleness, 86n

Lament of Tasso, 42n

'Letter to the Editor of *My Grandmother's Review*', 214n, 215, 216, 224 and n

Manfred, 14; Italian version, 15 and n

Marino Faliero, 207n

Mazeppa, 59n, 71, 76, 92, 123, 126n, 187; B.'s instructions, 95–6

Memoirs, 59n, 62 and n, 63–4, 235–6, 257; sold to Murray by Moore, 235n; destroyed after B.'s death, 235n; for publication after his death, 261; and Lady Byron, 261

Occasional verses, 3–6, 27, 28–9, 68; 'ballads' on Knight, 27, 28–9

Ode on Venice, 58, 76, 123, 126n, 187; B.'s instructions, 95 and n

Prophecy of Dante, 225, 235, 239

Sonnet: 'To be the father of the fatherless', 209

Verse epistles: 'My dear Mr Murray', 3–6

'A Very Mournful Ballad on the Seige and Conquest of Alhama' (trns. from Spanish), 71 and n

Byron, Capt. John, f. of B. and Augusta, 62n

Byron, Commander John, and Patagonian giants, 212 and n

Callcott, Augustus, painter, 172n

Callcott (née Dundas), Mrs. Mariá, *Little Arthur's History of England*, 172n
Campbell, Thomas, 47
Canning, George, 11n, 86
Canova, Antonio, 190, 191
Carbonari organization, B.'s connection with, 276
Carlile, Richard, 240n; trial and imprisonment, 240 and n, 256; *The Republican*, 240n
Caroline, Queen, 90
Cartwright, Major John, 165 and n, 187; challenges Hobhouse, 211
Castelli, Advocate, 213, 234, 254–5
Casti, Giambattista, *Animale parlanti*, 24n
Castlereagh, Robert Stewart, Viscount, 86, 89, 143; stanzas on in *Don Juan*, 91, 94, 105; B.'s opinion of, 104, 229
Cavalli, Marchese Antonio, 262 and n
Caylus, Comte de, 205 and n
Centlivre, Mrs. Susannah, *A Bold Stroke for a Wife*, 148n
Chalmers, George, *Life of Mary Queen of Scots*, 4n
Charles IV, King of Spain, 178n
Chatham, William Pitt, Earl of, 30
Chatterton, Thomas, 85
Chaucer, Geoffrey, 91
Clairmont, Claire, [*Vol. 5, 293–4*], 39n, 126; to Este with Allegra, 69
Clare, John Fitzgibbon, Earl of, 86
Clarke, Dr. E. D., 56
Claudianus, Claudius, 95
Cogni, Margarita (the Fornarina), 68n, 93; Harlow's drawing, 192n; B. relates her story, 192–4, 205; keeps her hold over him, 195–8; her parting behaviour 196–7; Genevan 'story', 238
Cohen, *see* Palgrave
Coleridge, John Taylor, 83n
Coleridge, Samuel Taylor, 83
Collins, William, 85
Congreve, William, 253
Contarini, Mme, incident with Margarita at masked ball, 194, 205
Cowley, Abraham, 85
Cowper, William, 85; translation from Homer, 47n
Crabbe, George, 10, 95
Croker, John Wilson, 11 and n, 24
Curran, John Philpot, 86, 237–8, 243

da Bezzi, Eleanora, 92
da Mosta, Elena, 14, 19
Dante, 122, 154, 181, 188, 189, 200; *Commedia*, 188n; *Inferno*, 129
Davies, Scrope Berdmore, [*Vol. 1, 184n*], 19, 20, 37, 60, 201; effect of restricting him, 25; 'everybody's Huncamunca', 32; hit hard on the turf, 74; agrees *Don Juan* should not be published, 97n; never writes to B., 109; quarrels with Lamb, 138; Augusta's report on, 187; B.'s debt to his landlord, 233; to get in touch with B., 242
Davison, Thomas, printer to the 'Board of Longitude', 29n; and to Murray, 200n
Dawkins, Edward, 'Pisan Affray', 142 and n
D'Israeli, Isaac, 30; *The Literary character*, 83 and n
Dodd, John, stranded sailor, 184–5
Dorville, Henry, Vice-Consul in Venice, 174 and n, 175, 183, 191; to have authority over B.'s affairs, 203, 204
Douglas, Hon. Frederick Sylvester North, 243n, 243
Drummond, Sir William, 125, 132
Dryden, John, 85, 166, 181, 234, 253
Dundas, Rear-Admiral, 172n

Eastlake, (Sir) Charles Lock, PRA, 172n, 173; 'Byron's Dream', 173n
Edgecombe, clerk, 143 and n, 144, 147, 163, 174, 175, 183, 237; to bring Allegra to Bologna, 213, 218; imputed peculations, 229–30, 231, 233–4; B.'s messages to, 177, 191, 203–4
Edgecombe, Mrs., 213
Eldon, John Scott, first Earl of, 252; judgment against Shelley, 252; against Southey, 253n
Elise, nurse to Allegra, 39n
Ellice, Edward, MP, 225 and n
Elmò, Teresa's dog, 203 and n
Erizzo, Andrea, sings Haydn and Handel, 19
Erskine, Lord, Hobhouse's pamphlet against, 187 and n
Este, B.'s villa, 16–17, 69
Euganean hills, 16
Eusebius, 29

Farebrother, auctioneer, 114 and n
Farquhar, George, *The Beaux Stratagem*, 46n
Ferrara, 145, 236–7; cemetery, 148–9, 150
Fielding, Henry, 91, 253; *Joseph Andrews*, 40n; *Tom Jones*, 80 and n, 82, 108 and n, 234, 253; *Tom Thumb*, 214 and n
Fitzgerald, Lord Edward, [*Vol. 3, 249 and n*], 209
Fitzgerald, William Thomas, poetaster, 27, 47 and n, 209 and n
Flahau[l]t (née Mercer), Mme, 146
Fletcher, William, 44n, 62, 64n, 74, 108, 145; amorous adventure with 'Tiretta', 48 and n; frightened by the baker's wife, 70; witnesses B.'s conveyances, 87; malapropism, 138; disarms La Fornarina, 197; and B.'s illness, 239; 'Tiretta' to be denied a passport, 255
Fletcher, Mrs., refused a character by Lady Byron, 171, 181
Foote, Samuel, *The Mayor of Garratt*, 141 and n, 187 and n
Ford, John, 95
Fornarina, The, *see* Cogni, Margarita
Foscarini family, B. leases La Mira from them, 204 and n
Foscolo, Ugo, 51, 105, 172n; and Countess Benzoni, 276; 'Essay on the present Literature of Italy' (in Hobhouse's notes to *Childe Harold*, Canto IV), 51n, 72n; *Ultime Lettere di Jacopo Ortis*, 51n
Fox, Charles James, 12n, 47, 48, 86, 89
Fox, Henry, s. of Lord Holland, 278
Francesca da Rimini, 181, 182, 189
Francis, Sir Philip (Junius), 18, 19
Fremont (?), Julia, 140
Frere, John Hookham, 78; 'Whistlecraft', 4n, 24

Galignani, Jean Antoine, *Messenger*, 89, 114n, 119, 205, 223–4, 233, 262
Galliani, Angelica, mistress, then second wife of Guiccioli, 276
Gamba Ghiselli, Count Ruggero, f. of Teresa, 245, 275–6, 277
Garrick, David, 30, 166 and n
Gibbon, Edward, 189
Gifford, William, 11, 20–1, 26, 59
Giorgi, Countess, 109

Godwin, Mary, [*Vol. 5, 293–4*], 125n, 126; *Frankenstein*, 126
Godwin, William, 76, 82, 126
Goldsmith, Oliver, 85; *The Good-humoured Man*, 106n, 244 and n; *She Stoops to Conquer*, 207 and n; *The Vicar of Wakefield*, 63, 123
Gordon, Pryse Lockhart, 24n
Gordon, Thomas, career, 4n; *History of the Greek Revolution*, 4n
Graham (née Dundas), Mariá, 172n; *Indian Journal, Letters on India*, 172n *see also* Callcott
Graham, Capt. Thomas, RN, 172n
Grattan, Henry, 86
Gray, Thomas, 30, 85
Grenville, William Wyndham Grenville, Lord, [*Vol. 1, 186 and n*], 79
Grey, Charles, second Earl, 18, 79
Griffiths, Ralph, 32; publisher of *Monthly Review*, 32n
Grimm, Friedrich Melchior, story of Comte de Caylus (*Correspondance Littéraire*), 205 and n
Gritti, Count, 25n
Guarini, Giovanni Battista, *Il Pastor Fido*, 118 and n
Guatimozin, Aztec chief, 216 and n
Guiccioli, Count Alessandro, 107, 114, 128 and n, 141, 276–7; his reputation, 130, 144, 164; at the theatre, 152; friendship with B., 157, 168, 176, 276–7; wealth, 164, 168, 186, 276; B. supports his wish to be Vice-Consul, 164 and n, 208, 235, 277; due in Venice, 237, 239; lays down conditions for Teresa, 239, 244; quarrels with her over B., 241, 248; first wife, 276; attitude to his wife's liaison, 277
Guiccioli, Ferdinando, s. of above, 177 and n, 201
Guiccioli (née Gamba Ghiselli), Countess Teresa, 107n, 189, 190, 277–8; B. in love with, 107–8, 114–15, 151, 168; wonders if she has his letters, 120; miscarriage, 130, 141, 165, 167; instructions to B., 144; illness, 151, 163, 167–8, 173, 175, 176; keeps B.'s handkerchief, 154n; popularity, 162–3; improves in health, 177; gossip about her and B., 178–80; writes to Scott, 182–3, 183n; described by B., 185–6, 248–9;

Mengaldo (Mingaldo), Cavalier Angelo, *51n*, *96*, 144 and n, 146, 147, 180; swimming matches with B., 51 and n, 54, 60, 191, 279; unsuccessful suit of Dr. Aglietti's daughter, 190 and n; B. on, 191

Merryweather, Francis, 213 and n, 233–4

Milman, Henry Hart, *Fazio*, 18 and n; *History of Christianity, History of the Jews*, 18n

Milton, John, 85

Missiagli, Signor Giorgione Battista, Venetian publisher, 59, 177 and n, 183–4, 205; proprietor of Apollo Library, 30; B. feels unable to assist, 224–5; to send B. *Minerva*, 262

Montagu, Lady Mary Wortley, 30, 64; and Algarotti, 60

Monti, Vincenzo, 91 and n, *96*

Moore, Barbara, d. of Thomas, death, 9–10

Moore, Thomas, [*Vol. 2, 284–5*], 59n, 78, 83; cottage at Sloperton, 24n; Registrar to the Admiralty, Bermuda, 205 and n; embezzlement by his deputy, 205 and n, 209; with B. in Venice, 230, 232, 236, 238; sells B.'s *Memoirs* to Murray, 235n; *The Fudge Family in Paris*, 46; *Lalla Rookh*, 11, 46, 232; *Life of Sheridan*, 68 and n; Irish National Songs (*Irish Melodies*), 67n, 206 and n; 'Little's' poems, 91, 95, 232, 234

Morelli, Abbate, 35

Moretto, B.'s bulldog, 235 and n

Morgan, Lady (Sydney), 12; *France*, 12n; attacked in *Quarterly Review*, 12n, 13

Morgan, Sir Thomas Charles (Dr.), 13

Morland and Ransom, 6–7

Mossi, translator of *Manfred*, 15

Mosti, Count, 144, 146, 148

Muratori, Lodovico Antonio, *Antiquitates Italicae*, 188n

Murphy, Arthur, *The Citizen*, 48n

Murray, Joe, to be looked after, 41, 43

Murray, John, [*Vol. 2, 285–6*], 3n, 126; called the 'coxcomb' of booksellers, 11 and n, 102; financial dealings with B., 39, 52, 56, 136–7, 138, 143, 145, 187; sends B. a kaleidoscope, 77n;

books for him, 78n, 83–4; and D'Israeli, 83n; B.'s complaints about, 102–3, 166; publishes *Don Juan* (I and II), 200 and n, 210; in a 'state of perturbation', 200, 205; B. recommends Guiccioli to him, 208–9; buys B.'s *Memoirs* from Moore, 235n; obtains an injunction on piracy of *Don Juan*, 252 and n, 256;

Mutz, B.'s dog, 108, 235 and n

Neipperg, Adam Albert, Comte de, 219 and n, 220

Newstead Abbey, sale of, 13, 34, 48, 65, 74, 173; disposal of purchase money, 6, 7, 39, 41, 79, 143n, 222n; amount of, 52; Wildman, at, 81

Noel, Lady, 138, 171, 232

Noel, Sir Ralph (formerly Milbanke), money due from, 7, 41, 48, 221

O'Hara, Kane, adaptation of *Tom Thumb*, 214n

Opie, Amelia, 11

Origo, Iris, 58n, 111n, 156n, 178n, 183n

Osborne, Lord Sydney Godolphin, 62 and n

Ostheid, Capt., sells B. a horse, 219

Otway, Thomas, 85

Ovid, *Metamorphoses*, 206n

Padua, 143

Paine, Thomas, *Age of Reason* (published by Carlile), 240n

Palgrave (née Cohen), Sir Francis, contributor to *Reviews*, 207n

Park, Mungo, 244 and n

Parr, Samuel, 68 and n

Peel, Sir Robert, 89, 145

Perelli, Don Gaspare, 159; go-between for B. and Teresa, 117n, 152, 247 and n; B.'s suspicions, 155

Perry, James, ed. *Morning Chronicle*, 206, 225–6

Persius, *Satires*, 204 and n

Peruzzi, Il Cavaliere Vincenzo, recommended to Lady Jersey and Hobhouse, 38, 39

Petrotini, 8, 14, 19

Pictet, Marc-Auguste, 127 and n